P9-DNP-741

576 Family-Style Recipes Right at Your Fingertips

THE SAYING "The third time is a charm" certainly is true for our *Taste of Home Annual Recipes* cookbook. The 1999 edition—our third in a series—sold over 1 million copies! It seems that lots of folks love having an entire year's worth of recipes from *Taste of Home*, North America's most popular food magazine, in one convenient, thoroughly indexed collection.

Like the three previous editions, this *2000 Taste of Home Annual Recipes* collection will become a valued reference in your kitchen for a number of reasons:

1. Its 324 pages are organized into 16 handy chapters for easy reference. Between its covers, you have at hand every single *Taste of Home* recipe we published in 1999.
2. Plus we've included *dozens* of bonus recipes—42 to be exact! So you'll have a whole group of new home-style recipes to try.
3. Finding all of the 576 recipes is a snap with this book's *three different indexes*—one indexes dishes by food category, one tells you which issue of *Taste of Home* it originally appeared in, and one designates every recipe that includes Nutritional Analysis and Diabetic Exchanges. These handy indexes can be found on pages 306-318.
4. The full-color pictures in this cookbook are *bigger* than ever so you can plainly see what many of these dishes will look like before you begin preparing them.
5. We've used larger print for easy reading while cooking. And each recipe is presented "all-on-a-page", so you never have to turn back and forth while cooking.
6. This volume is printed on the highest quality coated paper to make the foods more attractive and appealing. More importantly, it lets you wipe away spatters easily.
7. The book lies open and *stays open* as you cook. Its durable hard cover will give you *years* of use (you'll never have to worry about dog-earring your magazine collection again).

But the real proof of this volume's value is in the tasting. Your family will *rave* at the results of these recipes, all of which are favorites of other families.

Tight on time? The 18 fast-to-fix recipes in our "Meals in Minutes" chapter offer complete meals that go from stovetop to tabletop in less than 30 minutes.

On a budget? The "centsible" menu on page 284—featuring "Turkey Tetrazzini", "Lettuce with French Dressing" and "Chewy Almond Cookies"—costs just 96¢ a plate!

Family picnic? When you need to feed 10, 100 or any number in between, 47 "Potluck Pleasers" recipes will fill the bill (they start on page 178).

Planning a special supper? For 12 delectable menus that come straight from the kitchens of fellow country cooks, turn to the "My Mom's Best Meal" (page 212) and "Editors' Meals" (page 238) chapters.

With 576 down-home dishes, this taste treasury sets the table for delicious dining in your home year after year!

2000 Taste of Home Annual Recipes

Editors: Julie Schnittka, Jean Steiner
Art Director: Linda Dzik
Food Editor: Coleen Martin
Associate Editor: Kristine Krueger
Production: Ellen Lloyd, Claudia Wardius
Cover Photography: Scott Anderson

Taste of Home®

Executive Editor: Kathy Pohl
Food Editor: Coleen Martin
Associate Food Editor: Corinne Willkomm
Senior Recipe Editor: Sue A. Jurack
Senior Editor: Bob Ottum
Managing Editor: Ann Kaiser
Assistant Managing Editor: Faithann Stoner
Associate Editors: Kristine Krueger, Sharon Selz
Test Kitchen Home Economists: Sue Draheim, Julie Herzfeldt, Wendy Stenman, Diane Werner, Karen Wright
Test Kitchen Assistants: Sherry Smalley, Sue Hampton
Editorial Assistants: Barb Czysz, Mary Ann Koebernik
Design Director: Jim Sibilski
Art Director: Vicky Marie Moseley
Food Photography: Scott Anderson, Glenn Thiesenhusen
Food Photography Artist: Stephanie Marchese
Photo Studio Manager: Anne Schimmel
Production: Ellen Lloyd, Claudia Wardius
Publisher: Roy Reiman

Taste of Home Books

5400 S. 60th St., Greendale WI 53129

International Standard Book Number: 0-89821-265-0
International Standard Serial Number: 1094-3463

Printed in U.S.A.

PICTURED AT RIGHT. Clockwise from upper left: Savory Pot Roast (p. 88); Strawberry Meringue Cake and Cool Lime Pie (p. 150); Spiced Cider, Frozen Mud Pie, Sauerkraut Apple Salad, Classic Crab Cakes and Grandma's Popovers (pp. 258 and 259); Rainbow Pasta Salad (p. 192).

Taste of Home 2000 Annual Recipes

PICTURED ON FRONT COVER. Clockwise from upper left: Summer Spaghetti Salad (p. 30), Friendship Brownies (p. 131) and Golden Glazed Fryer (p. 100).

PICTURED ON BACK COVER. Clockwise from upper left: Mint Brownie Pie (p. 146), Dipped Coconut Shortbread (p. 129) and Lemon Meringue Torte (p. 146).

Additional Photographs: pp. 23, 34, 35, 39, 148, 149, 154, 155. Mike Huibregste, Photographer; Vicky Marie Moseley, Art Director.

FOR ADDITIONAL COPIES of this book or information on other books, write: *Taste of Home* Books, P.O. Box 990, Greendale WI 53129. **Credit card orders call toll-free 1-800/558-1013.**

snacks

Snacks & Beverages

Satisfy the "munchies" anytime of day with an appealing assortment of lip-smackin' snacks, thirst-quenching beverages and hearty appetizers.

SNACK ATTACK. Clockwise from upper left: Corn and Bacon Dip (p. 20), Mini Chicken Turnovers (p. 11), Ground Beef Snack Quiches (p. 18), Spicy Party Mix (p. 21) and Chilled Mocha Eggnog (p. 9).

Sunrise Mini Pizzas

(Pictured above)

I created this recipe for "something different" at breakfast. Even though they look like I went to a lot of trouble, these little pizzas do go together quickly—I even make them for our three children on rushed school mornings. —*Teresa Silver, Melba, Idaho*

8 to 10 eggs
3 tablespoons milk
Salt and pepper to taste
1 tablespoon butter *or* margarine
10 frozen white dinner rolls, thawed
10 bacon strips, cooked and crumbled
2 cups (8 ounces) shredded cheddar cheese

In a bowl, beat the eggs. Add milk, salt and pepper. Melt butter in a skillet; add the egg mixture. Cook and stir over medium heat until the eggs are set. Remove from the heat and set aside. Roll each dinner roll into a 5-in. circle. Place on greased baking sheets. Spoon egg mixture evenly over crusts. Sprinkle with bacon and cheese. Bake at 350° for 15 minutes or until the cheese is melted. **Yield:** 10 pizzas.

Traditional Popcorn Balls

Kids of all ages enjoy these old-fashioned holiday treats. One batch goes a long way. —*Cathy Karges Hazen, North Dakota*

7 quarts popped popcorn
1 cup sugar
1 cup light corn syrup
1/4 cup water
1/4 teaspoon salt
3 tablespoons butter *or* margarine
1 teaspoon vanilla extract
Food coloring, optional

Place popcorn in a large baking pan; keep warm in a 200° oven. In a heavy saucepan, combine sugar, corn syrup, water and salt. Cook over medium heat until a candy thermometer reads 235° (soft-ball stage). Remove from the heat. Add butter, vanilla and food coloring if desired; stir until butter is melted. Immediately pour over popcorn and stir until evenly coated. When mixture is cool enough to handle, quickly shape into 3-in. balls, dipping hands in cold water to prevent sticking. **Yield:** 20 servings. ***Editor's Note:** The accuracy of your candy thermometer is very important. See page 162 for information.

Sugar-Free Russian Tea

My mother always had Russian tea mix on hand for a quick warm-up. Our son has diabetes, so I carry on the tradition using this sugar-free alternative. —*Kim Marie Van Rheenen, Mendota, Illinois*

✓ Uses less fat, sugar or salt. Includes Nutritional Analysis and Diabetic Exchanges.

4-1/2 teaspoons sugar-free orange drink mix
3-1/2 teaspoons sugar-free lemonade mix
Artificial sweetener equivalent to 16 teaspoons sugar
1 teaspoon ground cinnamon
1/2 teaspoon ground cloves

Combine all ingredients; mix well. Store in an airtight container. To prepare one serving, add 1/4 teaspoon of mix to 3/4 cup of hot water; stir well. **Yield:** 1/4 cup mix. **Nutritional Analysis:** One 3/4-cup serving equals 2 calories, trace sodium, 0 cholesterol, trace carbohydrate, trace protein, trace fat. **Diabetic Exchange:** Free food.

Curried Olive Canapes

These special snacks are fast to assemble—you can make them in advance and heat them up at the last minute. —*Robert Ulis, Alexandria, Virginia*

1-1/2 cups (6 ounces) shredded cheddar cheese
1 cup sliced ripe olives

1/2 cup mayonnaise
1/4 cup sliced green onions
1/2 teaspoon curry powder
1/4 to 1/2 teaspoon salt
3 English muffins, split

In a bowl, combine the first six ingredients and mix well. Spread over English muffins. Cut into quarters. Place on an ungreased baking sheet. Broil 4 in. from the heat for 1-2 minutes or until cheese is melted. Serve warm. **Yield:** 2 dozen.

Baked Egg Rolls

These crisp egg rolls are packed with tasty ingredients and also low in fat. —*Barbra Lierman, Lyons, Nebraska*

✓ Uses less fat, sugar or salt. Includes Nutritional Analysis and Diabetic Exchanges.

2 cups grated carrots
1 can (14 ounces) bean sprouts, drained
1/2 cup chopped water chestnuts
1/4 cup chopped green pepper
1/4 cup chopped green onions
1 garlic clove, minced
2 cups diced cooked chicken
4 teaspoons cornstarch
1 tablespoon water
1 tablespoon light soy sauce
1 teaspoon vegetable oil
1 teaspoon brown sugar
Pinch cayenne pepper
16 egg roll wrappers*

Coat a large skillet with nonstick cooking spray; add the first six ingredients. Cook and stir over medium heat until vegetables are crisp-tender, about 3 minutes. Add chicken; heat through. In a small bowl, combine cornstarch, water, soy sauce, oil, brown sugar and cayenne until smooth; stir into chicken mixture. Bring to a boil. Cook and stir for 2 minutes; remove from the heat. Spoon 1/4 cup of chicken mixture on the bottom third of one egg roll wrapper; fold sides toward center and roll tightly. Place seam side down on a baking sheet coated with nonstick cooking spray. Repeat with remaining wrappers and filling. Spray tops of egg rolls with nonstick cooking spray. Bake at 425° for 10-15 minutes or until lightly browned. **Yield:** 8 servings. **Nutritional Analysis:** One serving (2 egg rolls) equals 261 calories, 518 mg sodium, 27 mg cholesterol, 45 gm carbohydrate, 13 gm protein, 3 gm fat. **Diabetic Exchanges:** 3 starch, 1 lean meat. ***Editor's Note:** Fill egg roll wrappers one at a time, keeping the others covered until ready to use.

Chilled Mocha Eggnog

(Pictured below and on page 6)

Eggnog gets a delightful twist with a hint of mocha flavor in this recipe. Instant coffee and a sweetened cream topping make this beverage one of the holiday season's super sippers. —*Debbi Smith, Crossett, Arkansas*

1-1/2 teaspoons instant coffee granules
1 tablespoon hot water
4 cups eggnog*
2 tablespoons brown sugar
1/8 teaspoon ground cinnamon
1/2 cup whipping cream
2 tablespoons confectioners' sugar
1/2 teaspoon vanilla extract

In a bowl, dissolve coffee in water. Add eggnog, brown sugar and cinnamon; whisk until sugar is dissolved. Chill. In a mixing bowl, beat cream, confectioners' sugar and vanilla until soft peaks form. Pour eggnog mixture into glasses and top with whipped cream. **Yield:** 4 cups. ***Editor's Note:** This recipe was tested with commercially prepared eggnog.

Creamy Crab Cheesecake

(Pictured below)

A savory appetizer cheesecake such as this one, dotted with tender crabmeat, is sure to grab the attention and tempt the taste buds of guests. It's an elegant spread that you make ahead, so there's no last-minute fuss.
—Cathy Sarrels, Tucson, Arizona

1 cup crushed butter-flavored crackers (about 25 crackers)
3 tablespoons butter *or* margarine, melted
2 packages (8 ounces *each*) cream cheese, softened
3/4 cup sour cream, *divided*
3 eggs
2 teaspoons grated onion
1 teaspoon lemon juice
1/4 teaspoon seafood seasoning
2 drops hot pepper sauce
1/8 teaspoon pepper
1 cup crabmeat, drained, flaked and cartilage removed
Additional seafood seasoning, optional

In a small bowl, combine the cracker crumbs and butter. Press onto the bottom of a greased 9-in. springform pan. Bake at 350° for 10 minutes. Cool on a wire rack. Reduce heat to 325°. In a mixing bowl, beat cream cheese and 1/4 cup of sour cream until smooth. Add eggs; beat on low just until combined. Add onion, lemon juice, seafood seasoning, hot pepper sauce and pepper; beat just until blended. Fold in crab. Pour over crust. Bake for 35-40 minutes or until center is almost set. Cool on a wire rack for 10 minutes. Carefully run a knife around edge of pan to loosen. Cool 1 hour longer. Spread remaining sour cream over top. Refrigerate overnight. Remove sides of pan. Let stand at room temperature for 30 minutes before serving. Sprinkle with seafood seasoning if desired. **Yield:** 20-24 appetizer servings.

Roasted Garlic Spread

Since garlic is so easy to grow, it's one of the favorite plants in our garden. This thick spread has a mild mellow flavor, making it perfect for topping any bread.
—Janice Mitchell, Aurora, Colorado

2 large garlic heads
1 teaspoon olive *or* vegetable oil
1 to 2 tablespoons butter *or* margarine
1 to 2 tablespoons all-purpose flour
1 teaspoon chicken bouillon granules
2/3 cup boiling water
Italian *or* French bread, sliced

Remove papery outer skin from garlic (do not peel or separate cloves). Brush with oil. Wrap each head in heavy-duty aluminum foil. Bake at 425° for 30-35 minutes or until softened. Cool for 10-15 minutes. Cut top off garlic heads, leaving root end intact. In a small saucepan, melt butter. Squeeze softened garlic into pan. Stir in flour until blended. Dissolve bouillon in water; gradually add to garlic mixture. Bring to a boil; cook and stir for 2 minutes. Serve with bread. **Yield:** about 1/2 cup.

Hot Tamale Meatballs

This zippy appetizer is my family's favorite dish using cumin. I often serve this at parties because the recipe is so easy. *—Darlene Babineaux, Arabi, Louisiana*

4 cups tomato juice, *divided*
3/4 cup cornmeal
2 tablespoons ground cumin, *divided*
2 tablespoons chili powder, *divided*
3/4 teaspoon salt, *divided*
2 garlic cloves, minced
1/4 to 1/2 teaspoon cayenne pepper

1/2 pound ground beef
1/2 pound bulk pork sausage

In a bowl, combine 1/3 cup tomato juice, cornmeal, 1 tablespoon cumin, 1 tablespoon chili powder, 1/4 teaspoon salt, garlic and cayenne. Add the beef and sausage; mix well. Shape into 1-1/4-in. balls. In a Dutch oven, combine the remaining tomato juice, cumin, chili powder and salt; bring to a boil. Add meatballs; cover and simmer for 45 minutes or until meat is no longer pink. **Yield:** 8-10 servings.

Crispy Fudge Treats

These chocolaty treats keep well in the refrigerator, but I never have to store them for very long!
—Joyce Jackson, Bridgetown, Nova Scotia

6 cups crisp rice cereal
3/4 cup confectioners' sugar
1-3/4 cups semisweet chocolate chips
1/2 cup corn syrup
1/3 cup butter *or* margarine
2 teaspoons vanilla extract

Combine the cereal and sugar in a large bowl; set aside. Place chocolate chips, corn syrup and butter in a 1-qt. microwave-safe dish. Microwave, uncovered, on high for about 1 minute; stir gently until smooth. Stir in vanilla. Pour over cereal mixture and mix well. Spoon into a greased 13-in. x 9-in. x 2-in. baking pan. Refrigerate for 30 minutes, then cut into squares. Store in the refrigerator. **Yield:** 3 dozen.

Mini Chicken Turnovers

(Pictured above right and on page 6)

I've been making these hearty tiny turnovers for several years. They take a little extra time to assemble, but it's worth it since they taste so special.
—Mary Detweiler, West Farmington, Ohio

FILLING:
3 tablespoons chopped onion
3 tablespoons butter *or* margarine
1-3/4 cups shredded cooked chicken
3 tablespoons chicken broth
1/4 teaspoon *each* garlic salt, poultry seasoning and pepper
1 package (3 ounces) cream cheese, cubed
PASTRY:
1-1/2 cups all-purpose flour

1/2 teaspoon salt
1/2 teaspoon paprika
1/2 cup cold butter *or* margarine
4 to 5 tablespoons cold water

In a large skillet, saute onion in butter until tender. Stir in chicken, broth, seasonings and cream cheese; set aside. For pastry, combine the flour, salt and paprika in a bowl; cut in butter until the mixture resembles coarse crumbs. Gradually add water, tossing with a fork until a ball forms. On a floured surface, roll out pastry to 1/16-in. thickness. Cut with a 2-1/2-in. round cookie cutter. Reroll scraps and cut more circles. Mound a heaping teaspoon of filling on half of each circle. Moisten edges with water; fold pastry over filling and press edges with a fork to seal. Place on ungreased baking sheets. Repeat with remaining pastry and filling. Prick tops with a fork. Bake at 375° for 15-20 minutes or until golden brown. **Yield:** about 2-1/2 dozen. **Editor's Note:** Turnovers can be baked, frozen and reheated at 375° for 5-7 minutes.

Terrific Iced Tea

Looking for ways to make your iced tea even more refreshing and inviting? Try stirring in 1/4 cup of raspberry juice into each tall glass. Or stir in a few drops of lemon and orange extracts into every batch. Don't forget to garnish individual glasses with some lemon and lime slices.

Sip and Savor Super Shakes

COOL and creamy or frosty and fruity, shakes and malts are a sure way to beat the summer heat. Treat family and friends to one of these blended beverages.

Their ice-cream-parlor flavor will have everyone clamoring for a sip!

Cherry Cranberry Shakes

(Pictured below)

My family has enjoyed this frothy pink drink for many years. The combination of cranberry juice and cherry soda is tongue tingling. —*Gayle Lewis*
Yucaipa, California

1 cup cranberry juice, chilled
1 cup cherry soda, chilled
1 tablespoon milk *or* half-and-half cream
3/4 teaspoon vanilla extract
1 cup vanilla ice cream, softened

Place all of the ingredients in a blender; cover and process until smooth. Pour into chilled glasses. **Yield:** 3-1/2 cups.

Tropical Milk Shakes

(Pictured below)

This fruity shake has a bold banana flavor. It's a tasty

SHAKE THINGS UP a bit with Cherry Cranberry Shakes, Tropical Milk Shakes and Chocolate Malts (shown above, left to right). They're easy to whip up, yummy and make any occasion special.

tradition to serve this beverage whenever the family is together. —*DeEtta Rasmussen, Ogden, Iowa*

3/4 cup milk
2 medium ripe bananas
3 cups vanilla ice cream, softened
1 can (8 ounces) chunk pineapple, undrained
2 tablespoons flaked coconut, toasted
2 tablespoons chopped pecans

In a blender, combine the milk, bananas, ice cream and pineapple; cover and process until smooth. Pour into chilled glasses. Top with coconut and pecans. **Yield:** 5 cups.

Chocolate Malts

(Pictured at left)

I can whip up this decadent ice cream drink in just minutes. It's a favorite with kids after a day in the pool or for dessert after a barbecue. —*Marion Lowery Medford, Oregon*

3/4 cup milk
1/2 cup caramel ice cream topping
2 cups chocolate ice cream, softened
3 tablespoons malted milk powder
2 tablespoons chopped pecans, optional
Grated chocolate, optional

In a blender, combine the first five ingredients; cover and process until blended. Pour into chilled glasses. Sprinkle with grated chocolate if desired. **Yield:** 2-1/2 cups.

Granola Chip Shakes

Packed with irresistible ingredients and served with a spoon, this shake makes a super snack or dessert. —*Elaine Anderson, Aliquippa, Pennsylvania*

3/4 to 1 cup milk
4 tablespoons butterscotch ice cream topping, *divided*
2 cups vanilla ice cream, softened
1/2 cup granola cereal
2 tablespoons miniature semisweet chocolate chips

In a blender, combine milk, 2 tablespoons butterscotch topping and ice cream; cover and process until smooth. Pour into chilled glasses. Drizzle with remaining topping; sprinkle with half of the granola and chocolate chips. Use a knife to swirl topping into shake. Top with remaining granola and chips. **Yield:** 2-1/2 cups.

Piece-o'-Cheesecake Shakes

My grandpa, who loves cheesecake, decided a shake made from his favorite dessert would be extra wonderful. He was right! —*Rebekah Ann Snow Star City, Arkansas*

4 ounces cream cheese, softened
1 can (14 ounces) sweetened condensed milk
1/4 cup lemon juice
1-1/4 cups whipped topping
1 graham cracker crust (9 inches)
ADDITIONAL INGREDIENTS:
1/2 cup plus 2 tablespoons milk
1/2 teaspoon vanilla extract
1 cup vanilla ice cream, softened

In a mixing bowl, beat cream cheese until fluffy. Add condensed milk and lemon juice; beat until thickened and blended. Fold in whipped topping. Spoon into the crust. Refrigerate for 2 hours or until set. Cut into eight pieces. For each shake, place one piece of cheesecake in a blender; add the additional ingredients. Cover and process until smooth. Pour into a chilled glass. **Yield:** 8 servings.

Peachy Buttermilk Shakes

The tang of buttermilk blended with the sweet peaches prompts frequent requests for this beverage from my husband and grandchildren. —*Anna Mayer Ft. Branch, Indiana*

1 cup buttermilk
3 cups sliced peaches
1 cup vanilla ice cream, softened
1/4 cup sugar
3/4 teaspoon ground cinnamon

Place all of the ingredients in a blender; cover and process until smooth. Pour into chilled glasses. **Yield:** 3 cups.

Toasting Coconut

Spread coconut in a single layer on a baking sheet. Bake at 375° for about 10 minutes or until golden brown, stirring occasionally. Watch closely so it doesn't get too brown.

Asparagus Roll-Ups

(Pictured above)

These roll-ups are simply divine. A friend shared the recipe after serving them at a church brunch, where they disappeared fast. They make a unique finger food, a side dish at supper or a lovely lunch served with soup. —*Clara Nenstiel, Pampa, Texas*

16 fresh asparagus spears
16 slices sandwich bread, crusts removed
1 package (8 ounces) cream cheese, softened
8 bacon strips, cooked and crumbled
2 tablespoons minced chives
1/4 cup butter *or* margarine, melted
3 tablespoons grated Parmesan cheese

Place asparagus in a skillet with a small amount of water; cook until crisp-tender, about 6-8 minutes. Drain and set aside. Flatten bread with a rolling pin. Combine the cream cheese, bacon and chives; spread 1 tablespoonful on each slice of bread. Top with an asparagus spear. Roll up tightly; place seam side down on a greased baking sheet. Brush with butter and sprinkle with Parmesan cheese. Cut roll-ups in half. Bake at 400° for 10-12 minutes or until lightly browned. **Yield:** 32 appetizers.

Critter Crunch

I make a big batch of this fun sweet snack throughout the year to keep on hand for hungry kids of all ages. Once you get started eating, it's hard to stop. Plus, it makes a great take-along treat. —*Wilma Miller Port Angeles, Washington*

1/4 cup butter *or* margarine
3 tablespoons brown sugar
1 teaspoon ground cinnamon
1-1/2 cups Crispix
1-1/2 cups Cheerios
1-1/2 cups animal crackers
1-1/2 cups bear-shaped honey graham snacks
1 cup bite-size Shredded Wheat
1 cup miniature pretzels

In a saucepan or microwave-safe bowl, heat butter, brown sugar and cinnamon until butter is melted; mix well. In a large bowl, combine the remaining ingredients. Add butter mixture and toss to coat. Place in a greased 15-in. x 10-in. x 1-in. baking pan. Bake, uncovered, at 300° for 30 minutes, stirring every 10 minutes. Store in an airtight container. **Yield:** about 8 cups.

Fruit Delight

I'm a 12-year-old who likes to experiment in the kitchen. This thick fruity beverage, which is refreshing as a snack or dessert, has become one of my family's favorites. —*Jonathan Weber, Atmore, Alabama*

2 cups frozen unsweetened strawberries *or* other fruit, partially thawed
5 ice cubes
1 carton (8 ounces) vanilla yogurt
1 tablespoon orange juice
1 to 2 teaspoons sugar
1 to 2 teaspoons brown sugar
1-1/2 teaspoons honey
1 teaspoon lemon juice
Whipped topping, optional

In a blender, combine the first eight ingredients. Cover and process until smooth. Pour into glasses. Garnish with whipped topping if desired. Serve immediately. **Yield:** 3-4 servings.

Lime Cucumber Salsa

This unique salsa tastes terrific with chicken and fish, on top of baked potatoes or eaten as a dip with tortilla chips. —*Marcia Kwiecinski, Lansing, Michigan*

✓ Uses less fat, sugar or salt. Includes Nutritional Analysis and Diabetic Exchanges.

1 large cucumber, seeded and finely chopped
1 to 2 garlic cloves, minced
1 jalapeno pepper,* finely chopped
3 green onions, sliced
2 tablespoons minced fresh cilantro
2 tablespoons lime juice
2 tablespoons olive *or* vegetable oil
1 teaspoon grated lime peel
1/2 teaspoon salt, optional
1/4 teaspoon pepper

In a bowl, combine all ingredients. Refrigerate for at least 2 hours before serving. **Yield:** 2-1/2 cups. **Nutritional Analysis:** One 3-tablespoon serving (prepared without salt) equals 25 calories, 1 mg sodium, 0 cholesterol, 1 gm carbohydrate, 2 gm protein, 2 gm fat. **Diabetic Exchange:** 1/2 fat. ***Editor's Note:** When cutting or seeding hot peppers, use rubber or plastic gloves to protect your hands. Avoid touching your face.

Hot Diggety Dogs

My family has always enjoyed this quick and easy snack. When our children were young, they used to help me fix these. Now they prepare them with their own families. —*Linda Blankenmyer Conestoga, Pennsylvania*

20 saltine crackers
5 slices process American cheese, quartered
Ketchup, mustard and pickle relish
2 hot dogs

Place crackers on a lightly greased baking sheet. Top with cheese, ketchup, mustard and relish. Cut each hot dog into 10 slices; place one slice on each cracker. Bake at 350° for 10-12 minutes or until the cheese is melted. **Yield:** 20 snacks. **Editor's Note:** If serving small children, cut hot dog slices in half; double the amount of crackers and cheese.

Spicy Mustard Spread

This zippy spread makes taste buds sit up and take notice. It's super on vegetables and a variety of different meats. —*Audrey Thibodeau, Gilbert, Arizona*

1/4 cup butter *or* margarine, softened
2 tablespoons ground mustard
2 tablespoons vinegar
1/4 teaspoon garlic salt
4 drops hot pepper sauce

In a mixing bowl, combine all ingredients; beat until smooth. Serve with hot dogs, vegetables, hamburgers, chicken or steak. Store in the refrigerator. **Yield:** about 1/3 cup.

Cheddar Pepper Crisps

(Pictured below)

I got the idea for these cheesy, peppery, crispy snacks at my bridal shower some 4 years ago. They're popular for munching by themselves or with a dip. —*Wendy Prevost, Cody, Wyoming*

1-3/4 cups all-purpose flour
1/2 cup cornmeal
1/2 teaspoon baking soda
1/2 teaspoon sugar
1/2 teaspoon salt
1/2 cup cold butter *or* margarine
1-1/2 cups (6 ounces) shredded sharp cheddar cheese
1/2 cup cold water
2 tablespoons vinegar
Coarsely ground pepper

In a large bowl, combine the first five ingredients. Cut in butter until crumbly. Stir in cheese. Sprinkle with water and vinegar. Toss with a fork until a ball forms. Wrap tightly in plastic wrap; refrigerate for 1 hour or until dough is firm. Divide into six portions. On a lightly floured surface, roll each portion of dough into an 8-in. circle. Cut into eight wedges and place on greased baking sheets. Sprinkle with pepper; lightly press into dough. Bake at 375° for 10-14 minutes or until golden brown and crisp. Cool on wire racks. Store in an airtight container. **Yield:** 4 dozen.

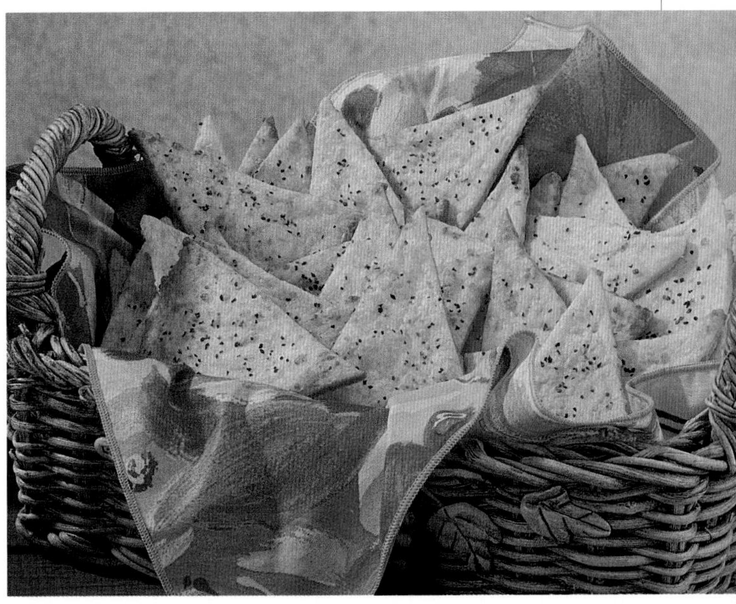

Cheese-Stuffed Cherry Tomatoes

(Pictured below)

We live close to some of the best tomato fields, so my husband and I go handpick enough for these easy-to-fix appetizers. It's impossible to eat just one.
—Mary Lou Robison, Miami, Florida

1 pint cherry tomatoes
4 ounces crumbled feta *or* blue cheese
1/2 cup finely chopped red onion
1/2 cup olive *or* vegetable oil
1/4 cup cider *or* red wine vinegar
1 tablespoon dried oregano
Salt and pepper to taste

Cut a thin slice off the top of each tomato. Scoop out and discard pulp. Invert tomatoes onto paper towels to drain. Combine cheese and onion; spoon into tomatoes. In a jar with a tight-fitting lid, combine oil, vinegar, oregano, salt and pepper; shake well. Spoon over tomatoes. Cover and refrigerate for 30 minutes or until ready to serve. **Yield:** about 1 dozen.

Pizza Sticks

When I saw the recipe for these pepperoni-filled snacks, I knew my three young daughters would like making them. They're quick and fun to assemble—especially when they work together. *—Darlene Sutton Boise, Idaho*

1 tube (11 ounces) refrigerated breadsticks
24 pepperoni slices
2 tablespoons grated Parmesan cheese
1/2 teaspoon Italian seasoning
1/4 teaspoon garlic powder
1/2 cup pizza sauce, warmed

Unroll breadstick dough and separate into eight pieces. Place three pepperoni slices on the bottom half of each breadstick, leaving about 3/4 in. of dough at the end. Fold top of dough over pepperoni and pinch end to seal; twist breadsticks. Place on ungreased baking sheets. Combine the Parmesan cheese, Italian seasoning and garlic powder; sprinkle over breadsticks. Bake at 350° for 15-20 minutes or until golden brown. Serve with pizza sauce. **Yield:** 8 breadsticks.

Salmon Tartlets

These make great party appetizers, but sometimes I forgo the crust and make the filling into a loaf for a family meal. *—Carolyn Kyzer, Alexander, Arkansas*

1/2 cup butter *or* margarine, softened
1 package (3 ounces) cream cheese, softened
1 cup all-purpose flour
FILLING:
2 eggs
1/2 cup milk
1 tablespoon butter *or* margarine, melted
1 teaspoon lemon juice
1/2 cup dry bread crumbs
1-1/2 teaspoons dried parsley flakes
1/2 teaspoon rubbed sage
1/2 teaspoon salt
1/4 teaspoon pepper
1 can (14-3/4 ounces) salmon, drained and bones removed
1 green onion, sliced

In a mixing bowl, beat butter, cream cheese and flour until smooth. Shape tablespoonfuls of dough into balls; press onto the bottom and up the sides of greased miniature muffin cups. In a bowl, combine eggs, milk, butter and lemon juice. Stir in crumbs, parsley, sage, salt and pepper. Fold in salmon and onion. Spoon into shells. Bake at 350° for 30-35 minutes or until browned. **Yield:** 2 dozen.

Cheesy Soft Pretzels

Fresh and warm from the oven, these chewy twists are a yummy snack even kids can make. Watch them disappear! *—Ruth Ann Stelfox, Raymond, Alberta*

1-1/2 cups all-purpose flour
1/2 cup shredded cheddar cheese

2 teaspoons baking powder
1 teaspoon sugar
3/4 teaspoon salt
2 tablespoons cold butter *or* margarine
2/3 cup milk
1 egg, beaten
Coarse salt

In a bowl, combine flour, cheese, baking powder, sugar and salt. Cut in butter until crumbly. Stir in milk just until moistened. Knead on a floured surface for 1 minute; divide in half. Roll each portion into a 12-in. x 8-in. rectangle; cut each into 8-in.-long strips. Fold strips in half, pinching the edges, and twist into pretzel shapes. Place on greased baking sheets. Brush with egg and sprinkle with coarse salt. Bake at 400° for 12-15 minutes or until golden brown. Serve immediately. **Yield:** 1-1/2 dozen.

Ginger Lime Dip

This creamy snack is tangy and refreshing. It's a fun alternative to sweet fruit dips. —*Shirley Glaab, Hattiesburg, Mississippi*

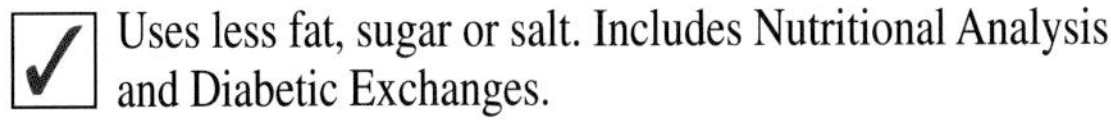
Uses less fat, sugar or salt. Includes Nutritional Analysis and Diabetic Exchanges.

1/2 cup sour cream
1/2 cup mayonnaise
1 tablespoon honey
1 tablespoon lime juice
1 teaspoon grated lime peel
1/4 teaspoon ground ginger
Cantaloupe and honeydew slices

In a small bowl, combine the sour cream, mayonnaise, honey, lime juice, lime peel and ginger. Cover and refrigerate until serving. Serve with melon. **Yield:** about 1 cup. **Nutritional Analysis:** 3 tablespoons of dip (prepared with nonfat sour cream and fat-free mayonnaise) equals 54 calories, 177 mg sodium, 2 mg cholesterol, 11 gm carbohydrate, 2 gm protein, trace fat. **Diabetic Exchange:** 1 fruit.

Colorful Crab Appetizer Pizza

(Pictured above right)

If you're looking for a really easy and special appetizer, this one stands out. It's a fresh-tasting and lovely variation on a cold vegetable pizza. I make it as a snack for parties all the time. —*Diane Caron, Des Moines, Iowa*

1 tube (8 ounces) refrigerated crescent rolls
1 package (8 ounces) cream cheese, softened
1-1/2 cups coarsely chopped fresh spinach, *divided*
1 green onion, thinly sliced
1-1/2 teaspoons minced fresh dill *or* 1/2 teaspoon dill weed
1 teaspoon grated lemon peel, *divided*
1/2 teaspoon lemon juice
1/8 teaspoon pepper
1-1/4 cups chopped imitation crabmeat
1/4 cup chopped ripe olives

Unroll the crescent roll dough and place on an ungreased 12-in. pizza pan. Flatten dough, sealing seams and perforations. Bake at 350° for 8-10 minutes or until lightly browned; cool. In a small mixing bowl, beat cream cheese until smooth. Stir in 1 cup of spinach, onion, dill, 1/2 teaspoon of lemon peel, lemon juice and pepper. Spread over the crust. Top with crab, olives and remaining spinach and lemon peel. Cut into bite-size squares. **Yield:** 8-10 servings.

Tortilla Turnaround

Cut leftover tortillas into wedges, then fry on both sides in a lightly oiled skillet until golden. Remove from the pan and sprinkle with sugar and cinnamon.

Ground Beef Snack Quiches

(Pictured above and on page 6)

My husband, Cory, farms, so supper can sometimes be quite late. A hearty appetizer like these meaty mini quiches is a perfect way to start the meal. They taste super made with ground beef, but I sometimes substitute bacon, ham, ground pork or sausage.
—Stacey Atkinson, Rugby, North Dakota

1/4 pound ground beef
1/8 to 1/4 teaspoon garlic powder
1/8 teaspoon pepper
1 cup biscuit/baking mix
1/4 cup cornmeal
1/4 cup cold butter *or* margarine
2 to 3 tablespoons boiling water
1 egg
1/2 cup half-and-half cream
1 tablespoon chopped green onion
1 tablespoon chopped sweet red pepper
1/8 to 1/4 teaspoon salt
1/8 to 1/4 teaspoon cayenne pepper
1/2 cup finely shredded cheddar cheese

In a saucepan over medium heat, cook beef, garlic powder and pepper until meat is no longer pink; drain and set aside. In a bowl, combine the biscuit mix and cornmeal; cut in butter. Add enough water to form a soft dough. Press onto the bottom and up the sides of greased miniature muffin cups. Place teaspoonfuls of beef mixture into each shell. In a bowl, combine the egg, cream, onion, red pepper, salt and cayenne; pour over beef mixture. Sprinkle with cheese. Bake at 375° for 20 minutes or until a knife inserted near the center comes out clean. **Yield:** 1-1/2 dozen.

Pretty Granola Treats

With chocolate chips, pecans, coconut and oats, these unforgettable chewy granola treats are enjoyed by adults and children alike. *—Dorothy Pritchett*
Wills Point, Texas

1-1/4 cups quick-cooking oats
1 cup flaked coconut
1/2 cup all-purpose flour
1/2 teaspoon baking powder
1/2 teaspoon ground cinnamon
1/4 teaspoon salt
1/8 teaspoon ground nutmeg
1/2 cup butter *or* margarine
3/4 cup packed brown sugar
3 tablespoons honey
1/2 cup semisweet chocolate chips
32 pecan halves

In a large bowl, combine the first seven ingredients and set aside. In a small saucepan, combine butter, brown sugar and honey; cook and stir over medium heat until sugar is dissolved. Pour over the oat mixture and mix well. Fill greased miniature muffin cups with 1 tablespoon of oat mixture. Bake at 350° for 12-14 minutes or until golden brown. Cool for 10 minutes; run a knife around edges before removing to a wire rack to cool completely. In a microwave, melt chocolate chips; stir until smooth. Dip bottoms of granola treats into melted chocolate. Place on waxed paper with chocolate side up; top each with a pecan half. Let stand until hardened. **Yield:** 32 servings.

Bell Pepper Nachos

When you're hungry for an out-of-the-ordinary snack, give this delicious recipe a try. Instead of tortilla chips, pretty pepper pieces hold a savory cheese and rice topping in this colorful appetizer. Our family really digs into a plate of these nachos. *—Aneta Kish*
La Crosse, Wisconsin

2 medium green peppers
1 medium sweet red pepper

1 medium sweet yellow pepper
2 medium plum tomatoes, seeded and chopped
1/3 cup finely chopped onion
1 teaspoon chili powder
1/2 teaspoon ground cumin
1-1/2 cups cooked rice
1/2 cup shredded Monterey Jack cheese
1/4 cup minced fresh cilantro *or* parsley
1/4 teaspoon hot pepper sauce
1/2 cup shredded sharp cheddar cheese

Cut peppers into 1-1/2- to 2-in. squares. Cut each square in half diagonally to form two triangles; set aside. In a lightly greased skillet, cook the tomatoes, onion, chili powder and cumin over medium heat for 3 minutes or until onion is tender, stirring occasionally. Remove from the heat. Add rice, Monterey Jack cheese, cilantro and hot pepper sauce; stir well. Spoon a heaping tablespoonful onto each pepper triangle. Place on greased baking sheets. Sprinkle with cheddar cheese. Broil 6-8 in. from the heat for 3-4 minutes or until cheese is bubbly and rice is heated through. **Yield:** 3-1/2 dozen. **Editor's Note:** These appetizers can be assembled ahead of time. Place on baking sheets, cover and refrigerate for up to 8 hours before broiling.

Cheesy Onion Roll-Ups

These roll-ups are very fast to fix, plus you can make them ahead and keep them wrapped in the refrigerator until you're ready to serve. So they're perfect when you're looking for fuss-free food for parties.
—Barbara Keith, Faucett, Missouri

1 cup (8 ounces) sour cream
1 package (8 ounces) cream cheese, softened
3/4 cup sliced green onions
1/2 cup finely shredded cheddar cheese
1 tablespoon lime juice
1 tablespoon minced seeded jalapeno pepper*
10 to 12 flour tortillas (6 inches)
Picante sauce

Combine the first six ingredients in a bowl; mix well. Spread on one side of tortillas. Roll up tightly; wrap in plastic wrap. Refrigerate for at least 1 hour. Slice into 1-in. pieces. Serve with picante sauce. **Yield:** about 5 dozen. ***Editor's Note:** When cutting or seeding hot peppers, use rubber or plastic gloves to protect your hands. Avoid touching your face.

No-Yolk Deviled Eggs

(Pictured below)

This lighter recipe still provides traditional deviled egg flavor and appearance. A mashed-potato mixture magically replaces the yolk filling. *—Dottie Burton*
Cincinnati, Ohio

Uses less fat, sugar or salt. Includes Nutritional Analysis and Diabetic Exchanges.

10 hard-cooked eggs
3/4 cup mashed potatoes (prepared with skim milk and margarine)
1 tablespoon fat-free mayonnaise
1 teaspoon prepared mustard
2 to 3 drops yellow food coloring, optional
Paprika

Slice eggs in half lengthwise; remove yolks and refrigerate for another use. Set whites aside. In a small bowl, combine mashed potatoes, mayonnaise, mustard and food coloring if desired; mix well. Stuff or pipe into egg whites. Sprinkle with paprika. Refrigerate until serving. **Yield:** 10 servings. **Nutritional Analysis:** One serving equals 35 calories, 118 mg sodium, trace cholesterol, 3 gm carbohydrate, 4 gm protein, 1 gm fat. **Diabetic Exchanges:** 1/2 very lean meat, 1/2 vegetable.

Corn and Bacon Dip

(Pictured below and on page 6)

The recipe for this creamy appetizer or snack dip was given to me about 20 years ago by a friend. It becomes a favorite wherever I share it. People are constantly asking me for the recipe. Sometimes I simply serve it with corn chips. —*Carolyn Zaschak, Corning, New York*

1 package (8 ounces) cream cheese, softened
1 cup (8 ounces) sour cream
1/4 cup mayonnaise
2 garlic cloves, minced
1/4 teaspoon hot pepper sauce
1 can (15-1/4 ounces) whole kernel corn, drained
8 bacon strips, cooked and crumbled
Assorted raw vegetables *and/or* crackers

In a mixing bowl, combine the first five ingredients. Stir in corn and bacon. Cover and refrigerate for several hours. Serve with vegetables and/or crackers. **Yield:** 3 cups.

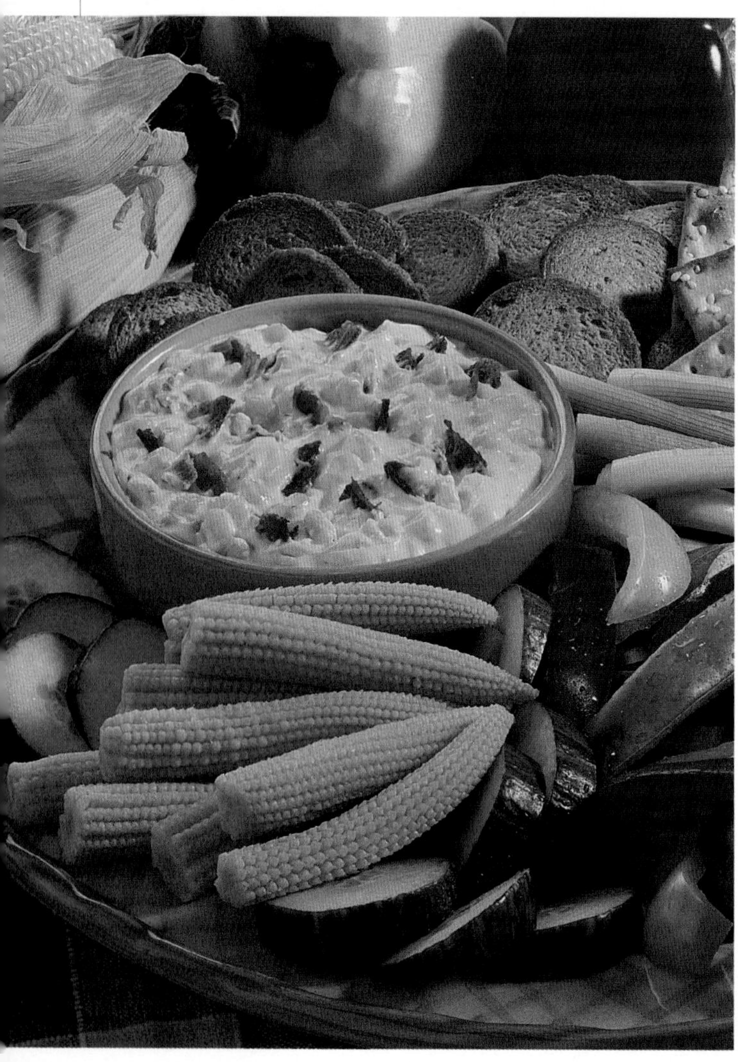

Broccoli Dip in a Bread Bowl

For a delicious herb dip, try this recipe. It's great on a holiday buffet or just for good munching and fun to serve in a loaf of bread. —*Lisa Hawes, Dallas, Texas*

✓ Uses less fat, sugar or salt. Includes Nutritional Analysis and Diabetic Exchanges.

1 cup plain nonfat yogurt
1 cup fat-free mayonnaise
1 package (10 ounces) frozen chopped broccoli, thawed and squeezed dry
1 jar (2 ounces) diced pimientos, drained
2 tablespoons minced fresh parsley
1 tablespoon chopped green onion
1/2 teaspoon dill weed
1/8 teaspoon garlic powder
1 loaf (1 pound) unsliced French bread

In a large bowl, combine the yogurt and mayonnaise. Stir in broccoli, pimientos, parsley, onion, dill and garlic powder. Cover and refrigerate for 3 hours or overnight. Cut the top fourth off the loaf of bread; carefully hollow out bottom of loaf, leaving a 1/2-in. shell. Set the shell aside. Cut top and removed bread into cubes; place on an ungreased baking sheet. Bake at 350° for 8-10 minutes or until golden brown. Fill bread shell with dip. Serve with toasted bread cubes. **Yield:** 3 cups. **Nutritional Analysis:** 2 tablespoons of dip (calculated without bread) equals 16 calories, 83 mg sodium, trace cholesterol, 3 gm carbohydrate, 1 gm protein, trace fat. **Diabetic Exchange:** Free food.

Stuffed Apple Treats

With apple trees right in my own yard, it's no wonder I love to pack these nutritious and tasty treats in my children's school lunches. —*Margaret Slocum Ridgefield, Washington*

2 tablespoons mayonnaise *or* softened cream cheese
2 tablespoons chopped nuts
2 tablespoons raisins, dried cranberries *or* dates
2 medium apples, cored

Combine mayonnaise or cream cheese, nuts and raisins. Stuff into apples. **Yield:** 2 servings.

Tumbleweeds

I like making these crisp and creamy treats because they require only four ingredients. It's hard to stop eating them. —*Virginia Johnson, Mims, Florida*

FINGER FOODS like Spicy Party Mix and Pizza by the Scoop (above, left to right) will be the hit at your next party or get-together.

- **1 can (12 ounces) salted peanuts**
- **1 can (7 ounces) potato sticks**
- **3 cups butterscotch chips**
- **3 tablespoons peanut butter**

Combine peanuts and potato sticks in a bowl; set aside. In a microwave, heat the butterscotch chips and peanut butter at 70% power for 1-2 minutes or until melted, stirring every 30 seconds. Add to peanut mixture; stir to coat evenly. Drop by rounded tablespoonfuls onto waxed paper-lined baking sheets. Refrigerate until set, about 5 minutes. Store in an airtight container. **Yield:** about 4-1/2 dozen. **Editor's Note:** This recipe was tested in an 850-watt microwave.

Spicy Party Mix

(Pictured above and on page 6)

Sesame seeds are a fun addition in this savory snack mix. Children and adults go for the crispy combo.
—June Mullins, Livonia, Missouri

- **10 cups Crispix cereal**
- **2 cups salted peanuts**
- **1-1/2 cups pretzel sticks**
- **1/2 cup sesame seeds, toasted**
- **1/2 cup vegetable oil**
- **2 tablespoons lemon juice**
- **1 tablespoon chili powder**
- **1 tablespoon curry powder**
- **1 teaspoon garlic salt**
- **1 teaspoon onion salt**
- **1/2 teaspoon ground cumin**

In a large bowl, combine the cereal, peanuts, pretzels and sesame seeds. In a saucepan, combine the remaining ingredients; bring to a boil. Pour over the cereal mixture and stir to coat. Spread in a greased 15-in. x 10-in. x 1-in. baking pan. Bake at 250° for 10 minutes or until golden brown, stirring once. Cool completely. Store in an airtight container. **Yield:** 4 quarts.

Pizza by the Scoop

(Pictured above)

This tasty cold snack dip is one of my most-requested recipes and always pleases friends at get-togethers. People keep scooping until the platter is clean.
—Georgene Robertson, Pikeville, Kentucky

- **2 packages (8 ounces *each*) cream cheese, softened**
- **1 bottle (12 ounces) chili sauce**
- **1 package (6 ounces) Canadian bacon, chopped**
- **1 small onion, chopped**
- **1 small green pepper, chopped**
- **3/4 cup shredded mozzarella cheese**
- **3/4 cup shredded cheddar cheese**
- **Corn chips**

Spread cream cheese on an ungreased 12-in. pizza pan. Spread with chili sauce. Sprinkle with the Canadian bacon, onion, green pepper and cheeses. Serve with chips. **Yield:** 14-16 servings.

Toasted Almond Crab Spread

(Pictured above)

I got the recipe for this super spread from my sister-in-law years ago, and it's always popular at social gatherings. It's so easy to make, yet it looks and tastes fancy. —*Sonja Blow, Groveland, California*

1 package (8 ounces) cream cheese, softened
1-1/2 cups (6 ounces) shredded Swiss cheese
1/3 cup sour cream
1/8 teaspoon ground nutmeg
1/8 teaspoon pepper
1 can (6 ounces) crabmeat, drained, flaked and cartilage removed *or* 1/2 cup imitation crabmeat, chopped
3 tablespoons finely chopped green onions, *divided*
1/3 cup sliced almonds, toasted
Assorted crackers

In a mixing bowl, combine the first five ingredients. Stir in crab and 2 tablespoons onions. Spread into an ungreased 9-in. pie plate. Bake at 350° for 15 minutes or until heated through. Sprinkle with almonds and remaining onions. Serve with crackers. **Yield:** 2 cups.

Kids' Crepe Roll-Ups

My grandson Craig loves to help make a batch of these light and airy bite-size crepes. This is the snack my seven grandchildren most often request. —*Phyllis Grodahl, Lytton, Iowa*

1-1/2 cups milk
2 eggs
1 cup all-purpose flour
1/2 teaspoon salt
1 tablespoon butter *or* margarine, melted
Maple syrup

In a blender, combine the milk, eggs, flour and salt. Cover and process until smooth. Heat a lightly greased nonstick 6-in. skillet. Add 1/4 cup of batter. Lift and tilt pan to evenly coat bottom. Cook on each side until golden. Repeat with remaining batter. Roll up and slice into bite-size pieces. Brush with butter and syrup. **Yield:** 5 servings.

Tuna Cheese Spread

The flavor of tuna is very subtle in this thick, creamy spread. It's terrific on crackers or carrot and celery sticks, stuffed in a tomato or used for a sandwich. —*Dorothy Anderson, Ottawa, Kansas*

1 package (8 ounces) cream cheese, softened
1 can (6 ounces) tuna, drained and flaked
1/2 cup finely sliced green onions
1/4 cup mayonnaise
1 tablespoon lemon juice
3/4 teaspoon curry powder
Dash salt
Bread *or* crackers

In a bowl, combine the first seven ingredients; mix well. Spread on bread or crackers. **Yield:** 2 cups.

Mini Corn Dogs

For satisfying homemade flavor, try this snack of golden cornmeal dough baked around mini hot dogs served with a tangy dipping sauce. —*Geralyn Harrington, Floral Park, New York*

1-2/3 cups all-purpose flour
1/3 cup cornmeal
3 teaspoons baking powder
1 teaspoon salt
3 tablespoons cold butter *or* margarine
1 tablespoon shortening
1 egg
3/4 cup milk
24 miniature hot dogs

HONEY MUSTARD SAUCE:
1/3 cup honey
1/3 cup prepared mustard
1 tablespoon molasses

In a large bowl, combine the first four ingredients. Cut in butter and shortening until mixture resembles coarse crumbs. Beat egg and milk; stir into crumb mixture until a soft dough forms. Turn onto a lightly floured surface; knead 6-8 times or until smooth. Roll out to 1/4-in. thickness. Cut with a 2-1/4-in. biscuit cutter. Fold each dough circle over a hot dog and press edges to seal (dough will be sticky). Place on greased baking sheets. Bake at 450° for 10-12 minutes or until golden brown. Meanwhile, combine sauce ingredients in a small bowl; mix well. Serve with the corn dogs. **Yield:** 2 dozen.

Creamy Green Onion Spread

All you need to make this snack is some crackers and four ingredients. —Sue Seymour, Valatie, New York

1 package (8 ounces) cream cheese, softened
2 tablespoons milk
2 green onions with tops, chopped
1/4 cup crushed pineapple, drained, optional
Crackers

In a small bowl, beat cream cheese and milk until smooth. Stir in onions and pineapple if desired. Serve with crackers. **Yield:** 1 cup.

Pumpkin Cheese Ball

No one will guess this make-ahead spread has pumpkin in it, but that subtle ingredient lends harvest color and added nutrition. —Linnea Rein, Topeka, Kansas

1 package (8 ounces) cream cheese, softened
1/2 cup canned *or* cooked pumpkin
1 can (8 ounces) crushed pineapple, well drained
2 cups (8 ounces) shredded sharp cheddar cheese
1 package (2-1/2 ounces) dried beef, finely chopped
1 tablespoon finely chopped onion
Celery leaves
Assorted crackers *and/or* raw vegetables

In a mixing bowl, beat cream cheese, pumpkin and pineapple. Stir in cheddar cheese, beef and onion. Shape into a ball; place on a serving platter. Score sides with a knife to resemble a pumpkin and add celery leaves for a stem. Serve with crackers and/or vegetables. **Yield:** 3 cups.

Softening Cream Cheese

To soften an 8-ounce package of cream cheese, place unwrapped cheese on a microwave-safe plate. Microwave at 50% power for about 1 minute.

Dairy Delicious Dip

(Pictured below)

Munching on fruit becomes so much more fun when there's a sweet, creamy dip to dunk your slices in. I enjoy its ease of preparation. —Karen Kenney Harvard, Illinois

1 package (8 ounces) cream cheese, softened
1/2 cup sour cream
1/4 cup sugar
1/4 cup packed brown sugar
1 to 2 tablespoons maple syrup
Assorted fresh fruit

In a small mixing bowl, combine cream cheese, sour cream, sugars and syrup to taste; beat until smooth. Chill. Serve with fruit. **Yield:** 2 cups.

Salads & Dressings

A brimming bowl of salad makes a refreshing accompaniment to any dinner or a hearty meal in itself. And don't forget to toss in a simple-to-prepare dressing.

SENSATIONAL SALADS. Clockwise from upper left: Colorful Vegetable Salad (p. 26), Seven-Fruit Salad (p. 27), Spinach Salad with Red Potatoes (p. 41) and Tangy Cucumber Salad (p. 39).

Colorful Vegetable Salad

(Pictured above and on page 24)

With its Christmasy colors, this salad is a very merry part of my holiday menu. It serves a big group, but since it also keeps well in the refrigerator, you can look forward to the tasty leftovers, too. —Pauline Phalen St. Louis, Missouri

✓ Uses less fat, sugar or salt. Includes Nutritional Analysis and Diabetic Exchanges.

6 cups broccoli florets
6 cups caulifloweretS
2 cups cherry tomatoes, halved
1 large red onion, sliced
1 can (6 ounces) pitted ripe olives, drained and sliced
1 envelope ranch salad dressing mix
2/3 cup vegetable oil
1/4 cup vinegar

In a large bowl, toss the broccoli, cauliflower, tomatoes, onion and olives. In a jar with a tight-fitting lid, combine dressing mix, oil and vinegar; shake well. Pour over salad and toss. Refrigerate for at least 3 hours. **Yield:** 20 servings. **Nutritional Analysis:** One 3/4-cup serving equals 94 calories, 130 mg sodium, 0 cholesterol, 5 gm carbohydrate, 1 gm protein, 8 gm fat. **Diabetic Exchanges:** 1-1/2 fat, 1 vegetable.

Low-Fat Ranch Dressing

No one will believe this creamy, fresh-tasting dressing is low in fat. It has wonderful traditional ranch flavor. —Connie Simon, Reed City, Michigan

✓ Uses less fat, sugar or salt. Includes Nutritional Analysis and Diabetic Exchanges.

4 teaspoons olive *or* vegetable oil
2 teaspoons cider vinegar
Artificial sweetener equivalent to 2 teaspoons sugar
1/4 teaspoon dried marjoram
3/4 cup buttermilk
3 tablespoons plain nonfat yogurt
2 tablespoons fat-free mayonnaise
2 tablespoons finely chopped onion
2 tablespoons minced fresh parsley
1 garlic clove, minced

In a bowl, combine oil, vinegar, sweetener and marjoram. Whisk in buttermilk, yogurt and mayonnaise. Stir in onion, parsley and garlic. Cover and refrigerate for 6 hours or overnight to thicken. Whisk before serving. Serve over salad greens and vegetables of your choice. Refrigerate leftover dressing. **Yield:** 1-1/4 cups. **Nutritional Analysis:** One 2-tablespoon serving equals 30 calories, 44 mg sodium, 1 mg cholesterol, 2 gm carbohydrate, 1 gm protein, 2 gm fat. **Diabetic Exchange:** 1/2 fat.

Molded Cranberry Salad

Cranberries add tang to this whipped gelatin treat. This molded salad makes for a pretty presentation on a holiday dinner table. —Bobbie Talbott Veneta, Oregon

1 package (12 ounces) fresh *or* frozen cranberries
3/4 cup plus 2 tablespoons sugar, *divided*
1-1/2 cups water, *divided*
1 can (8 ounces) pineapple tidbits, drained
1 medium tart apple, peeled and diced
1/4 cup chopped walnuts
1 envelope unflavored gelatin
1/4 teaspoon salt
1/2 cup mayonnaise
2 tablespoons lemon juice
1 teaspoon grated lemon peel

In a saucepan, combine cranberries, 3/4 cup sugar and 1/2 cup water. Bring to a boil; boil for 3-4 minutes or until berries pop. Remove from the heat; stir in pineapple, apple and walnuts. Refrigerate until completely cooled. Meanwhile, place gelatin and remaining water in another saucepan; let stand for 1 minute. Add salt and remaining sugar. Cook and stir over low heat until dissolved. Remove from the heat; stir in the mayonnaise, lemon juice and peel. Transfer to a mixing bowl; refrigerate until partially set, about 1 hour. Beat until fluffy. Fold in the cranberry mixture. Pour into a 6-cup mold that has been coated with nonstick cooking spray. Refrigerate until firm, about 8 hours. **Yield:** 10-12 servings.

Spinach Salad with Peanut Dressing

I use my own spinach and strawberries in this eye-catching salad. The dressing gives it a big peanut taste that draws compliments. —*Susan Taul, Birmingham, Alabama*

1/2 cup vegetable oil
1/4 cup water
1/4 cup salted peanuts
3 tablespoons honey
1 tablespoon lemon juice
2 teaspoons cider *or* white wine vinegar
8 cups torn fresh spinach
2 cups halved fresh strawberries

In a blender, combine the first six ingredients. Cover and process until smooth. Arrange spinach and strawberries on salad plates or bowls; drizzle with dressing. **Yield:** 8 servings.

Ham and Wild Rice Salad

We cut the grass on our farm only once a year. That's because we want our aquatic grass to produce nutty, tasty grains of wild rice. I look forward to my wife, Marian, making this salad. —*Art Hedstrom, St. Paul, Minnesota*

3/4 cup golden raisins
1-1/2 cups hot water
4 cups cooked wild rice
2 cups julienned fully cooked ham
4 green onions, thinly sliced
1/3 cup olive *or* vegetable oil
1/4 cup cider *or* white wine vinegar
1/2 teaspoon salt
1/4 teaspoon pepper
Lettuce leaves and toasted pecan halves

In a large bowl, soak the raisins in water for 5 minutes; drain. Add rice, ham and onions. In a small bowl or jar with tight-fitting lid, combine oil, vinegar, salt and pepper; mix well. Pour over rice mixture and toss to coat. Cover and refrigerate for at least 1 hour. Serve on lettuce; garnish with pecans. **Yield:** 4-5 servings.

Seven-Fruit Salad

(Pictured below and on page 24)

A tongue-tingling lime dressing complements the colorful variety of fruit in this delightful salad. It's always a hit at summer get-togethers. It looks beautiful on a buffet and is very refreshing on a hot day. —*Judi Cottrell, Grand Blanc, Michigan*

1/2 cup lime juice
1/2 cup water
1/2 cup sugar
2 medium nectarines, thinly sliced
1 large firm banana, thinly sliced
1 pint blueberries
1 pint fresh strawberries, sliced
1-1/2 cups watermelon balls
1 cup green grapes
1 kiwifruit, peeled and chopped

In a bowl, combine the lime juice, water and sugar; stir until sugar is dissolved. Add nectarines and banana; toss to coat. In a 2-1/2-qt. glass bowl, combine the remaining fruits. Add nectarine mixture; stir gently. Cover and refrigerate for 1 hour. Serve with a slotted spoon. **Yield:** 8-10 servings.

Warm Mustard Potato Salad

(Pictured below)

This tangy mixture is wonderful and so different from traditional potato salads. The Dijon mustard and dill spark the flavor. It's a comforting and tasty side dish that's really simple to assemble. —Tiffany Mitchell Susanville, California

2 pounds small red potatoes
1 cup mayonnaise
1/4 cup Dijon mustard
1/2 to 3/4 cup chopped red onion
2 green onions with tops, sliced
2 garlic cloves, minced
3 tablespoons snipped fresh dill *or* 1 tablespoon dill weed
1/2 teaspoon salt
1/2 teaspoon pepper
1/4 teaspoon lime juice

Place the potatoes in a saucepan and cover with water. Cover and bring to a boil; cook until tender, about 25 minutes. Drain thoroughly and cool slightly. Meanwhile, combine the remaining ingredients. Cut potatoes into chunks; place in a bowl. Add the mustard mixture and toss to coat. Serve warm. **Yield:** 8-10 servings.

Fruited Cranberry Gelatin

A neighbor gave my mom this recipe, and it's become an annual favorite during the holidays. I appreciate that it feeds a lot of people. —Linda Fox Soldotna, Alaska

1 package (6 ounces) cranberry *or* raspberry gelatin
1/2 cup sugar
1-1/2 cups boiling water
1 package (12 ounces) fresh *or* frozen cranberries
3 medium unpeeled green apples, cored and cut into wedges
1 medium navel orange, peeled and quartered
1 cup diced celery
1 cup chopped pecans
1 cup cold water
1 tablespoon cider vinegar
2 teaspoons grated orange peel
1-1/2 teaspoons lemon juice
1/2 teaspoon salt
3/4 cup mayonnaise
2 tablespoons orange juice

In a large bowl, dissolve gelatin and sugar in boiling water. In a blender or food processor, process cranberries until coarsely chopped; add to gelatin mixture. Repeat with apples and orange. Stir in celery, pecans, water, vinegar, orange peel, lemon juice and salt. Pour into a 13-in. x 9-in. x 2-in. dish or a 2-1/2-qt. serving bowl. Refrigerate until set, about 3 hours. Whisk mayonnaise and orange juice; serve with the salad. **Yield:** 12-16 servings.

Curried Bean Salad

Beans are perfect for a budget meal. This cool, tangy salad is a hit when our six children and nine grandchildren come to eat. —Veta Chapman St. Clair, Michigan

1 pound dry great northern beans
4 green onions with tops, sliced
1/2 cup grated carrots
1/2 cup sliced radishes

DRESSING:

1/2 cup vegetable oil
1/4 cup cider *or* white wine vinegar
2 tablespoons mango chutney
1 teaspoon curry powder
1/2 teaspoon salt
1/4 teaspoon pepper

Place beans in a Dutch oven; add water to cover by

2 in. Bring to a boil; boil for 2 minutes. Remove from the heat; cover and let stand for 1 hour. Drain and discard liquid. Return beans to pan; add water to cover by 2 in. Bring to a boil; cover and simmer for 45 minutes or until beans are tender. Drain and discard liquid. Place beans in a large bowl; add onions, carrots and radishes. In another bowl, whisk dressing ingredients. Pour over bean mixture and toss gently. Cover and refrigerate for several hours or overnight. **Yield:** 10-12 servings.

Cumin Vinaigrette

This pretty dressing is wonderful served over a variety of salad greens. Or use it to marinate garden-fresh vegetables. —*Yolanda Maciejewski Land O'Lakes, Florida*

1/3 cup lemon juice
1/3 cup olive oil
1/3 cup vegetable oil
1/4 cup water
2 teaspoons sugar
2 teaspoons ground cumin
2 teaspoons paprika
1-1/2 teaspoons salt
2 garlic cloves, minced
1/4 teaspoon hot pepper sauce

In a jar with a tight-fitting lid, combine all ingredients and shake well. Shake again before serving. Store in the refrigerator. **Yield:** 1-1/2 cups.

Cukes for Kids

My boys enjoy this cool pickle-like salad so much that they're willing to overlook the onions and gobble it up! —*Cindy Winter-Hartley, Cary, North Carolina*

3 medium cucumbers, peeled and thinly sliced
2 teaspoons salt
1 tablespoon vegetable oil
1 tablespoon vinegar
1 teaspoon sugar
Dash pepper
2 tablespoons sliced green onions
Dash paprika

Place cucumbers in a strainer. Sprinkle with salt; let stand for 30 minutes, tossing occasionally. Rinse and drain well. In a bowl, combine the oil, vinegar, sugar and pepper; add the cucumbers and stir well. Sprinkle with onions and paprika. Refrigerate until serving. **Yield:** 4 servings.

Creamy Orange Fluff

(Pictured above)

I got this yummy recipe from a friend but came up with my own tasty topping. Creamy, fruity and refreshing, this salad is simple to make ahead and cuts nicely into squares for ease in serving. —*Nancy Callis Woodinville, Washington*

1 package (6 ounces) orange gelatin
2-1/2 cups boiling water
2 cans (11 ounces *each*) mandarin oranges, drained
1 can (8 ounces) crushed pineapple, undrained
1 can (6 ounces) frozen orange juice concentrate, thawed
TOPPING:
1 package (8 ounces) cream cheese, softened
1 cup cold milk
1 package (3.4 ounces) instant vanilla pudding mix

In a bowl, dissolve gelatin in boiling water. Stir in oranges, pineapple and orange juice concentrate. Coat a 13-in. x 9-in. x 2-in. dish with nonstick cooking spray; add gelatin mixture. Refrigerate until firm. In a mixing bowl, beat cream cheese until light. Gradually add milk and pudding mix; beat until smooth. Spread over orange layer. Chill until firm. **Yield:** 12-16 servings.

A Parade of Pasta Salads

AT SUMMERTIME picnics, barbecues and reunions, pasta salads are popular fare. We asked cooks from across the country for their best blends, and they came through with flying colors!

Each good-for-you variation will take your taste buds in deliciously different directions. Plus, you're sure to appreciate their make-ahead convenience.

Summer Spaghetti Salad

(Pictured below and on front cover)

This attractive, fresh-tasting salad features a bounty of garden vegetables and starts with a bottle of store-bought dressing. The recipe yields a big bowl!

—Lucia Johnson, Massena, New York

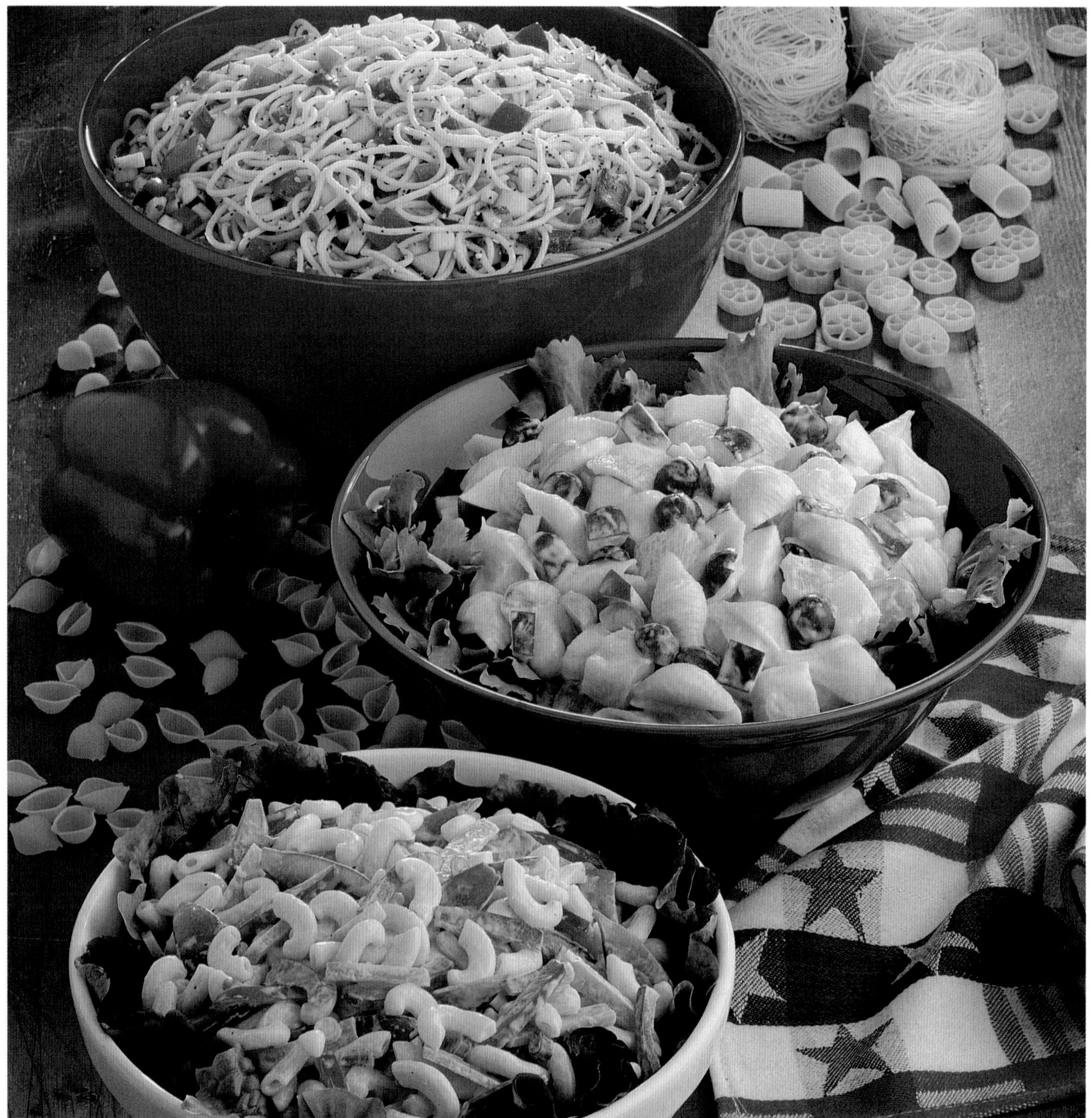

POPULAR PASTA SALADS at summertime gatherings—or any time of year—include Summer Spaghetti Salad, Pasta Fruit Salad and Oriental Pasta Salad (shown above, top to bottom).

✓ Uses less fat, sugar or salt. Includes Nutritional Analysis and Diabetic Exchanges.

1 package (16 ounces) thin spaghetti, halved
3 medium tomatoes, diced
3 small zucchini, diced
1 large cucumber, halved, seeded and diced
1 medium green pepper, diced
1 medium sweet red pepper, diced
1 bottle (8 ounces) Italian salad dressing
2 tablespoons grated Parmesan cheese
1-1/2 teaspoons sesame seeds
1-1/2 teaspoons poppy seeds
1/2 teaspoon paprika
1/4 teaspoon celery seed
1/8 teaspoon garlic powder

Cook spaghetti according to package directions; drain and rinse in cold water. Place in a large bowl; add tomatoes, zucchini, cucumber and peppers. Combine remaining ingredients; pour over salad and toss to coat. Cover and refrigerate for at least 2 hours. **Yield:** 16 servings. **Nutritional Analysis:** One 1-cup serving (prepared with fat-free salad dressing and nonfat Parmesan cheese topping) equals 137 calories, 150 mg sodium, trace cholesterol, 27 gm carbohydrate, 5 gm protein, 1 gm fat. **Diabetic Exchanges:** 1-1/2 starch, 1 vegetable.

Oriental Pasta Salad

(Pictured at left)

With a wonderful combination of colors and flavors, this one-of-a-kind salad goes great with barbecued chicken or pork. —*Diane Molberg*
Emerald Park, Saskatchewan

✓ Uses less fat, sugar or salt. Includes Nutritional Analysis and Diabetic Exchanges.

2 cups uncooked elbow macaroni
2 large carrots, cut into 1-inch strips
1 cup snow peas, halved
2 green onions with tops, sliced
1/2 cup thinly sliced sweet red pepper

DRESSING:

1/2 cup mayonnaise
1/2 cup sour cream
1 tablespoon cider *or* red wine vinegar
1 tablespoon soy sauce
1/2 teaspoon ground ginger
1/4 teaspoon pepper

Cook macaroni according to package directions; drain and rinse in cold water. Place in a large bowl; add carrots, peas, onions and red pepper. In a small bowl, whisk dressing ingredients until smooth. Pour over salad and toss to coat. Cover and refrigerate for 1-2 hours. **Yield:** 7 servings. **Nutritional Analysis:** One 1-cup serving (prepared with fat-free mayonnaise, nonfat sour cream and light soy sauce) equals 139 calories, 216 mg sodium, 1 mg cholesterol, 27 gm carbohydrate, 5 gm protein, 1 gm fat. **Diabetic Exchanges:** 1-1/2 starch, 1 vegetable.

Pasta Fruit Salad

(Pictured at far left)

Pasta and a creamy yogurt dressing give traditional fruit salad a new twist in this unusual but delicious dish. When I serve it at a buffet dinner or picnic, it always draws favorable comments. Give it a try!
—*Dixie Terry, Marion, Illinois*

✓ Uses less fat, sugar or salt. Includes Nutritional Analysis and Diabetic Exchanges.

3 cups uncooked medium pasta shells
1 can (20 ounces) unsweetened pineapple chunks, drained
1 large navel orange, peeled, sectioned and halved
1 cup halved red grapes
1 cup halved green grapes
1 medium apple, chopped
1 large firm banana, cut into 1/4-inch slices
1 carton (8 ounces) plain yogurt
1/4 cup orange juice concentrate

Cook pasta according to package directions; drain and rinse in cold water. Place in a large bowl; add the fruit. Combine yogurt and orange juice concentrate; pour over salad and toss to coat. Cover and chill for several hours. **Yield:** 10 servings. **Nutritional Analysis:** One 1-cup serving (prepared with nonfat yogurt) equals 192 calories, 20 mg sodium, trace cholesterol, 42 gm carbohydrate, 6 gm protein, 1 gm fat. **Diabetic Exchanges:** 2 starch, 1 fruit.

Cooking Pasta

Be sure to first bring water to a full rolling boil. For flavor, stir in 1 tablespoon salt to every 3 quarts water. To prevent noodles from sticking together, add 1 tablespoon vegetable or olive oil. Stir in pasta all at once and return to a boil. Boil, uncovered, stirring occasionally. As soon as the pasta tests done, drain in a colander. If using the pasta in a salad, rinse with cold water.

Cashew Pea Salad

(Pictured above)

My son-in-law frequently requests this crisp pea salad of mine. It has plenty of fresh ingredients and a tangy dressing. Peas are positively palate-pleasing paired with cashews in the cool side dish.
—Barbara Birk, American Fork, Utah

- **3/4 cup vegetable oil**
- **1/4 cup cider *or* red wine vinegar**
- **1 garlic clove, minced**
- **2 to 3 teaspoons Dijon mustard**
- **1 teaspoon Worcestershire sauce**
- **1/2 to 3/4 teaspoon salt**
- **1/2 teaspoon lemon juice**
- **1/4 teaspoon pepper**
- **1/4 teaspoon sugar**
- **1 package (10 ounces) frozen peas, thawed**
- **2 celery ribs, thinly sliced**
- **2 green onions, thinly sliced**
- **1/2 cup sour cream**
- **4 bacon strips, cooked and crumbled**
- **3/4 cup chopped cashews**
- **Lettuce leaves and tomato wedges, optional**

For dressing, combine the first nine ingredients in a small bowl; mix well. Cover and refrigerate for 1 hour. In a large bowl, combine peas, celery and onions. Combine sour cream and 2 tablespoons of dressing (refrigerate remaining dressing); mix well. Fold into the pea mixture. Just before serving, stir in bacon and cashews. If desired, serve on lettuce with a tomato garnish. **Yield:** 6-8 servings. **Editor's Note:** Remaining dressing may be served on a tossed salad.

Rice Salad with Cilantro Vinaigrette

I grow all my own herbs, including fresh cilantro. In fact, I first tried this recipe because it had cilantro in it. It's a delicious and colorful salad.
—Michele Montgomery, Lethbridge, Alberta

- **2 cups cooked long grain rice**
- **1 can (15 ounces) black beans, rinsed and drained**
- **1/2 cup diced sweet red pepper**
- **1/2 cup diced sweet yellow pepper**
- **4-1/2 teaspoons minced fresh cilantro**
- **3 tablespoons olive *or* vegetable oil**
- **2 tablespoons cider *or* white wine vinegar**
- **2 tablespoons water**
- **1 teaspoon ground cumin**
- **1/2 teaspoon salt**
- **1/2 teaspoon pepper**

In a bowl, combine the rice, beans, peppers and cilantro. Combine the remaining ingredients in a jar with a tight-fitting lid; shake well. Pour over rice mixture and toss to coat. Refrigerate until serving. **Yield:** 4-6 servings.

Creamy Egg Salad

This tasty egg salad can be served on greens, in a sandwich or on crackers. *—Cynthia Kohlberg Syracuse, Indiana*

- **1 package (3 ounces) cream cheese, softened**
- **1/4 cup mayonnaise**
- **1/2 teaspoon salt**
- **1/8 teaspoon pepper**
- **1/4 cup finely chopped green *or* sweet red pepper**
- **1/4 cup finely chopped celery**
- **1/4 cup sweet pickle relish**
- **2 tablespoons minced fresh parsley**
- **8 hard-cooked eggs, chopped**

In a mixing bowl, beat cream cheese, mayonnaise, salt and pepper until smooth. Add green pepper, celery, relish and parsley. Fold in eggs. Refrigerate until serving. **Yield:** 3 cups.

Fruity Carrot Salad

I get our kids to eat raw carrots by grating them and mixing them with lots of colorful, naturally sweet fruit. Toss in marshmallows and a creamy dressing, and the kids request this dish! —*Susan Stevens, Orange Park, Florida*

4 medium carrots, grated
1 package (10-1/2 ounces) miniature marshmallows
1 can (8 ounces) crushed pineapple, drained
1 cup raisins
1 cup flaked coconut
1/2 cup halved maraschino cherries
1/2 cup mayonnaise
1 tablespoon lemon juice
1 tablespoon orange juice
1/3 cup whipping cream, whipped

In a large bowl, combine the carrots, marshmallows, pineapple, raisins, coconut and cherries. In a small bowl, combine mayonnaise and juices. Fold in the whipped cream. Pour over carrot mixture and toss to coat. Serve immediately. **Yield:** 10-12 servings.

Southwestern Lentil Salad

Black beans and lentils pair so well with cumin in this refreshing salad. It's a colorful dish that works well at potlucks and picnics. —*Denise Baumert, Dalhart, Texas*

2 cans (15 ounces *each*) black beans, rinsed and drained
3 cups cooked lentils
1-1/2 cups fresh *or* frozen corn
1 cup chopped red onion
1 cup chopped green pepper
1/4 to 1/2 cup minced fresh cilantro *or* parsley
1 cup vegetable oil
1/2 cup cider vinegar
1 tablespoon Dijon mustard
1-1/2 teaspoons ground cumin
1 to 2 garlic cloves, minced
1/2 teaspoon salt
1/4 teaspoon pepper

In a large bowl, combine the first six ingredients. In a jar with a tight-fitting lid, combine the remaining ingredients and shake well. Pour over vegetables and toss. Cover and refrigerate for at least 2 hours. **Yield:** 8-10 servings.

Special Strawberry Spinach Salad

(Pictured below)

Any way you slice them, strawberries are extra-colorful and refreshing when paired with crisp greens in this salad. —*Jean Newnham, Peterborough, Ontario*

9 cups torn fresh spinach
1 pint fresh strawberries, halved
1/2 cup slivered almonds, toasted

DRESSING:

1/4 cup vegetable oil
2 tablespoons sugar
2 tablespoons cider vinegar
1 tablespoon chopped onion
1 teaspoon poppy seeds
1 teaspoon sesame seeds
1/4 teaspoon paprika
1/8 teaspoon Worcestershire sauce

In a large bowl, combine the spinach, strawberries and almonds. Place dressing ingredients in a blender; cover and process until combined. Pour over salad and toss to coat. Serve immediately. **Yield:** 6-8 servings.

Ambrosia Waldorf Salad

(Pictured below)

A light, lovely pink salad, this recipe puts a different spin on traditional Waldorf salad. It is super served with roast turkey or baked ham. People always go back for seconds. My family didn't think they liked cranberries until they tried this sweet crunchy salad.
—Janet Smith, Smithton, Missouri

2 cups fresh *or* frozen cranberry halves
1/2 cup sugar
3 cups miniature marshmallows
2 cups diced unpeeled apples
1 cup seedless green grape halves
3/4 cup chopped pecans
1 can (20 ounces) pineapple tidbits, drained
1 cup whipping cream, whipped
Shredded *or* flaked coconut

Combine cranberries and sugar. In a large bowl, combine the marshmallows, apples, grapes, pecans and pineapple. Add cranberries and mix well. Fold in whipped cream. Cover and chill. Sprinkle with coconut before serving. **Yield:** 12-14 servings.

Wilted Watercress Salad

When I was a girl growing up in Iowa, our whole family picked watercress. I modified my sister's recipe for spinach with hot bacon dressing to come up with this lovely, satisfying salad. The sweet dressing and crunchy bacon pieces really dress up plain watercress. It is a treat. *Judith Saeugling, Sun City, Arizona*

6 cups watercress
4 green onions, thinly sliced
5 bacon strips
2 tablespoons brown sugar
2 tablespoons vinegar
2 tablespoons lemon juice
1 tablespoon Worcestershire sauce

In a large bowl, toss watercress and onions; set aside. In a skillet, cook bacon until crisp. Remove bacon; crumble and add to watercress mixture. To the drippings, add brown sugar, vinegar, lemon juice and Worcestershire sauce; bring to a boil. Pour over salad and toss to coat; serve immediately. **Yield:** 6 servings.

Hot Bacon-Mustard Dressing

For a thick dressing that's irresistible on green salads, try this recipe. It has a bold, sweet and tangy flavor. *—Joyce Turley, Slaughters, Kentucky*

4 bacon strips, diced
2 cups honey-Dijon mustard
1/2 cup sugar
1/3 cup orange juice
1 tablespoon cider *or* red wine vinegar
1/4 teaspoon ground mustard
1/4 cup honey
Torn salad greens *or* fresh spinach

In a skillet, cook bacon until crisp. Drain, reserving 3 tablespoons drippings; set bacon aside. To the drippings, add Dijon mustard, sugar, orange juice, vinegar and ground mustard; bring to a boil. Stir in honey and bacon. Serve warm over salad greens or spinach. Refrigerate leftovers; reheat before serving. **Yield:** about 2 cups.

Marinated Tomato Salad

I've found this simple but tasty combination of ingredients turns tomatoes into a refreshing salad. It's best prepared at least 30 minutes ahead. *—Mary Tuthill*
Fort Myers Beach, Florida

✓ Uses less fat, sugar or salt. Includes Nutritional Analysis and Diabetic Exchanges.

8 medium tomatoes, sliced
1/4 cup minced fresh parsley
1/4 cup olive *or* vegetable oil
2 tablespoons cider *or* red wine vinegar
2 teaspoons prepared mustard

1 garlic clove, minced
1 teaspoon sugar
1 teaspoon salt, optional

Arrange tomatoes in a serving bowl; sprinkle with parsley. Combine the remaining ingredients in a jar with a tight-fitting lid; shake well. Pour over tomatoes. Cover and refrigerate for 30 minutes or until ready to serve. **Yield:** 8 servings. **Nutritional Analysis:** One 3/4-cup serving (prepared without salt) equals 90 calories, 29 mg sodium, 0 cholesterol, 7 gm carbohydrate, 1 gm protein, 7 gm fat. **Diabetic Exchanges:** 1-1/2 fat, 1 vegetable.

Missouri Peach and Applesauce Salad

Fresh peaches combine with applesauce in this tangy molded salad. It's a creamy-textured, refreshing side dish. —Bernice Morris, Marshfield, Missouri

1 cup lemon-lime soda
1 package (3 ounces) peach gelatin
1 cup applesauce
1 cup whipping cream
1 tablespoon sugar
1/8 teaspoon ground nutmeg
1/8 teaspoon vanilla extract
1 cup chopped peeled ripe peaches
Red grapes and mint leaves, optional

In a saucepan, bring soda to a boil. Remove from the heat; stir in gelatin until dissolved. Add applesauce. Chill until mixture mounds slightly when dropped from a spoon. In a mixing bowl, whip cream with sugar, nutmeg and vanilla until stiff. Fold into gelatin mixture along with the peaches. Transfer to a 1-1/2-qt. glass bowl. Chill until firm. Garnish with grapes and mint if desired. **Yield:** 8-12 servings.

Southern Sweet Potato Salad

(Pictured above right)

I do some catering, so I'm always looking for good new recipes. I love to take this deliciously different potato salad to potlucks and cookouts. —Marlyn Woods Lakeland, Florida

2 pounds sweet potatoes, peeled and cut into 1/2-inch cubes
2 tablespoons lemon juice
1 cup mayonnaise
2 tablespoons orange juice
1 tablespoon honey
1 teaspoon grated orange peel

1/2 teaspoon ground ginger
1/4 teaspoon salt
1/8 teaspoon ground nutmeg
1 cup sliced celery
1/3 cup chopped dates
1/2 cup chopped pecans
Lettuce leaves
1 can (11 ounces) mandarin oranges, drained

In a medium saucepan, cook sweet potatoes in boiling salted water just until tender, about 5-8 minutes (do not overcook). Drain; toss with the lemon juice. In a large bowl, combine mayonnaise, orange juice, honey, orange peel, ginger, salt and nutmeg. Add the warm potatoes, celery and dates. Toss to coat well. Cover and chill. Before serving, gently stir in the pecans. Spoon salad onto a lettuce-lined platter. Arrange oranges around salad. **Yield:** 6-8 servings.

Spaghetti Saver

Don't toss out leftover spaghetti noodles. Cut them into small pieces, then mix with mayonnaise, pickle juice, dill weed and whatever other potato salad ingredients you have on hand.

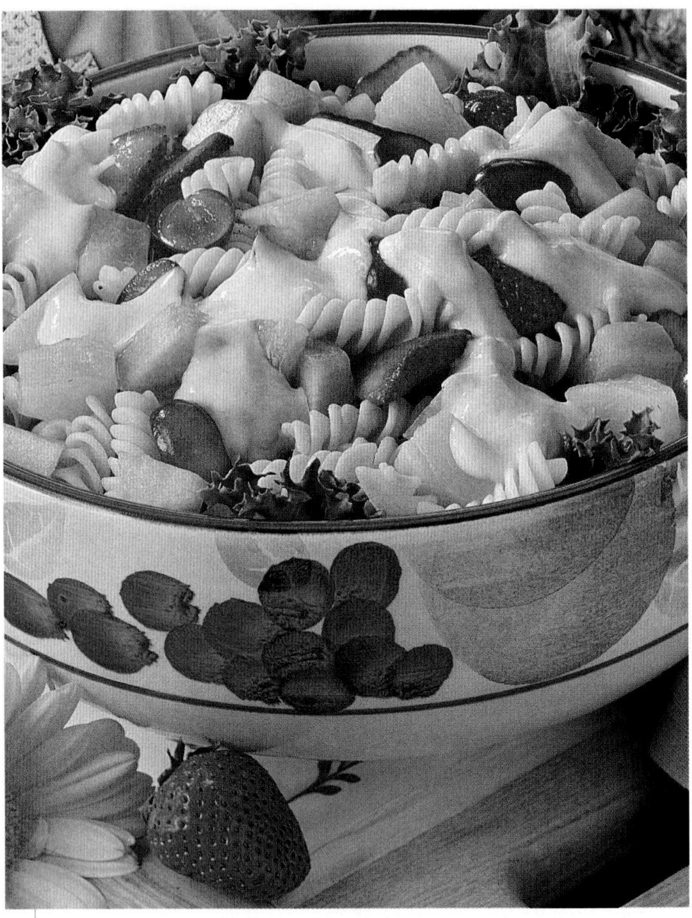

Fruited Pasta Salad

(Pictured above)

The vibrant colors, sweet fruit and tender pasta make this lovely, festive salad a hit with both men and women at picnics and potlucks. —*Sandra Pire Brookfield, Wisconsin*

✓ Uses less fat, sugar or salt. Includes Nutritional Analysis and Diabetic Exchanges.

1-1/2 cups uncooked spiral pasta
1 can (8 ounces) unsweetened pineapple chunks
1 carton (8 ounces) nonfat peach yogurt
2 tablespoons nonfat sour cream
1-1/2 cups cubed cantaloupe
1 cup halved seedless grapes
1-1/2 cups sliced fresh strawberries

Cook pasta according to package directions; rinse in cold water and drain. Cool completely. Drain pineapple, reserving 2 tablespoons juice (discard remaining juice or save for another use); set pineapple aside. In a small bowl, combine the yogurt, sour cream and reserved pineapple juice until smooth; cover and refrigerate. In a large bowl, combine pasta, pineapple, cantaloupe and grapes. Just before serving, stir in strawberries and drizzle with yogurt mixture. **Yield:** 13 servings. **Nutritional Analysis:** One 1/2-cup serving equals 90 calories, 15 mg sodium, 1 mg cholesterol, 19 gm carbohydrate, 3 gm protein, trace fat. **Diabetic Exchanges:** 1 fruit, 1/2 starch.

Confetti Cottage Salad

This pretty salad is a snap to fix. The cucumber, peppers and sunflower kernels give it a pleasant crunch. —*Kelly Thornberry, La Porte, Indiana*

✓ Uses less fat, sugar or salt. Includes Nutritional Analysis and Diabetic Exchanges.

1 carton (24 ounces) small-curd cottage cheese
1 large tomato, diced
1 cup diced cucumber
1 small sweet red pepper, diced
1 small sweet yellow pepper, diced
2 green onions with tops, sliced
1/3 cup sunflower kernels, toasted

In a bowl, combine all ingredients; toss lightly. Serve immediately. **Yield:** 8 servings. **Nutritional Analysis:** One 3/4-cup serving (prepared with fat-free cottage cheese and unsalted sunflower kernels) equals 102 calories, 305 mg sodium, 7 mg cholesterol, 7 gm carbohydrate, 11 gm protein, 3 gm fat. **Diabetic Exchanges:** 1-1/2 vegetable, 1 lean meat.

Cilantro Salad Dressing

Try using this zippy dressing over salad greens or hot or cold boiled potatoes. The flavor of fresh cilantro really shines through. —*Sara Laber Shelburne, Vermont*

✓ Uses less fat, sugar or salt. Includes Nutritional Analysis and Diabetic Exchanges.

1/2 cup fresh cilantro leaves
1/4 cup buttermilk
1/4 cup fat-free mayonnaise
1/8 teaspoon sugar
3 drops hot pepper sauce
Salad greens and vegetables of your choice

In a food processor or blender, place cilantro, buttermilk, mayonnaise, sugar and hot pepper sauce; cover and process until smooth. Serve over greens and vegetables. Store in the refrigerator. **Yield:** about 1/2 cup. **Nutritional Analysis:** 2 tablespoons of dressing equals 18 calories, 124 mg sodium, 1 mg cholesterol, 3 gm carbohydrate, 1 gm protein, trace fat. **Diabetic Exchange:** Free food.

Surprise Tuna Salad

Apple, raisins and pecans give tuna salad a harvest twist that makes a delicious cold or grilled sandwich.
—Vicki Reed, Kansas City, Missouri

- **2 cans (6 ounces *each*) tuna, drained and flaked**
- **1 medium apple, peeled and chopped**
- **1/2 cup golden raisins**
- **1/2 cup mayonnaise *or* salad dressing**
- **1/3 cup chopped pecans**
- **1 tablespoon sweet pickle relish**
- **12 bread slices, toasted**
- **6 slices Monterey Jack cheese**

In a bowl, combine the first six ingredients; spread over six slices of bread. Top each with a cheese slice and remaining bread. **Yield:** 6 servings.

Herbed Carrot Salad

We grow about 2,000 acres of carrots on our ranch. My whole family enjoys this colorful vegetable in a variety of recipes, including this refreshing salad.
—Bud Mercer, Prosser, Washington

- **1/2 cup water**
- **1 pound baby carrots**
- **1/4 cup minced fresh dill**
- **1/4 cup minced fresh oregano**
- **1 tablespoon minced fresh thyme**
- **3 tablespoons lemon juice**
- **2 tablespoons olive *or* vegetable oil**
- **1 tablespoon sugar**
- **1 teaspoon grated lemon peel**
- **8 cups torn romaine**

In a saucepan, bring water to a boil; add the carrots. Reduce heat; cover and simmer for 5-6 minutes or until crisp-tender. Drain; cool slightly. Meanwhile, in a bowl, combine the dill, oregano, thyme, lemon juice, oil, sugar and lemon peel. Add carrots and toss to coat. Cover and refrigerate. Serve over romaine. **Yield:** 4 servings.

Colorful Corn Salad

(Pictured at right)

This colorful, tasty corn salad is an excellent way to perk up a summer picnic. The seasonings add a bold, refreshing Southwestern flavor that brings people back for seconds. It's nice to have a different kind of salad to share.
—Helen Koedel, Hamilton, Ohio

- **2 packages (10 ounces *each*) frozen corn, thawed**
- **2 cups diced green pepper**
- **2 cups diced sweet red pepper**
- **2 cups diced celery**
- **1 cup minced fresh parsley**
- **1 cup chopped green onions**
- **1/2 cup shredded Parmesan cheese**
- **2 teaspoons ground cumin**
- **1-1/2 teaspoons salt**
- **3/4 teaspoon pepper**
- **1/2 teaspoon hot pepper sauce**
- **1/8 teaspoon cayenne pepper**
- **3 tablespoons olive *or* vegetable oil**
- **2 garlic cloves, minced**
- **6 tablespoons lime juice**

In a large bowl, combine the first 12 ingredients. In a microwave-safe dish, combine oil and garlic. Microwave, uncovered, on high for 1 minute. Cool. Whisk in lime juice. Pour over the corn mixture and toss to coat. Cover and refrigerate until serving. **Yield:** 16-18 servings.

Chili Corn Bread Salad

(Pictured below)

A co-worker brought this wonderful dish to a potluck several years ago. She had copies of the recipe next to the pan. Now I make it for get-togethers and also supply copies of the recipe. I never have any leftover salad or recipes. —Kelly Newsom, Jenks, Oklahoma

1 package (8-1/2 ounces) corn bread/muffin mix
1 can (4 ounces) chopped green chilies, undrained
1/8 teaspoon ground cumin
1/8 teaspoon dried oregano
Pinch rubbed sage
1 cup mayonnaise
1 cup (8 ounces) sour cream
1 envelope ranch salad dressing mix
2 cans (15 ounces *each*) pinto beans, rinsed and drained
2 cans (15-1/4 ounces *each*) whole kernel corn, drained
3 medium tomatoes, chopped
1 cup chopped green pepper
1 cup chopped green onions
10 bacon strips, cooked and crumbled
2 cups (8 ounces) shredded cheddar cheese

Prepare corn bread batter according to package directions. Stir in the chilies, cumin, oregano and sage. Spread in a greased 8-in. square baking pan. Bake at 400° for 20-25 minutes or until a toothpick inserted near the center comes out clean. Cool. In a small bowl, combine mayonnaise, sour cream and dressing mix; set aside. Crumble half of the corn bread into a 13-in. x 9-in. x 2-in. dish. Layer with half of the beans, mayonnaise mixture, corn, tomatoes, green pepper, onions, bacon and cheese. Repeat layers (dish will be very full). Cover and refrigerate for 2 hours. **Yield:** 12 servings.

Italian Tuna Salad

This fresh and colorful tuna salad has a nice crunch. It's a nice change of pace from plain tuna salad. —Lois Gelzer, Oak Bluffs, Massachusetts

✓ Uses less fat, sugar or salt. Includes Nutritional Analysis and Diabetic Exchanges.

1 can (15 ounces) white kidney *or* cannelini beans, rinsed and drained
1 medium sweet red pepper, chopped
1 medium green pepper, chopped
1 small red onion, chopped
1 celery rib, chopped
1/4 cup sliced green onions
1/4 cup sliced stuffed olives
1/4 cup sliced ripe olives
2 garlic cloves, minced
2 tablespoons minced fresh parsley
1 cup fat-free Italian salad dressing
2 cans (6 ounces *each*) low-sodium tuna, drained and flaked

In a large bowl, combine the first 10 ingredients. Add dressing and toss to coat. Fold in tuna. Cover and refrigerate for at least 1 hour before serving. **Yield:** 16 servings. **Nutritional Analysis:** One 1/2-cup serving equals 63 calories, 288 mg sodium, 6 mg cholesterol, 7 gm carbohydrate, 7 gm protein, 1 gm fat. **Diabetic Exchanges:** 1 very lean meat, 1/2 starch.

Mandarin Chicken Salad

Being raised on a chicken farm, I know lots of great ways to use this versatile meat. This fruity salad is one of my favorites. —Sylvia Watson, Dagsboro, Delaware

4 cups cubed cooked chicken
1 can (20 ounces) pineapple tidbits, drained

1 can (11 ounces) mandarin oranges, drained
1 cup chopped celery
1 cup mayonnaise *or* salad dressing
1/2 cup sliced ripe olives, optional
1/2 cup chopped green pepper
2 tablespoons grated onion
1 tablespoon prepared mustard
1/4 teaspoon salt
1/8 teaspoon pepper
Leaf lettuce, optional
1 can (5 ounces) chow mein noodles

In a large bowl, combine the first 11 ingredients. Refrigerate until serving. Serve on lettuce-lined plates if desired. Sprinkle with chow mein noodles. **Yield:** 8 servings.

Tangy Cucumber Salad

(Pictured on page 24)

You'll spark taste buds with this tangy and refreshing salad. The simple marinade gives mild cucumbers lots of zip. The tomatoes are a pretty addition. This is a super use of summer's garden bounty.
—Edna Hoffman, Hebron, Indiana

2 small cucumbers, thinly sliced
1 teaspoon salt, *divided*
2 medium tomatoes, chopped
1 medium onion, chopped
1/4 cup cider vinegar
2 tablespoons vegetable oil
1 tablespoon honey
1/2 teaspoon celery salt
1/2 teaspoon dried basil
1/2 teaspoon ground mustard
1/4 teaspoon garlic powder
1/4 teaspoon dried oregano
Dash cayenne pepper

Place cucumbers in a strainer; sprinkle with 1/2 teaspoon of salt and toss. Let stand for 30 minutes. Rinse and drain well. Place in a large bowl; add tomatoes and onion. In a small bowl, whisk together the remaining ingredients; pour over cucumber mixture and toss. Cover and refrigerate for several hours. Serve with a slotted spoon. **Yield:** 8 servings.

Grilled Chicken Salad

(Pictured above right)

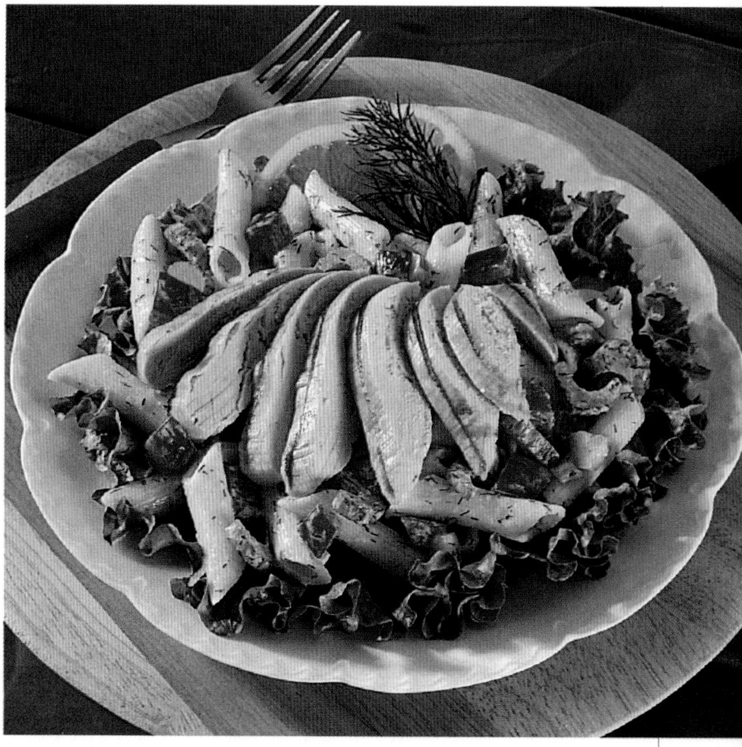

A few years back, I found this easy, light salad recipe and made it for a picnic for my boyfriend and me. Now that guy is my husband, and we still enjoy going on picnics and dining on this satisfying salad.
—Juli Stewart, Coppell, Texas

6 boneless skinless chicken breast halves
2 tablespoons fresh lemon juice
1 pound ziti, macaroni *or* corkscrew pasta, cooked and drained
1 medium sweet red pepper, chopped
2-1/2 cups sliced celery
1 medium red onion, chopped
1/4 cup minced fresh dill *or* 5 teaspoons dill weed
3 tablespoons white wine vinegar
2 tablespoons mayonnaise
2 tablespoons Dijon mustard
1/2 teaspoon salt
1/4 teaspoon pepper
2/3 cup olive *or* vegetable oil
Leaf lettuce, optional

Grill the chicken breasts over medium-hot heat for 15-18 minutes, turning once, or until tender and juices run clear. Remove from the grill and place in a single layer on a platter; sprinkle with lemon juice and set aside. In a large bowl, toss pasta, red pepper, celery, onion and dill. Remove chicken from platter; pour juices into a bowl. Slice chicken crosswise into thin strips; add to pasta mixture. To the juices, add vinegar, mayonnaise, mustard, salt and pepper; whisk well. Add oil very slowly in a stream until dressing is thickened. Pour over salad and toss. Serve in a lettuce-lined bowl or on individual lettuce-lined plates. **Yield:** 6 servings.

Curry Coleslaw

(Pictured above)

I inherited this coleslaw recipe from my mother. It's a snap to prepare, and the bacon gives it a tasty crunch.
—Joan Hallford, North Richland Hills, Texas

8 cups shredded cabbage
2/3 cup mayonnaise
1/4 cup cider vinegar
1/4 cup sugar
1 teaspoon salt
1/2 teaspoon curry powder
1/4 teaspoon pepper
4 bacon strips, cooked and crumbled

Place cabbage in a salad bowl. In a small bowl, combine the mayonnaise, vinegar, sugar, salt, curry and pepper. Pour over cabbage and toss to coat. Cover and refrigerate. Sprinkle with bacon just before serving. **Yield:** 6-8 servings.

Zucchini Orange Salad

The ingredients in this recipe may surprise you, but not as much as the delightful flavor and refreshing crunch the blend produces!
—Clarice Schweitzer, Sun City, Arizona

2 medium zucchini, thinly sliced
1 medium onion, thinly sliced
1 cup chopped celery
1 can (16 ounces) green beans,* drained
1 can (16 ounces) wax beans,* drained
1 can (15 ounces) mandarin oranges, drained
1 can (8 ounces) sliced water chestnuts, drained
1-1/2 cups sugar
1 cup vinegar
1 tablespoon water
1 teaspoon salt

In a large bowl, toss zucchini, onion and celery. Cover with boiling water; let stand for 1 hour. Drain. Add beans, oranges and water chestnuts. Combine remaining ingredients in a saucepan. Bring to a boil; boil for 1 minute. Pour over salad; cover and refrigerate for 24 hours before serving. **Yield:** 16-20 servings. ***Editor's Note:** Home-canned or fresh green and wax beans can be substituted for purchased canned beans. Use 2 cups of each, and if using fresh beans, cook until crisp-tender before adding to salad.

Apple Cider Salad

This cool, refreshing salad with crunchy nuts and apples makes me think of my mother and Thanksgiving. Mom prepared it each year for that holiday since apples were plentiful. She served it in a beautiful cut glass bowl.
—Jeannette Mack, Rushville, New York

✓ Uses less fat, sugar or salt. Includes Nutritional Analysis and Diabetic Exchanges.

2 envelopes unflavored gelatin
3-3/4 cups apple cider, *divided*
3 tablespoons lemon juice
3 tablespoons sugar
1/2 teaspoon salt
3-1/2 to 4 cups chopped peeled apples
1 cup chopped walnuts

In a small saucepan, sprinkle gelatin over 1/4 cup cider; let stand for 2 minutes. Add lemon juice, sugar, salt and remaining cider. Cook and stir over medium heat until sugar and gelatin are dissolved. Cover and refrigerate until slightly thickened, about 2-1/2 hours. Fold in the apples and walnuts. Transfer to a 2-qt. serving bowl. Cover and refrigerate overnight. **Yield:** 12 servings. **Nutritional Analysis:** One 1/2-cup serving equals 135 calories, 102 mg sodium, 0 cholesterol, 19 gm carbohydrate, 4 gm protein, 6 gm fat. **Diabetic Exchanges:** 1-1/2 fruit, 1 fat.

Fiddlehead Shrimp Salad

The stars of this salad are fiddleheads—the young, tightly curled fronds from bracken, ostrich and cinnamon ferns. Maine is considered a prime area for fiddleheads. —*Wilma Johnson, Thorndike, Maine*

3 cups fiddlehead ferns*
1 cup cooked shell macaroni
1/2 cup diced unpeeled apple
1/4 cup chopped celery
1 cup diced cooked shrimp
1/4 to 1/2 cup mayonnaise
1 tablespoon lemon juice
1 teaspoon grated lemon peel
Salt and pepper to taste

Cook ferns in a small amount of water until tender. Drain and place in a bowl. Add remaining ingredients and toss. Chill. **Yield:** 4 servings. ***Editor's Note:** As with any wild ingredient, be sure of what you're picking. Also be sure the ferns haven't been chemically treated.

Spinach Salad with Red Potatoes

(Pictured below right and on page 24)

My overflowing recipe collection includes many tried-and-true items like this lovely salad. Its hearty blend includes red potatoes, hard-cooked eggs and mushrooms. —*Mary Houchin, Swansea, Illinois*

 Uses less fat, sugar or salt. Includes Nutritional Analysis and Diabetic Exchanges.

1 package (10 ounces) fresh spinach, torn
3 small red potatoes, cooked and diced
2 hard-cooked eggs, chopped
1/2 cup sliced fresh mushrooms
2 bacon strips, diced
1/4 cup chopped red onion
1/2 teaspoon cornstarch
1/4 cup apple juice
2 tablespoons cider vinegar
Artificial sweetener equivalent to 2 teaspoons sugar
1/8 teaspoon pepper

In a salad bowl, combine spinach, potatoes, eggs and mushrooms. In a skillet, cook bacon until crisp. Remove bacon with a slotted spoon; drain on paper towels. In the drippings, saute onion until tender. Combine cornstarch, apple juice, vinegar, sweetener and pepper until smooth; stir into skillet. Bring to a boil; cook and stir for 1-2 minutes or until slightly thickened and bubbly. Pour over spinach mixture. Add bacon and toss. Serve immediately. **Yield:** 8 servings. **Nutritional Analysis:** One 1-cup serving equals 60 calories, 109 mg sodium, 56 mg cholesterol, 6 gm carbohydrate, 4 gm protein, 2 gm fat. **Diabetic Exchanges:** 1 vegetable, 1/2 meat.

Salami 'n' Shells Salad

Folks have commented on this salad's hearty blend of ingredients, calling it "a cut above" any deli salad. —*Carol Smith, New Berlin, Wisconsin*

7 ounces uncooked small pasta shells
1 cup halved cherry tomatoes
1 cup halved ripe olives
1 block (6 ounces) mozzarella cheese, cut into thin strips
4 ounces salami, cut into thin strips
1/2 cup chopped green pepper
4 green onions, sliced
DRESSING:
1/3 cup vegetable oil
3 tablespoons cider *or* red wine vinegar
1 teaspoon salt
1 teaspoon dried basil
1 teaspoon dried oregano
1/4 teaspoon garlic powder

Cook pasta according to package directions; drain and rinse in cold water. Place in a large bowl; add the next six ingredients. In a jar with a tight-fitting lid, combine the dressing ingredients; shake well. Pour over salad and toss to coat. Chill until serving. **Yield:** 8-10 servings.

Soups & Sandwiches

Pair a simmering pot of hearty soup and a platter of piled-high sandwiches for a comforting meal.

PERFECT PARTNERS. Clockwise from upper left: Super Sloppy Joes (p. 44), Champion Roast Beef Sandwiches and Hearty Hash Brown Soup (p. 54), Special Eggplant Subs (p. 50) and Spicy Cheeseburger Soup (p. 45).

Super Sloppy Joes

(Pictured above and on page 42)

Mother made these zesty sloppy joes many times when I was growing up. She passed the recipe on to me when I got married. My brother-in-law says they're the best sandwiches he's ever tasted. He ought to know—his name is Joe. —*Ellen Stringer, Fairmont, West Virginia*

2 pounds ground beef
1/2 cup chopped onion
2 celery ribs with leaves, chopped
1/4 cup chopped green pepper
1-2/3 cups canned crushed tomatoes
1/4 cup ketchup
2 tablespoons brown sugar
1 tablespoon vinegar
1 tablespoon Worcestershire sauce
1 tablespoon steak sauce
1/2 teaspoon garlic salt
1/4 teaspoon ground mustard
1/4 teaspoon paprika
8 to 10 hamburger buns, split

In a Dutch oven over medium heat, cook beef, onion, celery and green pepper until the meat is no longer pink and the vegetables are tender; drain. Add the next nine ingredients; mix well. Simmer, uncovered, for 35-40 minutes, stirring occasionally. Spoon 1/2 cup meat mixture onto each bun. **Yield:** 8-10 servings.

School Day Chowder

This hearty soup is a nice change-of-pace lunch for "brown-baggers". It stays hot for hours in a tightly sealed insulated container. It's a full meal with fresh fruit and a couple of cookies. —*Karen Ann Bland, Gove, Kansas*

1/2 pound hot dogs, halved lengthwise and sliced
1 cup sliced celery
1/2 cup sliced carrot
1/2 cup chopped green pepper
1/4 cup chopped onion
1/4 cup butter *or* margarine
1/4 cup all-purpose flour
1/8 teaspoon pepper
2-1/2 to 3 cups milk
2 cups (8 ounces) shredded cheddar cheese

In a large saucepan, combine hot dogs, celery, carrot, green pepper, onion and butter. Cook and stir over medium heat until vegetables are tender. Stir in flour and pepper until blended. Gradually add milk. Bring to a boil; cook and stir for 2 minutes or until thickened. Add cheese; stir until melted. **Yield:** 5 servings.

Florentine Tomato Soup

You'll come away satisfied after spooning into a bowl of this fresh-tasting soup. It's chock-full of delicious ingredients. —*Joan Clements, Wheatland, Indiana*

✓ Uses less fat, sugar or salt. Includes Nutritional Analysis and Diabetic Exchanges.

1/2 cup chopped green pepper
1/2 cup chopped onion
1 garlic clove, minced
1 teaspoon olive *or* vegetable oil
1 can (14-1/2 ounces) no-salt-added diced tomatoes, undrained
1-1/2 cups water
1 tablespoon minced fresh basil *or* 1 teaspoon dried basil
1 teaspoon chicken bouillon granules
1/4 teaspoon pepper
3/4 cup uncooked medium egg noodles
1 package (10 ounces) frozen chopped spinach, thawed

In a saucepan, saute the green pepper, onion and garlic in oil until tender. Add tomatoes, water, basil, bouillon and pepper; bring to a boil. Stir in noodles; reduce heat. Simmer for 10 minutes. Add spinach; cook until noodles are tender. **Yield:** 5 servings. **Nutritional Analysis:** One serving equals

72 calories, 301 mg sodium, 5 mg cholesterol, 13 gm carbohydrate, 4 gm protein, 2 gm fat. **Diabetic Exchange:** 1 starch.

Brussels Sprouts Soup

I've always liked brussels sprouts but had few ways to prepare them. Then I discovered this simple and sensational soup. —*Suzanne Strocsher, Bothell, Washington*

1 medium onion, chopped
1 medium potato, peeled and cubed
2 tablespoons butter *or* margarine
1 pound fresh brussels sprouts, quartered
3 cups chicken broth
1/2 to 1 teaspoon salt
1/4 to 1/2 teaspoon curry powder
1/8 teaspoon pepper
1 egg yolk
1/4 cup whipping cream
Sour cream and paprika, optional

In a large saucepan, saute onion and potato in butter until onion is tender. Add brussels sprouts, broth, salt, curry powder and pepper; bring to a boil. Reduce heat; cover and simmer for 10-12 minutes or until the vegetables are tender. Cool to room temperature. Puree in small batches in a blender or food processor; return all to pan. Combine egg yolk and cream; stir into soup. Cook and stir for 4-5 minutes over medium heat (do not boil). Garnish with sour cream and paprika if desired. **Yield:** 4-6 servings.

Golden Onion Soup

Mozzarella cheese gives this savory onion soup extra richness. It's simple to make and a joy to eat. —*Salvatore Bertolino, Indiana, Pennsylvania*

2 cups quartered thinly sliced onions
1/2 cup butter *or* margarine
1/4 cup all-purpose flour
2 cups chicken broth
2 cups milk
2 cups (8 ounces) shredded mozzarella cheese

In a saucepan over medium-low heat, cook onions in butter until tender, about 10 minutes. Stir in flour until blended. Gradually add broth and milk. Bring to a boil over medium heat, stirring constantly; cook and stir for 1 minute. Reduce heat. Add the cheese; heat just until cheese is melted (do not boil). **Yield:** 6 servings.

Spicy Cheeseburger Soup

(Pictured below and on page 42)

This creamy soup brings my family to the table in a hurry. I love the warming zip of cayenne, but it also tastes terrific without it if you prefer a milder flavor. —*Lisa Mast, White Cloud, Michigan*

1-1/2 cups water
2 cups cubed peeled potatoes
2 small carrots, grated
1 small onion, chopped
1/4 cup chopped green pepper
1 jalapeno pepper,* seeded and chopped
1 garlic clove, minced
1 tablespoon beef bouillon granules
1/2 teaspoon salt
1 pound ground beef, cooked and drained
2-1/2 cups milk, *divided*
3 tablespoons all-purpose flour
8 ounces process American cheese, cubed
1/4 to 1 teaspoon cayenne pepper, optional
1/2 pound sliced bacon, cooked and crumbled

In a large saucepan, combine the first nine ingredients; bring to a boil. Reduce heat; cover and simmer for 15-20 minutes or until potatoes are tender. Stir in beef and 2 cups of milk; heat through. Combine flour and remaining milk until smooth; gradually stir into soup. Bring to a boil; cook and stir for 2 minutes or until thickened and bubbly. Reduce heat; stir in cheese until melted. Add cayenne if desired. Top with bacon just before serving. **Yield:** 6-8 servings (about 2 quarts). ***Editor's Note:** When cutting or seeding hot peppers, use rubber or plastic gloves to protect your hands. Avoid touching your face.

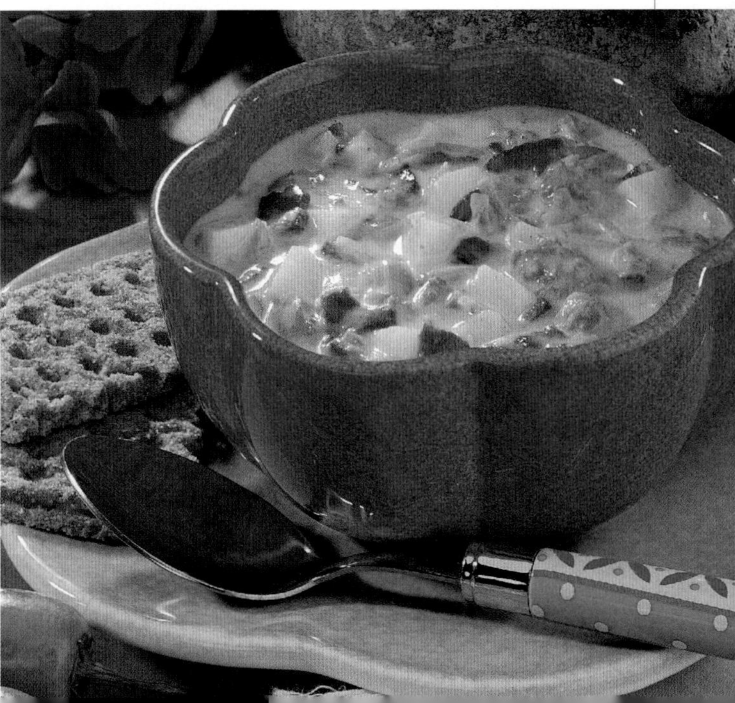

Fresh Tomato Soup

(Pictured below)

My husband doesn't care for traditional tomato soup, but he loves this garden-fresh version. It has an unexpected chicken-broth base and appealing chunks of tomatoes. It's an excellent first course and a great light lunch with a salad and garlic bread.

—Mrs. Donald Bong, Hager City, Wisconsin

✓ Uses less fat, sugar or salt. Includes Nutritional Analysis and Diabetic Exchanges.

2 cups sliced carrots
1 cup chopped celery
1 small onion, finely chopped
1/2 cup chopped green pepper
1/4 cup butter *or* margarine
4-1/2 cups chicken broth, *divided*
4 medium tomatoes, peeled and chopped (4 cups)
4 teaspoons sugar
1/2 teaspoon curry powder
1/2 teaspoon salt, optional
1/4 teaspoon pepper
1/4 cup all-purpose flour

In a Dutch oven, saute carrots, celery, onion and green pepper in butter until tender. Add 4 cups broth, tomatoes, sugar, curry powder, salt if desired and pepper; bring to a boil. Reduce heat; simmer for 20 minutes. In a small bowl, combine the flour and remaining broth until smooth. Gradually add to soup. Bring to a boil; cook and stir for 2 minutes. **Yield:** 9 servings (about 2 quarts). **Nutritional Analysis:** One 1-cup serving (prepared with margarine and low-sodium broth and without salt) equals 115 calories, 153 mg sodium, 2 mg cholesterol, 13 gm carbohydrate, 3 gm protein, 6 gm fat. **Diabetic Exchanges:** 1 starch, 1 fat.

Pork and Cabbage Sandwiches

When you think about cabbage, your first impression probably is a slowly simmering dish. Sometimes, though, you need the same savory results in just a matter of minutes. If so, turn to this tasty alternative!

—Elaine Fenton, Prescott, Arizona

1 pound bulk pork sausage
7 cups shredded cabbage
1 medium onion, chopped
1 medium sweet red pepper, thinly sliced
1/2 cup water
1/2 teaspoon salt
1/2 teaspoon sugar
1/4 cup sour cream
Hamburger buns *or* pita bread

In a large skillet, brown sausage; drain. Add cabbage, onion, red pepper, water, salt and sugar; mix well. Cover and cook for 20 minutes or until the vegetables are tender, stirring occasionally. Stir in sour cream and heat through. Serve on buns or in pita bread. **Yield:** 8-12 servings.

Alaskan Salmon Chowder

In this rich-tasting soup, we like to use some of the red salmon my husband and son catch. It's always a treat! *—Carol Ross, Anchorage, Alaska*

✓ Uses less fat, sugar or salt. Includes Nutritional Analysis and Diabetic Exchanges.

1/2 cup chopped onion
1/2 cup chopped celery
1/4 cup chopped green pepper
1 garlic clove, minced
1 can (14-1/2 ounces) chicken broth, *divided*
2 cups diced peeled potatoes

1 cup sliced carrots
1 teaspoon seasoned salt, optional
1/2 teaspoon dill weed
1 small zucchini, thinly sliced
1 can (14-3/4 ounces) cream-style corn
1 can (12 ounces) evaporated milk
2 cups cooked salmon chunks *or* 2 cans (7-1/2 ounces *each*) salmon, drained, bones and skin removed

In a saucepan, cook onion, celery, green pepper and garlic in 1/4 cup broth until tender. Add potatoes, carrots, seasoned salt if desired, dill and remaining broth. Cover and simmer for 20 minutes or until vegetables are tender. Add zucchini; simmer for 5 minutes. Add corn, milk and salmon; heat through. **Yield:** 7 servings. **Nutritional Analysis:** One 1-cup serving (prepared with low-sodium broth, no-salt-added corn and evaporated skim milk and without seasoned salt) equals 225 calories, 147 mg sodium, 27 mg cholesterol, 29 gm carbohydrate, 20 gm protein, 4 gm fat. **Diabetic Exchanges:** 2 lean meat, 1-1/2 starch, 1 vegetable.

Garlic Soup

I use many different herbs in cooking, but garlic is my favorite. Many family and friends enjoy this flavorful soup that resembles French onion soup.
—Marge Harris, Steubenville, Ohio

10 garlic cloves, minced
2 tablespoons butter *or* margarine
1 tablespoon all-purpose flour
4 cups water
2 cans (14-1/2 ounces *each*) beef broth
2 tablespoons minced fresh parsley
1/4 teaspoon pepper
5 egg yolks
1 tablespoon grated Parmesan cheese
14 slices Italian *or* French bread, toasted
Additional Parmesan cheese
7 slices Monterey Jack cheese, halved

In a soup kettle, saute garlic in butter until lightly browned. Stir in flour until blended. Gradually add the water, broth, parsley and pepper. Simmer for 1 hour. In a bowl, beat egg yolks with Parmesan cheese. Gradually stir 1 cup of hot soup into egg yolks; return all to the pan. Cook and stir until thickened (do not boil). Place toast in 8-oz. ovenproof bowls; sprinkle with Parmesan cheese. Ladle hot soup into bowls; top with Monterey Jack cheese. Broil 4 in. from the heat until cheese is melted. Serve immediately. **Yield:** 14 servings (3-1/2 quarts).

'I Wish I Had That Recipe...'

"WHILE visiting a friend in Washington, I ordered a Curry Chicken Croissant at the Victorian Rose Tea Room in Port Orchard," explains Merrilee Diers of Florissant, Colorado. "It was out of this world. I've since tried to duplicate it with no success."

Merilee requested *Taste of Home's* help in obtaining the raved-about recipe.

We contacted tea room owner Sandy O'Donnell, who was happy to share the pleasing filling. "Our Curry Chicken is a recipe from an employee's family collection," she says. "We serve it on a fresh-baked croissant with green leafy lettuce."

The creamy mayonnaise and sour cream base is specially seasoned with curry powder and Cajun seasoning. And chopped walnuts and celery lend to this salad's delightful crunch.

Located at 1130 Bethel Ave. in Port Orchard, the Victorian Rose Tea Room adjoins a doll and gift shop inspired by Sandy's love of doll collecting. Daily service includes breakfast (9 to 11 a.m.), lunch (11:30 a.m. to 3 p.m.) and tea (2:30 to 4:30 p.m.). Phone: 1-360/876-5695.

Curry Chicken Croissants

2-1/2 cups cubed cooked chicken
1/2 cup chopped walnuts
1/3 cup finely chopped celery
2 tablespoons grated onion
1/2 cup mayonnaise
2 tablespoons sour cream
3/4 teaspoon curry powder
1/8 teaspoon Cajun seasoning
Lettuce leaves
4 to 6 croissants, split

In a food processor or blender, process chicken until finely chopped. Transfer to a large bowl; add walnuts, celery and onion. In a small bowl, combine mayonnaise, sour cream, curry powder and Cajun seasoning; mix well. Pour over chicken mixture and stir well. Refrigerate for at least 1 hour. Place lettuce and about 3/4 cup chicken mixture on each croissant. **Yield:** 4-6 servings.

Baked Chili

(Pictured above)

This main dish is wonderful the first day and also makes outstanding leftovers. As a student living on my own, I love savory one-pot suppers like this that provide several days of tasty meals. —Michelle Gal Toronto, Ontario

1 pound ground beef
1 large onion, chopped
1 large green pepper, chopped
1 can (16 ounces) kidney beans, rinsed and drained
1 can (15-1/4 ounces) whole kernel corn, drained
1 can (15 ounces) tomato sauce
1 can (14-1/2 ounces) diced tomatoes, undrained
1 can (4 ounces) chopped green chilies
2 teaspoons chili powder
1 teaspoon salt
1 teaspoon ground cumin
1/2 teaspoon sugar
1/2 teaspoon garlic powder
CORN BREAD BISCUITS:
1 cup all-purpose flour
1 cup cornmeal
2 teaspoons baking powder
1/8 teaspoon salt
1 egg
1/2 cup milk
1/2 cup sour cream

In a Dutch oven over medium heat, cook beef, onion and green pepper until meat is no longer pink; drain. Add remaining ingredients; bring to a boil, stirring occasionally. Reduce heat; cover and simmer for 10 minutes. Meanwhile, combine flour, cornmeal, baking powder and salt in a bowl. Beat egg, milk and sour cream until smooth; stir into dry ingredients just until moistened. Transfer chili to an ungreased 13-in. x 9-in. x 2-in. baking dish. Drop batter by heaping teaspoonfuls onto hot chili. Bake, uncovered, at 400° for 15-17 minutes or until biscuits are lightly browned. **Yield:** 8 servings.

Short Rib Soup

This is one of my dad's most irresistible dishes. It has a flavorful broth, tender meat and colorful vegetables. It really hits the spot on a chilly fall or winter day. —Kathy Froehlich, Dix Hills, New York

1 can (15-1/4 ounces) lima beans
1 can (14-1/2 ounces) cut green beans
4 cups water
2 pounds beef short ribs
1 can (14-1/2 ounces) diced tomatoes, undrained
1 cup coarsely chopped carrot
3/4 cup chopped onion
1/3 cup pearl barley
1 tablespoon salt
1 tablespoon sugar
1/2 teaspoon dried basil
1 bay leaf

Drain beans, reserving liquid; set the beans aside. Place the liquid in a Dutch oven or soup kettle; add remaining ingredients. Bring to a boil. Reduce heat; cover and simmer for 2 hours or until the meat is tender. Remove meat from bones; discard bones. Cut the meat into bite-size pieces and return to kettle. Add beans and cook for 10 minutes or until heated through. Remove bay leaf before serving. **Yield:** 10 servings.

Peeling Garlic

To easily remove the skin from a clove of garlic, lay the clove on a flat rubber jar opener, fold one side of the opener over and roll the garlic a few times on a flat surface with the palm of your hand.

White Chili

Even without meat, this soup—packed with two kinds of beans simmered in a creamy broth—really sticks to the ribs. When I was a child, white beans were a staple at our table. —Gloria Hutchings, Troy, Michigan

1 pound dry navy beans
1 medium onion, chopped
2 garlic cloves, minced
1 tablespoon vegetable oil
1 can (10-3/4 ounces) condensed cream of chicken soup, undiluted
1 can (10-3/4 ounces) condensed cream of celery soup, undiluted
1 cup water
1 medium potato, peeled and cubed
2 tablespoons chili powder
1 chicken bouillon cube
1/2 teaspoon salt
1 can (15 ounces) garbanzo beans, rinsed and drained
1-1/2 cups half-and-half cream

Place navy beans in a Dutch oven or soup kettle; add water to cover by 2 in. Bring to a boil; boil for 2 minutes. Remove from the heat; cover and let stand for 1 hour. Drain and discard liquid; return beans to pan. Add water to cover by 2 in. Bring to a boil; cover and simmer for 45 minutes or until beans are tender. Drain and discard liquid; set the beans aside. In the same Dutch oven, saute onion and garlic in oil until tender. Add soups, 1 cup water, potato, chili powder, bouillon and salt; cover and cook over medium-low heat for 10 minutes. Add the garbanzo beans, cream and navy beans. Cook over medium heat for 10 minutes or until heated through (do not boil). **Yield:** 10 servings.

Hot Ham Hoagies

(Pictured below)

These satisfying sandwiches have a delicious hearty filling. They're very quick and simple to prepare and great for a gathering, too. —Maudie Raber Millersburg, Ohio

1 cup barbecue sauce
3/4 teaspoon ground mustard
3/4 teaspoon garlic salt
1/4 teaspoon ground cloves
1 pound thinly sliced fully cooked ham
Lettuce leaves and sliced tomato, onion and Swiss cheese
6 hoagie *or* submarine buns, split

In a saucepan over medium heat, combine the first five ingredients; bring to a boil. Reduce heat; cover and simmer for 15 minutes. Place lettuce, tomato, onion and cheese on buns; top with the ham mixture. **Yield:** 6 servings.

Special Eggplant Subs

(Pictured below and on page 43)

The idea for this unique sandwich was inspired by a light eggplant dish I made for hot summer evenings. I decided to use the golden eggplant slices as a base for sandwiches. My family goes wild for the delicious combination of toppings. —*Marie Maffucci, New Rochelle, New York*

2 eggs
1 cup dry bread crumbs
1 medium eggplant, peeled and sliced 1/4 inch thick
4 submarine sandwich buns (10 inches), split
Leaf lettuce
1 jar (7-1/4 ounces) roasted red peppers, drained and sliced
8 slices mozzarella cheese
2 medium tomatoes, thinly sliced
1 can (2-1/4 ounces) chopped ripe olives, drained
Italian *or* vinaigrette salad dressing

In a shallow bowl, beat the eggs. Place the bread crumbs in another bowl. Dip eggplant slices into egg, then coat with crumbs. Place on a greased baking sheet. Bake at 350° for 30 minutes or until crispy. Cool. On the bottom of each bun, layer lettuce, eggplant, red peppers, cheese, tomatoes and olives. Sprinkle with salad dressing; replace bun tops. **Yield:** 4 servings.

Lima Bean Soup

This colorful soup has a golden broth dotted with tender vegetables and lima beans. It makes an excellent lunch or first course. —*Betty Koreck, Bridgman, Michigan*

1 pound dry lima beans
1 large meaty ham bone *or* 2 ham hocks
2-1/2 quarts water
5 celery ribs, cut into chunks
5 medium carrots, cut into chunks
1 garlic clove, minced
2 tablespoons butter *or* margarine
2 tablespoons all-purpose flour
2 teaspoons salt
1/2 teaspoon pepper
Pinch paprika
1 cup cold water
1 can (14-1/2 ounces) stewed tomatoes

Place beans in a Dutch oven or soup kettle; add water to cover by 2 in. Bring to a boil; boil for 2 minutes. Remove from the heat; cover and let stand for 1 hour. Drain and discard liquid; return beans to pan. Add ham bone and the 2-1/2 qts. of water; bring to a boil. Reduce heat; cover and simmer for 1-1/2 hours. Debone ham and cut into chunks; return to pan. Add celery and carrots. Cover and simmer for 1 hour or until beans are tender. In a skillet, saute garlic in butter for 1 minute. Stir in flour, salt, pepper and paprika. Add cold water; bring to a boil. Reduce heat; cook and stir for 2 minutes or until thickened. Add to the soup with tomatoes; simmer for 10 minutes. **Yield:** 14 servings (3-1/2 quarts).

Lentil Vegetable Soup

I highly recommend this hearty variation of lentil soup. Curry and ginger give the broth zip, and spinach and squash are tasty, nutritious additions. —*Beverly Sterling, Gasport, New York*

✓ Uses less fat, sugar or salt. Includes Nutritional Analysis and Diabetic Exchanges.

1 medium yellow summer squash, cut into 1/2-inch cubes

3 teaspoons vegetable oil, *divided*
2 medium carrots, sliced
1 large potato, peeled and cut into 1/2-inch cubes
1 medium onion, chopped
2 garlic cloves, minced
1 teaspoon curry powder
1/4 teaspoon ground ginger
6 cups low-sodium chicken broth
1-1/4 cups dry lentils, rinsed
3 tablespoons no-salt-added tomato paste
1 tablespoon cider *or* red wine vinegar
1/2 teaspoon pepper
4 cups coarsely chopped fresh spinach

In a large saucepan, saute squash in 1 teaspoon oil until crisp-tender. Remove and set aside. Add carrots, potato, onion, garlic and remaining oil to the pan. Cook and stir over low heat for 8-10 minutes. Stir in curry powder and ginger; cook for 1 minute. Add the broth, lentils, tomato paste, vinegar and pepper; bring to a boil. Reduce heat; cover and simmer for 30 minutes or until lentils and potatoes are tender. Add spinach and squash; heat through. **Yield:** 6 servings. **Nutritional Analysis:** One 1-cup serving equals 236 calories, 145 mg sodium, 4 mg cholesterol, 37 gm carbohydrate, 15 gm protein, 5 gm fat. **Diabetic Exchanges:** 2 starch, 1 meat, 1 vegetable.

Corny Tomato Dumpling Soup

(Pictured above right)

I have a big garden on our farm and enjoy cooking with my harvest. In this savory tomato soup, corn stars in both the broth and dumplings. Ground beef makes it a hearty first course or satisfying light main dish.
—Jackie Ferris, Tiverton, Ontario

1 pound ground beef
3 cups fresh *or* frozen corn
1 can (28 ounces) diced tomatoes, undrained
2 cans (14-1/2 ounces *each*) beef broth
1 cup chopped onion
1 garlic clove, minced
1-1/2 teaspoons dried basil
1-1/2 teaspoons dried thyme
1/2 teaspoon dried rosemary, crushed
Salt and pepper to taste

CORN DUMPLINGS:
1 cup all-purpose flour
1/2 cup cornmeal
2-1/2 teaspoons baking powder
1/2 teaspoon salt
1 egg

2/3 cup milk
1 cup fresh *or* frozen corn
1/2 cup shredded cheddar cheese
1 tablespoon minced fresh parsley

In a large saucepan or Dutch oven over medium heat, cook beef until no longer pink; drain. Stir in corn, tomatoes, broth, onion, garlic and seasonings. Bring to a boil. Reduce heat; cover and simmer for 30-45 minutes. For dumplings, combine flour, cornmeal, baking powder and salt in a bowl. In another bowl, beat egg; stir in milk, corn, cheese and parsley. Stir into the dry ingredients just until moistened. Drop by tablespoonfuls onto simmering soup. Cover and simmer for 15 minutes or until a toothpick inserted in a dumpling comes out clean (do not lift cover while simmering). **Yield:** 8 servings (about 2 quarts).

Tasty Tomato Soup

Even if you don't have time to make tomato soup from scratch, you can still offer homemade flavor. Simply dilute canned tomato or vegetable soup with V-8 juice instead of water. Simmer in a saucepan, then top the bubbling mixture with your favorite homemade dumplings.

Teriyaki Chicken Sandwiches

(Pictured above)

After trying a similar sandwich in Hawaii, I was inspired to create my own. My sister-in-law contributed the marinade, and together we came up with this hearty version. —*Opal Reed, Tyler, Texas*

1/2 cup vegetable oil
1/4 cup soy sauce
3 tablespoons honey
2 tablespoons white wine vinegar
1 teaspoon ground ginger
3/4 teaspoon garlic powder
4 boneless skinless chicken breast halves (about 1-1/2 pounds)
4 hard rolls *or* croissants
1 cup finely shredded lettuce
8 tomato slices
4 green pepper rings
1/4 cup mayonnaise, optional

Combine the first six ingredients in a blender; process for 30 seconds. Reserve 1/4 cup. Pour remaining sauce into a large resealable plastic bag. Add chicken; seal and refrigerate overnight. Drain, discarding marinade. Broil chicken 4 in. from the heat for 5 minutes on each side or until juices run clear. On the bottom half of each roll or croissant, layer lettuce, tomato, chicken and green pepper. Drizzle with reserved sauce; spread with mayonnaise if desired. Top with other half of roll or croissant. **Yield:** 4 servings. **Editor's Note:** Chicken may be grilled, covered, over low heat for 10-12 minutes or until juices run clear.

Lentil Barley Soup

I get many requests from my family for this thick, full-flavored soup in the winter, especially on -35° days, which are not uncommon here! —*Myrtle Brandt*
Morris, Manitoba

✓ Uses less fat, sugar or salt. Includes Nutritional Analysis and Diabetic Exchanges.

1 medium onion, chopped
3/4 cup thinly sliced celery
1 garlic clove, minced
1 tablespoon margarine
2 quarts water
1 can (28 ounces) diced tomatoes, undrained
1 package (1.7 ounces) vegetable soup mix
3/4 cup dry lentils
3/4 cup medium pearl barley
1/4 teaspoon pepper
2 medium carrots, thinly sliced
1/2 cup reduced-fat shredded Swiss cheese, optional

In a soup kettle or Dutch oven, saute onion, celery and garlic in margarine until tender. Add water, tomatoes, soup mix, lentils, barley and pepper; bring to a boil. Reduce heat; cover and simmer for 45 minutes or until lentils and barley are tender. Add carrots; simmer 20-25 minutes longer or until the carrots are tender. Garnish with cheese if desired. **Yield:** 12 servings (3 quarts). **Nutritional Analysis:** One 1-cup serving (served without cheese) equals 125 calories, 405 mg sodium, trace cholesterol, 23 gm carbohydrate, 5 gm protein, 1 gm fat. **Diabetic Exchanges:** 1-1/2 starch, 1 vegetable.

Zucchini Beef Soup

My garden produces a bumper crop of zucchini, and I hate to see even one go to waste. This satisfying soup is a simple solution. The broth is delicious.
—*Robert Keith, Rochester, Minnesota*

1 pound beef stew meat, cut into 1-inch cubes
1 tablespoon vegetable oil

6 cups water
1 can (8 ounces) tomato sauce
1 medium onion, chopped
1-1/2 teaspoons salt
3/4 teaspoon dried oregano
1/4 teaspoon pepper
2 cups thinly sliced zucchini
1 cup uncooked broken spaghetti

In a Dutch oven, brown beef in oil; drain. Add the water, tomato sauce, onion, salt, oregano and pepper. Bring to a boil. Reduce heat; cover and simmer for 2 hours. Add zucchini and spaghetti; return to a boil. Cover and cook for 15-18 minutes or until zucchini and spaghetti are tender. **Yield:** 8 servings (2 quarts).

Jeff's Potato Soup

Chicken gravy mix, cumin and Cajun seasoning give this hearty and comforting soup a distinctive flavor.
—Jeff Gill, Valdosta, Georgia

1 celery rib, thinly sliced
1 small onion, chopped
1 green onion, thinly sliced
2 tablespoons butter *or* margarine
2 envelopes chicken gravy mix
1/4 teaspoon celery salt
1/4 teaspoon ground cumin
1/4 teaspoon Cajun seasoning
1/4 teaspoon pepper
4 cups milk
5 medium potatoes, peeled, cubed and cooked
1 cup cubed process American cheese

In a large saucepan, saute celery and onions in butter until tender. Stir in gravy mix and seasonings; gradually add milk. Bring to a boil; cook and stir for 2 minutes. Reduce heat; stir in potatoes and cheese. Cook and stir until the potatoes are heated through and the cheese is melted. **Yield:** 6-8 servings.

Roasted Squash Soup

A friend gave me this wonderful recipe that calls for sage. My family frequently requests this rich and nicely seasoned soup.
—Cathy Edge
Lake Oswego, Oregon

✓ Uses less fat, sugar or salt. Includes Nutritional Analysis and Diabetic Exchanges.

1 butternut squash (2-1/2 pounds)
1 cup chopped onion
1 tablespoon minced fresh sage *or* 1 teaspoon rubbed sage
Pinch ground allspice
2 tablespoons butter *or* margarine
4 cups chicken broth
1 small tart apple, peeled and chopped
1-1/2 teaspoons lemon *or* lime juice
Pepper to taste
TOPPING:
1/3 cup sour cream
1/2 teaspoon lemon *or* lime juice
1/4 teaspoon grated lemon *or* lime peel

Cut squash in half lengthwise; scoop out seeds. Place squash cut side down in a greased baking dish. Bake, uncovered, at 400° for 50-60 minutes or until tender. When cool enough to handle, scoop out squash. Place squash in a bowl and mash; set aside 2 cups. In a large saucepan, saute onion, sage and allspice in butter until tender. Add broth and apple; bring to a boil. Reduce heat; cover and simmer until apple is tender, about 8 minutes. Add reserved squash; simmer 5 minutes longer. Cool until lukewarm. Process in small batches in a blender or food processor until smooth; return to pan. Add lemon juice and pepper; heat through. Combine topping ingredients; place a dollop on each serving. **Yield:** 6 servings. **Nutritional Analysis:** One 1-cup serving (prepared with margarine, low-sodium broth and fat-free sour cream) equals 119 calories, 121 mg sodium, 3 mg cholesterol, 17 gm carbohydrate, 3 gm protein, 5 gm fat. **Diabetic Exchanges:** 1 starch, 1 fat.

Top-Dog Hot Dogs

Our two sons love the pizza-like flavor these hot dogs get from chili sauce and cheese. They're creative and delicious, too!
—Kathy Burggraaf
Plainfield Township, Michigan

8 hot dogs
8 hot dog buns, sliced
1 jar (10 ounces) hot dog relish *or* chili sauce
1 small green pepper, chopped
1 small onion, chopped
1 small tomato, chopped and seeded
Shredded mozzarella cheese

Cook hot dogs according to package directions. Place in buns; top with relish or chili sauce, green pepper, onion and tomato. Sprinkle with mozzarella cheese. **Yield:** 8 servings.

Hearty Hash Brown Soup

(Pictured below and on page 43)

Once they take a spoonful of this soup chock-full of potatoes and ham, folks will think you fussed. Since it uses frozen hash browns, it's simple and fast to make.
—Frances Rector, Vinton, Iowa

2 pounds frozen hash brown potatoes
4 cups water
1 large onion, chopped
3/4 cup sliced celery
4 chicken bouillon cubes
1/2 teaspoon celery seed
1/4 teaspoon pepper
4 cans (10-3/4 ounces *each*) condensed cream of chicken soup, undiluted
1 quart milk
2 cups cubed fully cooked ham
1 tablespoon dried parsley flakes
1-1/2 teaspoons garlic salt
8 bacon strips, cooked and crumbled

In a Dutch oven or soup kettle, combine the first seven ingredients; bring to a boil. Reduce heat; cover and simmer for 20 minutes or until vegetables are tender. Mash vegetables with cooking liquid. Add soup and milk; stir until smooth. Add ham, parsley and garlic salt; simmer for 10 minutes or until heated through. Garnish with bacon. **Yield:** 12-16 servings (4 quarts).

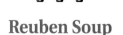

Champion Roast Beef Sandwiches

(Pictured below and on page 43)

When I have time, I like to prepare a roast with this much-requested recipe in mind. *—Ann Eastman, Greenville, California*

1/2 cup sour cream
1 tablespoon dry onion soup mix
1 tablespoon prepared horseradish, drained
1/8 teaspoon pepper
8 slices rye *or* pumpernickel bread
1/2 pound sliced roast beef
Lettuce leaves

In a small bowl, combine the first four ingredients; mix well. Spread 1 tablespoon on each slice of bread. Top four slices with roast beef and lettuce; cover with remaining bread. **Yield:** 4 servings.

Reuben Soup

When we're lucky (or have been good—I'm not certain

WINTER WARM-UP. When chilly winter winds blow, warm up with a classic combination like Champion Roast Beef Sandwiches and Hearty Hash Brown Soup (above).

which!), this soup is served in the staff cafeteria at the school where I work. The cooks have served it for years, and it remains a special favorite.
—Mary Lindell, Sanford, Michigan

1/2 cup chopped onion
1/2 cup sliced celery
2 tablespoons butter *or* margarine
1 cup chicken broth
1 cup beef broth
1/2 teaspoon baking soda
2 tablespoons cornstarch
2 tablespoons cold water
3/4 cup sauerkraut, rinsed and drained
2 cups half-and-half cream
2 cups chopped cooked corned beef
1 cup (4 ounces) shredded Swiss cheese
Salt and pepper to taste
Rye croutons, optional

In a large saucepan, saute the onion and celery in butter until tender. Add broth and baking soda. Combine cornstarch and water; add to pan. Bring to a boil; boil for 2 minutes, stirring occasionally. Reduce heat. Add sauerkraut, cream and corned beef; simmer and stir for 15 minutes. Add cheese; heat until melted. Add salt and pepper. Garnish with croutons if desired. **Yield:** about 6 servings.

Carrot Leek Soup

Loaded with leeks, carrots and potatoes, steaming bowlfuls of this colorful soup are sure to please.
—Norma Meyers, Huntsville, Arkansas

 Uses less fat, sugar or salt. Includes Nutritional Analysis and Diabetic Exchanges.

1 medium leek, thinly sliced
4 teaspoons low-fat margarine
6 medium carrots, sliced
2 medium potatoes, peeled and cubed
3 cans (14-1/2 ounces *each*) low-sodium chicken broth
2 cups skim milk
1/8 teaspoon pepper

In a large saucepan, saute leek in margarine until tender. Add carrots, potatoes and broth; bring to a boil. Reduce heat; cover and simmer until vegetables are tender. Cool to room temperature. Remove vegetables with a slotted spoon to a blender or food processor. Add enough cooking liquid to cover; blend until smooth. Return to pan. Stir in milk and pepper; heat through. **Yield:** 10 servings (2-1/2 quarts). **Nutritional Analysis:** One 1-cup serving equals 89 calories, 113 mg sodium, 4 mg cholesterol, 15 gm carbohydrate, 4 gm protein, 2 gm fat. **Diabetic Exchanges:** 1/2 starch, 1/2 skim milk, 1/2 fat.

Bologna Salad Sandwiches

This spread makes a filling sandwich perfect for a big appetite. *—Joyce Walker, Ridgeway, Virginia*

1-1/2 pounds bologna *or* ham, ground
1 to 1-1/4 cups mayonnaise
3/4 cup sweet pickle relish, well drained
3 tablespoons chopped onion
1 tablespoon Worcestershire sauce
30 slices bread
15 slices process American cheese
Lettuce leaves, optional

In a bowl, mix bologna, mayonnaise, relish, onion and Worcestershire sauce. Use about 1/3 cupful for each sandwich; top with a slice of cheese and lettuce if desired. **Yield:** 15 sandwiches. **Editor's Note:** All of the sandwiches don't have to be made at once. Salad will keep for 4-5 days stored in a covered container in the refrigerator.

Steak Chili

Why make ordinary ground beef chili when you can create this version using round steak? It's sure to earn you raves among family and friends.
—DeAnn Hill, Indianapolis, Indiana

1-1/2 pounds lean round steak, cut into 1/2-inch cubes
1 cup chopped onion
3 garlic cloves, minced
1 can (15 ounces) tomato sauce
1-1/4 cups water, *divided*
1 cup V-8 juice
1/2 teaspoon hot pepper sauce
1 tablespoon chili powder
1 tablespoon paprika
1-1/2 teaspoons ground cumin
1 teaspoon pepper
2 tablespoons all-purpose flour

In a large saucepan over medium heat, cook steak until no longer pink. Drain, reserving 2 tablespoons drippings. Set meat aside. Saute onion and garlic in drippings for 3 minutes. Return meat to pan. Add tomato sauce, 1 cup water, V-8 juice, hot pepper sauce and spices; bring to a boil. Reduce heat; cover and simmer for 2-1/2 hours. Combine flour and remaining water; whisk into chili. Cook for 10 minutes. **Yield:** 6 servings.

MINUTE MINDER

Side Dishes

Round out your everyday dinners and special-occasion meals with a country-style side dish featuring garden-fresh vegetables, tender pasta, hearty beans or tasty rice.

TASTES THAT ARE TOPS. Clockwise from upper left: Salsa Corn Cakes (p. 66), Company Mac and Cheese (p. 58), Calico Chowchow (p. 68) and Vegetables Mornay (p. 59).

Company Mac and Cheese

(Pictured above and on page 56)

This is by far the creamiest, tastiest and most special macaroni and cheese I have ever tried. I'm not usually a fan of homemade macaroni and cheese, but when a friend served this, I had to have the recipe. Since it's so little fuss and well received, it's a terrific potluck dish. —Catherine Odgen, Middlegrove, New York

- **1 package (7 ounces) elbow macaroni**
- **6 tablespoons butter *or* margarine, *divided***
- **3 tablespoons all-purpose flour**
- **2 cups milk**
- **1 package (8 ounces) cream cheese, cubed**
- **2 cups (8 ounces) shredded cheddar cheese**
- **2 teaspoons spicy brown mustard**
- **1/2 teaspoon salt**
- **1/4 teaspoon pepper**
- **3/4 cup dry bread crumbs**
- **2 tablespoons minced fresh parsley**

Cook macaroni according to package directions. Meanwhile, melt 4 tablespoons butter in a large saucepan. Stir in flour until smooth. Gradually add milk. Bring to a boil; cook and stir for 2 minutes. Reduce heat; add cheeses, mustard, salt and pepper. Stir until cheese is melted and sauce is smooth. Drain macaroni; add to the cheese sauce and stir to coat. Transfer to a greased shallow 3-qt. baking dish. Melt the remaining butter; toss with bread crumbs and parsley. Sprinkle over macaroni. Bake, uncovered, at 400° for 15-20 minutes or until golden brown. **Yield:** 6-8 servings.

Baked Potato Strips

These tender potatoes are excellent alongside everything from beef tenderloin to hot dogs. They're delicately seasoned with garlic powder and Parmesan cheese. —Mae Dean Williams, Charlotte, North Carolina

✓ Uses less fat, sugar or salt. Includes Nutritional Analysis and Diabetic Exchanges.

- **3 large baking potatoes**
- **2 egg whites**
- **2 tablespoons grated Parmesan cheese**
- **1 teaspoon garlic powder**

Cut potatoes lengthwise into thin 1/4-in. strips. Pat dry with paper towels. In a bowl, combine the egg whites, Parmesan cheese and garlic powder. Add the potatoes; toss to coat. Place in a single layer in a 15-in. x 10-in. x 1-in. baking pan coated with nonstick cooking spray. Bake, uncovered, at 375° for 35-40 minutes or until potatoes are golden brown and tender, turning several times. **Yield:** 4 servings. **Nutritional Analysis:** One serving equals 190 calories, 98 mg sodium, 2 mg cholesterol, 39 gm carbohydrate, 7 gm protein, 1 gm fat. **Diabetic Exchange:** 2-1/2 starch.

Steamed Broccoli and Squash

This side dish pairs two colorful vegetables and a savory dressing. When I serve it, I never have leftovers. —Dorothy Smith, El Dorado, Arkansas

✓ Uses less fat, sugar or salt. Includes Nutritional Analysis and Diabetic Exchanges.

- **1 pound broccoli, cut into spears**
- **1 medium yellow summer squash, halved lengthwise and cut into 1/4-inch slices**
- **2 tablespoons olive *or* vegetable oil**
- **1 garlic clove, minced**
- **1/2 teaspoon dried oregano**

Combine the broccoli and squash in a steamer basket; place in a saucepan over 1 in. of water. Bring to a boil; reduce heat. Cover and steam for 5-8 minutes or until crisp-tender. Meanwhile, combine the remaining ingredients. Remove vegetables from steamer; drizzle with oil mixture and toss to coat. **Yield:** 4 servings. **Nutritional Analysis:** One 3/4-

cup serving equals 86 calories, 18 mg sodium, 0 cholesterol, 5 gm carbohydrate, 2 gm protein, 7 gm fat. **Diabetic Exchanges:** 1 vegetable, 1 fat.

Cheesy Broccoli-Rice Bake

With cheese and sour cream, this lovely low-fat casserole is perfect to serve to guests or share on a buffet.
—Martha Myers, Ash Grove, Missouri

✓ Uses less fat, sugar or salt. Includes Nutritional Analysis and Diabetic Exchanges.

1 can (10-3/4 ounces) low-fat condensed cream of broccoli soup, undiluted
1 can (10-3/4 ounces) low-fat cream of chicken soup, undiluted
2 cups skim milk
1/2 cup light sour cream
2 cups (8 ounces) shredded part-skim mozzarella cheese
1 cup (4 ounces) shredded reduced-fat cheddar cheese
2 cups uncooked instant rice
2 cups chopped fresh broccoli
1 small onion, chopped
1 teaspoon paprika, *divided*
1/2 teaspoon pepper

In a large bowl, combine soups, milk and sour cream. Stir in cheeses, rice, broccoli, onion, 3/4 teaspoon of paprika and pepper. Transfer to a 13-in. x 9-in. x 2-in. baking dish coated with nonstick cooking spray. Sprinkle with remaining paprika. Cover and bake at 350° for 35 minutes. Uncover; bake 5-10 minutes longer or until rice and broccoli are tender. **Yield:** 16 servings. **Nutritional Analysis:** One 1/2-cup serving equals 194 calories, 291 mg sodium, 14 mg cholesterol, 27 gm carbohydrate, 10 gm protein, 5 gm fat. **Diabetic Exchanges:** 2-1/2 starch, 1 meat, 1 vegetable.

Vegetables Mornay

(Pictured at right and on page 56)

These saucy vegetables are a colorful and satisfying side dish we enjoy often. Our daughter, a 4-H member, earned the Reserve Grand Champion ribbon at our local county fair with this recipe. *—Jo Anne Remmele*
Echo, Minnesota

6 to 8 medium carrots, sliced 1/4 inch thick
1/4 cup water
1 package (10 ounces) frozen chopped broccoli
1 package (10 ounces) frozen cauliflowerets
2 jars (4-1/2 ounces *each*) whole mushrooms, drained
2 tablespoons cornstarch
1 teaspoon salt
1/4 teaspoon pepper
1-1/2 cups milk
8 tablespoons butter *or* margarine, melted, *divided*
1 cup (4 ounces) shredded Swiss cheese
2 tablespoons Parmesan cheese
1/2 cup seasoned croutons

Place the carrots and water in a 3-qt. microwave-safe dish. Cover and microwave on high for 2 minutes. Add broccoli and cauliflower. Cover and microwave for 8-12 minutes or until vegetables are tender; drain. Add mushrooms; cover and set aside. In another microwave-safe dish, combine cornstarch, salt, pepper, milk and 6 tablespoons butter until smooth. Cover and microwave on high for 4-6 minutes or until thickened and smooth. Add cheeses and stir until melted. Pour over the vegetables. Cover and microwave for 3-5 minutes or until heated through. Combine croutons and remaining butter; stir into vegetables. **Yield:** 8-10 servings. **Editor's Note:** This recipe was tested in an 850-watt microwave.

Stir-Fried Vegetables

(Pictured below)

For a colorful nutritious blend of crisp-tender vegetables in a mildly seasoned sauce, try this recipe. There's no restriction on good taste! —Cindy Winter-Hartley Cary, North Carolina

Uses less fat, sugar or salt. Includes Nutritional Analysis and Diabetic Exchanges.

2 medium green peppers, julienned
2 medium sweet red peppers, julienned
2 medium carrots, julienned
2 cups broccoli florets
3 tablespoons vegetable oil
2 tablespoons light soy sauce
1 teaspoon ground ginger
6 green onions, thinly sliced
2 tablespoons cornstarch
1 cup low-sodium chicken broth
1/4 cup cold water

In a large skillet or wok, saute the peppers, carrots and broccoli in oil until crisp-tender, about 3 minutes. Combine soy sauce and ginger; add to pan with onions. Cook and stir for 1 minute. Combine cornstarch, broth and water until smooth; gradually stir into vegetables. Bring to a boil; cook and stir for 2 minutes or until thickened. **Yield:** 4 servings. **Nutritional Analysis:** One 1/2-cup serving equals 183 calories, 308 mg sodium, 1 mg cholesterol, 20 gm carbohydrate, 4 gm protein, 1 gm fat. **Diabetic Exchanges:** 2 vegetable, 2 fat, 1/2 starch.

Fried Rice

(Pictured below)

Instead of reheating leftover cooked rice, turn it into this tasty new side dish. It's a snap to put together and tastes as good as any restaurant variety. —Suzanne McKinley, Lyons, Georgia

Uses less fat, sugar or salt. Includes Nutritional Analysis and Diabetic Exchanges.

1/2 cup chopped green pepper
Egg substitute equivalent to 2 eggs
4 cups cooked rice
2 tablespoons light soy sauce

In a skillet coated with nonstick cooking spray, saute green pepper until crisp-tender. Add egg substitute; cook and stir until egg is completely set. Chop egg into small pieces. Add rice and soy sauce; heat through. **Yield:** 9 servings. **Nutritional**

FLAVORS from the Far East like Stir-Fried Vegetables and Fried Rice (shown above) make any meal memorable.

Analysis: One 1/2-cup serving equals 105 calories, 226 mg sodium, trace cholesterol, 20 gm carbohydrate, 4 gm protein, 1 gm fat. **Diabetic Exchanges:** 1 starch, 1 vegetable.

Bacon Hash Brown Bake

This tasty side dish has wonderful from-scratch flavor since it starts with fresh potatoes. It's very popular with guests at my bed-and-breakfast.
—Mark Clark, Twin Mountain, New Hampshire

4 cups grated cooked potatoes
12 bacon strips, cooked and crumbled
1/2 cup milk
1/3 cup chopped onion
1/2 teaspoon salt
1/4 teaspoon pepper
1/4 teaspoon garlic powder
1 tablespoon butter *or* margarine, melted
1/2 teaspoon paprika

In a bowl, combine the first seven ingredients. Transfer to a greased 9-in. pie plate. Drizzle with butter and sprinkle with paprika. Bake at 350° for 35-45 minutes or until lightly browned. **Yield:** 6-8 servings.

Mushroom-Filled Tomatoes

A creamy herb stuffing makes these tomatoes a special part of any meal. They're even a tasty light lunch served with hot rolls.
—Roberta Hammond, Warrington, Florida

6 medium tomatoes
1-1/2 cups chopped fresh mushrooms
3 tablespoons butter *or* margarine, *divided*
2 egg yolks
1/2 cup sour cream
1/4 cup plus 3 tablespoons dry bread crumbs, *divided*
1 teaspoon salt
1/4 teaspoon dried thyme
Dash pepper

Cut a thin slice off the top of each tomato. Scoop out pulp, leaving a 1/2-in. shell. Invert tomatoes on paper towels to drain. Chop the pulp, reserving 1 cup. In a skillet, saute mushrooms in 2 tablespoons butter until tender. Combine egg yolks and sour cream; add to mushrooms. Stir in 1/4 cup bread crumbs, salt, thyme, pepper and reserved tomato pulp. Simmer, uncovered, until thickened, about 1 minute. Spoon about 1/3 cupful into each tomato. Place in an ungreased 11-in. x 7-in. x 2-in. baking dish. Melt remaining butter; toss with remaining bread crumbs. Sprinkle over tomatoes. Bake, uncovered, at 350° for 30-35 minutes or until heated through. **Yield:** 6 servings.

Stuffed Sweet Potatoes

These potatoes make a simple side dish that's extra nutritious. Stuffed with ham and onion, they're both hearty and delicious.
—Marion Lowery, Medford, Oregon

✓ Uses less fat, sugar or salt. Includes Nutritional Analysis and Diabetic Exchanges.

2 large sweet potatoes
1 tablespoon butter *or* margarine
1/3 cup chopped fully cooked low-fat ham
1 tablespoon finely chopped onion
Dash pepper

Scrub and pierce potatoes. Bake at 350° for 65-75 minutes or until tender. Cool. Cut a thin slice off the top of each potato. Scoop out pulp, leaving a 1/4-in. shell. Place pulp in a bowl; add butter and mash. Stir in ham, onion and pepper. Spoon into potato shells. Bake, uncovered, at 350° for 20-25 minutes or until heated through. **Yield:** 2 servings.
Nutritional Analysis: One serving (prepared with margarine) equals 220 calories, 417 mg sodium, 11 mg cholesterol, 32 gm carbohydrate, 7 gm protein, 7 gm fat. **Diabetic Exchanges:** 2 starch, 1-1/2 fat.

Almond-Mushroom Wild Rice

The delightful combination of ingredients in this dish makes a perfect accompaniment for beef, poultry or pork. It's very flavorful and hearty.
—Shirley Goehring, Lodi, California

1 cup uncooked wild rice
2-1/2 cups chicken broth
1 cup sliced fresh mushrooms
1/2 cup slivered almonds, toasted
2 tablespoons butter *or* margarine, melted
2 tablespoons chopped green onions

Rinse and drain rice; place in a 1-1/2-qt. baking dish coated with nonstick cooking spray. Add the remaining ingredients; mix well. Cover and bake at 325° for 1-1/2 to 2 hours or until liquid is absorbed and rice is tender. **Yield:** 6 servings.

Peppered Corn Fritters

(Pictured above)

Cumin complements the corn and peppers in these pretty fritters. These are nice to serve alongside a variety of meaty entrees. —*Precious Owens Elizabethtown, Kentucky*

1-1/4 cups fresh *or* frozen corn, thawed
1 cup finely chopped sweet red pepper
1 cup finely chopped green onions
1-1/4 cups all-purpose flour
2 teaspoons baking powder
1 teaspoon ground cumin
1/4 teaspoon salt
1/8 teaspoon pepper
1 cup milk
2 to 4 tablespoons vegetable oil

In a bowl, combine the corn, red pepper and onions. Combine flour, baking powder, cumin, salt and pepper; stir into corn mixture. Gradually add milk, stirring until blended. In a skillet over medium heat, heat 2 tablespoons of oil. Drop batter by 1/4 cupfuls into skillet. Cook for 2 minutes on each side or until golden brown. Repeat with remaining batter, adding more oil as needed. **Yield:** 13-14 fritters.

Garlic Cauliflower Stir-Fry

Garlic and lemon-pepper give pleasant flavor to this special side dish while parsley adds a splash of color. It's a fun and innovative way to serve cauliflower. —*Jesse and Anne Foust, Bluefield, Virginia*

✓ Uses less fat, sugar or salt. Includes Nutritional Analysis and Diabetic Exchanges.

3 tablespoons butter *or* margarine
1 large head cauliflower (about 3 pounds), broken into florets
2 garlic cloves, minced
1 tablespoon minced fresh parsley *or* 1 teaspoon dried parsley flakes
1-1/2 teaspoons lemon-pepper seasoning

In a skillet over medium heat, melt butter. Add cauliflower and garlic. Sprinkle with parsley and lemon-pepper. Cook and stir for 12-15 minutes or until lightly browned and tender. **Yield:** 8 servings. **Nutritional Analysis:** One 1/2-cup serving (prepared with margarine and salt-free lemon-pepper) equals 63 calories, 78 mg sodium, 0 cholesterol, 5 gm carbohydrate, 2 gm protein, 4 gm fat. **Diabetic Exchanges:** 1 vegetable, 1 fat.

Tomato-Garlic Angel Hair

The light olive oil and Parmesan cheese-based sauce is so fresh tasting. But fresh basil is the key ingredient in this pasta dish. —*Salvatore Bertolino Indiana, Pennsylvania*

1 package (1 pound) angel hair pasta
3 large ripe tomatoes, peeled, seeded and chopped
1/3 cup olive *or* vegetable oil
1/4 cup grated Parmesan cheese
1/4 cup minced fresh parsley
1 to 2 garlic cloves, minced
1 tablespoon minced fresh basil
1/4 teaspoon garlic salt

Cook pasta according to package directions. Meanwhile, combine remaining ingredients in a large bowl. Rinse and drain pasta; add to tomato mixture and toss to coat. Serve immediately. **Yield:** 8-10 servings.

Ripening Tomatoes

To ripen fresh tomatoes, store them at room temperature in a brown paper bag. Contrary to popular belief, it's best not to ripen tomatoes on the windowsill because exposure to the sun can make them mushy. When they're ripe, tomatoes will yield slightly to gentle pressure.

Herbed Macaroni 'n' Cheese

Herbs make this dish different from other macaroni and cheese recipes. —*Lois McAtee Oceanside, California*

✓ Uses less fat, sugar or salt. Includes Nutritional Analysis and Diabetic Exchanges.

1 tablespoon margarine
3 tablespoons all-purpose flour
2 cups skim milk
3/4 to 1 teaspoon dried marjoram
1/2 teaspoon dried thyme
1/8 teaspoon ground nutmeg
1/8 teaspoon paprika
1 tablespoon Dijon mustard
1/2 cup grated Parmesan cheese, *divided*
1 package (7 ounces) elbow macaroni, cooked and drained
1 cup low-fat cottage cheese

In a large saucepan, melt margarine. Stir in flour until smooth. Gradually add milk, stirring constantly. Bring to a boil over medium heat; boil for 2 minutes or until thickened. Add the marjoram, thyme, nutmeg and paprika; stir until blended. Remove from the heat. Stir in mustard and 1/3 cup Parmesan cheese; mix well. Add macaroni and cottage cheese; stir until coated. Pour into an 8-in. square baking dish coated with nonstick cooking spray. Sprinkle with remaining Parmesan. Bake, uncovered, at 350° for 30 minutes or until top is golden brown. **Yield:** 4 servings. **Nutritional Analysis:** One serving equals 372 calories, 615 mg sodium, 20 mg cholesterol, 50 gm carbohydrate, 23 gm protein, 9 gm fat. **Diabetic Exchanges:** 3 starch, 2 meat.

Red Potato Wedges

My husband and I enjoy these tempting potato wedges instead of fries with hamburgers or any meat. —*Jennie Freeman, Crescent City, California*

✓ Uses less fat, sugar or salt. Includes Nutritional Analysis and Diabetic Exchanges.

4 medium red potatoes, cut into wedges
1 tablespoon vegetable oil
1-1/2 teaspoons minced fresh rosemary *or* 1/2 teaspoon dried rosemary, crushed
1/4 teaspoon garlic powder
1/4 teaspoon pepper

Place potatoes in a large bowl. Sprinkle with oil, rosemary, garlic powder and pepper; toss to coat. Place potatoes on a baking sheet coated with nonstick cooking spray. Cover and bake at 425° for 20 minutes. Turn potatoes. Bake, uncovered, 20 minutes longer or until browned. **Yield:** 4 servings. **Nutritional Analysis:** One serving equals 104 calories, 4 mg sodium, 0 cholesterol, 15 gm carbohydrate, 3 gm protein, 4 gm fat. **Diabetic Exchanges:** 1 starch, 1/2 fat.

Asparagus with Orange Sauce

(Pictured below)

This dish has the inspiring taste of spring. The light, creamy orange sauce makes asparagus a treat for the whole family. —*Cathee Bethel, Lebanon, Oregon*

✓ Uses less fat, sugar or salt. Includes Nutritional Analysis and Diabetic Exchanges.

2 pounds fresh asparagus, trimmed
1/4 cup plain nonfat yogurt
2 tablespoons light mayonnaise
2 tablespoons orange juice
1 teaspoon grated orange peel
Dash cayenne pepper
Orange slices and additional orange peel, optional

Place asparagus and a small amount of water in a skillet; bring to a boil. Cook for 6-8 minutes or until crisp-tender. Meanwhile, combine yogurt, mayonnaise, orange juice, peel and cayenne. Drain asparagus; top with orange sauce. Garnish with orange slices and peel if desired. **Yield:** 8 servings. **Nutritional Analysis:** One serving equals 44 calories, 45 mg sodium, trace cholesterol, 6 gm carbohydrate, 3 gm protein, 2 gm fat. **Diabetic Exchanges:** 1 vegetable, 1/2 fat.

TEMPT TASTE BUDS with Creamy Sprouts 'n' Noodles, Lemon Garlic Sprouts and Marinated Brussels Sprouts (shown above, clockwise from top right).

Lemon Garlic Sprouts

(Pictured above)

Lemon, garlic and Parmesan cheese are the perfect complement for brussels sprouts. I often rely on this easy recipe. —Mary Steiner, West Bend, Wisconsin

Uses less fat, sugar or salt. Includes Nutritional Analysis and Diabetic Exchanges.

1 pound fresh brussels sprouts, quartered
1 small onion, finely chopped
3 tablespoons butter *or* margarine
1 to 2 garlic cloves, minced
3 tablespoons lemon juice
1 teaspoon grated lemon peel
1/2 teaspoon salt, optional
1/4 teaspoon pepper
1/4 cup shredded Parmesan cheese

In a skillet, saute brussels sprouts and onion in butter for 5 minutes. Add garlic, lemon juice and peel, salt if desired and pepper; saute for 1 minute. Reduce heat to medium; cook and stir for 5-6 minutes or until the sprouts are tender. Sprinkle with Parmesan cheese. **Yield:** 8 servings. **Nutritional Analysis:** One 1/2-cup serving (prepared with margarine and nonfat Parmesan cheese topping and without salt) equals 73 calories, 113 mg sodium, 1 mg cholesterol, 7 gm carbohydrate, 3 gm protein, 4 gm fat. **Diabetic Exchanges:** 1 vegetable, 1 fat.

Creamy Sprouts 'n' Noodles

(Pictured above)

This comforting casserole is great with pork roast or pork chops. Plus, it makes a delicious side dish for company. —Dixie Terry, Marion, Illinois

1 pound fresh brussels sprouts, quartered
2 medium onions, finely chopped
4 tablespoons butter *or* margarine, *divided*
1 cup (8 ounces) sour cream
1 cup small-curd cottage cheese

1 garlic clove, minced
1 teaspoon paprika
1/2 teaspoon salt
1/4 to 1/2 teaspoon caraway seeds
3 cups medium egg noodles, cooked and drained
1 cup soft bread crumbs

Place the brussels sprouts and a small amount of water in a saucepan; cover and cook until tender. Meanwhile, in a skillet, saute onions in 2 tablespoons butter until golden brown. Remove from the heat; stir in the sour cream, cottage cheese, garlic, paprika, salt and caraway. Drain sprouts; add to onion mixture with noodles. Spread into a greased shallow 2-qt. baking dish. Melt remaining butter and toss with bread crumbs. Sprinkle over casserole. Bake, uncovered, at 375° for 20-25 minutes or until golden brown. **Yield:** 6-8 servings.

Marinated Brussels Sprouts

(Pictured at left)

This unique and refreshing relish makes a lovely addition to any table. I especially like serving it at backyard barbecues on summer days. —Marie Hattrup The Dalles, Oregon

Uses less fat, sugar or salt. Includes Nutritional Analysis and Diabetic Exchanges.

1 package (10 ounces) frozen brussels sprouts
1 cup Italian salad dressing
1 tablespoon finely chopped onion
1 garlic clove, minced
1/2 teaspoon dill weed

Cook brussels sprouts according to package directions; drain. Combine remaining ingredients; pour over sprouts and toss to coat. Cover and refrigerate. **Yield:** 2-1/2 cups. **Nutritional Analysis:** One 1/2-cup serving (prepared with fat-free salad dressing) equals 41 calories, 470 mg sodium, 0 cholesterol, 8 gm carbohydrate, 2 gm protein, trace fat. **Diabetic Exchange:** 1-1/2 vegetable.

Cheesy Broccoli Bake

Our children refused to eat broccoli, then I discovered this simple recipe. It has tender rice in a cheese sauce. The kids hardly notice the broccoli. —Dawn Trapp, West Fargo, North Dakota

1 package (10 ounces) frozen chopped broccoli
1 can (10-3/4 ounces) condensed cream of chicken soup, undiluted
1 jar (8 ounces) process cheese spread
3/4 cup uncooked instant rice
3 tablespoons seasoned bread crumbs
1 tablespoon butter *or* margarine, melted

In a bowl, combine the broccoli, soup, cheese spread and rice. Transfer to a greased 1-1/2-qt. baking dish. Toss bread crumbs and butter; sprinkle over the top. Cover and bake at 350° for 30 minutes; uncover and bake 15 minutes longer. **Yield:** 4 servings.

Tomato Crouton Casserole

This baked dish uses lots of delicious tomatoes and seasonings that give it an Italian twist. Every time I serve this dish, someone asks for the recipe. —Norma Nelson, Punta Gorda, Florida

8 medium tomatoes, peeled and cut into wedges
8 slices bread, crusts removed and cubed
1/2 cup plus 2 tablespoons butter *or* margarine, melted
1 teaspoon salt
1 teaspoon dried basil
1 teaspoon dried thyme
3/4 cup grated Parmesan cheese

Arrange tomatoes in a greased 13-in. x 9-in. x 2-in. baking dish. Top with bread cubes. Combine butter, salt, basil and thyme; drizzle over bread and tomatoes. Sprinkle with cheese. Bake, uncovered, at 350° for 30-35 minutes or until tomatoes are tender. **Yield:** 8-10 servings.

Dilly Mashed Potatoes

Liven up ordinary mashed potatoes with dill. Plus, sour cream makes them deliciously creamy. —Annie Tompkins, Deltona, Florida

6 medium potatoes, peeled and cubed
1/2 cup milk
1 cup (8 ounces) sour cream
2 tablespoons minced fresh dill *or* 2 teaspoons dill weed
1 tablespoon dried minced onion
3/4 teaspoon seasoned salt

In a saucepan, cover potatoes with water; cook until very tender. Drain; mash with milk. Stir in remaining ingredients. **Yield:** 6-8 servings.

Salsa Corn Cakes

(Pictured below and on page 56)

This recipe is super with fresh or canned corn. I whip up these patties to serve alongside nachos or tacos on hot summer evenings. The salsa is subtle but adds flavor. —*Lisa Boettcher, Rosebush, Michigan*

- **1-1/2 cups all-purpose flour**
- **1/2 cup cornmeal**
- **1 teaspoon baking powder**
- **1 teaspoon salt**
- **2 packages (3 ounces *each*) cream cheese, softened**
- **6 eggs**
- **1 cup milk**
- **1/4 cup butter *or* margarine, melted**
- **1 can (15-1/4 ounces) whole kernel corn, drained**
- **1/2 cup salsa, drained**
- **1/4 cup minced green onions**
- **Sour cream and additional salsa**

Combine flour, cornmeal, baking powder and salt; set aside. In a mixing bowl, beat cream cheese and eggs; add milk and butter. Add the dry ingredients just until moistened. Fold in the corn, salsa and onions. Pour the batter by 1/4 cupfuls onto a greased hot griddle. Turn when bubbles form on top; cook until the second side is golden brown. Serve with sour cream and salsa. **Yield:** 6-8 servings.

Alien Noodles

In an attempt to get my son to eat vegetables, I fixed an Alfredo sauce and stirred in fresh spinach and pasta. He started to complain, but when I called it "Alien Noodles", he took a bite. It's now his favorite side dish! —*Laura Hodges, Shallowater, Texas*

- **12 ounces uncooked angel hair pasta**
- **3 tablespoons butter *or* margarine**
- **3 tablespoons all-purpose flour**
- **1 teaspoon salt**
- **1/8 teaspoon pepper**
- **2 cups milk**
- **1/4 cup grated Parmesan cheese**
- **1-1/2 cups finely chopped fresh spinach *or* 1 package (10 ounces) frozen chopped spinach, thawed and drained**

Cook the pasta according to package directions. Meanwhile, in a saucepan, melt butter over medium heat. Stir in the flour, salt and pepper until smooth. Gradually stir in milk. Bring to a boil; cook and stir for 2 minutes. Remove from the heat; stir in Parmesan cheese until melted. Stir in spinach. Drain pasta and transfer to a serving bowl. Pour sauce over pasta and toss to coat. **Yield:** 8 servings.

Flavorful Fettuccine

Parmesan and cottage cheese make this side dish extra cheesy. I'll often add leftover ham, pork or shrimp. —*Edna Coburn, Tucson, Arizona*

✓ Uses less fat, sugar or salt. Includes Nutritional Analysis and Diabetic Exchanges.

- **1 package (12 ounces) fettuccine**
- **1 package (10 ounces) frozen chopped spinach, thawed**
- **3/4 cup diced sweet red pepper**
- **1 teaspoon cornstarch**
- **1 tablespoon chicken bouillon granules**
- **1 cup milk**
- **1 cup small-curd cottage cheese**
- **1/4 teaspoon ground nutmeg**
- **1/2 cup grated Parmesan cheese, optional**

In a large saucepan or Dutch oven, cook fettuccine in boiling water for 5 minutes. Add spinach and red pepper; return to a boil. Cook for 4-5 minutes or until the pasta is tender; drain and set aside. In a saucepan, combine cornstarch, bouillon and milk until smooth. Bring to a boil; cook and stir for 2 minutes or until thickened. Remove from the heat. Stir in cottage cheese and nutmeg. Add fettuccine and vegetables; toss to coat. Sprinkle with Parmesan cheese if desired. **Yield:** 8 servings. **Nutritional Analysis:** One 3/4-cup serving (prepared with skim milk, fat-free cottage cheese and low-sodium bouillon and without Parmesan cheese) equals 161 calories, 229 mg sodium, 3 mg cholesterol, 29 gm carbohydrate, 10 gm protein, 1 gm fat. **Diabetic Exchanges:** 2 starch, 1 lean meat.

Chive Potato Souffle

I've enjoyed cooking with herbs since I was a teenager. Chives, which are one of my favorites, enhance the flavor of this cheesy souffle. —*Wendy Nickel Kiester, Minnesota*

2 cups hot mashed potatoes (without added milk and butter)
3/4 cup shredded sharp cheddar cheese
1/2 cup sour cream
3 to 4 tablespoons minced chives
1/2 teaspoon salt
3 eggs, *separated*
Additional chives

In a large bowl, combine the potatoes, cheese, sour cream, chives and salt. Beat egg yolks; stir into potato mixture. In a small mixing bowl, beat egg whites until stiff peaks form; gently fold into the potato mixture. Transfer to a greased 1-1/2-qt. baking dish. Bake, uncovered, at 350° for 40-45 minutes or until a knife inserted near the center comes out clean. Sprinkle with chives. Serve immediately. **Yield:** 6 servings.

Cabbage with Herb Butter

Even folks who don't usually care for cabbage will love this side dish. A perfectly seasoned herb butter makes it irresistible. —*Iola Egle, McCook, Nebraska*

1 medium head cabbage (about 2 pounds), cut into wedges
1/2 cup butter *or* margarine, melted
1/2 cup minced chives
1/4 cup thinly sliced green onions
1/4 cup minced fresh parsley
1 tablespoon lemon juice
1-1/2 teaspoons minced fresh thyme *or* 1/2 teaspoon dried thyme
1/4 cup shredded cheddar cheese

Place cabbage in a large saucepan or Dutch oven; cover with water. Bring to a boil. Reduce heat; cover and cook for 8-10 minutes or until tender. Meanwhile, combine the butter, chives, onions, parsley, lemon juice and thyme. Drain cabbage; transfer to a serving platter. Drizzle with the herb butter; sprinkle with cheese. **Yield:** 6 servings.

Texas Two-Step Corn Medley

(Pictured above)

I came up with this pleasing pairing of corn and summer squash as a side dish for a Mexican buffet. Family and friends who have tried it are generous with their compliments and recipe requests. This delicious dish is a regular menu item when husband Bob and I entertain. —*Pauline Howard, Lago Vista, Texas*

1 medium onion, chopped
1/4 cup butter *or* margarine
2 medium yellow summer squash, sliced
2 garlic cloves, minced
2 tablespoons canned chopped green chilies
1/4 teaspoon salt
1/8 teaspoon pepper
2 cans (11 ounces *each*) Mexicorn, drained
3/4 cup shredded Co-Jack cheese

In a skillet, saute onion in butter until tender. Add the squash, garlic, chilies, salt and pepper. Saute until squash is crisp-tender, about 5 minutes. Add corn; cook and stir for 2 minutes. Sprinkle with cheese; cover and let stand until the cheese is melted. **Yield:** 4 servings.

Cheesy Corn Spoon Bread

(Pictured above)

Homey and comforting, this custard-like side dish is a much-requested recipe at potlucks and holiday dinners. The jalapeno pepper adds just the right "bite".
—Katherine Franklin, Carbondale, Illinois

1 medium onion, chopped
1/4 cup butter *or* margarine
2 eggs
2 cups (16 ounces) sour cream
1 can (15-1/4 ounces) whole kernel corn, drained
1 can (14-3/4 ounces) cream-style corn
1/4 teaspoon salt
1/4 teaspoon pepper
1 package (8-1/2 ounces) corn bread/muffin mix
1 medium jalapeno pepper, minced*
2 cups (8 ounces) shredded cheddar cheese, *divided*

In a skillet, saute onion in butter until tender; set aside. In a bowl, beat the eggs; add sour cream, both cans of corn, salt and pepper. Stir in corn bread mix just until blended. Fold in sauteed onion, jalapeno and 1-1/2 cups of cheese. Transfer to a greased shallow 3-qt. baking dish. Sprinkle with the remaining cheese. Bake, uncovered, at 375° for 35-40 minutes or until a toothpick inserted near the center comes out clean; cool slightly. **Yield:** 12-15 servings. ***Editor's Note:** When cutting or seeding hot peppers, use rubber or plastic gloves to protect your hands. Avoid touching your face or eyes.

Calico Chowchow

(Pictured on page 56)

I make this special garden-fresh relish each fall. It goes well with both hot and cold meats. —Doris Haycroft Westbank, British Columbia

7 cups shredded cabbage (about 1 small head)
4 cups fresh corn (about 5 ears)
4 cups caulifloweretes (about 1 small head)
2 cups diced sweet red pepper
1 cup diced green pepper
1 cup chopped onion
1/4 cup canning salt
7 cups water, *divided*
3-1/2 cups packed brown sugar
1/2 cup all-purpose flour
1/4 cup ground mustard
1 tablespoon celery seed
2 teaspoons ground turmeric
1-1/2 teaspoons salt
5 cups vinegar

In a large bowl, combine the first six ingredients; sprinkle with canning salt. Add 6 cups water; cover and refrigerate for 4 hours. Drain and rinse well. In a large heavy saucepan or Dutch oven, combine the brown sugar, flour, mustard, celery seed, turmeric and salt. Stir in vinegar and remaining water until smooth. Bring to a boil; cook and stir for 5 minutes or until thickened. Add vegetables; bring to a boil. Simmer, uncovered, for 8-10 minutes or until crisp-tender. Pack the hot mixture into hot jars, leaving 1/4-in. headspace. Adjust caps. Process for 15 minutes in a boiling-water bath. **Yield:** 7 pints.

Ruby Red Cabbage

I usually serve this great side dish with pork roast or sausages. You can't beat the sweet-and-sour taste.
—Keri Lawson, Fullerton, California

1 cup dried cranberries
1 tablespoon butter *or* margarine
1 large head red cabbage (about 3 pounds), thinly sliced
1/4 cup cider *or* red wine vinegar
1/4 cup apple juice
1/4 cup plum *or* currant jelly
2 tablespoons brown sugar
1/2 teaspoon salt
1/2 teaspoon pepper

In a Dutch oven or large saucepan, cook cranberries in butter until softened, about 3 minutes. Add the remaining ingredients. Cover and cook over medium-low heat until cabbage is wilted, about 5-7 minutes. Transfer to a greased 2-qt. baking dish. Cover and bake at 350° for 1 hour or until tender. Serve with a slotted spoon. **Yield:** 8-10 servings.

Spinach Potato Pancakes

These dressed-up potato pancakes are extra tasty and nutritious. —Mildred Sherrer, Bay City, Texas

✓ Uses less fat, sugar or salt. Includes Nutritional Analysis and Diabetic Exchanges.

- **1 package (10 ounces) frozen chopped spinach, thawed and squeezed dry**
- **2 cups shredded zucchini**
- **1 medium potato, peeled and shredded**
- **1/4 cup finely chopped onion**
- **1/4 cup all-purpose flour**
- **1/4 to 3/4 teaspoon salt**
- **1/2 teaspoon pepper**
- **1/4 to 1/2 teaspoon ground nutmeg**
- **1 egg, beaten**
- **Applesauce, optional**

In a bowl, combine the first eight ingredients. Stir in egg; mix well. Drop batter by 1/4 cupfuls onto a well-greased hot griddle. Flatten to form patties. Fry until golden brown; turn and cook until second side is lightly browned. Drain on paper towels. Serve with applesauce if desired. **Yield:** 1 dozen. **Nutritional Analysis:** One pancake (prepared with 1/4 teaspoon salt and egg substitute equivalent to one egg and served without applesauce) equals 32 calories, 77 mg sodium, trace cholesterol, 6 gm carbohydrate, 2 gm protein, trace fat. **Diabetic Exchange:** 1/2 starch.

Stuffing Surprise

With its mild flavor, tender squash is easy to blend into recipes to please the palates of picky eaters. —Suzanne Zick, Osceola, Arkansas

- **2 cups mashed cooked butternut *or* acorn squash**
- **1 can (10-3/4 ounces) condensed cream of chicken soup, undiluted**
- **1 cup (8 ounces) sour cream**
- **1/2 cup chopped onion**
- **1 medium carrot, finely shredded**
- **1/4 teaspoon salt**
- **1/8 teaspoon pepper**
- **2 cups crushed herb-seasoned stuffing, *divided***
- **2 tablespoons butter *or* margarine, melted**

In a bowl, combine the squash, soup, sour cream, onion, carrot, salt and pepper. Sprinkle 1 cup stuffing into a greased 1-1/2-qt. baking dish. Top with squash mixture and remaining stuffing; drizzle with butter. Bake, uncovered, at 350° for 35 minutes or until lightly browned. **Yield:** 6-8 servings.

Mushroom Corn Casserole

(Pictured below)

I decided to create a casserole that combined corn, mushrooms and a rich cheesy sauce. I succeeded with this recipe. Corn's sunny color brightens any meal. —Mary Jones, Cumberland, Maine

- **1/3 cup chopped green pepper**
- **1/3 cup finely chopped onion**
- **3 tablespoons butter *or* margarine, *divided***
- **1/4 cup all-purpose flour**
- **1 can (14-3/4 ounces) cream-style corn**
- **1/2 teaspoon salt**
- **1/8 teaspoon pepper**
- **1 package (3 ounces) cream cheese, cubed**
- **1 can (15-1/4 ounces) whole kernel corn, drained**
- **1 can (4 ounces) mushroom stems and pieces, drained**
- **1/2 cup shredded Swiss cheese**
- **1-1/2 cups soft bread crumbs**

In a saucepan, saute green pepper and onion in 1 tablespoon butter until tender. Stir in flour, cream corn, salt and pepper until blended. Add cream cheese; stir until melted. Stir in the whole kernel corn, mushrooms and Swiss cheese. Transfer to a greased 1-1/2-qt. baking dish. Melt remaining butter; toss with bread crumbs. Sprinkle over the corn mixture. Bake, uncovered, at 400° for 20-25 minutes or until heated through. **Yield:** 4-6 servings.

Slow-Cooked Broccoli

(Pictured below)

This casserole is quick to assemble and full of good flavor. Even those who don't usually like broccoli enjoy it served this way. Since it simmers in a slow cooker, it frees up my oven for other things when I'm preparing a big meal. —*Connie Slocum*
St. Simons Island, Georgia

2 packages (10 ounces *each*) frozen chopped broccoli, partially thawed
1 can (10-3/4 ounces) condensed cream of celery soup, undiluted
1-1/2 cups (6 ounces) shredded sharp cheddar cheese, *divided*
1/4 cup chopped onion
1/2 teaspoon Worcestershire sauce
1/4 teaspoon pepper
1 cup crushed butter-flavored crackers (about 25)
2 tablespoons butter *or* margarine

In a large bowl, combine broccoli, soup, 1 cup cheese, onion, Worcestershire sauce and pepper. Pour into a greased slow cooker. Sprinkle crackers on top; dot with butter. Cover and cook on high for 2-1/2 to 3 hours. Sprinkle with remaining cheese. Cook 10 minutes longer or until the cheese is melted. **Yield:** 8-10 servings.

Basil Pasta Shells

Pepper, basil and cherry tomatoes add pizzazz to this cheesy noodle dish. It not only tastes good, it's good for you! —*Marcia Hostetter, Canton, New York*

✓ Uses less fat, sugar or salt. Includes Nutritional Analysis and Diabetic Exchanges.

2-1/2 cups uncooked medium shell pasta
8 green onions, thinly sliced
2 teaspoons olive *or* vegetable oil
1 pint cherry tomatoes, halved
1/4 pound Canadian bacon, diced
1/4 cup minced fresh basil *or* 1-1/2 teaspoons dried basil
1/2 teaspoon coarsely ground pepper
3/4 cup shredded reduced-fat mozzarella cheese, *divided*

Cook pasta according to package directions. Meanwhile, in a large skillet, saute onions in oil until tender. Stir in tomatoes, bacon, basil and pepper; cook and stir until tomatoes are softened. Rinse and drain pasta; stir into tomato mixture. Add half of the cheese. Transfer to a 1-1/2-qt. baking dish coated with nonstick cooking spray. Sprinkle with the remaining cheese. Bake, uncovered, at 375° for 8-10 minutes or until cheese is melted. **Yield:** 4 servings. **Nutritional Analysis:** One 1-cup serving equals 360 calories, 523 mg sodium, 26 mg cholesterol, 49 gm carbohydrate, 20 gm protein, 9 gm fat. **Diabetic Exchanges:** 3 starch, 2 meat.

Wild Rice Medley

For an autumn feel at any meal, serve this distinctive side dish starring wild rice. Green pepper, mushrooms, tomatoes and cheese are flavorful additions.
—*Antonia Seguin, Westlock, Alberta*

✓ Uses less fat, sugar or salt. Includes Nutritional Analysis and Diabetic Exchanges.

1-3/4 cups low-sodium chicken broth
1 teaspoon dill weed
1/2 teaspoon dried basil
1/8 teaspoon pepper
Pinch dried thyme
3/4 cup uncooked wild rice
1 cup chopped green pepper

1 small onion, chopped
1 garlic clove, minced
1 tablespoon olive *or* vegetable oil
6 fresh mushrooms, sliced
1 large tomato, diced
1/4 cup reduced-fat shredded mozzarella cheese

In a saucepan, combine broth and seasonings; bring to a boil. Add rice; cover and simmer for 55-60 minutes or until the liquid is absorbed. In a skillet, saute green pepper, onion and garlic in oil. Add mushrooms; saute until tender. Stir in rice and tomato. Transfer to a greased 1-1/2-qt. baking dish. Cover and bake at 350° for 25 minutes. Sprinkle with cheese. Bake, uncovered, 5 minutes longer or until cheese is melted. **Yield:** 8 servings. **Nutritional Analysis:** One 1/2-cup serving equals 110 calories, 48 mg sodium, 3 mg cholesterol, 17 gm carbohydrate, 5 gm protein, 3 gm fat. **Diabetic Exchanges:** 1 starch, 1 fat.

Sage Dressing Patties

These pretty little patties are loaded with flavor and hold their shape well. Celery, onion, bread crumbs and seasonings cook up tender. —*Anna Jean Allen West Liberty, Kentucky*

1 medium onion, chopped
3/4 cup chopped celery with leaves
3 tablespoons butter *or* margarine, *divided*
6 slices day-old bread, toasted and crumbled (about 3 cups)
3/4 to 1 cup chicken *or* turkey broth
2 tablespoons minced fresh sage *or* 2 teaspoons rubbed sage
2 teaspoons minced fresh parsley
2 teaspoons minced chives
1/2 teaspoon dried basil

In a skillet, saute the onion and celery in 1 tablespoon butter until tender. Add bread, broth and seasonings; mix well. Shape into six patties. In another skillet, melt remaining butter over medium heat. Cook patties on both sides until lightly browned. **Yield:** 6 servings.

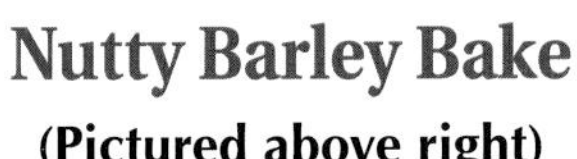

Nutty Barley Bake

(Pictured above right)

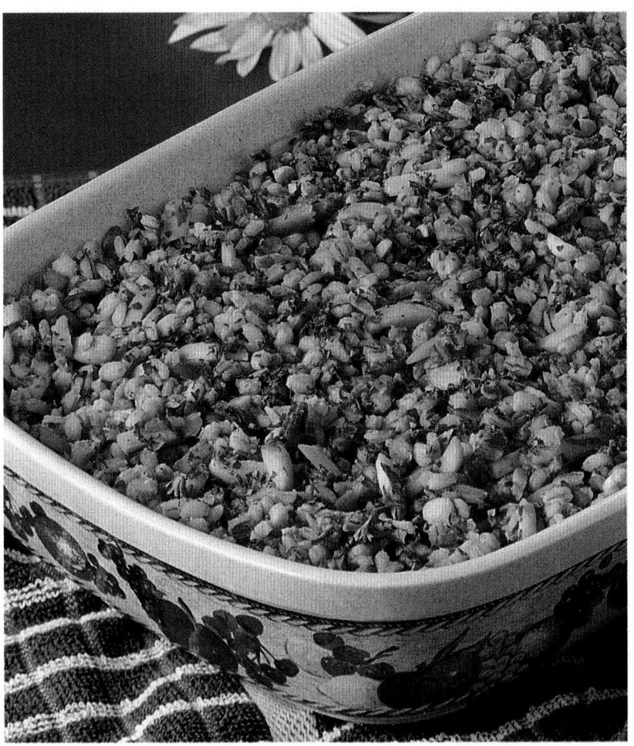

When I started bringing this hearty, distinctive dish to geranium club holiday dinners, a lot of people had never seen barley in anything but soup. They've since dubbed me "the barley lady", and now I wouldn't dare bring anything but this harvest side dish. Even if I double the recipe, I come home with an empty pan.
—*Renate Crump, Los Angeles, California*

1 medium onion, chopped
1 cup medium pearl barley
1/2 cup slivered almonds *or* pine nuts
1/4 cup butter *or* margarine
1/2 cup minced fresh parsley
1/4 cup thinly sliced green onions
1/4 teaspoon salt
1/8 teaspoon pepper
2 cans (14-1/2 ounces *each*) beef broth
Additional parsley, optional

In a skillet over medium heat, saute onion, barley and nuts in butter until barley is lightly browned. Stir in parsley, green onions, salt and pepper. Transfer to a greased 2-qt. baking dish. Stir in broth. Bake, uncovered, at 350° for 1 hour and 15 minutes or until the barley is tender and the liquid is absorbed. Sprinkle with parsley if desired. **Yield:** 6 servings.

Green Onion Tips

When purchasing green onions, choose those with healthy-looking green tops and clean white ends. Store wrapped in the refrigerator for up to 5 days. One green onion equals 2 tablespoons sliced.

Main Dishes

From morning 'til night, these down-home oven entrees, skillet suppers, grilled favorites and microwave specialties will surely satisfy every hearty appetite.

THE MAIN EVENTS. Clockwise from upper left: Microwave Tuna Casserole (p. 96), Classic Cabbage Rolls (p. 81), Two-Meat Pizza with Wheat Crust (p. 84) and Barbecued Sage Spareribs (p. 94).

Steak Diane

(Pictured above)

When I want to provide a memorable dinner but don't want to spend hours in the kitchen, this is the recipe I rely on. I've used it many times on holidays or other occasions for a quick, impressive main dish. We relish the savory sauce poured over the steaks.
—Phoebe Carre, Mullica Hill, New Jersey

- **4 beef rib eye steaks (1/2 inch thick)**
- **1/4 teaspoon pepper**
- **1/8 teaspoon salt**
- **4 tablespoons butter *or* margarine, *divided***
- **2 tablespoons finely chopped green onions**
- **1/2 teaspoon ground mustard**
- **1 tablespoon lemon juice**
- **1-1/2 teaspoons Worcestershire sauce**
- **1 tablespoon minced fresh parsley**
- **1 tablespoon minced fresh chives**

Sprinkle steaks with pepper and salt. In a skillet, melt 2 tablespoons butter. Stir in onions and mustard; cook for 1 minute. Add steaks; cook for 2 minutes on each side or until the meat reaches desired doneness. Remove to a serving platter and keep warm. Add lemon juice, Worcestershire sauce and remaining butter to skillet; cook for 2 minutes. Add parsley and chives. Pour over steaks. **Yield:** 4 servings.

Italian Turkey Breast

My husband, Hal, and I enjoy this Italian-style turkey dish as a delightful change of pace. The dressed-up turkey slices are never dry, and they cook in minutes.
—Helen Vail, Glenside, Pennsylvania

✓ Uses less fat, sugar or salt. Includes Nutritional Analysis and Diabetic Exchanges.

- **1 tablespoon all-purpose flour**
- **1/8 teaspoon pepper**
- **2 turkey breast slices (3 ounces *each*)**
- **2 teaspoons olive *or* vegetable oil**
- **1 teaspoon margarine**
- **1 can (8 ounces) no-salt-added tomato sauce**
- **1 teaspoon *each* dried oregano, basil and thyme**
- **2 teaspoons reduced-fat shredded mozzarella cheese**
- **1 teaspoon nonfat Parmesan cheese topping**

In a shallow bowl, combine flour and pepper; dredge the turkey slices. In a skillet over medium heat, brown turkey in oil and margarine. Combine tomato sauce, oregano, basil and thyme; pour over turkey. Bring to a boil; reduce heat. Cover and simmer for 3-4 minutes or until meat is no longer pink. Sprinkle with cheeses. **Yield:** 2 servings. **Nutritional Analysis:** One serving equals 220 calories, 103 mg sodium, 63 mg cholesterol, 13 gm carbohydrate, 25 gm protein, 8 gm fat. **Diabetic Exchanges:** 3 lean meat, 2 vegetable.

Ground Turkey Stroganoff

I like to experiment in the kitchen. This stick-to-your-ribs main dish calls for ground turkey instead of the traditional beef. *—Jeff Gill, Valdosta, Georgia*

- **1 pound ground turkey**
- **1 small onion, grated**
- **1 cup sliced mushrooms**
- **2 cans (10-3/4 ounces *each*) condensed cream of mushroom soup, undiluted**
- **1/3 cup buttermilk**
- **1 teaspoon garlic powder**
- **1/2 teaspoon salt**
- **1/4 to 1/2 teaspoon pepper**
- **1 cup (8 ounces) sour cream**

Hot cooked noodles
Minced fresh parsley, optional

In a skillet, cook turkey and onion until meat is no longer pink; drain. Add mushrooms; cook and stir for 1 minute. Stir in soup, buttermilk, garlic powder, salt and pepper. Bring to a boil; reduce heat. Simmer, uncovered, for 5-10 minutes. Stir in sour cream; heat gently but do not boil. Serve over noodles. Garnish with parsley if desired. **Yield:** 4 servings.

Festive Fillets

When the weather's not right for outdoor cooking and you want an outstanding steak, this recipe is the answer. We like the zippy gravy so much we don't wait for inclement evenings to fix this!

—Donna Cline, Pensacola, Florida

✓ Uses less fat, sugar or salt. Includes Nutritional Analysis and Diabetic Exchanges.

1 envelope brown gravy mix
1 jar (4-1/2 ounces) sliced mushrooms, drained
2 teaspoons prepared horseradish
4 beef tenderloin fillets (5 ounces *each*)
1/8 teaspoon pepper

Prepare gravy according to package directions; add mushrooms and horseradish. Set aside and keep warm. In a nonstick skillet, cook fillets over medium-high heat until meat reaches desired doneness (about 10-13 minutes for medium), turning once. Season with pepper. Serve with the gravy. **Yield:** 4 servings. **Nutritional Analysis:** One serving equals 268 calories, 714 mg sodium, 88 mg cholesterol, 7 gm carbohydrate, 33 gm protein, 11 gm fat. **Diabetic Exchanges:** 4 lean meat, 1/2 starch. **Editor's Note:** Fillets can be baked. First brown in a skillet for 1 minute on each side, then transfer to an 8-in. square baking pan. Bake, uncovered, at 350° for 10-20 minutes or until meat reaches desired doneness.

Pleasing Potato Pizza

(Pictured at right)

I first heard of this delicious and distinctive pizza when a friend tried it at a restaurant. It sounded great, so I experimented to come up with my own recipe. The way the slices disappear, there's no doubt about their popularity. Guests are always excited when my potato pizza is on the menu.

—Barbara Zimmer
Wanless, Manitoba

3 large potatoes, peeled and cubed
1 tube (10 ounces) refrigerated pizza crust
1/4 cup milk
1/2 teaspoon salt
1 pound sliced bacon, diced
1 large onion, chopped
1/2 cup chopped sweet red pepper
1-1/2 cups (6 ounces) shredded cheddar cheese
1-1/2 cups (6 ounces) shredded mozzarella cheese
Sour cream, optional

Place potatoes in a saucepan and cover with water. Bring to a boil; cook for 20-25 minutes or until very tender. Meanwhile, unroll the pizza crust onto an ungreased 14-in. pizza pan; flatten dough and build up edges slightly. Prick dough several times with a fork. Bake at 350° for 15 minutes or until lightly browned. Cool on a wire rack. Drain potatoes and transfer to a mixing bowl. Mash with milk and salt until smooth. Spread over crust. In a skillet, partially cook the bacon. Add onion and red pepper; cook until bacon is crisp and vegetables are tender. Drain well; sprinkle over potatoes. Top with cheeses. Bake at 375° for 20 minutes or until cheese is melted. Serve with sour cream if desired. **Yield:** 8 slices.

Better Bread

After boiling potatoes, drain the cooking liquid but don't discard it. Instead, save the potato water in a covered container in the refrigerator. Then use it in place of ordinary water the next time you make homemade bread.

Mashed Potato Beef Casserole

(Pictured below)

This recipe came out of my mother's cookbook. The smudges and splatters show that Mom used it extensively to feed our large family. The tarragon really comes through to make a flavorful dish. Now I prepare it for our four children and six grandchildren.
—Helen McGeorge, Abbotsford, British Columbia

2 bacon strips, diced
1 pound ground beef
1 large onion, finely chopped
1/4 pound fresh mushrooms, sliced
1 large carrot, finely chopped
1 celery rib, finely chopped
3 tablespoons all-purpose flour
1 cup beef broth
1 tablespoon Worcestershire sauce
1 teaspoon dried tarragon
1/4 teaspoon pepper
3 cups hot mashed potatoes
3/4 cup shredded cheddar cheese, *divided*
Paprika

In a skillet, cook bacon until crisp; drain, reserving 1 teaspoon drippings. Set bacon aside. Cook beef in drippings over medium heat until no longer pink; drain. Toss onion, mushrooms, carrot and celery in flour; add to skillet with the broth, Worcestershire sauce, tarragon and pepper. Bring to a boil; reduce heat. Simmer, uncovered, for 15-20 minutes or until the vegetables are tender. Add bacon; transfer to a greased 2-qt. baking dish. Combine potatoes and 1/2 cup of cheese; spread over beef mix-

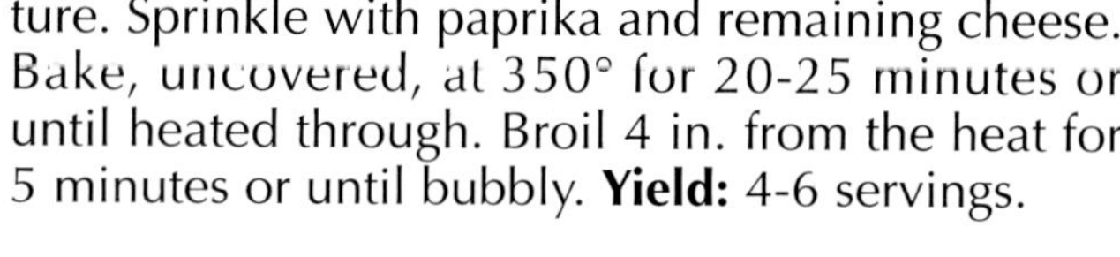
ture. Sprinkle with paprika and remaining cheese. Bake, uncovered, at 350° for 20-25 minutes or until heated through. Broil 4 in. from the heat for 5 minutes or until bubbly. **Yield:** 4-6 servings.

Peanutty Chicken

We use peanuts in a variety of dishes. This tender chicken, covered in a tasty gravy and sprinkled with peanuts, has a zip that perks up taste buds.
—Mary Kay Dixson, Decatur, Alabama

1 teaspoon chili powder
1 teaspoon salt
1/4 teaspoon pepper
1 broiler-fryer chicken (3-1/2 to 4 pounds), cut up
5 tablespoons butter *or* margarine
1 cup orange juice
2/3 to 1 cup salted peanuts
Orange slices and minced fresh cilantro *or* parsley, optional

Combine chili powder, salt and pepper; rub over chicken. In a large skillet, saute chicken in butter until golden brown. Reduce heat; cover and cook until juices run clear, about 30 minutes. Transfer chicken to a serving platter and keep warm. Add orange juice to skillet, stirring to loosen browned bits from pan; simmer for 5 minutes. Pour over chicken. Sprinkle with peanuts. Garnish with orange slices and cilantro if desired. **Yield:** 4 servings.

Company Seafood Pasta

This was my first original recipe. It blends seafood, angel hair pasta, which I love, and an awesome, cheesy white sauce. *—Robert Ulis, Alexandria, Virginia*

2 tablespoons all-purpose flour
2 cups (16 ounces) sour cream
3 cups (12 ounces) shredded Monterey Jack cheese
2 tablespoons butter *or* margarine
1 package (8 ounces) imitation flaked crabmeat
1/8 teaspoon pepper
1 pound fresh *or* frozen bay scallops, thawed, rinsed and drained
1 pound angel hair pasta
1 pound medium shrimp, cooked, peeled and deveined
Minced fresh parsley, optional

In a saucepan, whisk flour and sour cream. Stir in cheese and butter; bring to a boil over medium-low

heat, stirring frequently. Cook and stir for 2 minutes. Remove from the heat. Stir in crab and pepper; set aside and keep warm. Place the scallops in a saucepan with a small amount of water. Cover and cook over medium heat for 5-7 minutes or just until opaque. Meanwhile, cook pasta according to package directions. Drain scallops; add to crab mixture. Stir in shrimp; cook over low heat just until heated through, about 3 minutes. Drain pasta; top with seafood mixture. Garnish with parsley if desired. **Yield:** 6-8 servings.

Sesame Salmon Fillet

A tangy honey-mustard sauce, green onions and sesame seeds dress up broiled salmon for a delightful meal. —Karen Gorman, Gunnison, Colorado

- **1 salmon fillet (1-1/2 to 2 pounds)**
- **2 tablespoons cider vinegar**
- **2 tablespoons soy sauce**
- **1 tablespoon honey**
- **1 teaspoon vegetable oil**
- **1 teaspoon spicy brown *or* horseradish mustard**
- **1/8 to 1/4 teaspoon ground ginger**
- **2 tablespoons sesame seeds, toasted**
- **3 green onions, sliced**

Place salmon in a shallow dish. Combine vinegar, soy sauce, honey, oil, mustard and ginger; pour over salmon. Cover and refrigerate for 1 hour, turning once. Drain and discard marinade. Broil the salmon or grill, covered, over medium-high heat for 15-20 minutes or until the fish flakes easily with a fork. Sprinkle with sesame seeds and onions. **Yield:** 4 servings.

Garlic Beef Enchiladas

(Pictured above right)

I use flour tortillas in this saucy casserole that has irresistible home-cooked flavor and a subtle kick. —Jennifer Standridge, Dallas, Georgia

- **1 pound ground beef**
- **1 medium onion, chopped**
- **2 tablespoons all-purpose flour**
- **1 tablespoon chili powder**
- **1 teaspoon salt**
- **1 teaspoon garlic powder**
- **1/2 teaspoon ground cumin**
- **1/4 teaspoon rubbed sage**
- **1 can (14-1/2 ounces) stewed tomatoes**

SAUCE:

- **4 to 6 garlic cloves, minced**
- **1/3 cup butter *or* margarine**
- **1/2 cup all-purpose flour**
- **1 can (14-1/2 ounces) beef broth**
- **1 can (15 ounces) tomato sauce**
- **1 to 2 tablespoons chili powder**
- **1 to 2 teaspoons ground cumin**
- **1 to 2 teaspoons rubbed sage**
- **1/2 teaspoon salt**
- **10 flour tortillas (7 inches)**
- **2 cups (8 ounces) shredded Co-Jack cheese**

In a saucepan over medium heat, cook beef and onion until meat is no longer pink; drain. Add flour and seasonings; mix well. Stir in tomatoes; bring to a boil. Reduce heat; cover and simmer for 15 minutes. Meanwhile, in another saucepan, saute garlic in butter until tender. Stir in flour until blended. Gradually stir in broth; bring to a boil. Cook and stir for 2 minutes or until bubbly. Stir in tomato sauce and seasonings; heat through. Pour about 1-1/2 cups sauce into an ungreased 13-in. x 9-in. x 2-in. baking dish. Spread about 1/4 cup beef mixture down the center of each tortilla; top with 1-2 tablespoons cheese. Roll up tightly; place seam side down over sauce. Top with the remaining sauce. Cover and bake at 350° for 30-35 minutes. Sprinkle with the remaining cheese. Bake, uncovered, 10-15 minutes longer or until the cheese is melted. **Yield:** 4-6 servings.

Roasted Wild Turkey

(Pictured above)

Since we have avid hunters in our family, I will quite often prepare game. Once it's stuffed with apples and topped with a unique combination of sauces, this wild bird requires no basting and cooks up nice and moist.
—Tammy Rose, Garnavillo, Iowa

- **1 wild turkey (10 to 15 pounds)**
- **2 large apples, quartered**
- **6 to 8 medium red potatoes, quartered**
- **2 pounds baby carrots**
- **2 medium onions, sliced**
- **2 cups water**
- **1-1/2 teaspoons seasoned salt**
- **1 teaspoon salt**
- **1 teaspoon pepper**
- **1/2 cup maple syrup**
- **1/4 cup French salad dressing**
- **1/4 cup barbecue sauce**
- **2 tablespoons ketchup**
- **2 tablespoons steak sauce**
- **1 tablespoon lemon juice**

Place turkey on a rack in a roasting pan; place apples in turkey cavity. Place potatoes, carrots and onions around turkey. Pour water over vegetables. Combine seasoned salt, salt and pepper; rub over turkey. Combine remaining ingredients; brush over the turkey. Cover and bake at 325° for 3-1/2 hours or until a meat thermometer reads 180°; baste if desired. Turkey may be uncovered for the last 30 minutes for additional browning if desired. **Yield:** 10-12 servings.

Michigan Beans 'n' Sausage

A hot bean dish like this warms the body and the house...I'm glad my husband, Jim, is also crazy about beans. We welcome this simmering entree in the cold winter. *—Elaine Schuster, Southfield, Michigan*

- **1 pound dry navy beans**
- **6 bacon strips, diced**
- **3 medium onions, sliced into rings**
- **1 pound chicken gizzards, trimmed and halved, optional**
- **4 cups water**
- **2 garlic cloves, minced**
- **1 teaspoon salt**
- **1/2 teaspoon dried marjoram**
- **1 bay leaf**
- **1/8 teaspoon pepper**
- **1 pound fully cooked kielbasa *or* Polish sausage, halved lengthwise and cut into 1/4-inch slices**
- **1 can (8 ounces) tomato sauce**
- **1 cup soft bread crumbs**
- **2 tablespoons butter *or* margarine, melted**

Place beans in a Dutch oven; add water to cover by 2 in. Bring to a boil; boil for 2 minutes. Remove from the heat; cover and let stand for 1 hour. Drain and discard liquid. Return beans to pan and set aside. In a skillet, cook bacon until crisp. Drain, reserving 2 tablespoons of drippings; set bacon aside. Saute onions and gizzards if desired in the drippings until the onions are tender and the gizzards are browned. Add the 4 cups of water, garlic, salt, marjoram, bay leaf, pepper, bacon and onion mixture to the beans. Cover and bake at 350° for 3 hours or until the beans are tender. Discard bay leaf. Stir in sausage and tomato sauce. Toss bread crumbs and butter; sprinkle over top. Bake, uncovered, 25 minutes longer or until golden. **Yield:** 10-12 servings.

Don't Be Bugged

To keep insects out of dry beans, place the beans and a few dried chili peppers in an airtight container. Store in a cool dry place for up to 1 year.

Tangy Pineapple Chicken

Tender chicken in a tangy sauce, topped with pretty pineapple, makes a mouth-watering main dish. It's nice to offer guests an entree low in fat. —Jean Ecos Waukesha, Wisconsin

✓ Uses less fat, sugar or salt. Includes Nutritional Analysis and Diabetic Exchanges.

4 boneless skinless chicken breast halves (1 pound)
1 teaspoon dried thyme
1/2 teaspoon salt
1/8 teaspoon pepper
1 tablespoon vegetable oil
1 can (20 ounces) unsweetened sliced pineapple
1 tablespoon cornstarch
1/4 cup Dijon mustard
1/4 cup honey
2 garlic cloves, minced
Hot cooked rice

Sprinkle chicken with thyme, salt and pepper. In a skillet, brown chicken in oil. Meanwhile, drain pineapple, reserving the juice. Cut the pineapple rings in half and set aside. Combine cornstarch and 2 tablespoons juice until smooth; set aside. Combine mustard, honey, garlic and remaining pineapple juice; mix well. Add to pan; bring to a boil. Reduce heat; cover and simmer for 15-20 minutes or until chicken juices run clear. Remove chicken and keep warm. Stir cornstarch mixture and add to pan; bring to a boil. Boil and stir for 2 minutes. Return chicken to pan. Top with pineapple; heat through. Serve over rice. **Yield:** 4 servings. **Nutritional Analysis:** One serving (calculated without rice) equals 351 calories, 736 mg sodium, 73 mg cholesterol, 44 gm carbohydrate, 28 gm protein, 8 gm fat. **Diabetic Exchanges:** 4 very lean meat, 3 fruit, 1/2 fat.

Roasted Veggie Pizza

(Pictured at right)

A bold, flavorful garlic and basil pesto sauce is an awesome change of pace from traditional tomato-based pizza sauce. Roasted vegetables are a fantastic topping. Whenever I serve it alongside a standard meat pizza, this one's always the first to go! —Cindy Elsbernd, Des Moines, Iowa

8 to 10 medium fresh mushrooms, sliced
1 small onion, sliced
1/2 cup sliced green pepper
1/2 cup sliced sweet red pepper
2 teaspoons olive *or* vegetable oil
2 garlic cloves, minced
1/4 teaspoon *each* dried rosemary, oregano and thyme
PESTO SAUCE:
1/2 cup coarsely chopped fresh basil
1/4 cup olive *or* vegetable oil
1/4 cup grated Parmesan cheese
4 garlic cloves, minced
1 prebaked Italian bread shell crust (1 pound)
1 large tomato, thinly sliced
2 cups (8 ounces) shredded mozzarella cheese

Place mushrooms, onion and peppers in a roasting pan or baking pan lined with heavy-duty foil. Combine oil, garlic, rosemary, oregano and thyme; drizzle over vegetables and toss to coat. Cover and bake at 400° for 20 minutes. Meanwhile, for sauce, combine basil, oil, Parmesan cheese and garlic in a food processor or blender; cover and process until smooth, scraping sides often. Set aside. Place the crust on an ungreased 12-in. pizza pan. Spread with sauce; top with the tomato slices. Sprinkle with mozzarella cheese. Top with roasted vegetables. Bake for 15 minutes or until cheese is melted and bubbly. **Yield:** 8 slices.

Pizza with Stuffed Crust

(Pictured below)

Cheese baked into the edge of the crust makes this extra-special pizza our favorite. It tastes like a restaurant-style pizza with mild ingredients. I sometimes substitute Canadian bacon for the pepperoni and stuffed olives for the ripe ones. —*Sandy McKenzie, Braham, Minnesota*

- **2 teaspoons cornmeal**
- **2 tubes (10 ounces *each*) refrigerated pizza crust**
- **8 ounces string cheese***
- **1 tablespoon butter *or* margarine, melted**
- **1-1/2 teaspoons minced fresh basil *or* 1/2 teaspoon dried basil**
- **1 can (8 ounces) pizza sauce**
- **1 package (3-1/2 ounces) sliced pepperoni**
- **1 can (4 ounces) mushroom stems and pieces, drained**
- **1 can (2-1/4 ounces) sliced ripe olives, drained**
- **2 cups (8 ounces) shredded mozzarella cheese**

Sprinkle cornmeal evenly over a greased 15-in. x 10-in. x 1-in. baking pan. Unroll pizza dough and place on pan, letting dough drape 1 in. over the edges. Pinch center seam to seal. Place pieces of string cheese around edges of pan. Fold dough over cheese; pinch to seal. Brush the crust with butter; sprinkle with basil. Bake at 425° for 5 minutes. Spread sauce over crust. Place two-thirds of the pepperoni in a single layer over sauce. Sprinkle with mushrooms, olives and cheese. Top with remaining pepperoni. Bake for 10-12 minutes or until crust and cheese are lightly browned. **Yield:** 8-10 slices. ***Editor's Note:** 8 ounces of bulk mozzarella cheese, cut into 4-in. x 1/2-in. sticks, may be substituted for the string cheese.

Mustard Salmon Puff

This easy baked entree is a delicious way to use leftover salmon. It makes a great second-time around dish. —*Perlene Hoekema, Lynden, Washington*

- **2 eggs**
- **2/3 cup milk**
- **1/2 cup sour cream**
- **3/4 cup dry bread crumbs**
- **1 teaspoon seafood seasoning**
- **1/2 teaspoon lemon-pepper seasoning**
- **1/4 teaspoon dill weed**
- **3 cups cooked flaked salmon**
- **3 tablespoons chopped celery**
- **2 tablespoons chopped onion**
- **4-1/2 teaspoons lemon juice**

TOPPING:

- **1-1/3 cups mayonnaise***
- **1 tablespoon prepared mustard**
- **1 egg white**
- **2 tablespoons minced parsley**

In a bowl, stir eggs, milk and sour cream until smooth. Add bread crumbs, seafood seasoning, lemon-pepper and dill. Add salmon, celery, onion and lemon juice; mix well. Transfer to a greased 11-in. x 7-in. x 2-in. baking dish. Bake at 350° for 25-30 minutes or until a knife inserted near the center comes out clean. Meanwhile, combine mayonnaise and mustard in a bowl. In a mixing bowl, beat egg white until stiff peaks form; fold into mayonnaise mixture. Spread over salmon mixture. Bake 10-15 minutes longer or until lightly browned. Sprinkle with parsley. **Yield:** 8 servings. ***Editor's Note:** Light or fat-free mayonnaise may not be substituted for regular mayonnaise.

Purchasing Herbs

When buying fresh herbs, look for leaves that look healthy and have no brown spots. Fresh herbs are very perishable, so only buy them as you need them.

Roasted Tenderloin and Red Potatoes

I love thyme and cracked black peppercorns on beef, so I combined them in this recipe. Some family and friends have commented that this is the best beef they've ever tasted. —*Kathryn Heft*
Bullhead City, Arizona

Uses less fat, sugar or salt. Includes Nutritional Analysis and Diabetic Exchanges.

1 beef tenderloin (2-1/2 pounds), trimmed
2 garlic cloves, thinly sliced
1 tablespoon minced fresh thyme *or* 1 teaspoon dried thyme
1-1/2 teaspoons coarsely ground pepper, *divided*
3 tablespoons olive *or* vegetable oil
7 small red potatoes, cut into chunks
1/2 cup low-sodium beef broth

Cut small slits in the tenderloin; place a garlic slice in each slit. Combine thyme and 1 teaspoon pepper; rub over beef. In a skillet, brown beef in oil. Remove to a roasting pan; cover and keep warm. Toss potatoes with remaining pepper; add to skillet. Cook and stir until lightly browned. Remove to the roasting pan. Gradually add broth to skillet; bring to a boil. Stir to loosen browned bits. Pour over meat and potatoes. Bake, uncovered, at 375° for 25-40 minutes or until meat reaches desired doneness (for rare, a meat thermometer should read 140°; medium, 160°; well-done, 170°). **Yield:** 10 servings. **Nutritional Analysis:** One serving equals 284 calories, 62 mg sodium, 71 mg cholesterol, 16 gm carbohydrate, 25 gm protein, 13 gm fat. **Diabetic Exchanges:** 3 meat, 1 starch.

Classic Cabbage Rolls

(Pictured above right)

I've always enjoyed cabbage rolls but didn't make them since most methods were too complicated. This recipe is fairly simple and results in the best cabbage rolls. My husband, Sid, requests them often. They're terrific to share at gatherings with our children and grandchildren. —*Beverly Zehner*
McMinnville, Oregon

1 medium head cabbage, cored
1-1/2 cups chopped onion, *divided*
1 tablespoon butter *or* margarine
2 cans (14-1/2 ounces *each*) Italian stewed tomatoes
4 garlic cloves, minced
2 tablespoons brown sugar
1-1/2 teaspoons salt, *divided*
1 cup cooked rice
1/4 cup ketchup
2 tablespoons Worcestershire sauce
1/4 teaspoon pepper
1 pound lean ground beef
1/4 pound bulk Italian sausage
1/2 cup V-8 juice, optional

In a Dutch oven, cook cabbage in boiling water for 10 minutes or until outer leaves are tender; drain. Rinse in cold water; drain. Remove eight large outer leaves (refrigerate remaining cabbage for another use); set aside. In a saucepan, saute 1 cup onion in butter until tender. Add tomatoes, garlic, brown sugar and 1/2 teaspoon salt. Simmer for 15 minutes, stirring occasionally. Meanwhile, in a bowl, combine the rice, ketchup, Worcestershire sauce, pepper and remaining onion and salt. Add beef and sausage; mix well. Remove thick vein from cabbage leaves for easier rolling. Place about 1/2 cup meat mixture on each leaf; fold in sides. Starting at an unfolded edge, roll up leaf to completely enclose filling. Place seam side down in a skillet. Top with the sauce. Cover and cook over medium-low heat for 1 hour. Add V-8 juice if desired. Reduce heat to low; cook 20 minutes longer or until rolls are heated through and meat is no longer pink. **Yield:** 4 servings.

Spinach Beef Biscuit Bake

(Pictured above)

My family is from Greece, and I grew up on Greek food. I also like comfort food like casseroles, so I combined the two in this deliciously different main dish. I've served this to both family and friends, and it's a hit with everyone. —Bonnie Bootz, Scottsdale, Arizona

2 tubes (7-1/2 ounces *each*) refrigerated buttermilk biscuits
1-1/2 pounds ground beef
1/2 cup finely chopped onion
2 eggs
1 package (10 ounces) frozen chopped spinach, thawed and squeezed dry
1 can (4 ounces) mushroom stems and pieces, drained
4 ounces crumbled feta *or* shredded Monterey Jack cheese
1/4 cup grated Parmesan cheese
1-1/2 teaspoons garlic powder
Salt and pepper to taste
1 to 2 tablespoons butter *or* margarine, melted

Press and flatten biscuits onto the bottom and up the sides of a greased 11-in. x 7-in. x 2-in. baking dish; set aside. In a skillet over medium heat, cook beef and onion until meat is no longer pink; drain. In a bowl, beat eggs. Add spinach and mushrooms; mix well. Stir in the cheeses, garlic powder, salt, pepper and beef mixture; mix well. Spoon into prepared crust. Drizzle with butter. Bake, uncovered, at 375° for 25-30 minutes or until crust is lightly browned. **Yield:** 6 servings.

Chicken Artichoke Casserole

This creamy chicken dish is so easy to prepare that it's perfect for serving to guests for lunch or supper. —Diane Hixon, Niceville, Florida

1 pound boneless skinless chicken breasts, cut into 2-inch cubes
4 tablespoons butter *or* margarine, *divided*
Salt and pepper to taste
1 package (9 ounces) frozen artichoke hearts, thawed *or* 1 can (14 ounces) water-packed artichoke hearts, drained and halved
1/4 cup all-purpose flour
1/8 teaspoon ground nutmeg
2 cups chicken broth
1 cup (4 ounces) shredded cheddar cheese
1/4 cup dry bread crumbs
1 tablespoon minced fresh savory *or* 1 teaspoon dried savory
1 tablespoon minced fresh thyme *or* 1 teaspoon dried thyme
Hot cooked noodles *or* rice

In a skillet, saute chicken in 1 tablespoon butter until no longer pink. Season with salt and pepper. Place chicken and artichokes in a greased 11-in. x 7-in. x 2-in. baking dish; set aside. In a saucepan, melt remaining butter; stir in the flour and nutmeg until smooth. Gradually add broth. Bring to a boil; cook and stir for 2 minutes or until thickened and bubbly. Stir in cheese until melted; spoon over the chicken. Combine bread crumbs, savory and thyme; sprinkle over chicken. Bake, uncovered, at 350° for 25-35 minutes or until golden brown. Serve over noodles or rice. **Yield:** 4-6 servings.

Mushroom Quiche

Fresh mushrooms and Swiss cheese complement each other in this wonderful dish. Served with fresh fruit, it makes a hearty meal any time of day. —Sheila Hart Evanston, Wyoming

1 unbaked pastry shell (9 inches)
4 cups sliced fresh mushrooms
1 tablespoon butter *or* margarine
1 cup (4 ounces) shredded Swiss cheese

2 tablespoons all-purpose flour
3 eggs, lightly beaten
1-1/4 cups milk
1 tablespoon minced fresh savory *or* 1 teaspoon dried savory
1/2 teaspoon salt
1/4 teaspoon pepper

Line unpricked pastry shell with a double thickness of heavy-duty foil. Bake at 425° for 10 minutes or until edges begin to brown. Remove foil; set the crust aside. In a skillet, saute mushrooms in butter. Remove with a slotted spoon; set aside. In a bowl, toss cheese with flour; add eggs, milk, savory, salt and pepper. Stir in mushrooms. Pour into crust. Bake at 350° for 1 hour or until a knife inserted near the center comes out clean. Let stand for 10 minutes before cutting. **Yield:** 6-8 servings.

Breakfast Quiche

I enjoy preparing hearty country breakfasts for the guests at my bed-and-breakfast. This fluffy golden pie, which has lots of cheese and bacon, is a most satisfying entree.
—Mark Clark
Twin Mountain, New Hampshire

1 unbaked pastry shell (9 inches)
12 bacon strips, cooked and crumbled
1/2 cup shredded pepper Jack *or* Monterey Jack cheese
1/2 cup shredded sharp cheddar cheese
1/3 cup finely chopped onion
4 eggs
2 cups whipping cream
3/4 teaspoon salt
1/4 teaspoon sugar
1/8 teaspoon cayenne pepper

Line unpricked pastry shell with a double thickness of heavy-duty foil. Bake at 450° for 5 minutes; remove foil. Bake 5 minutes longer; remove from the oven and let cool. Reduce heat to 425°. Sprinkle bacon, cheeses and onion over the crust. In a bowl, beat eggs, cream, salt, sugar and cayenne; pour into the crust. Bake for 15 minutes. Reduce heat to 300°; bake 30 minutes longer or until a knife inserted near the center comes out clean. **Yield:** 6-8 servings.

Chicken Fajita Pizza

(Pictured at right)

Our family loves pizza, and this variation is one we enjoy often—the chicken is unexpected but delicious. On hectic days, I can make it in a snap using a prepared crust. Either way, it disappears in a hurry.
—Rosemary Miller, Lagrange, Indiana

 Uses less fat, sugar or salt. Includes Nutritional Analysis and Diabetic Exchanges.

1 package (1/4 ounce) active dry yeast
1 cup warm water (110° to 115°)
2-1/2 cups all-purpose flour
4 tablespoons vegetable oil, *divided*
2 teaspoons salt, *divided*
1 teaspoon sugar
1 pound boneless skinless chicken breasts, cut into strips
2 cups sliced onions
2 cups sliced green peppers
2 teaspoons chili powder
1 teaspoon garlic powder
1 cup salsa
2 cups (8 ounces) shredded Monterey Jack *or* mozzarella cheese

In a bowl, dissolve yeast in water. Add flour, 2 tablespoons oil, 1 teaspoon salt and sugar. Beat vigorously by hand 20 strokes. Cover and let rest about 15 minutes. Divide dough in half; press each portion into a greased 12-in. pizza pan. Prick the dough several times with a fork. Bake at 425° for 6-8 minutes. In a skillet, saute chicken in remaining oil until juices run clear. Add onions, peppers, chili powder, garlic powder and remaining salt; cook until vegetables are tender. Spoon over crusts; top with salsa and cheese. Bake for 14-18 minutes or until crust is golden and cheese is melted. **Yield:** 2 pizzas (8 slices each). **Nutritional Analysis:** One slice (prepared with reduced-fat cheese) equals 193 calories, 544 mg sodium, 23 mg cholesterol, 20 gm carbohydrate, 12 gm protein, 7 gm fat. **Diabetic Exchanges:** 1 starch, 1 meat, 1 vegetable, 1/2 fat.

Scalloped Potatoes with Ham

(Pictured below)

This dish is a crowd-pleaser with its creamy sauce, chunks of ham and potato slices. I always enjoyed it when Mother made it. I added the parsley and thyme, and now my husband and five children request it.
—Wendy Rhoades, Yacolt, Washington

6 tablespoons butter *or* margarine, *divided*
1/4 cup all-purpose flour
1 teaspoon dried parsley flakes
1 teaspoon salt
1/2 teaspoon dried thyme
1/4 teaspoon pepper
3 cups milk
6 cups thinly sliced peeled potatoes
1-1/2 cups chopped fully cooked ham
1 small onion, grated

In a saucepan, melt 4 tablespoons of butter. Stir in flour, parsley, salt, thyme and pepper until smooth. Gradually add milk; bring to a boil. Cook and stir for 2 minutes. Combine potatoes, ham and onion; place half in a greased 2-1/2-qt. baking dish. Top with half of the sauce; repeat layers. Cover and bake at 375° for 65-75 minutes or until potatoes are almost tender. Dot with remaining butter. Bake, uncovered, 15-20 minutes longer or until potatoes are tender. **Yield:** 4 servings.

Two-Meat Pizza with Wheat Crust

(Pictured on page 72)

When our children were younger, I made this tasty, from-scratch pizza for their birthday parties. Everyone loved it so much there was never any left over. It has a thick, chewy crust plus hearty toppings.
—Kathy Mulville, Sterling Heights, Michigan

CRUST:
1 package (1/4 ounce) active dry yeast
1-1/2 cups warm water (110° to 115°)
2 tablespoons vegetable oil
1-1/4 cups whole wheat flour
2 tablespoons sugar
1/2 teaspoon salt
1-3/4 to 2 cups all-purpose flour
TOPPINGS:
1 can (15 ounces) pizza sauce
1 teaspoon sugar
1/2 cup sliced mushrooms
1/4 cup chopped onion
1/4 cup sliced ripe olives
1/2 pound bulk Italian sausage, cooked and drained
4 ounces Canadian bacon, chopped
2 cups (8 ounces) shredded mozzarella cheese

In a bowl, dissolve yeast in water; add oil. Combine whole wheat flour, sugar and salt; add to yeast mixture and stir until smooth. Stir in enough all-purpose flour to form a soft dough. Turn onto a floured surface; knead until smooth and elastic, about 6-8 minutes. Place in a greased bowl, turning once to grease top. Cover and let rise in a warm place for 15-20 minutes. Punch dough down. Pat dough onto the bottom and 1 in. up the sides of a greased 14-in. pizza pan. Combine pizza sauce and sugar; spread over crust. Sprinkle with mushrooms, onion and olives. Layer with sausage, Canadian bacon and cheese. Bake at 350° for 25-30 minutes or until crust is golden and cheese is melted. **Yield:** 8 slices.

Cilantro Chicken

Our family would eat Mexican food every day if we could, and this recipe is a favorite! Chicken breasts stay moist and tender topped with salsa, cilantro and cheese. —Juline Goelzer, Arroyo Grande, California

2 tablespoons lime juice
2 tablespoons vegetable oil
1 teaspoon honey
4 boneless skinless chicken breast halves (1 pound)

1 cup finely crushed tortilla chips
1 jar (16 ounces) salsa
2 tablespoons minced fresh cilantro
1/3 cup shredded Monterey Jack cheese

In a shallow bowl, combine lime juice, oil and honey. Dip chicken in lime juice mixture, then coat with tortilla chips. Place in an ungreased 11-in. x 7-in. x 2-in. baking dish. Bake, uncovered, at 350° for 25 minutes or until the juices run clear. Combine salsa and cilantro; pour over chicken. Sprinkle with cheese. Bake 5-7 minutes longer or until cheese is melted. **Yield:** 4 servings.

South-of-the-Border Meat Loaf

My zesty meat loaf calls for black beans, jalapeno and green peppers and crushed taco shells. It's a savory twist on a longtime favorite. —*Ruth Bogdanski, Grants Pass, Oregon*

1 can (15 ounces) black beans, rinsed and drained
4 taco shells, crushed
1/2 cup chopped onion
1/2 cup chopped green pepper
1/3 cup minced fresh cilantro
2 egg whites
2 tablespoons chopped jalapeno pepper*
2 teaspoons ground cumin
2 teaspoons chili powder
3 garlic cloves, minced
1 teaspoon salt
1/2 teaspoon pepper
2 pounds lean ground beef
Salsa, optional

In a bowl, combine the first 12 ingredients. Add beef and mix well. Press into a 9-in. x 5-in. x 3-in. loaf pan coated with nonstick cooking spray. Bake, uncovered, at 375° for 1 hour or until meat is no longer pink and a meat thermometer reads 160°. Cool for 10 minutes before removing from pan. Drizzle with salsa if desired. **Yield:** 6-8 servings.

***Editor's Note:** When cutting or seeding hot peppers, use rubber or plastic gloves to protect your hands. Avoid touching your face and eyes.

No-Fuss Pork Chops

(Pictured above right)

These tender, mouth-watering chops taste a bit like sweet-and-sour pork but require little attention or time. I prepare them year-round whenever I'm on a tight schedule but still would like something scrumptious. —*Sally Jones, Lancaster, New Hampshire*

4 boneless pork loin chops (3/4 inch thick)
2 tablespoons olive *or* vegetable oil
2 medium onions, chopped
1/2 cup pineapple juice
2 tablespoons brown sugar
2 tablespoons cider vinegar
1/2 teaspoon salt
Hot cooked noodles, optional

In a skillet, cook pork chops in oil until browned on both sides, about 8 minutes. Add the onions; cook until tender. Combine pineapple juice, brown sugar, vinegar and salt; pour over pork chops. Cover and simmer until the meat is tender, about 15 minutes. Serve over noodles if desired. **Yield:** 4 servings.

Cilantro Secret

Cilantro can be stored for several days in the refrigerator by standing the stems in a jar of water and loosely covering the leaves with a plastic bag. Use cilantro sparingly when cooking until you become accustomed to the strength of the flavor.

Saucy Skillet Fish

(Pictured above)

The main industry here on Kodiak Island is fishing, so I'm always on the lookout for new seafood recipes. This is my favorite way to fix halibut since it's quick and tasty. I often get recipe requests when I serve this to guests. —*Merle Powell, Kodiak, Alaska*

- **1/2 cup all-purpose flour**
- **1-1/4 teaspoons salt**
- **1 teaspoon paprika**
- **1/8 teaspoon pepper**
- **2 pounds halibut, haddock *or* salmon fillets *or* steaks**
- **1 medium onion, sliced**
- **1/3 cup butter *or* margarine**
- **1-1/2 cups (12 ounces) sour cream**
- **1 teaspoon dried basil**
- **1 tablespoon minced fresh parsley**

In a large resealable plastic bag, combine the flour, salt, paprika and pepper. Add fish and shake to coat (if using fillets, cut into serving-size pieces first). In a skillet, saute onion in butter until tender; remove and set aside. Add fish to the skillet; cook over medium heat for 3-5 minutes on each side or until the fish flakes easily with a fork. Remove fish to a serving plate and keep warm. Add sour cream, basil and onion to the skillet; heat through (do not boil). Serve over fish. Garnish with parsley. **Yield:** 6-8 servings.

Pepperoni Pan Pizza

I've spent years trying to come up with the perfect pizza crust and sauce, and they're paired up in this recipe. I fix this crispy, savory pizza for my family often...it really satisfies my husband and three sons.
—*Susan Lindahl, Alford, Florida*

- **2-3/4 to 3 cups all-purpose flour**
- **1 package (1/4 ounce) active dry yeast**
- **1/4 teaspoon salt**
- **1 cup warm water (120° to 130°)**
- **1 tablespoon vegetable oil**

SAUCE:

- **1 can (14-1/2 ounces) diced tomatoes, undrained**
- **1 can (6 ounces) tomato paste**
- **1 tablespoon vegetable oil**
- **1 teaspoon salt**
- **1/2 teaspoon *each* dried basil, oregano, marjoram and thyme**
- **1/4 teaspoon garlic powder**
- **1/4 teaspoon pepper**
- **1 package (3-1/2 ounces) sliced pepperoni**
- **5 cups (20 ounces) shredded mozzarella cheese**
- **1/4 cup grated Parmesan cheese**
- **1/4 cup grated Romano cheese**

In a mixing bowl, combine 2 cups flour, yeast and salt. Add water and oil; beat until smooth. Add enough remaining flour to form a soft dough. Turn onto a floured surface; knead until smooth and elastic, about 5-7 minutes. Cover and let stand for 10 minutes. Meanwhile, in a bowl, combine tomatoes, tomato paste, oil and seasonings. Divide dough in half; press each portion into a greased 15-in. x 10-in. x 1-in. baking pan coated with nonstick cooking spray. Prick the dough generously with a fork. Bake at 425° for 12-16 minutes or until crust is lightly browned. Spread sauce over each crust; top with pepperoni and cheeses. Bake 8-10 minutes longer or until cheese is melted. Cut into squares. **Yield:** 2 pizzas (9 slices each).

Western-Style Beef 'n' Beans

This crowd-pleasing dish is a comforting meal on a chilly night with bread and a salad. It doesn't take long to make but tastes like it simmered all day.
—*Jolene Lopez, Wichita, Kansas*

- **3 pounds ground beef**
- **2 medium onions, chopped**
- **2 celery ribs, chopped**
- **2 teaspoons beef bouillon granules**

2/3 cup boiling water
2 cans (28 ounces *each*) baked beans with molasses
1-1/2 cups ketchup
1/4 cup prepared mustard
3 garlic cloves, minced
1-1/2 teaspoons salt
1/2 teaspoon pepper
1/2 pound sliced bacon, cooked and crumbled

In a Dutch oven over medium heat, cook beef, onions and celery until the meat is no longer pink and vegetables are tender; drain. Dissolve bouillon in water; stir into beef mixture. Add the beans, ketchup, mustard, garlic, salt and pepper; mix well. Cover and bake at 375° for 60-70 minutes or until bubbly; stir. Top with bacon. **Yield:** 12 servings.

Citrus Cod

We enjoy fish frequently, and this baked version has a tempting mild orange flavor. —*Jacquelyn Dixon*
La Porte City, Iowa

✓ Uses less fat, sugar or salt. Includes Nutritional Analysis and Diabetic Exchanges.

1 pound frozen cod fillets, thawed
1 tablespoon minced fresh parsley
1/8 teaspoon pepper
1/2 cup chopped onion
1 garlic clove, minced
2 tablespoons butter *or* margarine
1/3 cup orange juice
1 tablespoon lemon juice
1 teaspoon grated orange peel

Cut fillets into serving-size pieces; place in an 11-in. x 7-in. x 2-in. baking dish coated with nonstick cooking spray. Sprinkle with parsley and pepper. In a skillet, saute onion and garlic in butter until tender; sprinkle over fish. Combine juices and orange peel; drizzle over fish. Bake, uncovered, at 375° for 20-25 minutes or until fish flakes easily with a fork. **Yield:** 4 servings. **Nutritional Analysis:** One serving (prepared with margarine) equals 153 calories, 139 mg sodium, 37 mg cholesterol, 5 gm carbohydrate, 19 gm protein, 6 gm fat. **Diabetic Exchanges:** 2 lean meat, 1 vegetable.

Frozen Fish Fact

Store well-wrapped frozen fish in the freezer for up to 6 months.

'I Wish I Had That Recipe...'

"THEY SERVE terrific lamb shanks at Schreiner's Restaurant in Fond du Lac, Wisconsin," reports Dale Grantman of Des Moines, Iowa. "I'd love to have the recipe.

"Our family has enjoyed the food there for over 40 years. Schreiner's is a 'must stop' for good food for folks traveling from Chicago to Green Bay."

Paul and Joan Cunningham, who now own the restaurant founded by the Schreiner family in 1938, were happy to share the recipe.

"It's been on the menu for decades," recalled Paul. "I started working for Bernard Schreiner as a busboy 29 years ago, and baked lamb shanks were a favorite then, too. The recipe was passed down from his mother. We feature comfort foods made from scratch."

An average of 1,800 people a day patronize Schreiner's for the down-home food and friendly service.

Located at 168 Pioneer Rd., just off Highway 41 at Fond du Lac, the restaurant is open daily from 6:30 a.m. to 9 p.m., except for Easter, Thanksgiving and Christmas. 1-920/922-0590.

Schreiner's Baked Lamb Shanks

4 lamb shanks (14 to 16 ounces *each*)
1/2 teaspoon salt
1/8 teaspoon pepper
4 cups beef broth
1/2 cup finely chopped onion
2 teaspoons dried rosemary, crushed
1 teaspoon garlic powder
1 teaspoon ground mustard
Mint jelly, optional

Place the lamb shanks in an ungreased 13-in. x 9-in. x 2-in. baking pan. Sprinkle with salt and pepper. Bake, uncovered, at 400° for 30 minutes. Remove from the oven and reduce heat to 350°. Add broth to the pan. Combine onion, rosemary, garlic powder and mustard; sprinkle over lamb. Cover tightly and bake for 2-1/2 to 3 hours or until very tender. If desired, make gravy from pan drippings. Serve lamb with gravy and mint jelly if desired. **Yield:** 4 servings.

Savory Pot Roast

(Pictured below)

My husband and I used to raise cattle, so I prepared a lot of beef in several different ways. This old-fashioned pot roast is the best—smooth gravy is a tempting topper for the tender, flavorful meat. I like to serve it with crisp potato pancakes. —*Lee Leuschner, Calgary, Alberta*

1 rolled boneless chuck roast* (6 pounds)
2 tablespoons vegetable oil
1 large onion, coarsely chopped
2 medium carrots, coarsely chopped
1 celery rib, coarsely chopped
2 cups water
1 can (14-1/2 ounces) beef broth
2 bay leaves
GRAVY:
1/4 cup butter *or* margarine
1/4 cup all-purpose flour
1 teaspoon lemon juice
4 to 5 drops hot pepper sauce

In a large skillet over medium-high heat, brown roast on all sides in oil. Transfer to a large roasting pan; add onion, carrots and celery. In a saucepan, bring water, broth and bay leaves to a boil. Pour over roast and vegetables. Cover and bake at 350° for 2-1/2 to 3 hours or until meat is tender, turning once. Remove roast to a serving platter and keep warm. For gravy, strain pan juices, reserving 2 cups. Discard vegetables and bay leaves. In a saucepan over medium heat, melt butter. Stir in flour until smooth. Gradually stir in pan juices; bring to a boil. Cook and stir for 2 minutes. Add lemon juice and hot pepper sauce; mix well. Serve with the roast. **Yield:** 14-16 servings. ***Editor's Note:** Ask your butcher to tie two 3-pound chuck roasts together to form a rolled chuck roast.

Meatballs with Cream Sauce

I get raves from my husband and even our three fussy children when I serve these satisfying meatballs with mashed potatoes. The savory cream sauce gives a tasty new twist to meatballs and always makes a memorable meal. —*Michelle Thompson, Smithfield, Utah*

1 egg, lightly beaten
1/4 cup milk
2 tablespoons ketchup
1 teaspoon Worcestershire sauce
3/4 cup quick-cooking oats
1/4 cup finely chopped onion
1/4 cup minced fresh parsley
1 teaspoon salt
1/4 teaspoon pepper
1-1/2 pounds lean ground beef
3 tablespoons all-purpose flour
CREAM SAUCE:
2 tablespoons butter *or* margarine
2 tablespoons all-purpose flour
1/4 teaspoon dried thyme
Salt and pepper to taste
1 can (14-1/2 ounces) chicken broth
2/3 cup whipping cream
2 tablespoons minced fresh parsley

In a bowl, combine the first nine ingredients. Add beef and mix well. Shape into 1-1/2-in. balls. Roll in flour, shaking off excess. Place 1 in. apart on greased 15-in. x 10-in. x 1-in. baking pans. Bake, uncovered, at 400° for 10 minutes. Turn meatballs; bake 12-15 minutes longer or until the meat is no longer pink. Meanwhile, for sauce, melt butter in a saucepan over medium heat. Stir in flour, thyme, salt and pepper until smooth. Gradually add broth and cream; bring to a boil. Cook and stir for 2 minutes or until thickened and bubbly. Drain meatballs on paper towels; transfer to a serving dish. Top with sauce; sprinkle with parsley. **Yield:** 6 servings.

Grilled Pork Roast

We enjoy the mild mustard flavor of this juicy, tender pork roast. With a little advance preparation, this roast is simple since it creates no dirty dishes, and I get the rest of the meal ready while it cooks. —*Myra Innes Auburn, Kansas*

- **2/3 cup vegetable oil**
- **1/3 cup soy sauce**
- **1/4 cup cider *or* red wine vinegar**
- **2 tablespoons lemon juice**
- **2 tablespoons Worcestershire sauce**
- **2 garlic cloves, minced**
- **1 to 2 tablespoons ground mustard**
- **1 to 2 teaspoons pepper**
- **1 teaspoon salt**
- **1 boneless pork loin roast (2-1/2 to 3 pounds)**

In a large resealable plastic bag or shallow glass container, combine the first nine ingredients; add pork and turn to coat. Seal or cover and refrigerate overnight. Drain, discarding the marinade. Grill roast, covered, over indirect heat for 1-1/2 hours or until a meat thermometer reads 160°-170°. Let stand 10 minutes before slicing. **Yield:** 8 servings.

Bacon Cheeseburger Pizza

Kids of all ages love pizza and cheeseburgers...and this recipe combines them both. My grandchildren usually request pizza for supper when they visit me. They like to help me assemble this version, and they especially enjoy eating it! —*Cherie Ackerman Lakeland, Minnesota*

- **1/2 pound ground beef**
- **1 small onion, chopped**
- **1 prebaked Italian bread shell crust (1 pound)**
- **1 can (8 ounces) pizza sauce**
- **6 bacon strips, cooked and crumbled**
- **20 dill pickle coin slices**
- **2 cups (8 ounces) shredded mozzarella cheese**
- **2 cups (8 ounces) shredded cheddar cheese**
- **1 teaspoon pizza *or* Italian seasoning**

In a skillet, cook beef and onion until meat is no longer pink; drain and set aside. Place crust on an ungreased 12-in. pizza pan. Spread with pizza sauce. Top with beef mixture, bacon, pickles and cheeses. Sprinkle with pizza seasoning. Bake at 450° for 8-10 minutes or until cheese is melted. **Yield:** 8 slices.

Li'l Cheddar Meat Loaves

(Pictured above)

I got this recipe from my aunt when I was a teen and have made these lip-smacking miniature loaves many times. My husband and three children count this main dish among their favorites. The recipe is also great for company since it's easily doubled or tripled. —*Katy Bowron, Cocolalla, Idaho*

- **1 egg**
- **3/4 cup milk**
- **1 cup (4 ounces) shredded cheddar cheese**
- **1/2 cup quick-cooking oats**
- **1/2 cup chopped onion**
- **1 teaspoon salt**
- **1 pound lean ground beef**
- **2/3 cup ketchup**
- **1/2 cup packed brown sugar**
- **1-1/2 teaspoons prepared mustard**

In a bowl, beat the egg and milk. Stir in cheese, oats, onion and salt. Add beef and mix well. Shape into eight loaves; place in a greased 13-in. x 9-in. x 2-in. baking dish. Combine ketchup, brown sugar and mustard; spoon over loaves. Bake, uncovered, at 350° for 45 minutes or until the meat is no longer pink and a meat thermometer reads 160°. **Yield:** 8 servings.

Deep-Dish Sausage Pizza

(Pictured above)

My grandma made the tastiest snacks for us when we stayed the night at her farm. Her wonderful pizza, hot from the oven, was covered with cheese and had fragrant herbs in the crust. Now this pizza frequently is a meal for my husband and me and our two young daughters. —*Michele Madden, Washington Court House, Ohio*

1 package (1/4 ounce) active dry yeast
2/3 cup warm water (110° to 115°)
1-3/4 to 2 cups all-purpose flour
1/4 cup vegetable oil
1 teaspoon *each* dried oregano, basil and marjoram
1/2 teaspoon garlic salt
1/2 teaspoon onion salt
TOPPINGS:
4 cups (16 ounces) shredded mozzarella cheese, *divided*
1 large onion, chopped
2 medium green peppers, chopped
1/2 teaspoon *each* dried oregano, basil and marjoram
1 tablespoon olive *or* vegetable oil
1 cup grated Parmesan cheese
1 pound bulk pork sausage, cooked and drained
1 can (28 ounces) diced tomatoes, well drained
2 ounces sliced pepperoni

In a mixing bowl, dissolve yeast in water. Add 1 cup flour, oil and seasonings; beat until smooth. Add enough remaining flour to form a soft dough. Turn onto a floured surface; knead until smooth and elastic, 6-8 minutes. Place in a greased bowl; turn once to grease top. Cover and let rise in a warm place until doubled, about 1 hour. Punch dough down; roll out into a 15-in. circle. Transfer to a well-greased 12-in. heavy ovenproof skillet, letting dough drape over the edges. Sprinkle with 1 cup mozzarella. In another skillet, saute onion, green peppers and seasonings in oil until tender; drain. Layer half of the mixture over crust. Layer with half of the Parmesan, sausage and tomatoes. Sprinkle with 2 cups mozzarella. Repeat layers. Fold crust over to form an edge. Bake for 400° for 20 minutes. Sprinkle with pepperoni and remaining mozzarella. Bake 10-15 minutes longer or until crust is browned. Let stand 10 minutes before slicing. **Yield:** 8 slices.

Cottage Cheese Meat Loaf

Cottage cheese makes this meat loaf wonderfully moist. Folks are delighted when I tell them my "secret ingredient". —*Maggie Slocum, Lindon, Utah*

1 cup small-curd cottage cheese
1 egg, lightly beaten
1/4 cup ketchup
2 tablespoons chopped onion
1 tablespoon prepared mustard
1/2 cup quick-cooking oats
1 teaspoon salt
1/8 teaspoon pepper
1 pound lean ground beef
1/3 cup grated Parmesan cheese

In a bowl, combine the first eight ingredients. Add beef and mix well. Press into an ungreased 8-in. square baking pan. Bake at 350° for 20 minutes. Sprinkle with Parmesan cheese; bake 10-15 minutes longer or until meat is no longer pink. Drain; let stand 10 minutes before cutting. **Yield:** 4 servings.

Firecracker Casserole

I loved this Southwestern-style casserole when my mother made it years ago. Now my husband enjoys it when I prepare it. The flavor reminds us of enchiladas, but this handy recipe doesn't require the extra time to roll them up. —Teressa Eastman, El Dorado, Kansas

2 pounds ground beef
1 medium onion, chopped
1 can (15 ounces) black beans, rinsed and drained
1 to 2 tablespoons chili powder
2 to 3 teaspoons ground cumin
1/2 teaspoon salt
4 flour tortillas (7 inches)
1 can (10-3/4 ounces) condensed cream of mushroom soup, undiluted
1 can (10 ounces) diced tomatoes and green chilies, undrained
1 cup (4 ounces) shredded cheddar cheese

In a skillet, cook the beef and onion until the meat is no longer pink; drain. Add beans, chili powder, cumin and salt. Transfer to a greased 13-in. x 9-in. x 2-in. baking dish. Arrange tortillas over the top. Combine soup and tomatoes; pour over the tortillas. Sprinkle with cheese. Bake, uncovered, at 350° for 25-30 minutes or until heated through. **Yield:** 8 servings.

Blue Plate Beef Patties

A friend and I discovered this recipe together and both consider it a staple menu item. —Phyllis Miller Danville, Indiana

1 egg
2 green onions with tops, sliced
1/4 cup seasoned bread crumbs
1 tablespoon prepared mustard
1-1/2 pounds ground beef
1 jar (12 ounces) beef gravy
1/2 cup water
2 to 3 teaspoons prepared horseradish
1/2 pound fresh mushrooms, sliced

In a bowl, beat the egg; stir in onions, bread crumbs and mustard. Add beef and mix well. Shape into four 1/2-in.-thick patties. In an ungreased skillet, cook patties for 4-5 minutes on each side or until meat is no longer pink; drain. In a small bowl, combine gravy, water and horseradish; add mushrooms. Pour over patties. Cook, uncovered, for 5 minutes or until mushrooms are tender and heated through. **Yield:** 4 servings.

Mushroom Math

One pound of fresh whole mushrooms yields 6 cups raw slices or 2 cups cooked slices.

Rice-Stuffed Squab

(Pictured below)

For company or family, you'll be proud to serve these golden game birds. The rich-tasting dark meat goes well with the savory rice stuffing, which includes onion, celery, fresh mushrooms and raisins. —Peggy Lecza, Branford, Connecticut

1 cup chopped celery
1/2 cup chopped onion
3 tablespoons butter *or* margarine
1-1/2 cups cooked rice
1-1/2 cups chopped fresh mushrooms
1/3 to 1/2 cup raisins
6 tablespoons orange juice concentrate, *divided*
1 tablespoon minced fresh parsley
1-1/2 teaspoons salt, *divided*
3/4 teaspoon dried marjoram
6 dressed squab (about 1 pound *each*)
3/4 cup vegetable oil

In a skillet, saute celery and onion in butter until tender. Add rice, mushrooms, raisins, 3 tablespoons orange juice concentrate, parsley, 3/4 teaspoon salt and marjoram. Sprinkle cavities of squab lightly with remaining salt; stuff with rice mixture. Place on a rack in a roasting pan. Combine the oil and remaining orange juice concentrate; brush over squab. Bake, uncovered, at 375° for 1 hour or until meat juices run clear and a meat thermometer inserted into the stuffing reads 165°, basting frequently. **Yield:** 6 servings.

Please 'Em with Pancakes

HOMEMADE PANCAKES are a traditional treat most folks "flip" over. The delightful varieties here will wake up your taste buds any time of the day.

Rolled Swedish Pancakes

(Pictured below)

We love the hint of lemon wrapped inside these rich pancakes. They taste even more terrific topped with sour cream and cherry preserves. —*Tami Escher Dumont, Minnesota*

1/2 cup plus 1 tablespoon sugar, *divided*
2 tablespoons grated lemon peel
1-1/2 cups all-purpose flour
1/2 teaspoon salt
8 eggs
3 cups milk
3 tablespoons butter *or* margarine, melted
Sour cream and cherry preserves

Combine 1/2 cup sugar and the lemon peel; set aside. In a bowl, combine flour, salt and remaining sugar. Beat eggs, milk and butter; stir into dry ingredients and mix well. Pour batter by 1/2 cupfuls onto a lightly greased hot griddle; cook until set

FLAT-OUT FANTASTIC are these pleasing platefuls of Rolled Swedish Pancakes and Sunrise Orange Pancakes (shown above).

and lightly browned. Turn; cook 1 minute longer. Immediately sprinkle each pancake with lemon sugar mixture; roll up and keep warm. Top with sour cream and preserves. **Yield:** 1 dozen.

Sunrise Orange Pancakes

(Pictured below left)

These delectable citrusy pancakes make any breakfast special. Plus, they're simple to prepare.
—Dorothy Smith, El Dorado, Arkansas

- **7 tablespoons sugar, *divided***
- **1-1/2 teaspoons cornstarch**
- **1-1/2 cups orange juice, *divided***
- **2 cups biscuit/baking mix**
- **2 eggs**
- **3/4 cup milk**

In a saucepan, combine 4 tablespoons sugar, cornstarch and 3/4 cup orange juice; stir until smooth. Bring to a boil; cook and stir for 2 minutes. Remove from the heat; cool to lukewarm. Meanwhile, combine biscuit mix and remaining sugar in a bowl. Beat the eggs, milk and remaining orange juice; stir into dry ingredients just until moistened. Pour the batter by 1/4 cupfuls onto a lightly greased hot griddle; turn when bubbles form on top of pancakes. Cook until second side is golden brown. Serve with the orange sauce. **Yield:** 1 dozen.

Buttermilk Pecan Pancakes

With flecks of pecans in each bite, these light pancakes are an elegant morning entree. *—Jann Braun Chatham, Illinois*

- **3 eggs, *separated***
- **3 tablespoons butter *or* margarine, melted**
- **1-1/2 cups all-purpose flour**
- **1/2 to 1 cup chopped pecans**
- **1 tablespoon sugar**
- **1 teaspoon baking powder**
- **1 teaspoon baking soda**
- **1/2 teaspoon salt**
- **1-2/3 cups buttermilk**

In a bowl, beat the egg yolks and butter. Combine flour, pecans, sugar, baking powder, baking soda and salt; add to the egg mixture alternately with buttermilk. Beat egg whites until stiff peaks form; fold into batter. Pour batter by 1/4 cupfuls onto a lightly greased hot griddle; turn when bubbles form on top of pancakes. Cook until second side is golden brown. **Yield:** 16 pancakes.

Banana Nut Pancakes

I enjoy these versatile pancakes since they're a satisfying breakfast and can even be a deliciously different dessert. *—Diane Hixon, Niceville, Florida*

- **1 package (3 ounces) cream cheese, softened**
- **1/2 cup whipped topping**
- **1 cup pancake mix**
- **1 tablespoon sugar**
- **1 egg**
- **3/4 cup milk**
- **2 teaspoons vegetable oil**
- **1 medium ripe banana, mashed**
- **1/2 cup chopped pecans**

In a small mixing bowl, beat the cream cheese until smooth. Mix in whipped topping (mixture will be stiff); set aside. In a bowl, combine pancake mix and sugar. Beat egg, milk and oil; add to pancake mix and mix well. Fold in banana and pecans. Pour batter by 1/4 cupfuls onto a lightly greased hot griddle; turn when bubbles form on top of pancakes. Cook until second side is golden brown. Serve with cream topping. **Yield:** 8-10 pancakes.

Pancakes with Orange Honey Butter

Whenever I ask my family what they want for breakfast, they invariably ask for these pancakes. My homemade orange honey butter adds a sweet flavor.
—LaDonna Reed, Ponca City, Oklahoma

- **1-3/4 cups all-purpose flour**
- **1 teaspoon baking powder**
- **1 teaspoon baking soda**
- **1/2 teaspoon salt**
- **1-1/2 cups buttermilk**
- **3 eggs, lightly beaten**
- **2 tablespoons vegetable oil**
- **1 tablespoon honey**

ORANGE HONEY BUTTER:

- **1/2 cup butter *or* margarine, softened**
- **1/3 cup honey**
- **2 tablespoons orange juice concentrate**

In a mixing bowl, combine flour, baking powder, baking soda and salt. Combine buttermilk, eggs, oil and honey; add to dry ingredients and mix well. Pour batter by 1/4 cupfuls onto a lightly greased hot griddle; turn when bubbles form on top of pancakes. Cook until second side is golden brown. For orange honey butter, combine butter and honey in a mixing bowl; beat well. Stir in orange juice concentrate until smooth. Serve with pancakes. **Yield:** 12 pancakes.

Grilled Steak Fajitas

(Pictured below)

This tasty main dish is as quick and easy to assemble as tacos. Marinating the meat overnight makes it very tender. We like the hearty and flavorful steak slices. I serve the fajitas with Spanish rice, refried beans and a gelatin dessert. —Pamela Pogue, Quitman, Texas

1 flank steak (1-1/2 pounds)
1 large onion, cut into wedges
1 medium green pepper, julienned
1 can (4 ounces) chopped green chilies
1/2 cup lemon juice
1/2 cup cider *or* red wine vinegar
1/2 cup vegetable oil
4 garlic cloves, minced
1 tablespoon Worcestershire sauce
1 teaspoon dried oregano
1/2 teaspoon salt
1/2 teaspoon pepper
12 flour tortillas (6 inches)
1 medium avocado, peeled and sliced, optional
Sour cream, optional

Place steak in a shallow glass container or large resealable plastic bag. Place onion and green pepper in another container or bag. Combine the chilies, lemon juice, vinegar, oil, garlic, Worcestershire sauce, oregano, salt and pepper. Pour 1-1/2 cups over meat. Pour remaining marinade over vegetables. Cover and refrigerate overnight. Drain meat and vegetables, discarding marinade. Grill steak, covered, over medium-hot heat for 10 minutes on each side or until meat reaches desired doneness (for rare, a meat thermometer should read 140°; medium, 160°; well-done, 170°). Meanwhile, cut two pieces of heavy-duty foil into 18-in. x 12-in. rectangles. Wrap tortillas in one piece and vegetables in the other; seal foil tightly. Grill, covered, over indirect heat for 5-7 minutes, turning occasionally. Cut steak into 1/8-in. slices across the grain; place on tortillas. Top with vegetables and roll up. Serve with avocado and sour cream if desired. **Yield:** 6 servings.

Barbecued Sage Spareribs

(Pictured on page 72)

Folks love to see a huge platter of these tender barbecued ribs arrive at the table. Since the ribs are cooked ahead, they simply need to be browned and reheated on the grill. I love the easy last-minute preparation and magnificent results. Raves begin with the first bite. —Linda Caray, Fruitland, Idaho

6 pounds country-style pork spareribs
1 medium onion, chopped
2 to 3 garlic cloves, minced
2 tablespoons mixed pickling spices
1 tablespoon minced fresh sage *or* 1 teaspoon rubbed sage
1/2 teaspoon hot pepper sauce
1 bottle (18 ounces) barbecue sauce

Place ribs in a Dutch oven and cover with water. Add onion, garlic, pickling spices, sage and hot pepper sauce. Bring to a boil; reduce heat. Cover and simmer for 1-1/2 hours or until tender. Cool slightly; rinse ribs with water to remove spices. Pour barbecue sauce into a large resealable plastic bag or shallow baking dish. Add ribs; cover and refrigerate overnight. Bring to room temperature. Drain, reserving marinade. Grill ribs, uncovered, over medium heat, turning several times until browned and heated through, about 10 minutes. Place marinade in a saucepan; bring to a boil, stirring constantly. Brush over the ribs. **Yield:** 6 servings.

Spicy Skillet Supper

This recipe comes from my cousin. Using brown rice and turkey, she concocted this hearty, flavorful main course. I think it's a winner. —Dorothea Roberts Tulsa, Oklahoma

✓ Uses less fat, sugar or salt. Includes Nutritional Analysis and Diabetic Exchanges.

1 pound ground turkey breast
1 can (15-1/2 ounces) chili beans in chili sauce, undrained
1-1/2 cups cooked brown rice
1 cup salsa
1 tablespoon vinegar
2 to 3 teaspoons chili powder
1 teaspoon sugar
1 teaspoon ground cumin
1/4 teaspoon garlic powder
1/4 teaspoon pepper
1/4 cup shredded light cheddar cheese, optional

In a skillet coated with nonstick cooking spray, brown turkey over medium heat; drain if necessary. Add chili beans, rice, salsa, vinegar and seasonings; mix well. Bring to a boil. Reduce heat; cover and simmer for 20 minutes. Sprinkle with cheese if desired. **Yield:** 5 servings. **Nutritional Analysis:** One 1-cup serving (prepared without cheese) equals 248 calories, 944 mg sodium, 45 mg cholesterol, 32 gm carbohydrate, 28 gm protein, 3 gm fat. **Diabetic Exchanges:** 3 very lean meat, 2 starch.

Creamy Spaghetti Casserole

Cottage cheese is the secret to the sauce for this hearty main dish that my family calls "Norwegian spaghetti".
—Denise Baumert, Dalhart, Texas

1/2 cup sliced green onions
1/2 cup sliced celery
1 can (4 ounces) mushroom stems and pieces, drained
2 tablespoons butter *or* margarine
8 ounces spaghetti, cooked and drained
3 cups cubed fully cooked ham
2 cups (8 ounces) shredded Monterey Jack cheese, *divided*
1 cup (8 ounces) sour cream
1 cup small-curd cottage cheese
1 cup frozen cut green beans, thawed
1 jar (2 ounces) diced pimientos, drained
1/4 teaspoon garlic salt
1/8 teaspoon pepper

In a large saucepan or Dutch oven, saute onions, celery and mushrooms in butter until tender. Add the spaghetti, ham, 1-1/2 cups of Monterey Jack cheese, sour cream, cottage cheese, beans, pimientos, garlic salt and pepper; mix well. Transfer to a greased shallow 2-qt. baking dish. Bake, uncovered, at 350° for 20 minutes; sprinkle with the remaining Monterey Jack cheese. Bake 10 minutes longer or until bubbly and the cheese is melted. **Yield:** 8-10 servings.

Honey-Fried Walleye

(Pictured above)

We fish on most summer weekends, so we have lots of fresh fillets. Everyone who tries this crisp, golden fish loves it.
—Sharon Collis, Colona, Illinois

1 egg
1 teaspoon honey
1 cup coarsely crushed saltines (about 22 crackers)
1/3 cup all-purpose flour
1/4 teaspoon salt
1/4 teaspoon pepper
4 to 6 walleye fillets (about 1-1/2 pounds), skin removed
Vegetable oil
Additional honey
Lemon *or* lime slices, optional

In a shallow bowl, beat egg and honey. In another bowl, combine the cracker crumbs, flour, salt and pepper. Dip fillets into egg mixture, then coat with crumb mixture. In a large skillet, heat 1/4 in. of oil; fry fillets over medium-high heat for 3-4 minutes on each side or until fish flakes easily with a fork. Drizzle with honey; garnish with lemon or lime if desired. **Yield:** 4-6 servings.

Corn Tortilla Pizzas

(Pictured above)

These tasty individual pizzas have the zippy flavor of tacos. When I created this recipe and served these pizzas to my husband and day-care kids, they made them disappear. The recipe produces a big batch of the meat mixture, but leftovers can be frozen for up to 3 months. —Karen Housley-Raatz, Walworth, Wisconsin

- **1-1/4 pounds ground beef**
- **1 small onion, chopped**
- **1/2 cup chopped green pepper**
- **3 cans (6 ounces *each*) tomato paste**
- **1-1/4 cups water**
- **1 cup salsa**
- **2 cups fresh *or* frozen corn**
- **1-1/2 cups chopped fresh tomatoes**
- **3/4 cup chopped ripe olives**
- **1 envelope taco seasoning**
- **3 teaspoons garlic powder**
- **1-1/2 teaspoons dried parsley flakes**
- **1/2 teaspoon dried oregano**
- **1/8 teaspoon salt**
- **1/4 teaspoon pepper**
- **32 corn *or* flour tortillas (6 inches)**
- **8 cups (2 pounds) shredded mozzarella cheese**

In a skillet over medium heat, cook beef, onion and green pepper until meat is no longer pink; drain. In a bowl, combine the tomato paste and water until blended; add salsa. Stir into meat mixture. Stir in the corn, tomatoes, olives and seasonings. Place tortillas on ungreased baking sheets. Spread each with 1/4 cup meat mixture to within 1/2 in. of edge and sprinkle with 1/4 cup of cheese. Bake at 375° for 5-7 minutes or until the cheese is melted. **Yield:** 32 pizzas.

Microwave Tuna Casserole

(Pictured on page 72)

My family digs into this moist, flavorful tuna casserole. Crisp celery along with zucchini and tomato give it a fresh twist. When I get home from work and we have to be somewhere else in a hurry, this is the recipe I use. —Laura Montoya, Williams Lake, British Columbia

- **1/2 cup sour cream**
- **1/2 cup mayonnaise***
- **2 teaspoons prepared mustard**
- **1/2 teaspoon salt**
- **1/2 teaspoon dried thyme**
- **1/4 teaspoon dill weed**
- **5 cups cooked egg noodles**
- **2 cans (6 ounces *each*) tuna, drained and flaked**
- **1/2 cup chopped celery**
- **1/3 cup sliced green onions**
- **1 small zucchini, sliced**
- **1 cup (4 ounces) shredded cheddar cheese**
- **1 medium tomato, chopped**

In a small bowl, combine the first six ingredients; mix well. In a large bowl, combine noodles, tuna, celery and onions. Stir in the sour cream mixture. Spoon half into a greased 2-qt. microwave-safe dish; top with half of the zucchini. Repeat layers. Microwave, uncovered, on high for 6-8 minutes or until heated through. Sprinkle with cheese and tomato. Microwave, uncovered, 2 minutes longer. Let stand for 3 minutes before serving. **Yield:** 6 servings. ***Editor's Note:** Light or fat-free mayonnaise may not be substituted for regular mayonnaise. This recipe was tested in an 850-watt microwave.

Chicken Stroganoff

I came up with this recipe, a variation on beef Stroganoff, as a way to use up roasted chicken. It was a hit. I'm usually the only one in my family who enjoys noodles, but even our young son will have more when they're topped with this creamy chicken. —Laura Schimanski, Coaldale, Alberta

- 4 bacon strips, diced
- 1 pound boneless skinless chicken breasts, cut into 1/4-inch strips
- 1 medium onion, chopped
- 2 jars (4-1/2 ounces *each*) sliced mushrooms, drained
- 1-1/2 cups chicken broth
- 2 garlic cloves, minced
- 1/2 teaspoon salt
- 1/8 teaspoon paprika
- Pepper to taste
- 2 tablespoons all-purpose flour
- 1 cup (8 ounces) sour cream
- Hot cooked noodles
- Additional paprika, optional

In a skillet, cook bacon until crisp. Drain, reserving 2 tablespoons drippings; set bacon aside. In the drippings, cook the chicken, onion and mushrooms until the chicken is no longer pink. Add the broth, garlic, salt, paprika, pepper and bacon. Cover and simmer for 10 minutes. Combine the flour and sour cream until smooth; add to the skillet. Bring to a boil; cook and stir for 2 minutes or until thickened. Serve over noodles. Sprinkle with paprika if desired. **Yield:** 4 servings.

Beef Noodle Bake

Everyone eagerly digs into this dish's delicious layers of ground beef, egg noodles and cheese. Chives offer a subtle sweet onion flavor. —*Pam Laaker Quincy, Illinois*

- 1 pound ground beef
- 1 can (8 ounces) tomato sauce
- 1 teaspoon salt
- 1/2 teaspoon garlic powder
- 1/2 teaspoon onion powder
- 1/4 teaspoon pepper
- 1 cup small-curd cottage cheese
- 1 cup (8 ounces) sour cream
- 1/2 cup minced chives
- 8 ounces medium egg noodles, cooked and drained
- 3/4 cup shredded cheddar cheese

In a skillet over medium heat, cook beef until no longer pink; drain. Add tomato sauce, salt, garlic powder, onion powder and pepper; bring to a boil. Reduce heat; cover and simmer for 5 minutes. Meanwhile, combine the cottage cheese, sour cream and chives; fold in noodles. In a greased 3-qt. baking dish, layer half of the noodle mixture and meat mixture. Repeat layers. Cover and bake at 350° for 35 minutes. Uncover; sprinkle with cheddar cheese. Bake 5 minutes longer or until cheese is melted. **Yield:** 6 servings.

Crustless Cheese Quiche

(Pictured below)

Olives and zesty chilies add dash to the rich flavor of this pie. With no crust, it's easy to prepare.
—*Beverly Gottfried, Candler, North Carolina*

- 2 cups small-curd cottage cheese
- 2 cups (8 ounces) shredded Monterey Jack cheese
- 2 cups (8 ounces) shredded cheddar cheese
- 4 eggs, lightly beaten
- 2 tablespoons butter *or* margarine, melted
- 1 can (4 ounces) chopped green chilies
- 2 tablespoons chopped ripe olives
- 1/2 cup all-purpose flour
- 1 teaspoon baking powder
- 1/2 teaspoon salt
- Chopped tomatoes
- Additional chopped olives

In a bowl, combine the first seven ingredients. Combine flour, baking powder and salt; add to the cheese mixture and mix well. Transfer to a greased 9-in. pie plate. Bake at 400° for 15 minutes. Reduce heat to 350°; bake 30 minutes longer or until a knife inserted near the center comes out clean. Garnish with tomatoes and olives. **Yield:** 6-8 servings.

Egg and Corn Quesadilla

(Pictured below)

For a deliciously different breakfast or brunch, try this excellent quesadilla. It's also great for a light lunch or supper. Corn is a natural in Southwestern cooking and a tasty addition to this zippy egg dish.
—Stacy Joura, Stoneboro, Pennsylvania

1 medium onion, chopped
1 medium green pepper, chopped
1 garlic clove, minced
2 tablespoons olive *or* vegetable oil
3 cups fresh *or* frozen corn
1 teaspoon minced chives
1/2 teaspoon dried cilantro *or* parsley flakes
1/2 teaspoon salt
1/4 teaspoon pepper
4 eggs, beaten
4 flour tortillas (10 inches)
1/2 cup salsa
1 cup (8 ounces) sour cream
1 cup (4 ounces) shredded cheddar cheese
1 cup (4 ounces) shredded mozzarella cheese
Additional salsa and sour cream, optional

In a skillet, saute onion, green pepper and garlic in oil until tender. Add the corn, chives, cilantro, salt and pepper. Cook until heated through, about 3 minutes. Stir in eggs; cook until completely set, stirring occasionally. Remove from the heat. Place one tortilla on a lightly greased baking sheet or pizza pan; top with a third of the corn mixture, salsa and sour cream. Sprinkle with a fourth of the cheeses. Repeat layers twice. Top with the remaining tortilla and cheeses. Bake at 350° for 10 minutes or until the cheese is melted. Cut into wedges. Serve with salsa and sour cream if desired. **Yield:** 6-8 servings.

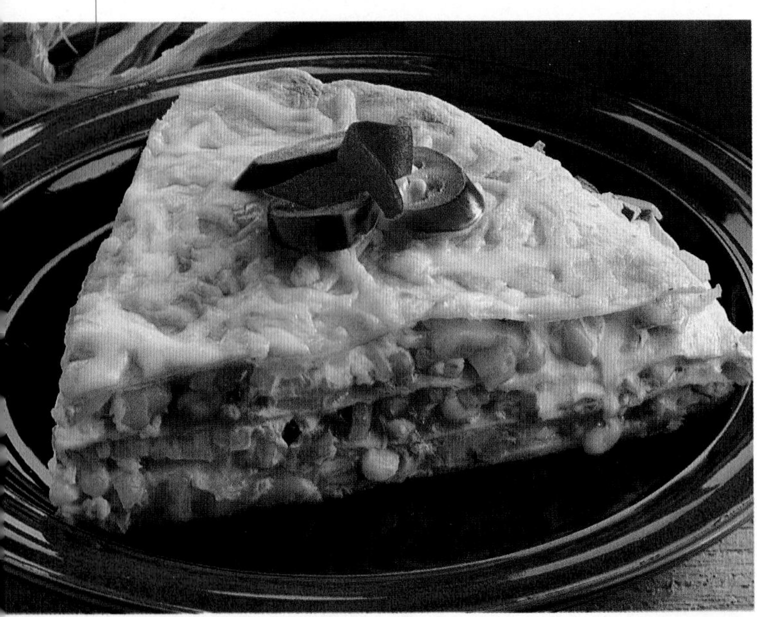

Italian Vegetable Bowl

I love to fix this hamburger vegetable stew on chilly fall and winter days. The tasty variety of ingredients and seasonings ensures this combination is a crowd-pleaser.
—Lynn Sager, North Richland Hills, Texas

✓ Uses less fat, sugar or salt. Includes Nutritional Analysis and Diabetic Exchanges.

1 pound lean ground beef
2 cups water
1 can (16 ounces) kidney beans, rinsed and drained
1 can (15 ounces) tomato sauce
1 can (14-1/2 ounces) Italian stewed tomatoes
1 cup chopped carrots
1 cup chopped celery
1 cup chopped onion
3 beef bouillon cubes
2 garlic cloves, minced
3/4 teaspoon dried oregano
3/4 teaspoon dried basil
1/2 teaspoon pepper
2 cups shredded cabbage
1 cup cooked elbow macaroni
1 tablespoon minced fresh parsley

In a Dutch oven or soup kettle over medium heat, cook beef until no longer pink; drain. Add the next 12 ingredients; bring to a boil. Reduce heat; cover and simmer for 1 hour or until the vegetables are tender. Add cabbage, macaroni and parsley. Cook 20 minutes longer or until cabbage is tender. **Yield:** 10 servings (2-1/2 quarts). **Nutritional Analysis:** One 1-cup serving equals 193 calories, 508 mg sodium, 17 mg cholesterol, 23 gm carbohydrate, 15 gm protein, 5 gm fat. **Diabetic Exchanges:** 1 starch, 1 meat, 1 vegetable.

Scalloped Ham and Cabbage

One of our daughters adores cabbage, so I fix this flavorful dish whenever her family comes to dinner.
—Ruth Peterson, Jenison, Michigan

2 cups cubed fully cooked ham
1/2 cup uncooked long grain rice
1/4 cup chopped onion
1/4 cup butter *or* margarine
1-1/2 cups milk

1 can (10-3/4 ounces) condensed cream of mushroom soup, undiluted
1 teaspoon prepared horseradish
1/2 teaspoon salt
3 to 4 cups chopped cabbage

In a large skillet, saute the ham, rice and onion in butter until rice is golden brown and onion is tender. Stir in the milk, soup, horseradish and salt. Add cabbage; cover and cook over low heat for 35-45 minutes or until the cabbage is tender, stirring occasionally. **Yield:** 4-6 servings.

Herbed Pork Pie

Folks savor this hearty meat pie. The flaky crust is filled with pork, potatoes, celery, onion and a blend of seasonings. —Marcella Moore, Washington, Illinois

Pastry for double-crust pie (9 inches)
1-1/2 pounds ground pork
1 medium onion, chopped
1 cup chopped celery
1 garlic clove, minced
2 medium potatoes, peeled and shredded
1-1/2 cups water
1 tablespoon minced fresh sage *or* 1 teaspoon rubbed sage
1 teaspoon salt
1/4 to 1/2 teaspoon ground cinnamon
1/4 teaspoon dried savory
1/4 teaspoon ground allspice
1 bay leaf
1 tablespoon all-purpose flour
2 tablespoons cold water
GLAZE:
1 egg, lightly beaten
1 teaspoon water

Line a 9-in. pie plate with bottom pastry; trim even with edge. Set aside. In a large skillet, cook the pork, onion, celery and garlic until meat is no longer pink and vegetables are tender; drain. Add potatoes, water and seasonings; bring to a boil. Reduce heat; cover and simmer for 15 minutes. Combine flour and cold water until smooth; stir into pork mixture. Bring to a boil. Reduce heat; cover and simmer for 5 minutes or until slightly thickened. Discard bay leaf. Beat egg and water; brush over bottom pastry. Bake at 400° for 5 minutes. Increase heat to 450°. Pour pork mixture into crust. Roll out remaining pastry to fit top of pie. Place over filling; cut slits in top. Trim, seal and flute edges. Bake for 10 minutes. Reduce heat to 350°; bake 10-15 minutes longer or until golden brown. **Yield:** 6 servings.

Moist Garlic Chicken

(Pictured above)

I created this version of oven-baked chicken by modifying a recipe to match my family's love of garlic with chicken. Just coat the chicken, pop it into the oven and forget it. The crispy coating really stays on. My family always enjoys this flavorful main dish. —Jan Walls, Camden, Delaware

✓ Uses less fat, sugar or salt. Includes Nutritional Analysis and Diabetic Exchanges.

1/3 cup butter *or* margarine, melted
2 garlic cloves, minced
1 teaspoon garlic powder
1/4 to 1/2 teaspoon salt, optional
1/2 cup seasoned bread crumbs
1/4 cup finely shredded cheddar cheese
2 tablespoons grated Parmesan cheese
Dash pepper
6 boneless skinless chicken breast halves (1-1/2 pounds)

In a shallow bowl, combine butter, garlic, garlic powder and salt if desired. In another bowl, combine bread crumbs, cheeses and pepper. Dip chicken in butter mixture, then coat with crumb mixture. Place in a 13-in. x 9-in. x 2-in. baking dish coated with nonstick cooking spray. Cover and bake at 350° for 45-50 minutes or until juices run clear. **Yield:** 6 servings. **Nutritional Analysis:** One serving (prepared with reduced-fat margarine and light cheddar cheese and without salt) equals 259 calories, 483 mg sodium, 78 mg cholesterol, 8 gm carbohydrate, 31 gm protein, 11 gm fat. **Diabetic Exchanges:** 4 lean meat, 1/2 starch.

Chicken Corn Fritters

(Pictured above)

I've always loved corn fritters, but they weren't satisfying as a main dish. I came up with this recipe and was thrilled when my husband and our three young boys gave the chicken and zesty sauce rave reviews.
—Marie Greene, Scottsbluff, Nebraska

1 can (15-1/4 ounces) whole kernel corn, drained
1 cup finely chopped cooked chicken
1 egg, lightly beaten
1/2 cup milk
2 tablespoons butter *or* margarine, melted
1/2 teaspoon salt
1/8 teaspoon pepper
1-3/4 cups all-purpose flour
1 teaspoon baking powder
Oil for deep-fat frying
GREEN CHILI SAUCE:
1/3 cup butter *or* margarine
1/4 cup all-purpose flour
1/4 teaspoon salt
1/8 teaspoon pepper
1/8 teaspoon garlic powder
1/8 teaspoon ground cumin
1 can (4 ounces) chopped green chilies
1 cup milk
Shredded cheddar cheese, optional

Place corn in a bowl; lightly crush with a potato masher. Stir in chicken, egg, milk, butter, salt and pepper. Combine flour and baking powder; stir into the corn mixture just until combined. In a deep-fat fryer or skillet, heat 2 in. of oil to 375°. Drop batter by 1/4 cupfuls into oil. Fry for 3 minutes on each side or until golden brown. Drain on paper towels; keep warm. In a saucepan, melt butter over medium-low heat. Stir in flour and seasonings until smooth. Add chilies. Gradually stir in milk. Bring to a boil; cook and stir for 2 minutes or until thickened. Serve with the corn fritters; sprinkle with cheese if desired. **Yield:** 1 dozen.

Tangy Cranberry Sauce

I use this fruity sauce with grilled and baked meats. For the holidays or anytime, this cranberry condiment brightens a menu with its sweet-tart goodness.
—Marlene Muckenhirn, Delano, Minnesota

1 can (14-1/2 ounces) Italian stewed tomatoes
1/2 cup chopped onion
2 tablespoons brown sugar
1 tablespoon cider vinegar
1 tablespoon molasses
2 garlic cloves, minced
1/2 teaspoon ground cumin
1/2 teaspoon paprika
1/4 teaspoon ground allspice
1 can (16 ounces) whole-berry cranberry sauce

Place the first nine ingredients in a blender; cover and process until almost smooth. Transfer to a saucepan; add cranberry sauce. Bring to a boil; reduce heat. Simmer, uncovered, for 30 minutes or until thickened, stirring occasionally. Serve warm or cold as an accompaniment to poultry or pork. Refrigerate leftovers. **Yield:** 3 cups.

Golden Glazed Fryer

(Pictured on front cover)

This moist grilled chicken has a savory coating that's a nice change of pace from tomato-based sauces. The recipe has been passed down for generations.
—Peggy West, Georgetown, Delaware

1 broiler-fryer chicken (3 to 4 pounds), cut up
1/2 cup vegetable oil
1/2 cup cider vinegar

1 egg, lightly beaten
4 teaspoons salt
1-1/2 teaspoons poultry seasoning
1/4 teaspoon pepper

Grill the chicken, skin side down, uncovered, over medium heat for 15 minutes. Turn; grill 15 minutes longer. Meanwhile, combine the remaining ingredients; brush over chicken. Grill for 5 minutes. Turn and brush with glaze; grill 5 minutes more or until meat juices run clear. Discard any unused glaze. **Yield:** 4-6 servings.

Honey Barbecue Meat Loaf

The addition of honey barbecue sauce creates a sweet, smoky flavor that gives meat loaf a tasty new twist.
—Jeff Gill, Valdosta, Georgia

1 teaspoon beef bouillon granules
1 tablespoon hot water
1 egg
1/2 cup quick-cooking oats
1/3 cup honey barbecue sauce
1/4 cup chopped onion
2 tablespoons brown sugar
1 tablespoon Worcestershire sauce
1 tablespoon prepared mustard
1/2 teaspoon garlic powder
1/4 teaspoon salt
1/4 teaspoon pepper
1/4 teaspoon chili powder
1 pound ground beef
Ketchup

In a large bowl, dissolve bouillon in water. Stir in egg, oats, barbecue sauce, onion, brown sugar, Worcestershire sauce, mustard, garlic powder, salt, pepper and chili powder. Add beef and mix well. Press into an ungreased 8-in. x 4-in. x 2-in. loaf pan. Bake at 350° for 1 hour. Top with ketchup. Bake 5-10 minutes longer or until meat is no longer pink and a meat thermometer reads 160°. Let stand 10 minutes before serving. **Yield:** 4-6 servings.

Chicken with Slippery Dumplings

(Pictured at right)

Thin dumplings are cooked in a mild broth and are served with chicken and gravy at church dinners. This old-fashioned dish reminds many of us of simpler days growing up on the farm. *—Betty Jean Boyd*
Wilmington, Delaware

✓ Uses less fat, sugar or salt. Includes Nutritional Analysis and Diabetic Exchanges.

1 stewing chicken (about 5 pounds), cut up
4 celery ribs, chopped
1 medium onion, chopped
4 medium carrots, coarsely chopped
1 tablespoon chicken bouillon granules
DUMPLINGS:
3 cups all-purpose flour
1 teaspoon salt, optional
1/2 teaspoon baking powder
Minced fresh parsley, optional

Place chicken, celery and onion in a Dutch oven. Cover with water; bring to a boil. Reduce heat; cover and simmer until chicken is tender. Remove chicken and keep warm. Skim fat from the pan juices; add water to measure 3 qts. Set aside 1-1/2 cups for dumplings; cool. Return remaining broth to the Dutch oven; add carrots and bouillon. For dumplings, combine flour, salt if desired and baking powder. Add enough reserved broth to form a stiff dough. Divide dough into thirds; cover and let rest for 10-15 minutes. Meanwhile, bring broth to a simmer. Roll each portion of dough to 1/8-in. thickness; cut into 2-in. squares. Drop one at a time into simmering broth. Cover and cook for 5-7 minutes, stirring occasionally. Serve immediately with the chicken. Sprinkle with parsley if desired. **Yield:** 8 servings. **Nutritional Analysis:** One serving (prepared with low-sodium bouillon and without salt) equals 414 calories, 134 mg sodium, 76 mg cholesterol, 42 gm carbohydrate, 33 gm protein, 11 gm fat. **Diabetic Exchanges:** 3-1/2 lean meat, 2-1/2 starch.

Turkey Stew with Dumplings

(Pictured below)

My husband and I love dumplings, and this mild-tasting, homey dish has flavorful ones floating on a tasty turkey and vegetable stew. It really hits the spot on chilly fall and winter days. —*Rita Taylor*
St. Cloud, Minnesota

8 medium carrots, cut into 1-inch chunks
4 celery ribs, cut into 1-inch chunks
1 cup chopped onion
1/2 cup butter *or* margarine
2 cans (10-1/2 ounces *each*) beef consomme
4-2/3 cups water, *divided*
2 teaspoons salt
1/4 teaspoon pepper
3 cups cubed cooked turkey
2 cups frozen cut green beans
1/2 cup all-purpose flour
2 teaspoons Worcestershire sauce
DUMPLINGS:
1-1/2 cups all-purpose flour
2 teaspoons baking powder
1 teaspoon salt
2 tablespoons minced fresh parsley
1/8 teaspoon poultry seasoning
3/4 cup milk
1 egg

In a Dutch oven or soup kettle, saute carrots, celery and onion in butter for 10 minutes. Add consomme, 4 cups water, salt and pepper. Cover and cook over low heat for 15 minutes or until vegetables are tender. Add turkey and beans; cook for 5 minutes. In a small bowl, combine flour, Worcestershire sauce and remaining water until smooth. Stir into turkey mixture; bring to a boil. Reduce heat; cover and simmer for 5 minutes, stirring occasionally. For dumplings, combine flour, baking powder and salt in a bowl. Stir in parsley and poultry seasoning. Combine milk and egg; stir into flour mixture just until moistened. Drop by tablespoons onto simmering stew. Cover and simmer for 10 minutes; uncover and simmer 10 minutes longer. **Yield:** 10-12 servings.

Chicken 'n' Biscuits

This comforting casserole has a colorful medley of vegetables and chunky chicken topped with golden from-scratch biscuits. We savor this easy version of an old-fashioned favorite. —*Marilyn Minnick*
Hillsboro, Indiana

✓ Uses less fat, sugar or salt. Includes Nutritional Analysis and Diabetic Exchanges.

1 medium onion, chopped
2 teaspoons vegetable oil
1/4 cup all-purpose flour
1/2 teaspoon dried basil
1/2 teaspoon dried thyme
1/4 teaspoon pepper
2-1/2 cups skim milk
1 tablespoon Worcestershire sauce
1 package (16 ounces) frozen mixed vegetables
2 cups cubed cooked chicken
2 tablespoons grated Parmesan cheese
BISCUITS:
1 cup all-purpose flour
1 tablespoon sugar
1-1/2 teaspoons baking powder
1/4 teaspoon salt
1/3 cup skim milk
3 tablespoons vegetable oil
1 tablespoon minced fresh parsley

In a saucepan, saute onion in oil until tender. Stir in flour, basil, thyme and pepper until blended. Gradually stir in milk and Worcestershire sauce until smooth. Bring to a boil; boil and stir for 2 minutes. Stir in the vegetables, chicken and Parmesan cheese; reduce heat to low. Meanwhile, combine flour, sugar, baking powder and salt in a bowl. Combine milk, oil and parsley; stir into dry ingredients just until combined. Transfer hot chicken mixture to a greased 2-1/2-qt. baking dish. Drop biscuit batter by rounded tablespoonfuls onto chicken mixture. Bake, uncovered, at 375° for 30-40 minutes or until biscuits are lightly browned. **Yield:** 8 servings. **Nutritional Analysis:** One serving equals 246 calories, 284 mg sodium, 24 mg cholesterol, 31 gm carbohydrate, 13 gm protein, 8 gm fat. **Diabetic Exchanges:** 2 starch, 1 meat, 1/2 fat.

Cabbage Patch Stew

On a chilly day, a hearty stew like this is a welcome treat when you come home in the evening. It's a wonderful change of pace from regular beef stew.
—Violet Beard, Marshall, Illinois

✓ Uses less fat, sugar or salt. Includes Nutritional Analysis and Diabetic Exchanges.

1-1/2 pounds ground beef
4 celery ribs, chopped
1 medium onion, chopped
7 cups chopped cabbage
2 cans (16 ounces *each*) kidney beans, rinsed and drained
3 cups beef broth
1 can (28 ounces) diced tomatoes, undrained
1 can (15 ounces) tomato sauce
2 medium carrots, chopped
1/2 teaspoon sugar
Pepper to taste

In a large saucepan or Dutch oven, cook beef, celery and onion until meat is no longer pink and vegetables are tender. Add the remaining ingredients; bring to a boil. Reduce heat; cover and simmer for 1 hour or until cabbage and carrots are tender. **Yield:** 14 servings (3-1/2 quarts). **Nutritional Analysis:** One 1-cup serving (prepared with lean ground beef, no-salt-added tomato sauce and low-sodium broth) equals 170 calories, 194 mg sodium, 18 mg cholesterol, 16 gm carbohydrate, 15 gm protein, 5 gm fat. **Diabetic Exchanges:** 1-1/2 meat, 1 starch.

Cabbage Equivalents

One small head of cabbage roughly weighs 1 pound and equals about 6 cups chopped cabbage.

Baked Almond Chicken

(Pictured above)

Tender, golden chicken, a creamy sauce and crisp almond slices make this entree one of my favorites.
—Ken Churches, San Andreas, California

1/2 cup all-purpose flour
1/3 cup plus 1 tablespoon butter *or* margarine, melted, *divided*
1 teaspoon celery salt
1 teaspoon paprika
1/2 teaspoon salt
1/2 teaspoon curry powder
1/2 teaspoon dried oregano
1/4 teaspoon pepper
6 boneless skinless chicken breast halves
1-1/2 cups whipping cream
1/3 cup dry bread crumbs
3/4 cup sliced almonds, toasted
Hot cooked pasta

Place flour in a shallow bowl. Combine 1/3 cup butter and seasonings in another bowl. Coat chicken with flour, then dip in butter mixture. Arrange in a greased shallow 3-qt. baking dish. Pour cream around chicken. Bake, uncovered, at 350° for 45 minutes. Combine bread crumbs and remaining butter; sprinkle over chicken. Top with almonds. Bake, uncovered, for 5-8 minutes or until golden brown. Serve over pasta. **Yield:** 6 servings.

Breads & Muffins

Homemade breads please palates around the clock.

BREAD BASKET. Clockwise from upper left: Frosted Pumpkin Doughnuts, Orange-Glazed Crullers and Applesauce Drop Doughnuts (pp. 116 and 117); Fudgy Banana Muffins (p. 120); Candy Cane Coffee Cakes (p. 109); and Traditional Hot Cross Buns (p. 118).

Italian Cheese Bread

(Pictured above)

People are astounded to learn I make savory Italian bread from scratch in less than an hour. With this recipe from my brother-in-law, warm slices are a delicious and easy alternative to garlic toast. I'll sometimes use this bread as a snack or appetizer.
—Sandra Wingert, Star City, Saskatchewan

2-1/2 cups all-purpose flour
1 teaspoon salt
1 teaspoon sugar
1 tablespoon quick-rise yeast
1 cup warm water (120° to 130°)
1 tablespoon vegetable oil
TOPPING:
1/4 to 1/3 cup prepared Italian salad dressing
1/4 teaspoon salt
1/4 teaspoon garlic powder
1/4 teaspoon dried oregano
1/4 teaspoon dried thyme
Dash pepper
1 tablespoon grated Parmesan cheese
1/2 cup shredded mozzarella cheese

In a bowl, combine the first four ingredients. Combine water and oil; add to flour mixture. Add additional flour if needed to form a soft dough. Turn onto a floured surface; knead for 1-2 minutes or until smooth and elastic. Place in a greased bowl, turning once to grease top. Cover and let rise in a warm place for 20 minutes. Punch the dough down; place on a greased 12-in. pizza pan and pat into a 12-in. circle. Brush with salad dressing. Combine the seasonings; sprinkle over top. Sprinkle with cheeses. Bake at 450° for 15 minutes or until golden brown. Serve warm. **Yield:** 1 loaf.

Aniseed Loaf

A pleasant anise flavor distinguishes this from other quick breads. I've found that the old-fashioned flavor appeals to all. —Henrietta Tenhage, Fergus, Ontario

1 cup sugar
1/2 cup honey
1 tablespoon vegetable oil
2 cups all-purpose flour
1 teaspoon baking soda
1 teaspoon salt
1 cup sour milk*
1 tablespoon aniseed

In a mixing bowl, beat the sugar, honey and oil. Combine flour, baking soda and salt; add to sugar mixture alternately with milk, beating well after each addition. Stir in aniseed. Pour into a greased 9-in. x 5-in. x 3-in. loaf pan. Bake at 350° for 35-45 minutes or until a toothpick comes out clean. Cool for 10 minutes; remove from pan to a wire rack to cool completely. **Yield:** 1 loaf. ***Editor's Note:** To sour milk, place 1 tablespoon white vinegar in a measuring cup. Add milk to measure 1 cup.

Lime Pineapple Jam

This refreshing chunky spread, packed with pineapple, is deliciously different. It's like sunshine in a jar! Use it to top a host of fresh-from-the-oven goodies.
—Rebecca Baird, Salt Lake City, Utah

4 cups finely chopped fresh pineapple
1-3/4 cups sugar
3 tablespoons lime juice
1 teaspoon grated lime peel

In a saucepan, combine all ingredients. Bring to a boil over medium heat, stirring occasionally. Boil until thickened, about 40 minutes. Pour into hot jars, leaving 1/4-in. headspace. Adjust caps. Process for 15 minutes in a boiling-water bath. **Yield:** about 3 half-pints.

Raisin Scones

Several years ago, my parents went to Scotland, where Mom was born. Mom asked Dad to re-create the scones they had on the trip. Mom agrees eating these is like being back in Scotland! —*Kathy Froehlich, Dix Hills, New York*

2 cups all-purpose flour
2 tablespoons sugar
2 teaspoons baking powder
1/2 teaspoon salt
1/2 teaspoon baking soda
1/2 teaspoon ground nutmeg
1/2 cup cold butter *or* margarine
1 cup raisins
3/4 cup buttermilk
1 egg white
Additional sugar

In a bowl, combine dry ingredients. Cut in butter until mixture resembles coarse crumbs. Stir in raisins and buttermilk just until moistened. Turn onto a floured surface; knead gently 6-8 times. Pat into an 8-in. circle and cut into 12 wedges. Place 1 in. apart on a greased baking sheet. Beat egg white until foamy; brush over scones. Sprinkle with sugar. Bake at 425° for 12-15 minutes or until golden brown. **Yield:** 1 dozen.

Red Currant Muffins

Currants hold up so nicely baked into these yummy, golden cake-like muffins. The berries add tartness to the sweet mixture. These are great for breakfast, brunch or a snack. —*Jane Larter, Hallock, Minnesota*

1/2 cup butter *or* margarine, softened
1/2 cup sugar
2 eggs
1 teaspoon grated orange peel
1 cup all-purpose flour
2 teaspoons baking powder
1/4 teaspoon salt
1 cup fresh red currants
Confectioners' sugar

In a mixing bowl, cream the butter and sugar. Add eggs and orange peel; beat well. Combine the flour, baking powder and salt; add to the creamed mixture just until blended. Fold in currants. Fill greased or paper-lined muffin cups two-thirds full. Bake at 375° for 20-25 minutes or until muffins test done. Cool for 5 minutes before removing from pan to a wire rack. Dust with confectioners' sugar. **Yield:** 1 dozen.

Sweet Onion Muffins

(Pictured below)

These savory muffins are wonderful alongside any main dish and also make a great snack warm or cold. It's hard to stop eating them. I've been cooking for 60 years, and this recipe from my niece is one of my favorites. —*Mildred Spinn, Cameron, Texas*

1-1/2 cups all-purpose flour
1/2 cup sugar
1-1/2 teaspoons baking powder
1/2 teaspoon salt
2 eggs
1 cup finely chopped onion
1/2 cup butter *or* margarine, melted
1-1/2 cups chopped walnuts

In a bowl, combine the flour, sugar, baking powder and salt. In another bowl, beat eggs, onion and butter until blended; stir into dry ingredients just until moistened. Fold in walnuts. Fill greased or paper-lined miniature muffin cups three-fourths full. Bake at 400° for 10-12 minutes or until muffins test done. Cool for 5 minutes before removing from pans to wire racks. **Yield:** 3 dozen mini muffins or 1 dozen regular muffins. **Editor's Note:** If using regular-size muffin cups, bake for 20-25 minutes.

Cherry Almond Muffins

(Pictured below)

As a kid, I loved doughnuts filled with custard or jelly. So I decided to experiment with fillings in muffins. The result was this recipe. These are almost like a pastry. —*John Montgomery, Fortuna, California*

1-3/4 cups all-purpose flour
1/2 cup plus 1 tablespoon sugar
1/2 teaspoon baking powder
1/2 teaspoon baking soda
1/4 teaspoon salt
1/2 cup cold butter *or* margarine
1 egg
3/4 cup sour cream
1 teaspoon almond extract

FILLING:
1 package (8 ounces) cream cheese, softened
1 egg
1/4 cup sugar
1/2 teaspoon vanilla extract
3/4 cup cherry preserves

TOPPING:
1/3 cup all-purpose flour
2 tablespoons sugar
2 tablespoons cold butter *or* margarine
1/3 cup chopped sliced almonds

In a bowl, combine flour, sugar, baking powder, baking soda and salt. Cut in butter until mixture resembles coarse crumbs. In another bowl, beat the egg, sour cream and extract until smooth. Stir into dry ingredients just until moistened (batter will be thick). In a mixing bowl, beat cream cheese, egg, sugar and vanilla until smooth. In a saucepan over low heat, warm the preserves. For topping, combine flour and sugar in a small bowl; cut in butter until crumbly. Stir in almonds. Fill greased jumbo muffin cups half full with batter. Divide cream cheese filling and preserves evenly between muffin cups; swirl gently. Cover with remaining batter. Sprinkle with topping. Bake at 350° for 30-35 minutes or until muffins test done. Cool for 5 minutes before removing from pans to wire racks. **Yield:** 7 jumbo muffins or 14 regular muffins. **Editor's Note:** If using regular-size muffin cups, bake for 20-25 minutes.

Herbed Biscuits

These savory biscuits bake up golden and tender. The blend of herb seasonings is irresistible. Keep the convenient seasoning mix on hand for a variety of uses.
—*Jane Everett, Pinehurst, North Carolina*

SEASONING MIX:
2 tablespoons *each* dried oregano, marjoram and basil
4 teaspoons dried savory
2 teaspoons dried rosemary, crushed
2 teaspoons rubbed sage

BISCUITS:
1/4 cup chopped onion
2 tablespoons butter *or* margarine, *divided*
1-1/2 cups all-purpose flour
2 teaspoons baking powder
1/2 teaspoon salt
1/4 cup shortening
1 egg
1/3 cup milk
2 tablespoons grated Parmesan *or* Romano cheese

Combine seasoning mix ingredients. Store in an airtight container in a cool dry place. For biscuits, saute 1 tablespoon mix and onion in 1 tablespoon butter in a skillet until onion is tender; set aside. In a bowl, combine flour, baking powder and salt. Cut in shortening until crumbly. Combine egg, milk and onion mixture; stir into dry ingredients just until moistened. Turn onto a floured surface; knead 10-15 times. Roll to 3/4-in. thickness; cut with a 2-1/2-in. biscuit cutter. Place on an ungreased baking sheet. Melt remaining butter; brush over biscuits. Sprinkle with cheese. Bake at 450° for 10-14 minutes or until golden brown. **Yield:** 6 biscuits (1/2 cup seasoning mix). **Editor's Note:** Seasoning mix is enough for eight batches of biscuits. It may also be used on chicken, pork, beef and steamed vegetables.

Morning Maple Muffins

Maple combines with a subtle touch of cinnamon and nuts to give these muffins the flavor of a hearty pancake breakfast. But you don't have to sit down to enjoy them. Our 2-year-old comes back for seconds...even my husband, who's not a muffin eater, likes these.
—Elizabeth Talbot, Lexington, Kentucky

2 cups all-purpose flour
1/2 cup packed brown sugar
2 teaspoons baking powder
1/2 teaspoon salt
3/4 cup milk
1/2 cup butter *or* margarine, melted
1/2 cup maple syrup
1/4 cup sour cream
1 egg
1/2 teaspoon vanilla extract

TOPPING:

3 tablespoons all-purpose flour
3 tablespoons sugar
2 tablespoons chopped nuts
1/2 teaspoon ground cinnamon
2 tablespoons cold butter *or* margarine

In a large bowl, combine the flour, brown sugar, baking powder and salt. In another bowl, combine the milk, butter, syrup, sour cream, egg and vanilla. Fill greased or paper-lined muffin cups two-thirds full. For topping, combine the flour, sugar, nuts and cinnamon; cut in butter until crumbly. Sprinkle over muffins. Bake at 400° for 16-20 minutes or until muffins test done. Cool for 5 minutes before removing from pans to wire racks. **Yield:** 16 muffins.

Candy Cane Coffee Cakes

(Pictured above right and on page 105)

For many years, I made these moist, jolly loaves as Christmas gifts for the elderly in our church or to share at holiday open houses. The hazelnut filling is a wonderful surprise. This is the kind of old-fashioned bread my mother baked when I was a girl. Now our daughter also makes them.
—Eleanor Gross
Bowdle, South Dakota

1 package (1/4 ounce) active dry yeast
3/4 cup warm water (110° to 115°)
1/2 cup warm milk (110° to 115°)
4 eggs
1 cup sugar
1/2 cup butter *or* margarine, melted
2 teaspoons salt
7 to 7-1/2 cups all-purpose flour

FILLING:

1 cup chopped hazelnuts
1 cup packed brown sugar
1 cup raisins
2 teaspoons ground cinnamon
3 tablespoons butter *or* margarine, melted

GLAZE:

2 cups confectioners' sugar
3 to 4 tablespoons warm milk
1 tablespoon butter *or* margarine, softened
1 teaspoon vanilla extract
1/2 teaspoon lemon extract
1/4 cup chopped hazelnuts

In a mixing bowl, dissolve yeast in water and milk. Add eggs, sugar, butter, salt and 3 cups of flour; beat until smooth. Add enough remaining flour to form a soft dough. Turn onto a floured surface; knead until smooth and elastic, 6-8 minutes. Place in a greased bowl; turn once to grease top. Cover and let rise in a warm place until doubled, about 1-1/2 hours. For filling, combine nuts, brown sugar, raisins and cinnamon; set aside. Punch the dough down and divide into fourths. Roll one portion into a 12-in. x 7-in. rectangle. Brush with some butter; sprinkle with 2/3 cup filling. Roll up, jelly roll-style, starting with a long side; pinch to seal. Place on a greased baking sheet; curve top to form a cane. Repeat with remaining dough, filling and butter. Cover and let rise until doubled, about 35 minutes. Bake at 350° for 25 minutes or until golden brown. Cool on wire racks. Combine the first five glaze ingredients; drizzle stripes over loaves. Sprinkle with nuts. **Yield:** 4 loaves.

Fresh Rolls Rise to the Occasion

THE ENTICING AROMA of rolls warm from the oven is a delightful invitation to good eating.

Honey Nut Sticky Buns

(Pictured below)

These sweet rolls are gooey and delicious around the clock. Enjoy them with coffee or tea for breakfast, a snack or dessert —Bobbie Talbott, Veneta, Oregon

2 packages (1/4 ounce *each*) active dry yeast
1/2 cup warm water (110° to 115°)
2 eggs
1/4 cup sugar

MMM...HOMEMADE ROLLS! Your reputation as a baker will surely rise after you serve delectable Oat Dinner Rolls, Basil Cloverleaf Rolls and Honey Nut Sticky Buns (shown above, top to bottom).

3 tablespoons butter *or* margarine, melted
2 teaspoons salt
1 teaspoon vanilla extract
3-1/4 cups all-purpose flour
TOPPING:
1/2 cup packed brown sugar
1/3 cup honey
1/4 cup butter *or* margarine
1/4 teaspoon salt
1/2 cup chopped pecans
FILLING:
2 tablespoons butter *or* margarine, melted
1/2 cup chopped pecans
1/4 cup packed brown sugar
1 teaspoon ground cinnamon

In a mixing bowl, dissolve yeast in water. Add eggs, sugar, butter, salt and vanilla; mix well. Add 2 cups of flour; beat until smooth. Stir in enough remaining flour to form a soft dough. Turn onto a floured surface; knead until smooth and elastic, about 6-8 minutes. Place in a greased bowl; turn once to grease top. Cover and let rise in a warm place until doubled, about 1-1/2 hours. In a saucepan, combine brown sugar, honey, butter and salt; bring to a boil, stirring occasionally. Boil for 1 minute. Pour into a greased 13-in. x 9-in. x 2-in. baking pan; sprinkle with pecans. Set aside. Punch the dough down. Turn onto a lightly floured surface; roll into a 24-in. x 8-in. rectangle; brush with butter to within 1 in. of edges. Combine pecans, brown sugar and cinnamon; sprinkle over butter. Roll up from a long side; seal seam. Cut into 1-in. slices; place cut side down in pan. Cover and let rise until doubled, about 30 minutes. Bake at 350° for 25-28 minutes or until golden brown. Cool for 1 minute; invert onto a serving platter. **Yield:** 2 dozen.

Oat Dinner Rolls

(Pictured at left)

These soft rolls are out of this world. The addition of oats makes them a little more hearty than other dinner rolls. —Patricia Rutherford, Winchester, Illinois

2-1/3 cups water, *divided*
1 cup quick-cooking oats
2/3 cup packed brown sugar
3 tablespoons butter *or* margarine
1-1/2 teaspoons salt
2 packages (1/4 ounce *each*) active dry yeast
5 to 5-3/4 cups all-purpose flour

In a saucepan, bring 2 cups water to a boil. Stir in oats; reduce heat. Simmer, uncovered, for 1 minute. Stir in brown sugar, butter, salt and remaining water. Transfer to a mixing bowl; let stand until mixture reaches 110°-115°. Stir in yeast. Add 3 cups flour; beat well. Add enough remaining flour to form a soft dough. Turn onto a floured surface; knead until smooth and elastic, about 6-8 minutes. Place in a greased bowl; turn once to grease top. Cover and let rise in a warm place until doubled, about 1 hour. Punch dough down; shape into 24 rolls. Place on greased baking sheets. Cover and let rise until doubled, about 30 minutes. Bake at 350° for 20-25 minutes or until golden brown. Cool on wire racks. **Yield:** 2 dozen.

Basil Cloverleaf Rolls

(Pictured at far left)

This dough will keep for 3 days in the refrigerator, so you can have fragrant, fresh-baked rolls every night. What a treat! —Audrey Thibodeau, Mesa, Arizona

2-1/2 to 3 cups all-purpose flour, *divided*
1 cup whole wheat flour
1/2 cup sugar
1 package (1/4 ounce) active dry yeast
3 to 4 teaspoons dried basil
1 teaspoon celery salt
2 medium potatoes, peeled and cubed
1-1/2 cups water
1/4 cup butter *or* margarine, melted
2 eggs, beaten
GLAZE:
1 egg yolk
1 tablespoon water

In a mixing bowl, combine 2 cups all-purpose flour, whole wheat flour, sugar, yeast, basil and celery salt; set aside. Place potatoes and water in a saucepan; cook until tender. Drain, reserving 1 cup cooking liquid; cool liquid to 120°-130°. Meanwhile, mash or rice potatoes; measure 1 cup (refrigerate remaining potato for another use). Combine potato liquid, butter, eggs and mashed potato; add to dry ingredients. Beat until smooth. Add enough of the remaining flour to form a soft dough. Turn onto a floured surface; knead until smooth and elastic, about 8-10 minutes. Place in a greased bowl; turn once to grease top. Cover and refrigerate overnight or up to 3 days, punching down daily. To bake, punch dough down. Pinch off small portions of dough; roll into 1-in. balls. Place three balls each in greased muffin cups. Cover and let rise until doubled, about 1-1/2 to 2 hours. Beat egg yolk and water; brush over rolls. Bake at 375° for 20 minutes or until golden brown. Cool on wire racks. **Yield:** 2 dozen.

Cappuccino Muffins

(Pictured above)

These are my favorite muffins to serve with a cup of coffee or a tall glass of cold milk. Not only are they great for breakfast, they make a tasty midnight snack or dessert. I get lots of recipe requests when I serve these. —*Janice Bassing, Racine, Wisconsin*

ESPRESSO SPREAD:
4 ounces cream cheese, cubed
1 tablespoon sugar
1/2 teaspoon instant coffee granules
1/2 teaspoon vanilla extract
1/4 cup miniature semisweet chocolate chips
MUFFINS:
2 cups all-purpose flour
3/4 cup sugar
2-1/2 teaspoons baking powder
1 teaspoon ground cinnamon
1/2 teaspoon salt
1 cup milk
2 tablespoons instant coffee granules
1/2 cup butter *or* margarine, melted
1 egg
1 teaspoon vanilla extract
3/4 cup miniature semisweet chocolate chips

In a food processor or blender, combine spread ingredients; cover and process until well blended. Cover and refrigerate until serving. In a bowl, combine flour, sugar, baking powder, cinnamon and salt. In another bowl, stir milk and coffee granules until the coffee is dissolved. Add butter, egg and vanilla; mix well. Stir into dry ingredients just until moistened. Fold in chocolate chips. Fill greased or paper-lined muffin cups two-thirds full. Bake at 375° for 17-20 minutes or until muffins test done. Cool for 5 minutes before removing from pans to wire racks. Serve with espresso spread. **Yield:** about 14 muffins (1 cup spread).

Low-Fat Corn Muffins

These quick-to-make corn muffins call for applesauce in place of oil. All of my friends say they're the best. You can also use the batter to make corn bread.
—*Gary Raymond, Seattle, Washington*

✓ Uses less fat, sugar or salt. Includes Nutritional Analysis and Diabetic Exchanges.

1-1/3 cups all-purpose flour
1-1/3 cups cornmeal
1/3 cup instant nonfat dry milk powder
1/4 cup sugar
4 teaspoons baking powder
1/4 teaspoon salt
1 can (8-1/2 ounces) cream-style corn
3/4 cup water
Egg substitute equivalent to 2 eggs
1/2 cup unsweetened applesauce

In a bowl, combine the first six ingredients. In another bowl, combine corn, water, egg substitute and applesauce; mix well. Stir into dry ingredients just until moistened. Fill muffin cups coated with nonstick cooking spray two-thirds full. Bake at 350° for 17-20 minutes or until muffins test done. Cool for 5 minutes before removing from pans to wire racks. **Yield:** 1-1/2 dozen. **Nutritional Analysis:** One muffin equals 105 calories, 199 mg sodium, trace cholesterol, 22 gm carbohydrate, 3 gm protein, 1 gm fat. **Diabetic Exchange:** 1-1/2 starch. **Editor's Note:** For corn bread, use a 13-in. x 9-in. x 2-in. baking pan coated with nonstick cooking spray; bake for 20-25 minutes.

Zucchini Dinner Rolls

Grated squash gives these golden dinner rolls wonderful moistness. They're scrumptious warm from the oven. —*Robert Keith, Rochester, Minnesota*

1 cup grated peeled zucchini
1 teaspoon salt, *divided*
3-1/2 cups all-purpose flour, *divided*
1 package (1/4 ounce) quick-rise yeast

5 tablespoons grated Parmesan cheese, *divided*
1 teaspoon sugar
1 cup warm water (120° to 130°)
1/4 cup butter *or* margarine, softened

Place zucchini in a bowl; sprinkle with 1/2 teaspoon salt. Let stand for 5 minutes; drain. Meanwhile, in another bowl, combine 3 cups of flour, yeast, 2 tablespoons Parmesan cheese, sugar and remaining salt. Add zucchini; toss to combine. Combine water and butter; add to dry ingredients. Add remaining flour to form a soft dough. Turn onto a floured surface; knead until smooth and elastic, about 6-8 minutes. Place in a greased bowl, turning once to grease top. Cover and let rise in a warm place until doubled, about 1 hour. Divide dough in half; shape each portion into 12 balls. Place in a greased 13-in. x 9-in. x 2-in. baking pan. Sprinkle with remaining cheese. Cover and let rise in a warm place until doubled, about 45 minutes. Bake at 375° for 20-25 minutes or until golden brown. Remove from pan to a wire rack. **Yield:** 2 dozen.

Sticky Cinnamon Rolls

These scrumptious rolls are made with convenient frozen bread dough and can be prepared the night before and baked the next morning. —*Mark Clark*
Twin Mountain, New Hampshire

1-1/4 cups confectioners' sugar
1/2 cup whipping cream
1 cup coarsely chopped pecans
2 loaves (1 pound *each*) frozen white bread dough, thawed
3 tablespoons butter *or* margarine, melted
1/2 cup packed brown sugar
1 teaspoon ground cinnamon
3/4 cup raisins, optional

In a small bowl, combine confectioners' sugar and cream. Divide evenly between two greased 9-in. square baking pans. Sprinkle with pecans; set aside. On a floured surface, roll each loaf of bread dough into a 12-in. x 8-in. rectangle; brush with butter. Combine brown sugar and cinnamon; sprinkle over butter. Top with raisins if desired. Roll up from a long side; pinch seam to seal. Cut each roll into 12 slices; place with cut side down in prepared pans. Cover and refrigerate overnight. Remove from the refrigerator; cover and let rise until doubled, about 2 hours. Cover loosely with foil. Bake at 375° for 10 minutes. Uncover and bake 8-10 minutes longer or until golden brown. **Yield:** 2 dozen.

Burst o' Lemon Muffins

(Pictured below)

While I visited my sister in Florida, she baked a batch of these incredible muffins. They have a cake-like texture, sweet coconut and a mouth-watering lemon zing. I went home with the recipe. —*Nancy Rader*
Westerville, Ohio

1-3/4 cups all-purpose flour
3/4 cup sugar
1 teaspoon baking powder
3/4 teaspoon baking soda
1/4 teaspoon salt
1 cup (8 ounces) lemon *or* vanilla yogurt
1 egg
1/3 cup butter *or* margarine, melted
1 to 2 tablespoons grated lemon peel
1 tablespoon lemon juice
1/2 cup flaked coconut
TOPPING:
1/3 cup lemon juice
1/4 cup sugar
1/4 cup flaked coconut, toasted

In a large bowl, combine the flour, sugar, baking powder, baking soda and salt. In another bowl, beat the yogurt, egg, butter, lemon peel and juice until smooth; stir into dry ingredients just until moistened. Fold in coconut. Fill greased muffin cups two-thirds full. Bake at 400° for 18-22 minutes or until golden brown and muffins test done. Cool for 5 minutes before removing from pan to a wire rack. In a saucepan, combine lemon juice and sugar; cook and stir until sugar is dissolved. Stir in coconut. Using a toothpick, poke 6-8 holes in each muffin. Spoon coconut mixture over muffins. Serve warm or cool to room temperature. **Yield:** 1 dozen.

Cinnamon Rolls in a Snap

(Pictured below)

A friend called one morning to see if I wanted company for coffee. I was going to make biscuits for breakfast but wanted something fancier to share. So I quickly turned those biscuits into hot cinnamon rolls. Was my friend impressed when she arrived to the sweet aroma! —Laura McDermott, Big Lake, Minnesota

4-1/2 cups biscuit/baking mix
1-1/3 cups milk
FILLING:
2 tablespoons butter *or* margarine, softened
1/4 cup sugar
1 teaspoon ground cinnamon
1/3 cup raisins, optional
ICING:
2 cups confectioners' sugar
2 tablespoons milk
2 tablespoons butter *or* margarine, melted
1 teaspoon vanilla extract

In a bowl, combine biscuit mix and milk. Turn onto a floured surface; knead 8-10 times. Roll into a 12-in. x 10-in. rectangle. Spread with butter. Combine sugar, cinnamon and raisins if desired; sprinkle over butter. Roll up from a long side; pinch seam to seal. Cut into 12 slices; place with cut side down on a greased baking sheet. Bake at 450° for 10-12 minutes or until golden brown. Meanwhile, combine the icing ingredients; spread over rolls. Serve warm. **Yield:** 1 dozen.

Sage Tea Bread

I grow my own sage just so I can bake this tasty bread. The incentive of a cup of tea served with a slice of this bread makes my efforts worthwhile. —Roberta Van Anda, Rumson, New Jersey

1/2 cup milk
2 tablespoons minced fresh sage *or* 2 teaspoons rubbed sage
1/2 cup butter *or* margarine, softened
1/2 cup sugar
2 eggs
2 cups all-purpose flour
1 teaspoon baking powder
1 teaspoon salt

In a small saucepan, heat milk and sage just until warm (do not boil); set aside to cool. In a mixing bowl, cream butter and sugar. Add eggs, one at a time, beating well after each. Combine flour, baking powder and salt; add to the creamed mixture alternately with milk mixture. Pour into a greased 9-in. x 5-in. x 3-in. loaf pan. Bake at 350° for 40-50 minutes or until a toothpick inserted near the center comes out clean. Cool for 10 minutes before removing from pan to a wire rack. **Yield:** 1 loaf.

Berry Mini Breads

This buttery, sweet-tart bread and its recipe were dropped at our doorstep one evening during the holidays. It was so tasty and festive that it has become a tradition at our house. Now we also leave the same gift pack on many doorsteps throughout the Christmas season. —Heidi Naylor, Boise, Idaho

1/2 cup butter *or* margarine, softened
1 cup sugar
2 eggs
3 cups all-purpose flour
1 teaspoon baking soda
1 teaspoon baking powder
1 teaspoon salt
1 cup buttermilk
1 cup whole-berry cranberry sauce
1 cup fresh *or* frozen blueberries

In a mixing bowl, cream butter and sugar. Add eggs, one at a time, beating well after each addition. Combine dry ingredients; add to the creamed mixture alternately with buttermilk. Stir in cranberry sauce and blueberries. Pour into four greased 5-3/4-in. x 3-in. x 2-in. loaf pans. Bake at 350° for 25-30 minutes or until a toothpick inserted near the center comes out clean. Cool for 10 minutes before removing from pans to wire racks. **Yield:** 4 loaves.

Spiced Pear Muffins

I got this delightful recipe from the custodian at our church, who fixes these moist fruity muffins and shares them with friends. He gave me one to try a couple years ago, and I was hooked. The combination of pears and spices is irresistible. —*Linda Jachimstal Manitowoc, Wisconsin*

2 cups all-purpose flour
1/2 cup packed brown sugar
2 teaspoons ground ginger
1 teaspoon baking soda
1 teaspoon ground cinnamon
1/2 teaspoon salt
1/8 teaspoon ground nutmeg
1/8 teaspoon ground cloves
1 egg
1 cup (8 ounces) plain yogurt
1/2 cup vegetable oil
3 tablespoons molasses
1-1/2 cups finely chopped peeled pears (about 2 medium)
1/2 cup raisins
1/3 cup chopped walnuts

In a large bowl, combine the first eight ingredients. In another bowl, beat the egg, yogurt, oil and molasses until smooth. Stir into dry ingredients just until moistened. Fold in pears, raisins and walnuts. Fill greased or paper-lined miniature muffin cups two-thirds full. Bake at 400° for 10-12 minutes or until muffins test done. Cool for 5 minutes before removing from pans to wire racks. Serve warm. **Yield:** 2 dozen mini muffins or 16 regular muffins.
Editor's Note: If using regular-size muffin cups, bake for 18-22 minutes.

Chocolate Cookie Muffins

(Pictured above right)

I'm always on the lookout for new ways to make muffins. This fun version includes crushed cream-filled chocolate cookies in the batter. They're a double treat. —*Jan Blue, Cuyahoga Falls, Ohio*

1-3/4 cups all-purpose flour
1/4 cup sugar
3 teaspoons baking powder
1/3 cup cold butter *or* margarine
1 egg
1 cup milk
16 cream-filled chocolate sandwich cookies, coarsely chopped

TOPPING:

3 tablespoons all-purpose flour
3 tablespoons sugar
5 cream-filled chocolate sandwich cookies, finely crushed
2 tablespoons cold butter *or* margarine
1 cup vanilla chips
1 tablespoon shortening

In a large bowl, combine flour, sugar and baking powder. Cut in butter until the mixture resembles coarse crumbs. Beat egg and milk; stir into dry ingredients just until moistened. Fold in chopped cookies. Fill greased muffin cups two-thirds full. For topping, combine flour, sugar and crushed cookies. Cut in butter until crumbly; sprinkle about 1 tablespoon over each muffin. Bake at 400° for 16-18 minutes or until muffins test done. Cool for 5 minutes before removing from pan to a wire rack. In a heavy saucepan over low heat, melt vanilla chips and shortening until smooth. Drizzle over cooled muffins. **Yield:** 1 dozen.

Foolproof Muffins

For best results, use the type of muffin cup directed in each recipe. Either paper liners or greased cups can be used if both are listed as an option. But if a recipe calls for greased muffin cups, do not use paper liners, and vice versa.

Homemade Doughnuts Are Dandy!

DOUGHNUTS sweeten any morning menu and make an irresistible snack. These special from-scratch varieties have been tempting taste buds for generations.

Applesauce Drop Doughnuts

(Pictured below and on page 104)

These tasty cake doughnuts are quick and easy to make since they aren't cut out. —*Frances Poste*
Wall, South Dakota

- **3 tablespoons butter *or* margarine, softened**
- **3/4 cup sugar**
- **3 eggs**
- **1 cup applesauce**
- **1 teaspoon vanilla extract**
- **4-1/2 cups all-purpose flour**
- **3-1/2 teaspoons baking powder**
- **1 teaspoon salt**
- **1/2 to 3/4 teaspoon ground cinnamon**
- **1/4 to 1/2 teaspoon ground nutmeg**
- **1/4 cup milk**
- **Oil for deep-fat frying**
- **Additional sugar**

In a mixing bowl, cream butter and sugar. Add the eggs, one at a time, beating well after each addition. Beat in applesauce and vanilla. Combine dry ingredients; add to creamed mixture alternately with milk (batter will be thick). In an electric skillet or deep-fat fryer, heat oil to 375°. Drop teaspoonfuls of batter a few at a time into hot oil. Turn with a slotted spoon; fry until golden, about 1 minute on each side. Drain on paper towels; roll in sugar while warm. **Yield:** about 5 dozen.

DELECTABLE DOUGHNUTS like Applesauce Drop Doughnuts, Orange-Glazed Crullers and Frosted Pumpkin Doughnuts (shown above, clockwise from upper right) will brighten any breakfast.

Orange-Glazed Crullers

(Pictured below left and on page 104)

The dough is made ahead, so this recipe is great for a gathering. —*Muriel Lerdal, Humboldt, Iowa*

1 package (1/4 ounce) active dry yeast
1/4 cup warm water (110° to 115°)
3/4 cup warm milk (110° to 115°)
1/2 cup butter *or* margarine, softened
1/4 cup sugar
1 teaspoon salt
2 eggs, beaten
4 cups all-purpose flour
Oil for deep-fat frying
GLAZE:
2 cups confectioners' sugar
3 tablespoons orange juice
1 teaspoon grated orange peel

In a mixing bowl, dissolve yeast in water. Add milk, butter, sugar, salt and eggs; mix well. Beat in 2 cups flour until smooth. Add remaining flour. Place in a greased bowl, turning once to grease top. Cover and refrigerate overnight. Punch dough down; divide in half. Return one portion to the refrigerator. On a floured surface, roll out second portion into an 18-in. x 9-in. rectangle; cut widthwise into 3/4-in. strips. Fold each strip in half lengthwise and twist several times. Pinch ends to seal. Place on greased baking sheets. Repeat with the remaining dough. Cover and let rise until almost doubled, about 35-45 minutes. In an electric skillet or deep-fat fryer, heat oil to 375°. Fry crullers, a few at a time, until golden, about 1 minute on each side, turning with a slotted spoon. Drain on paper towels. Combine glaze ingredients; brush over warm crullers. **Yield:** about 3 dozen.

Frosted Pumpkin Doughnuts

(Pictured at left and on page 104)

Our three children grow pumpkins to sell. At harvest, it's time to make these scrumptious doughnuts.
—*Connie Simon, Reed City, Michigan*

2 eggs
1 cup sugar
2 tablespoons butter *or* margarine, softened
1 cup cooked *or* canned pumpkin
1 tablespoon lemon juice
4-1/2 cups all-purpose flour
2 teaspoons baking powder
1 teaspoon baking soda
1/2 teaspoon salt
1/2 teaspoon ground cinnamon
1/2 teaspoon ground nutmeg
1 cup evaporated milk
Oil for deep-fat frying
FROSTING:
3 cups confectioners' sugar
2 to 3 tablespoons orange juice
1 tablespoon evaporated milk
1 teaspoon grated orange peel

In a mixing bowl, beat eggs, sugar and butter. Add pumpkin and lemon juice; mix well. Combine the dry ingredients; add to pumpkin mixture alternately with milk. Cover and refrigerate for 2 hours. Turn onto a lightly floured surface; knead 5-6 times. Roll out to 3/8-in. thickness. Cut with a 2-1/2-in. doughnut cutter. In an electric skillet or deep-fat fryer, heat oil to 375°. Fry doughnuts, a few at a time, until golden, about 3 minutes; turn once with a slotted spoon. Drain on paper towels. Combine frosting ingredients; spread over cooled doughnuts. **Yield:** about 3 dozen.

Baked Cinnamon Doughnuts

Baking these light raised pastries is a delicious alternative to frying. —*Kathi Grenier, Auburn, Maine*

2 packages (1/4 ounce *each*) active dry yeast
1/3 cup warm water (110° to 115°)
1-1/2 cups warm milk (110° to 115°)
1/3 cup shortening
2 eggs
1-1/4 cups sugar, *divided*
2 teaspoons ground nutmeg
1-1/2 teaspoons salt
4-1/2 to 5 cups all-purpose flour
1/3 cup butter *or* margarine, melted
1 teaspoon ground cinnamon

In a mixing bowl, dissolve yeast in water. Add milk and shortening; stir for 1 minute. Add eggs, 1/4 cup sugar, nutmeg, salt and 2 cups flour; beat on low speed until smooth. Stir in enough remaining flour to form a soft dough (do not knead). Cover and let rise in a warm place until doubled, about 1 hour. Punch dough down. Turn onto a floured surface; roll out to 1/2-in. thickness. Cut with a 2-3/4-in. doughnut cutter; place 1 in. apart on greased baking sheets. Cover and let rise in a warm place until doubled, about 30 minutes. Bake at 450° for 7-8 minutes or until lightly browned. Brush with butter. In a shallow bowl, combine cinnamon and remaining sugar; roll warm doughnuts in mixture. Serve immediately. **Yield:** about 2 dozen.

Traditional Hot Cross Buns

(Pictured above and on page 104)

On Easter morning, our family looked forward to a breakfast of dyed hard-boiled eggs and Mom's hot cross buns. It was a tradition for many years. I still serve them as part of special brunches or buffets.
—Barbara Jean Lull, Claremont, California

2 packages (1/4 ounce *each*) active dry yeast
2 cups warm milk (110° to 115°)
1/3 cup butter *or* margarine, softened
2 eggs, lightly beaten
1/4 cup sugar
1-1/2 teaspoons salt
6 to 7 cups all-purpose flour
1/2 cup raisins
1/2 cup dried currants
1 teaspoon ground cinnamon
1/4 teaspoon ground allspice
2 tablespoons water
1 egg yolk
Confectioners' sugar icing

In a mixing bowl, dissolve yeast in milk. Stir in butter, eggs, sugar and salt. Combine 3 cups flour, raisins, currants, cinnamon and allspice; add to the yeast mixture and mix well. Stir in enough remaining flour to form a soft dough. Turn onto a floured surface and knead until smooth and elastic, about 6-8 minutes. Place in a greased bowl, turning once to grease top. Cover and let rise in a warm place until doubled, about 1 hour. Punch dough down; shape into 1-1/2- to 2-in. balls. Place 2 in. apart on greased baking sheets. Using a sharp knife, cut a cross on top of each roll. Cover and let rise until doubled, about 30 minutes. Beat water and egg yolk; brush over rolls. Bake at 375° for 15-20 minutes or until golden brown. Cool on wire racks. Pipe icing over rolls. **Yield:** 2-1/2 dozen.

Cocoa Macaroon Muffins

This recipe is an old-time favorite that I've modified over the years depending on whether I served them for breakfast, a snack or as dessert. I love chocolate in any form, and these muffins pair it with coconut for yummy results. —Carol Wilson, Rio Rancho, New Mexico

2 cups all-purpose flour
1/2 cup sugar
3 tablespoons baking cocoa
3 teaspoons baking powder
1 teaspoon salt
1 cup milk
1 egg
1/3 cup vegetable oil
1-1/4 cups flaked coconut, *divided*
1/4 cup sweetened condensed milk
1/4 teaspoon almond extract

In a bowl, combine flour, sugar, cocoa, baking powder and salt. Combine milk, egg and oil; mix well. Stir into dry ingredients just until moistened. Spoon 2 tablespoonfuls into 12 greased or paper-lined muffin cups. Combine 1 cup coconut, condensed milk and extract; place 2 teaspoonfuls in the center of each cup (do not spread). Top with remaining batter; sprinkle with remaining coconut. Bake at 400° for 20-22 minutes or until muffins test done. Cool for 5 minutes before removing from pan to a wire rack. **Yield:** 1 dozen.

Confectioners' Sugar Icing

Here's a standard recipe for confectioners' sugar icing that you can use in a variety of ways: Combine 1 cup confectioners' sugar, 1/2 teaspoon vanilla extract and 1 to 2 tablespoons milk. If the icing is too thick, stir in more milk, 1/2 teaspoon at a time, until the desired consistency is reached.

Cake Doughnuts

I got the recipe for these tasty traditional treats from a camp cook who has prepared them for years, to the delight of campers. —*Dawn Fagerstrom Warren, Minnesota*

2 eggs
2-1/2 cups sugar
1/2 cup sour cream
5 tablespoons butter *or* margarine, melted
1 teaspoon vanilla extract
10 cups all-purpose flour
3 teaspoons baking soda
1 teaspoon salt
1/2 teaspoon ground nutmeg
2-1/2 cups buttermilk
Oil for deep-fat frying
Confectioners' sugar

In a bowl, beat eggs; add sugar, sour cream, butter and vanilla. Combine flour, baking soda, salt and nutmeg; add to sour cream mixture alternately with buttermilk. Turn onto a lightly floured surface; roll to 1/4-in. thickness. Cut with a 2-1/2-in. doughnut cutter. In an electric skillet or deep-fat fryer, heat oil to 375°. Fry doughnuts, a few at a time, until golden, about 2 minutes; turn once with a slotted spoon. Drain on paper towels. Dust with confectioners' sugar. **Yield:** about 6 dozen.

Apple Nut Muffins

(Pictured at right)

The inspiration for these muffins came from a favorite coffee cake. I wanted to put it in a form our four girls could munch while playing. For variety, I sometimes substitute prepared blueberry or lemon pie filling for the delectable from-scratch apple filling. —*Hollie Gregory, Mt. Vision, New York*

2 tablespoons butter *or* margarine
1/3 cup packed brown sugar
1 tablespoon all-purpose flour
1/2 teaspoon ground cinnamon
1/8 to 1/4 teaspoon ground nutmeg
2 cups finely chopped peeled apples
1/2 cup finely chopped nuts
MUFFINS:
3/4 cup butter *or* margarine, softened
1-1/2 cups sugar
3 eggs
1-1/2 teaspoons vanilla extract
3-1/2 cups all-purpose flour
1-1/2 teaspoons baking powder
1-1/2 teaspoons baking soda
3/4 teaspoon salt
1-1/2 cups (12 ounces) sour cream
Cinnamon-sugar

In a saucepan, melt butter. Stir in brown sugar, flour, cinnamon and nutmeg until smooth. Add apples; cook over medium-low heat for 10 minutes or until apples are tender, stirring frequently. Remove from the heat; stir in nuts. Set aside to cool. In a mixing bowl, cream butter and sugar. Add eggs, one at a time, beating well after each addition. Beat in vanilla. Combine the dry ingredients; add to the creamed mixture alternating with sour cream. Spoon 1/4 cupfuls of batter into greased jumbo muffins cups. Spoon apple mixture into the center of each (do not spread). Top with remaining batter. Sprinkle with cinnamon-sugar. Bake at 350° for 25-27 minutes or until muffins test done. Cool for 5 minutes before removing from pans to wire racks. **Yield:** 1 dozen jumbo muffins or 2 dozen regular muffins. **Editor's Note:** If using regular-size muffin cups, fill cups half full with batter; add a rounded teaspoonful of apple mixture and remaining batter. Bake for 16-18 minutes.

Fudgy Banana Muffins

(Pictured below and on page 105)

We love the flavor combination of chocolate and banana. Once when I didn't have chocolate chips on hand, I made these moist muffins with chunks of chocolate bars instead. My husband likes them even better this way, since they have big bites of chocolate.
—Kristin Wagner, Spokane, Washington

1-1/4 cups all-purpose flour
1 cup whole wheat flour
3/4 cup packed brown sugar
1-1/2 teaspoons baking powder
1 teaspoon baking soda
1/4 teaspoon salt
3 medium ripe bananas, mashed
1-1/4 cups milk
1 egg
1 tablespoon vegetable oil
2 teaspoons vanilla extract
6 milk chocolate candy bars (1.55 ounces *each*)

In a mixing bowl, combine the flours, brown sugar, baking powder, baking soda and salt. In another bowl, combine bananas, milk, egg, oil and vanilla; stir into dry ingredients just until moistened. Fill greased or paper-lined muffin cups one-third full. Break each candy bar into 12 pieces; place two pieces in each muffin cup. Top with remaining batter. Chop remaining candy bar pieces; sprinkle over muffins. Bake at 400° for 15 minutes or until muffins test done. Cool for 5 minutes before removing from pans to wire racks. **Yield:** 1-1/2 dozen.

Apple Raisin Quick Bread

Cloves are a subtle but effective complement to the abundant apple pieces in this fruity, golden quick bread. *—Gail Buss, Westminster, Maryland*

1-1/4 cups vegetable oil
4 eggs
4 teaspoons vanilla extract
3 cups all-purpose flour
2-1/2 cups sugar
2 teaspoons ground cinnamon
1-1/2 teaspoons salt
1-1/2 teaspoons baking soda
1 teaspoon ground cloves
1/2 teaspoon baking powder
3 cups diced peeled tart apples
2/3 cup raisins
1/2 cup chopped nuts

In a mixing bowl, beat oil, eggs and vanilla. Combine flour, sugar, cinnamon, salt, baking soda, cloves and baking powder; beat into egg mixture. Stir in the apples, raisins and nuts. Pour into two greased 9-in. x 5-in. x 3-in. loaf pans. Bake at 325° for 60-70 minutes or until a toothpick inserted near the center comes out clean. Cool for 10 minutes before removing from pans to wire racks. **Yield:** 2 loaves.

Chive Muffins

These savory muffins are chock-full of chives. They're great with a brimming bowl of soup or stew.
—Shirley Glaab, Hattiesburg, Mississippi

2 cups all-purpose flour
1/3 cup minced chives
1 tablespoon baking powder
1 tablespoon sugar
1 tablespoon brown sugar
1/2 teaspoon salt
1/4 to 1/2 teaspoon pepper
1 egg
1 cup buttermilk
1/4 cup butter *or* margarine, melted

In a bowl, combine the first seven ingredients. Combine egg, buttermilk and butter; stir into dry ingredients just until moistened. Fill greased muffin cups two-thirds full. Bake at 400° for 14-18 minutes or until golden brown. Cool for 5 minutes before removing from pan to a wire rack. **Yield:** 1 dozen.

Dijon Ham Muffins

For a nice change from sweet muffins, try this delightful hearty variety. They're easy to fix and great for breakfast. They're also super for lunch with soup.
—Karen Davis, Springfield, Missouri

1-2/3 cups all-purpose flour
1/3 cup cornmeal
1/4 cup sugar
2 teaspoons baking powder
1 to 2 teaspoons ground mustard
1/2 teaspoon salt
1/2 teaspoon baking soda
1/8 teaspoon ground cloves
2 eggs
1 cup buttermilk
1/3 cup vegetable oil
3 tablespoons Dijon mustard
1 cup finely chopped fully cooked ham

In a bowl, combine the first eight ingredients. Combine the eggs, buttermilk, oil and mustard; stir into dry ingredients just until moistened. Fold in ham. Fill greased or paper-lined muffin cups three-fourths full. Bake at 375° for 20-25 minutes or until muffins test done. Cool for 5 minutes before removing from pans to wire racks. **Yield:** 14 muffins.

Orange-Raisin Sticky Muffins

(Pictured above right)

These finger-lickin' muffins have the appeal of old-fashioned sticky buns without the fuss of yeast dough. They have a delightful blend of flavors, including walnuts, raisins, cinnamon and sunny orange zest.
—Sandi Ritchey, Silverton, Oregon

1/4 cup chopped raisins
1 tablespoon sugar
1/2 teaspoon ground cinnamon

TOPPING:
1/2 cup chopped nuts
1/3 cup packed brown sugar
2 tablespoons butter *or* margarine, melted
2 tablespoons honey
1/4 teaspoon ground cinnamon

MUFFINS:
2 cups all-purpose flour
3 teaspoons baking powder
1/2 teaspoon salt
1 egg
2/3 cup milk
1/4 cup honey
1/3 cup butter *or* margarine, melted
2 tablespoons grated orange peel

Combine the raisins, sugar and cinnamon; set aside. Combine topping ingredients; spoon 1 teaspoonful into 12 greased muffin cups. Set aside. In a bowl, combine the flour, baking powder and salt. Beat egg, milk, honey, butter and orange peel; stir into dry ingredients just until moistened. Spoon 1 tablespoon of batter into prepared muffin cups; sprinkle with raisin mixture. Top with remaining batter. Bake at 375° for 16-20 minutes or until muffins test done. Cool for 5 minutes; invert the pan onto a lightly buttered foil-lined shallow baking pan. Serve warm. **Yield:** 1 dozen.

Count on Chives

Chopped fresh chives can be put into plastic freezer bags and frozen for handy use. They keep their color and flavor well in the freezer.

Cookies & Bars

A cookie jar packed with tasty morsels or a platter of bars and brownies sweetens any day.

MOUTH-WATERING MORSELS. Clockwise from upper left: Cinnamon Crackle Cookies (p. 133), Best Cake Brownies (p. 124), Sally Ann Cookies (p. 126), Secret Treat Molasses Cookies (p. 130) and Chocolate Caramel Bars (p. 128).

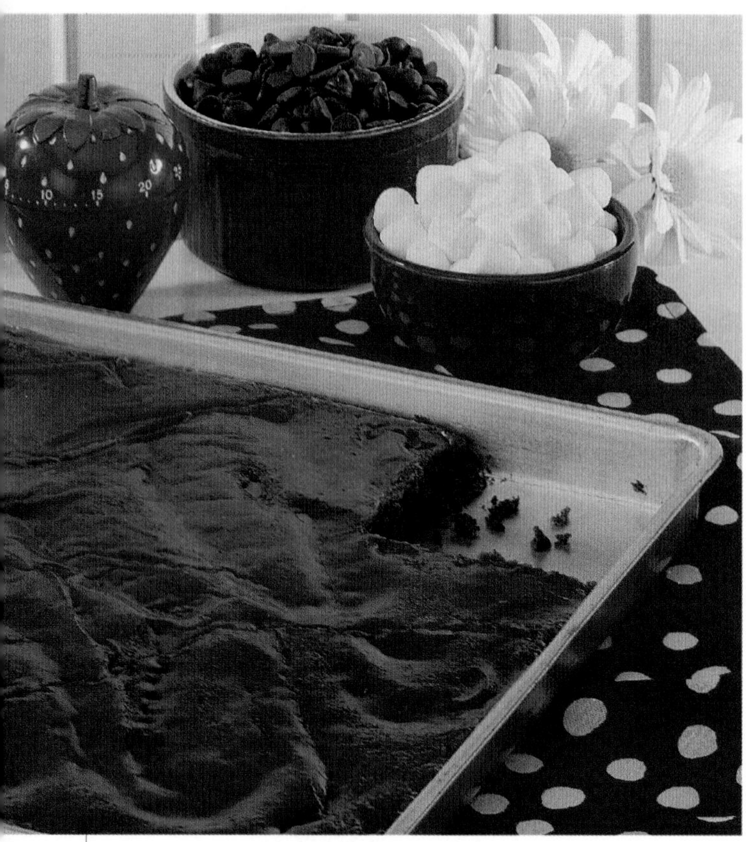

Best Cake Brownies

(Pictured above and on page 123)

This recipe caught my eye because it uses a whole can of chocolate syrup! I had searched for years for a brownie everyone likes, and this is it. My husband takes them to work, and they're gone in no time. They cut nicely after cooling a bit, but we don't often wait to dig in. —*Jean Kennedy, Springfield, Oregon*

1/2 cup butter *or* margarine, softened
1 cup sugar
4 eggs
1 can (16 ounces) chocolate syrup
1 teaspoon vanilla extract
1 cup all-purpose flour
1/2 teaspoon salt
GLAZE:
1 cup sugar
1/3 cup butter *or* margarine
1/3 cup milk
2/3 cup semisweet chocolate chips
2/3 cup miniature marshmallows

In a mixing bowl, cream butter and sugar. Add the eggs, one at a time, beating well after each addition. Beat in chocolate syrup and vanilla. Add the flour and salt until blended. Pour into a greased 15-in. x 10-in. x 1-in. baking pan. Bake at 350° for 20-25 minutes or until a toothpick inserted near the center comes out clean (top of brownies will still appear wet). Cool on a wire rack for 15-20 minutes. Meanwhile, in a small saucepan, combine sugar, butter and milk. Bring to a boil; boil until the sugar is dissolved. Remove from the heat; stir in chocolate chips and marshmallows until melted. Pour over the brownies and spread evenly. Refrigerate for 5 minutes before cutting. **Yield:** about 3 dozen.

Chunky Mocha Cookies

Every Christmas, my Home Economics Club has a cookie exchange. These cookies flavored with a hint of coffee are always a big hit. —*Janet Sparks*
Shirley, Indiana

1 cup butter-flavored shortening
3/4 cup sugar
1/2 cup packed brown sugar
2 eggs
2 tablespoons milk
1 tablespoon instant coffee granules
1 teaspoon vanilla extract
2-1/3 cups all-purpose flour
2 tablespoons baking cocoa
1 teaspoon baking soda
1/2 teaspoon salt
1 cup chopped pecans
1 cup (6 ounces) semisweet chocolate chips
3/4 cup raisins
3/4 cup flaked coconut

In a mixing bowl, cream shortening and sugars. Beat in eggs, milk, coffee granules and vanilla. Combine the flour, cocoa, baking soda and salt; add to the creamed mixture and mix well. Stir in pecans, chips, raisins and coconut. Drop by rounded tablespoonfuls 2 in. apart onto ungreased baking sheets. Bake at 375° for 10-12 minutes. Cool on wire racks. **Yield:** about 6 dozen.

Dad's Chocolate Chip Cookies

My dad, Art Winter, would tuck some of these cookies in the care packages he and my mom sent to me when I was in college. —*Kathy Froehlich*
Dix Hills, New York

2/3 cup butter *or* margarine, softened
2/3 cup shortening
1 cup sugar
1 cup packed brown sugar
2 eggs
2 teaspoons vanilla extract
3-1/2 cups all-purpose flour

1 teaspoon salt
1 teaspoon baking soda
2 cups (12 ounces) semisweet chocolate chips
1 cup chopped walnuts

In a mixing bowl, cream butter, shortening and sugars. Add eggs, one at a time, beating well after each addition. Add vanilla; mix well. Combine flour, salt and baking soda; add to the creamed mixture. Stir in chocolate chips and nuts. Drop by rounded tablespoonfuls onto ungreased baking sheets. Bake at 350° for 10-11 minutes or until golden brown. Cool on wire racks. **Yield:** about 6-1/2 dozen.

Chewy Chip Bars

These sweet granola bars are chock-full of butterscotch and chocolate chips. The bars freeze well, so they make a quick snack or dessert that's easily portable and handy. —Eileen Sears, Eagle, Wisconsin

4-1/2 cups old-fashioned oats
1 cup all-purpose flour
2/3 cup butter *or* margarine, softened
1/2 cup honey
1/3 cup packed brown sugar
1 teaspoon baking soda
1 teaspoon vanilla extract
1 cup semisweet chocolate chips
1 cup butterscotch chips

In a mixing bowl, combine the first seven ingredients; mix well. Stir in chips. Press into a greased 13-in. x 9-in. x 2-in. baking pan. Bake at 325° for 18-22 minutes or until golden brown. Cool for 10 minutes; cut into bars. Cool completely in the pan. **Yield:** 3 dozen.

Easy Peanut Butter Cookies

With only four ingredients, these cookies couldn't be easier for our son, Jacob, to help whip up. He thinks it's fun helping prepare meals and snacks. —Valerie Ellsworth, Belvidere, Illinois

1 cup peanut butter
1 cup sugar
1 egg, beaten
1 teaspoon vanilla extract

In a bowl, stir all ingredients until combined. Shape level tablespoonfuls into balls. Place 2 in. apart on ungreased baking sheets; flatten with a fork. Bake at 350° for 16-18 minutes or until set. Cool for 5 minutes; remove to wire racks. **Yield:** about 2 dozen. **Editor's Note:** These cookies do not contain flour.

Nutmeg Meltaways

(Pictured below)

My family and friends have enjoyed these melt-in-your-mouth cookies since I first began making them years ago. I love to bake and try to keep the cookie jar filled. For the holidays, the dusting of nutmeg is a tasty touch. —Judy Burdette, Kettering, Ohio

1 cup butter (no substitutes), softened
1/2 cup sugar
1 teaspoon vanilla extract
2 cups all-purpose flour
3/4 cup ground almonds (about 3 ounces), toasted
1 cup confectioners' sugar
1 tablespoon ground nutmeg

In a mixing bowl, cream butter, sugar and vanilla. Gradually add flour; mix well. Stir in the almonds. Shape into 1-in. balls; place 2 in. apart on ungreased baking sheets. Bake at 300° for 18-20 minutes or until bottoms are lightly browned. Cool on wire racks. Combine confectioners' sugar and nutmeg. Gently roll cooled cookies in sugar mixture. **Yield:** about 5 dozen.

Sally Ann Cookies

(Pictured below and on page 123)

These soft, cake-like cookies are especially satisfying because they're low in fat. I modified an old recipe, and my husband and I like this version even better.
—Sarah Jane Hayes, Dilworth, Minnesota

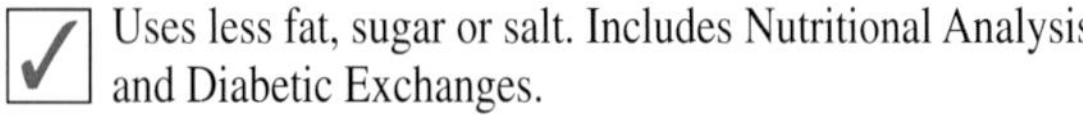
Uses less fat, sugar or salt. Includes Nutritional Analysis and Diabetic Exchanges.

1-1/2 cups sugar
1 cup molasses
1/2 cup brewed coffee, room temperature
5 cups all-purpose flour
2 teaspoons baking soda
3/4 teaspoon salt
1/2 teaspoon ground nutmeg
1/4 teaspoon ground cloves
1/4 teaspoon ground ginger
FROSTING:
1-1/2 cups sugar
1/2 cup water
1 teaspoon vinegar
1 cup miniature marshmallows
2 egg whites

In a mixing bowl, combine sugar, molasses and coffee. Combine dry ingredients; add to sugar mixture and mix well. Refrigerate for 2 hours. Roll dough on a floured surface to about 1/4-in. thickness. Cut with 3-in. to 4-in. cookie cutters. Place on baking sheets coated with nonstick cooking spray. Bake at 350° for 8-10 minutes or until set. Cool on wire racks. Meanwhile, for frosting, combine sugar, water and vinegar in a heavy saucepan. Cover and bring to a boil. Uncover and cook over medium-high heat until a candy thermometer reads 234°-240° (soft-ball stage), about 5-10 minutes. Remove from the heat; stir in marshmallows until smooth. In a mixing bowl, beat egg whites until frothy. Gradually beat in sugar mixture; beat on high for 7-8 minutes or until stiff peaks form. Frost the cookies. **Yield:** about 6 dozen. **Nutritional Analysis:** One cookie equals 79 calories, 63 mg sodium, 0 cholesterol, 19 gm carbohydrate, 1 gm protein, trace fat. **Diabetic Exchange:** 1 starch. **Editor's Note:** The accuracy of your candy thermometer is very important. See page 162 for information.

Angel Macaroons

These sweet, chewy coconut cookies are super simple since they start with a boxed angel food cake mix.
—Renee Schwebach, Dumont, Minnesota

✓ Uses less fat, sugar or salt. Includes Nutritional Analysis and Diabetic Exchanges.

1 package (16 ounces) one-step angel food cake mix
1/2 cup water
1-1/2 teaspoons almond extract
2 cups flaked coconut

In a mixing bowl, beat cake mix, water and extract on low speed for 30 seconds. Scrape bowl; beat on medium speed for 1 minute. Fold in the coconut. Drop by rounded teaspoonfuls onto a parchment paper-lined baking sheet. Bake at 350° for 10-12 minutes or until set. Remove paper with cookies to a wire rack to cool. **Yield:** 2-1/2 dozen. **Nutritional Analysis:** One cookie equals 89 calories, 164 mg sodium, 0 cholesterol, 16 gm carbohydrate, 2 gm protein, 2 gm fat. **Diabetic Exchange:** 1 starch.

Danish Apricot Bars

I've always found that these special fruity bars hold up well packed in lunches.
—Verona Koehlmoos, Pilger, Nebraska

1 cup all-purpose flour
1 teaspoon baking powder
1/2 cup butter *or* margarine, softened
1 egg
1 tablespoon milk
3/4 cup apricot preserves
TOPPING:
1/4 cup butter *or* margarine, softened
1 cup sugar

1 egg
1 teaspoon vanilla extract
1 cup flaked coconut

In a bowl, combine the flour, baking powder and butter. Add egg and milk; mix well. Press into a greased 9-in. square baking pan. Spread with preserves; set aside. In a mixing bowl, cream butter and sugar. Beat in egg and vanilla. Stir in coconut. Carefully spread over preserves. Bake at 350° for 25-30 minutes or until a toothpick inserted near the center comes out clean. Cool on a wire rack. **Yield:** 1-1/2 dozen.

Sam's Chocolate Sandwich Cookies

My soft, not-too-sweet chocolate cookies are filled with a heavenly cream filling. Kids of all ages devour them! Whenever my family comes to visit, these are the treats they always request. —*Salvatore Bertolino Indiana, Pennsylvania*

1 cup shortening
2 cups sugar
2 eggs
1 cup (8 ounces) sour cream
1 cup hot brewed coffee
1 teaspoon vanilla extract
4 cups all-purpose flour
3/4 cup baking cocoa
2 teaspoons baking soda
1/2 teaspoon baking powder

FILLING:

3 tablespoons all-purpose flour
1 cup milk
1/2 cup butter *or* margarine, softened
1/4 cup shortening
1 cup confectioners' sugar
1 teaspoon vanilla extract
1/4 teaspoon salt

In a mixing bowl, cream shortening and sugar. Add eggs, one at a time, beating well after each addition. Beat in sour cream, coffee and vanilla. Combine the dry ingredients and gradually add to the creamed mixture. Drop by tablespoonfuls 2 in. apart onto greased baking sheets. Bake at 350° for 9-11 minutes or until firm to touch. Cool on wire racks. In a saucepan, combine flour and milk until smooth. Bring to a boil; cook and stir for 2 minutes or until thickened. Cool to room temperature. In a mixing bowl, combine remaining filling ingredients; add the milk mixture and mix well. Spread 2 teaspoonfuls of filling on the bottom of half of the cookies; top with remaining cookies. **Yield:** about 4 dozen.

Almond Icebox Cookies

(Pictured above)

I frequently have a roll of this cookie dough on hand so I can serve freshly baked cookies in a snap.
—*Elizabeth Montgomery, Taylorville, Illinois*

1-1/2 cups butter *or* margarine, softened
1 cup sugar
1 cup packed brown sugar
3 eggs
4 cups all-purpose flour
1 tablespoon ground cinnamon
1 teaspoon baking soda
1/2 cup finely chopped almonds
2 packages (2-1/4 ounces *each*) whole unblanched almonds

In a mixing bowl, cream butter and sugars. Add eggs, one at a time, beating well after each addition. Combine flour, cinnamon and baking soda; gradually add to the creamed mixture. Fold in chopped almonds. Shape into two 15-in. rolls; wrap each in plastic wrap. Refrigerate for 2 hours or overnight. Unwrap and cut into 1/4-in. slices. Place 2 in. apart on ungreased baking sheets; top each with a whole almond. Bake at 375° for 8-10 minutes or until edges begin to brown. Cool on wire racks. **Yield:** 10 dozen.

It's in the Bag!

Save the plastic liner bags from empty cereal boxes. Next time you need to crush nuts, pop them inside a bag for less mess.

Chocolate Caramel Bars

(Pictured above and on page 122)

These rich, gooey bars are my most-requested treats. They're popular at school functions, family barbecues and picnics. We like them alone or topped with a scoop of ice cream. —*Betty Hagerty*
Philadelphia, Pennsylvania

2-1/4 cups all-purpose flour, *divided*
2 cups quick-cooking oats
1-1/2 cups packed brown sugar
1 teaspoon baking soda
1/2 teaspoon salt
1-1/2 cups cold butter *or* margarine
2 cups (12 ounces) semisweet chocolate chips
1 cup chopped pecans
1 jar (12 ounces) caramel ice cream topping

In a bowl, combine 2 cups flour, oats, brown sugar, baking soda and salt. Cut in butter until crumbly. Set half aside for topping. Press the remaining crumb mixture into a greased 13-in. x 9-in. x 2-in. baking pan. Bake at 350° for 15 minutes. Sprinkle with the chocolate chips and pecans. Whisk the caramel topping and remaining flour until smooth; drizzle over top. Sprinkle with the reserved crumb mixture. Bake for 18-20 minutes or until golden brown. Cool on a wire rack for 2 hours before cutting. **Yield:** about 4-1/2 dozen.

Flavorful Dried Fruit Bars

These yummy bars are packed with naturally sweet fruit and tasty spices, so no one will miss the sugar.
—*Ruth Seitz, Columbus Junction, Iowa*

✓ Uses less fat, sugar or salt. Includes Nutritional Analysis and Diabetic Exchanges.

1 cup water
1/2 cup chopped dates
1/2 cup chopped prunes
1/2 cup raisins
1/2 cup margarine
Egg substitute equivalent to 2 eggs
1 teaspoon vanilla extract
1 cup all-purpose flour
1 teaspoon baking soda
1/2 teaspoon ground cinnamon
1/4 teaspoon ground nutmeg
1/4 teaspoon salt

In a small saucepan, combine water, dates, prunes and raisins. Cook over medium heat until fruit is softened, about 10 minutes. Remove from the heat; add margarine and stir until melted. Cool. Stir in egg substitute and vanilla; mix well. Combine dry ingredients in a large bowl; stir in fruit mixture. Spread into an 11-in. x 7-in. x 2-in. baking pan that has been coated with nonstick cooking spray. Bake at 350° for 20-25 minutes or until a toothpick inserted near the center comes out clean. Cool on a wire rack. **Yield:** 12 servings. **Nutritional Analysis:** One serving equals 171 calories, 263 mg sodium, trace cholesterol, 23 gm carbohydrate, 3 gm protein, 8 gm fat. **Diabetic Exchanges:** 1-1/2 fat, 1 starch, 1/2 fruit.

Candy Bar Brownies

Two kinds of candy bars make these brownies extra special. —*Sharon Evans, Rockwell, Iowa*

3/4 cup butter *or* margarine, melted
2 cups sugar
4 eggs
2 teaspoons vanilla extract
1-1/2 cups all-purpose flour
1/3 cup baking cocoa
1/2 teaspoon baking powder
1/4 teaspoon salt
4 Snickers bars (2.07 ounces *each*), cut into 1/4-inch pieces
3 plain milk chocolate candy bars (1.55 ounces *each*), coarsely chopped

In a bowl, combine butter, sugar, eggs and vanilla. Combine flour, cocoa, baking powder and salt;

set aside 1/4 cup. Add remaining dry ingredients to the egg mixture; mix well. Toss Snickers pieces with reserved flour mixture; stir into batter. Transfer to a greased 13-in. x 9-in. x 2-in. baking pan. Sprinkle with milk chocolate candy bar pieces. Bake at 350° for 30-35 minutes or until a toothpick inserted near the center comes out clean (do not overbake). Cool on a wire rack. Chill before cutting. **Yield:** 3 dozen.

Toasted Anise Strips

Keep some of these unique crunchy cookies on hand to enjoy with a cup of hot coffee or a cold glass of milk.
—Elena Smoulder, Pittsburgh, Pennsylvania

1/4 cup butter (no substitutes), softened
1 cup sugar
3 eggs
1 tablespoon anise extract
2-1/2 cups cake flour
2 teaspoons baking powder
1/4 teaspoon salt

In a mixing bowl, cream butter and sugar. Add the eggs, one at a time, beating well after each addition. Add extract. Combine flour, baking powder and salt; add to creamed mixture and mix well. Spread half of the batter onto a greased baking sheet, forming an 11-in. x 5-in. rectangle. Repeat with remaining batter on a second baking sheet. Bake at 350° for 15 minutes. Remove from baking sheets; cut into 1-in. slices. Place with cut side down on baking sheets. Bake 15 minutes longer or until lightly browned. Cool on wire racks. **Yield:** about 2 dozen.

Cherry Macaroons

I received this recipe along with its ingredients at my bridal shower. Now these are a favorite of our sons.
—Sherma Talbot, Salt Lake City, Utah

1-1/3 cups shortening
1-1/2 cups sugar
2 eggs
1 teaspoon almond extract
3-1/2 cups all-purpose flour
2 teaspoons baking powder
2 teaspoons baking soda
1 teaspoon salt
1-1/2 cups flaked coconut
1 cup maraschino cherries, chopped

In a mixing bowl, cream shortening and sugar. Add eggs and extract; mix well. Combine flour, baking powder, baking soda and salt; gradually add to creamed mixture. Stir in the coconut and cherries (dough will be very stiff). Drop by rounded teaspoonfuls 2 in. apart onto greased baking sheets. Bake at 375° for 10-12 minutes or until lightly browned. Cool on wire racks. **Yield:** about 6 dozen.

Dipped Coconut Shortbread

(Pictured below and on back cover)

I often make these cookies for Valentine's Day. Coconut adds flavor and texture to the shortbread.
—Toni Petroskey, Lorain, Ohio

3/4 cup butter (no substitutes), softened
1/4 cup sugar
2 teaspoons vanilla extract
1-3/4 cups all-purpose flour
1/2 teaspoon baking powder
1 cup flaked coconut
1-1/2 cups semisweet chocolate chips
1 tablespoon shortening

In a mixing bowl, cream butter, sugar and vanilla until light and fluffy. Combine flour and baking powder; gradually add to the creamed mixture and mix well. Stir in coconut. Cover and refrigerate for 1 hour or until firm. On a floured surface, roll out dough to 1/4-in. thickness. Cut with a 2-1/2-in. round cookie cutter. Place 2 in. apart on ungreased baking sheets. Bake at 300° for 20-25 minutes or until edges begin to brown. Cool on wire racks. In a small saucepan over low heat, melt chocolate chips and shortening. Remove from the heat; dip cookies halfway into chocolate. Place on waxed paper-lined baking sheets until set. **Yield:** about 2 dozen.

Secret Treat Molasses Cookies

(Pictured below and on page 122)

This recipe has been passed down for generations. I've made these cookies for years, but like my mother, I only make them for special occasions. They're fun to decorate and delicious to eat, with a "surprise flavor" inside. —*Ruby Neese, Liberty, North Carolina*

1/2 cup butter *or* margarine, softened
1/2 cup packed brown sugar
1 egg
1/2 cup molasses
2-1/2 cups all-purpose flour
3/4 teaspoon baking soda
1/2 teaspoon salt
1/2 teaspoon ground cinnamon
1/2 teaspoon ground ginger
1/2 cup strawberry preserves
GLAZE:
1-2/3 cups confectioners' sugar
2 tablespoons water
1/4 teaspoon vanilla extract

In a large mixing bowl, cream butter and sugar. Add egg; mix well. Beat in molasses. Combine flour, baking soda, salt, cinnamon and ginger; add to creamed mixture and mix well (dough will be very stiff). Cover and chill several hours or overnight. On a lightly floured surface, roll dough to 1/8-in. thickness; cut into 2-1/4-in. to 2-1/2-in. circles. Place 1/2 teaspoon preserves on half of the circles; top with remaining circles. Pinch edges together to seal. Place on greased baking sheets. Bake at 350° for 10 minutes or until lightly browned. Cool on a wire rack. Combine glaze ingredients; spread over cooled cookies. **Yield:** 4 dozen.

Jeweled Cookie Slices

I often mark recipes with "G" for good, "VG" for very good; this seasonal favorite is marked "VVG!" I usually double the recipe. —*Rosella Peters*
Gull Lake, Saskatchewan

1/3 cup butter (no substitutes), melted
1/3 cup sugar
1/4 cup packed brown sugar
1 egg
1/2 teaspoon vanilla extract
1/2 cup chopped candied pineapple *or* red and green candied cherries
2 tablespoons chopped blanched almonds
1-1/2 cups all-purpose flour
1 teaspoon baking powder
1/8 teaspoon baking soda
1/8 teaspoon ground nutmeg

In a mixing bowl, beat butter and sugars. Add egg and vanilla; mix well. Stir in pineapple and almonds. Combine dry ingredients; add to butter mixture. Spread evenly into a foil-lined 8-in. x 4-in. x 2-in. loaf pan. Cover and refrigerate for at least 2 hours. Invert dough onto a cutting board; remove foil. Cut into 1/4-in. slices; place on greased baking sheets. Bake at 350° for 10-12 minutes or until lightly browned. Cool on wire racks. **Yield:** about 2-1/2 dozen.

Sugar-Free Raisin Bars

My mother is diabetic, so I keep these moist, golden bars on hand for dessert. I even serve them during the holidays. They're a nice light snack for everyone.
—*Betty Ruenholl, Syracuse, Nebraska*

✓ Uses less fat, sugar or salt. Includes Nutritional Analysis and Diabetic Exchanges.

1 cup raisins
1/2 cup water
1/4 cup margarine

1 teaspoon ground cinnamon
1/4 teaspoon ground nutmeg
1 cup all-purpose flour
1 egg, lightly beaten
3/4 cup unsweetened applesauce
1 tablespoon sugar substitute
1 teaspoon baking soda
1/4 teaspoon vanilla extract

In a saucepan over medium heat, cook raisins, water, margarine, cinnamon and nutmeg until margarine is melted; continue cooking for 3 minutes. Add all remaining ingredients. Spread into an 8-in. square baking dish that has been coated with nonstick cooking spray. Bake at 350° for 25-30 minutes or until lightly browned. **Yield:** 16 servings. **Nutritional Analysis:** One serving equals 92 calories, 97 mg sodium, 13 mg cholesterol, 15 gm carbohydrate, 2 gm protein, 3 gm fat. **Diabetic Exchanges:** 1 starch, 1/2 fat.

Refrigerator Confetti Brownies

When you want to keep your kitchen cool but have a taste for brownies, try this no-bake version.
—Marcia Dzikiewicz, Newfield, New York

3 cups graham cracker crumbs
2 cups colored miniature marshmallows
1 cup chopped walnuts *or* pecans
1 cup confectioners' sugar
2 cups (12 ounces) semisweet chocolate chips
1 cup evaporated milk
1/2 teaspoon peppermint extract, optional

In a large bowl, combine the crumbs, marshmallows, nuts and sugar. In a saucepan, melt chocolate chips and milk over low heat, stirring often until blended and smooth. Remove from the heat; add extract if desired. Set aside 1/2 cup. Pour remaining chocolate mixture over crumb mixture; stir until well blended. Pour batter into a greased 8-in. square baking pan. Press down evenly. Frost with reserved chocolate mixture. Chill for 1 hour. **Yield:** 2-1/2 dozen.

Friendship Brownies

(Pictured above right and on front cover)

I keep batches of the brownie mix on hand so my son Travis can whip up a pan of these chewy treats in a snap. All he has to do is add eggs, oil and vanilla.
—Twila Burkholder, Middleburg, Pennsylvania

BROWNIE MIX:
1 cup plus 2 tablespoons all-purpose flour
2/3 cup packed brown sugar
3/4 teaspoon salt
2/3 cup sugar
1 teaspoon baking powder
1/3 cup baking cocoa
1/2 cup semisweet chocolate chips
1/2 cup chopped walnuts
ADDITIONAL INGREDIENTS:
3 eggs
2/3 cup vegetable oil
1 teaspoon vanilla extract

Pour the flour into a 1-qt. glass container with a tight-fitting lid. On top of the flour, layer the brown sugar, salt, sugar, baking powder, cocoa, chocolate chips and nuts (do not mix). Cover and store in a cool dry place for up to 6 months. **To prepare brownies:** In a bowl, beat the eggs, oil and vanilla. Add the brownie mix; stir well. Spread into a greased 9-in. square baking pan. Bake at 350° for 34-38 minutes or until a toothpick inserted near the center comes out clean. Cool on a wire rack. **Yield:** 16 brownies.

M&M Oat Bars

(Pictured above)

These irresistible bars made with seasonally colored M&M's can sweeten any holiday. They're fun to make and eat! —Renee Schwebach, Dumont, Minnesota

1/2 cup butter *or* margarine, softened
1 cup packed brown sugar
1 egg
1 teaspoon vanilla extract
1-1/4 cups all-purpose flour
1/2 teaspoon baking soda
1/2 teaspoon salt
2 cups quick-cooking oats
1 package (14 ounces) caramels
3 tablespoons water
1 cup miniature semisweet chocolate chips
1 cup chopped walnuts
1 cup plain M&M's
3 ounces white confectionary coating*

In a mixing bowl, cream butter and brown sugar. Beat in egg and vanilla. Combine flour, baking soda and salt; add to the creamed mixture. Stir in oats. Press into a greased 15-in. x 10-in. x 1-in. baking pan. Bake at 350° for 10-15 minutes or until golden brown. Cool on a wire rack. In a microwave-safe bowl, melt the caramels and water. Spread over crust. Sprinkle with chips, nuts and M&M's. Gently press into the caramel mixture. Melt confectionary coating; drizzle over the top. Cut into bars. **Yield:** 6 dozen. ***Editor's Note:** Confectionary coating, sometimes called "almond bark" or "candy coating", is found in the baking section of most grocery stores. It is often sold in bulk packages of 1 to 1-1/2 pounds.

Welcome-to-the-Neighborhood Cookies

I always share a batch of these cookies with new neighbors. They're easy to make but taste like I fussed. —Susan Bice, Edwards Air Force Base, California

1 cup butter *or* margarine, softened
1/2 cup sugar
1/2 cup packed brown sugar
1 egg
2-1/4 cups all-purpose flour
2 to 3 teaspoons grated orange peel
1 teaspoon ground cinnamon
3/4 teaspoon baking soda
1/2 teaspoon salt
Pinch ground nutmeg
Pinch ground cloves
1 package (12 ounces) vanilla chips

In a mixing bowl, cream butter and sugars; beat in egg. Combine flour, orange peel, cinnamon, baking soda, salt, nutmeg and cloves; add to creamed mixture. Stir in the chips. Drop by rounded tablespoonfuls onto ungreased baking sheets. Bake at 350° for 12-14 minutes or until lightly browned. Cool on wire racks. **Yield:** about 3-1/2 dozen.

Anise Cutouts

This roll-out cookie dough is so easy to work with. —Katie Hutchison, Warrenton, Virginia

1/2 cup shortening
1 cup sugar
2 eggs
1 teaspoon vanilla extract
2 cups all-purpose flour
2 teaspoons baking powder
1/2 teaspoon salt
1 tablespoon aniseed

In a mixing bowl, cream shortening and sugar. Add eggs and vanilla; mix well. Combine flour, baking powder and salt; add to creamed mixture. Stir in aniseed. Chill for 2 hours or until dough is easy to handle. On a lightly floured surface, roll dough to 1/8-in. thickness. Cut with a 2-1/2-in. cookie cutter. Place 1 in. apart on ungreased baking sheets. Bake at 325° for 7-10 minutes. Cool on wire racks. **Yield:** about 3-1/2 dozen.

Sugar-Coated Cookies

For cookies that require balls of dough to be rolled in sugar, put a few balls in a covered container of sugar and shake to coat. It saves time.

Soft Spice Bars

These bars have the old-fashioned taste of ginger-snaps, but they're chewy and quick and easy to make.
—Sharon Nichols, Brookings, South Dakota

3/4 cup butter *or* margarine, melted
1 cup plus 2 tablespoons sugar, *divided*
1/4 cup molasses
1 egg
2 cups all-purpose flour
2 teaspoons baking soda
1 teaspoon ground cinnamon
1/2 teaspoon ground cloves
1/2 teaspoon ground ginger
1/2 teaspoon salt

In a mixing bowl, combine butter, 1 cup of sugar and molasses. Beat in egg until smooth. Combine flour, baking soda, cinnamon, cloves, ginger and salt; stir into the molasses mixture. Spread into a greased 15-in. x 10-in. x 1-in. baking pan. Sprinkle with remaining sugar. Bake at 375° for 10-12 minutes or until lightly browned. Do not overbake. Cool on a wire rack before cutting. **Yield:** 2-1/2 dozen.

Green Tomato Bars

Dessert doesn't spring to mind for most folks when tomatoes are mentioned. That's not true for my family, though. They often beg me to make these bars—they love the mixture of the sweet taste with the chewy oatmeal texture. *—Sharon Pratt, Cuba City, Wisconsin*

4 cups finely chopped green tomatoes
2 cups packed brown sugar, *divided*
2 tablespoons lemon juice
1 teaspoon lemon extract
3/4 cup butter *or* margarine, softened
1-1/2 cups all-purpose flour
1/2 teaspoon baking soda
1/2 teaspoon salt
2 cups old-fashioned oats
1/2 cup chopped walnuts

Drain tomatoes on paper towels for 10 minutes. In a saucepan, combine tomatoes, 1 cup of brown sugar and the lemon juice. Simmer, uncovered, for 20-25 minutes or until thickened. Remove from the heat and stir in extract; set aside. In a mixing bowl, cream the butter and remaining brown sugar. Add flour, baking soda and salt; mix well. Stir in oats and nuts. Press 2-1/2 cups on the bottom of a greased 13-in. x 9-in. x 2-in. baking pan. Spread tomato mixture over crust. Crumble remaining oat mixture on top. Bake at 375° for 30-35 minutes or until golden brown. Cool. **Yield:** 2 dozen.

Cinnamon Crackle Cookies

(Pictured below and on page 122)

This recipe is the compilation of many years of baking. I make these cookies for a holiday bazaar and year-round for our family. They freeze well. *—Vicki Lair*
Apple Valley, Minnesota

1/2 cup butter (no substitutes), softened
1/2 cup shortening
1 cup sugar
1/2 cup packed brown sugar
1 egg
1 teaspoon vanilla extract
1/2 teaspoon almond extract
2-1/2 cups all-purpose flour
1 tablespoon ground cinnamon
2 teaspoons baking soda
2 teaspoons cream of tartar
2 teaspoons ground nutmeg
2 teaspoons grated orange peel
1 teaspoon grated lemon peel
1/2 teaspoon salt
Additional sugar

In a mixing bowl, cream butter, shortening and sugars. Add the egg and extracts; mix well. Combine the next eight ingredients; gradually add to the creamed mixture. Shape into 1-in. balls; roll in sugar. Place 2 in. apart on ungreased baking sheets. Bake at 350° for 10-15 minutes or until lightly browned. **Yield:** about 6 dozen.

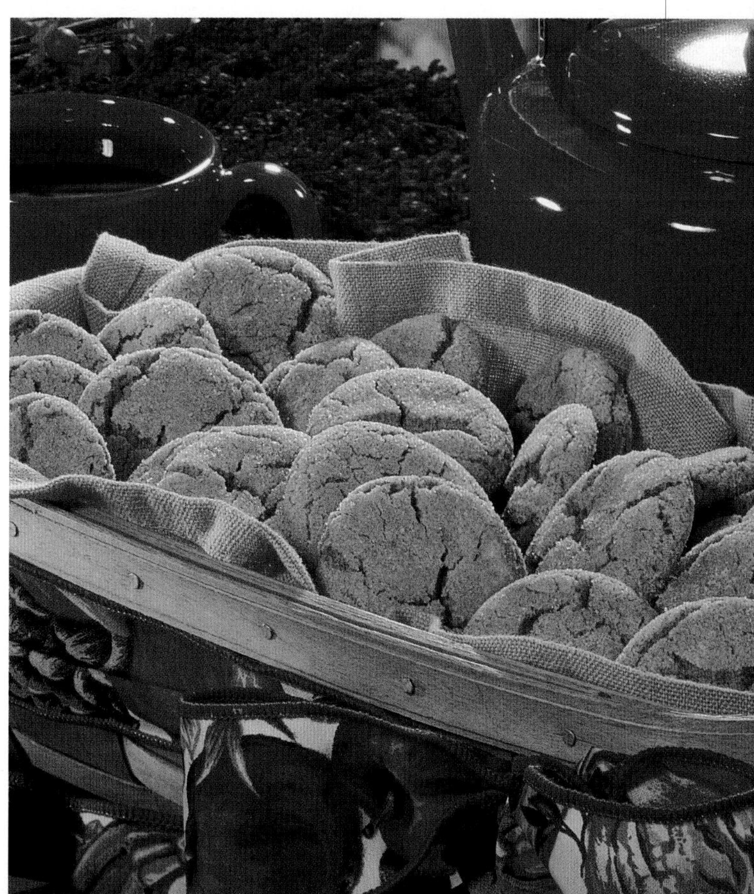

Polka-Dot Cookie Bars

(Pictured below)

To serve a group, these lightly sweet bars are a lot easier to make than fussing with individual cookies. They're my favorite to prepare and eat.
—Elizabeth Poire, Kailua-Kona, Hawaii

- **1 cup butter *or* margarine, softened**
- **3/4 cup sugar**
- **3/4 cup packed brown sugar**
- **2 eggs**
- **1/2 teaspoon almond extract**
- **2-1/4 cups all-purpose flour**
- **1/3 cup baking cocoa**
- **1 teaspoon baking soda**
- **1/2 teaspoon salt**
- **1 package (10 ounces) vanilla chips, *divided***

In a mixing bowl, cream butter and sugars. Add eggs, one at a time, beating well after each addition. Beat in extract. Combine flour, cocoa, baking soda and salt; gradually add to the creamed mixture. Set aside 1/4 cup vanilla chips; stir remaining chips into batter. Spread into a greased 15-in. x 10-in. x 1-in. baking pan. Sprinkle with reserved chips. Bake at 375° for 18-23 minutes or until a toothpick inserted near the center comes out clean. Cool before cutting. **Yield:** 4 dozen.

Oatmeal Cookies

These chewy, lightly sweet cookies are filled with great flavor. *—Laura Letobar, Livonia, Michigan*

- **3 cups quick-cooking oats**
- **2/3 cup all-purpose flour**
- **2/3 cup sugar**
- **1/3 cup packed brown sugar**
- **1 teaspoon baking powder**
- **1/4 teaspoon salt**
- **2 eggs**
- **1/3 cup light corn syrup**
- **1 teaspoon vanilla extract**

In a mixing bowl, mix oats, flour, sugars, baking powder and salt. Add eggs, corn syrup and vanilla; mix well. Drop by rounded teaspoonfuls onto greased baking sheets. Bake at 350° for 10-12 minutes. Cool on wire racks. **Yield:** 2 dozen. **Editor's Note:** These cookies do not contain shortening.

Sugar-Free Maple Cookies

My brother is diabetic, so our mom made batch after batch of cookies until she came up with this terrific recipe that he could eat. We all like these soft cookies.
—Brenda Wile, Winesburg, Ohio

✓ Uses less fat, sugar or salt. Includes Nutritional Analysis and Diabetic Exchanges.

- **1/2 cup reduced-fat margarine, softened**
- **1/2 cup sour cream**
- **1 cup shredded peeled tart apple**
- **2 eggs**
- **1 teaspoon maple flavoring**
- **1/2 teaspoon vanilla extract**
- **2 cups all-purpose flour**
- **Artificial brown sugar sweetener equivalent to 1/3 cup brown sugar**
- **1/2 teaspoon baking soda**
- **1/2 teaspoon baking powder**

In a mixing bowl, combine margarine, sour cream, apple, eggs, maple flavoring and vanilla. Combine flour, sweetener, baking soda and baking powder; add to apple mixture and mix well. Drop by heaping tablespoonfuls onto baking sheets coated with nonstick cooking spray. Bake at 375° for 9-10 minutes or until lightly browned. Cool on wire racks. Store in an airtight container. **Yield:** 42 cookies. **Nutritional Analysis:** One cookie equals 44 calories, 51 mg sodium, 11 mg cholesterol, 5 gm carbohydrate, 1 gm protein, 2 gm fat. **Diabetic Exchanges:** 1/2 starch, 1/2 fat.

Butterscotch Bars

I put three recipes together to make these great bars—they really satisfy the sweet tooth.
—Romagene Deuel, Clarkston, Michigan

- **1 cup butter-flavored shortening**
- **1 cup sugar**

1 cup packed brown sugar
2 eggs
1 teaspoon vanilla extract
2 cups all-purpose flour
1 cup old-fashioned oats
1/2 teaspoon baking soda
1 package (10 ounces) butterscotch chips
1 cup chopped pecans

FILLING:

1 package (3 ounces) cream cheese, softened
2 tablespoons butter *or* margarine, softened
1/4 cup sugar
1 egg
1 tablespoon all-purpose flour

In a mixing bowl, cream the shortening and sugars. Add eggs, one at a time, beating well after each addition. Beat in vanilla. Combine flour, oats and baking soda; gradually add to the creamed mixture. Stir in chips and pecans. Reserve 2 cups. Spread remaining dough into a greased 13-in. x 9-in. x 2-in. baking pan. In a mixing bowl, combine filling ingredients. Spread evenly over crust. Crumble reserved dough over filling. Bake at 375° for 40-42 minutes or until golden brown. Cool on a wire rack before cutting. **Yield:** about 1-1/2 dozen.

Peanut Butter Chocolate Cookies

This recipe was featured in our Sunday paper years ago, and I just had to try it. Kids really love the peanut butter surprise inside the cookie.
—June Formanek, Belle Plaine, Iowa

1/2 cup butter *or* margarine, softened
1/2 cup sugar
1/2 cup packed brown sugar
1 cup creamy peanut butter, *divided*
1 egg, lightly beaten
1 teaspoon vanilla extract
1-1/2 cups all-purpose flour
1/2 cup baking cocoa
1/2 teaspoon baking soda
3/4 cup confectioners' sugar

In a large mixing bowl, cream butter, sugars and 1/4 cup peanut butter. Add egg and vanilla; mix well. Combine flour, cocoa and baking soda; add to creamed mixture and mix well. Blend confectioners' sugar with remaining peanut butter until smooth. Roll into 24 balls, 1 in. each. Divide dough into 24 pieces; flatten each into a 3-in. circle. Place one peanut butter ball on each circle; bring edges over to completely cover it. (Dough may crack; reshape cookies as needed.) Place cookies with seam side down on ungreased baking sheets. Flatten each cookie slightly with the bottom of a glass dipped in sugar. Bake at 375° for 7-9 minutes or until set. Cool on wire racks. **Yield:** 2 dozen.

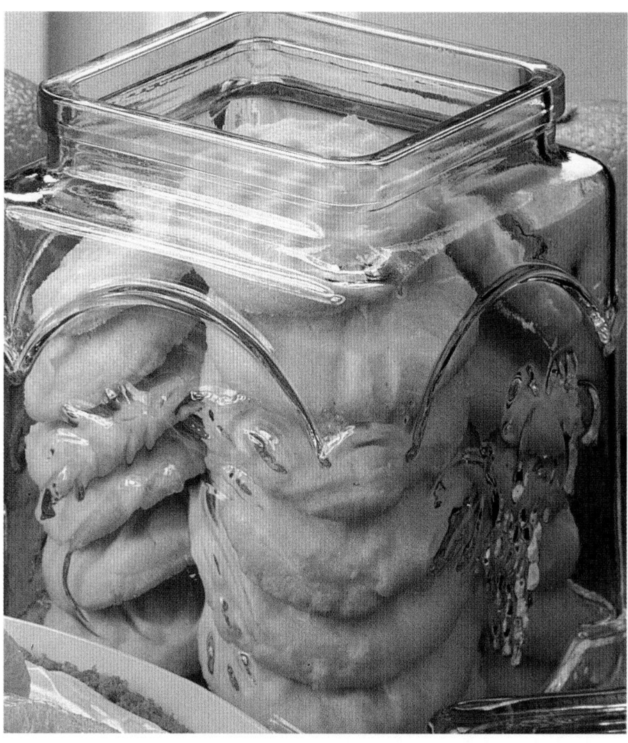

Butter Meltaways

(Pictured above)

Add variety to this cookie recipe by substituting lemon flavoring for the vanilla plus a teaspoon of lemon peel.
—Sue Call, Beech Grove, Indiana

1/2 cup butter (no substitutes), softened
1/2 cup vegetable oil
1/2 cup sugar
1/2 cup confectioners' sugar
1 egg
1/2 teaspoon vanilla extract
2-1/4 cups all-purpose flour
1/2 teaspoon baking soda
1/2 teaspoon cream of tartar
Additional sugar

In a mixing bowl, cream butter, oil and sugars. Add egg and vanilla. Combine flour, baking soda and cream of tartar; gradually add to the creamed mixture. Chill for several hours or overnight. Drop by rounded teaspoonfuls 2 in. apart onto ungreased baking sheets. Flatten with a fork dipped in flour; sprinkle with sugar. Bake at 350° for 13-15 minutes or until lightly browned. Cool on wire racks. **Yield:** about 4 dozen.

Cakes & Pies

Serving a palate-pleasing dessert is as easy as pie...and cake! Cut generous slices of these sweet treats and you'll receive rave reviews.

APPEALING CAKES AND PIES. Clockwise from upper left: Strawberry Meringue Cake and Cool Lime Pie (p. 150), Cherry Cheese Pizza (p. 141), Cherry Puddles Cake (p. 140) and Tin Roof Fudge Pie (p. 142).

Glazed Lemon Bundt Cake

(Pictured above)

A sunny lemon-flavored cake is just the dessert to brighten up any gloomy day. Lemon peel provides a nice zing in every bite. A light glaze gives the golden cake a delicate crust. Watch this dessert disappear at your next gathering. —*John Thompson Vandalia, Illinois*

1 cup butter *or* margarine, softened
2 cups sugar
4 eggs
1-1/2 teaspoons lemon extract
1-1/2 teaspoons vanilla extract
3 cups all-purpose flour
2 teaspoons baking powder
1/2 teaspoon salt
1 cup milk
1 tablespoon grated lemon peel
GLAZE:
1/4 cup lemon juice
1 tablespoon water
1/2 teaspoon lemon extract
3/4 cup sugar

In a mixing bowl, cream butter and sugar. Add the eggs, one at a time, beating well after each addition. Beat in extracts. Combine flour, baking powder and salt; add to the creamed mixture alternately with milk. Stir in lemon peel. Pour into a greased and floured 10-in. fluted tube pan. Bake at 350° for 60-70 minutes or until a toothpick inserted near the center comes out clean. Cool for 10 minutes; invert onto a wire rack. Cool 10 minutes longer. Place rack on waxed paper. Combine glaze ingredients; drizzle over the warm cake. Cool completely before serving. **Yield:** 12-16 servings.

Berry-Filled Lemon Cake

This delectable dessert starts with a convenient boxed cake mix. The cake and glaze have a mild lemon flavor that's delightful paired with fresh berries. —*Leanne Kistler, San Antonio, Texas*

✓ Uses less fat, sugar or salt. Includes Nutritional Analysis and Diabetic Exchanges.

1-1/4 cups water
Egg substitute equivalent to 3 eggs
1/4 cup plain nonfat yogurt
1 tablespoon grated lemon peel
1 package (18-1/4 ounces) light yellow cake mix
1/2 cup confectioners' sugar
3 teaspoons lemon juice
2 cups sliced strawberries

In a mixing bowl, combine water, egg substitute, yogurt and lemon peel; add dry cake mix. Beat on medium speed for 2 minutes. Pour into a greased and floured 10-in. fluted tube pan. Bake at 350° for 40-50 minutes or until a toothpick inserted near the center comes out clean. Cool for 10 minutes; remove from pan to a wire rack to cool completely. Combine sugar and lemon juice; drizzle over cake. Fill center of cake with strawberries. **Yield:** 14 servings. **Nutritional Analysis:** One serving equals 189 calories, 254 mg sodium, trace cholesterol, 38 gm carbohydrate, 4 gm protein, 3 gm fat. **Diabetic Exchanges:** 2 starch, 1/2 fruit, 1/2 fat. **Editor's Note:** Due to the egg substitute, this cake does not rise very high.

Strawberry Banana Split Cake

This scrumptious cake is so easy to make but so impressive to serve. I've used the recipe for potlucks, showers and birthdays. —*Joan Pacey Ennismore, Ontario*

2 cups graham cracker crumbs (about 32 squares)
1/2 cup butter *or* margarine, melted
1/4 cup sugar

FILLING:

1/2 cup butter *or* margarine, softened
2 cups confectioners' sugar
1 tablespoon milk
1 teaspoon vanilla extract
3 large firm bananas, cut into 1/4-inch slices
2 cans (8 ounces *each*) crushed pineapple, drained
2 quarts fresh strawberries, sliced

TOPPING:

2 cups whipping cream
1/4 cup confectioners' sugar
1-1/2 cups chopped walnuts

Combine the crumbs, butter and sugar; press into an ungreased 13-in. x 9-in. x 2-in. dish. Chill for 1 hour. In a mixing bowl, cream butter, confectioners' sugar, milk and vanilla. Spread over crust; chill for 30 minutes. Layer with bananas, pineapple and strawberries. In a small mixing bowl, beat cream until soft peaks form. Add confectioners' sugar; beat until stiff peaks form. Spread over fruit. Sprinkle with nuts. Chill until serving. **Yield:** 12-15 servings.

Ruby Grape Pie

My wife, Paula, and I produce red and green seedless table grapes on our 75-acre vineyard. Our crop is wonderful eaten out-of-hand or in salads. Paula also uses them in this unusual and tasty pie. —*Fred Smeds Reedley, California*

4 cups halved seedless red grapes (about 2 pounds)
2/3 cup sugar
1/2 teaspoon ground cinnamon
3 tablespoons cornstarch
2 tablespoons lemon juice
1 tablespoon grated lemon peel
Pastry for double-crust pie (9 inches)
2 tablespoons butter *or* margarine

In a saucepan, combine grapes, sugar and cinnamon; toss to coat. Let stand for 15 minutes. Combine cornstarch, lemon juice and peel; stir into grape mixture. Bring to a boil; cook and stir for 2 minutes or until thickened. Line a 9-in. pie plate with the bottom pastry. Add filling. Dot with butter. Roll out remaining pastry to fit top of pie; place over filling. Trim, seal and flute edges; cut slits in top. Cover edges loosely with foil. Bake at 425° for 20 minutes. Reduce heat to 350°; remove foil and bake 30-35 minutes longer or until the crust is golden brown. Cool on a wire rack. **Yield:** 6-8 servings.

Frosted Brownie Pizza

(Pictured below)

It's impossible to eat just one piece of this dessert pizza with a chewy, chocolaty crust, creamy peanut butter frosting and mouth-watering sweet and crunchy toppings. —*Paula Riehl, Boise, Idaho*

1/2 cup butter (no substitutes)
2 squares (1 ounce *each*) unsweetened chocolate
1 cup sugar
3/4 cup all-purpose flour
2 eggs, beaten

FROSTING:

1 cup confectioners' sugar
1/3 cup creamy peanut butter
1-1/2 teaspoons vanilla extract
2 to 4 tablespoons milk

TOPPINGS:

3/4 cup plain M&M's
1/2 cup flaked coconut, toasted
1/2 cup chopped pecans, toasted

In a saucepan over low heat, melt butter, chocolate and sugar. Remove from the heat; stir in flour until smooth. Add eggs and beat until smooth. Spread onto a greased 12-in. pizza pan. Bake at 350° for 15 minutes or until a toothpick inserted near the center comes out clean. Cool completely. For frosting, in a mixing bowl, beat sugar, peanut butter, vanilla and enough milk to achieve desired spreading consistency. Spread over brownie crust. Top with the M&M's, coconut and pecans. **Yield:** 8-10 servings.

Strawberry Heart Cake

(Pictured below)

My granddaughter, Leslie, was born on Valentine's Day, so every year I bake up this special strawberry heart-shaped cake for her. We love the berries folded right into the batter. It's a delightful dessert.
—Patricia Rutherford, Winchester, Illinois

1 package (18-1/4 ounces) white cake mix
1 package (3 ounces) strawberry gelatin
3 tablespoons all-purpose flour
1/3 cup vegetable oil
4 eggs
1 package (10 ounces) frozen sweetened strawberries, thawed
1/2 cup cold water
1/2 cup butter *or* margarine, softened
5 to 5-1/2 cups confectioners' sugar
Red-hot candies, optional

In a mixing bowl, combine cake mix, gelatin and flour. Beat in oil and eggs. Drain strawberries, reserving 1/2 cup syrup for frosting. Add berries and water to batter; mix well. Divide batter between two waxed paper-lined 8-in. baking pans, one square and one round. Bake at 350° for 30-35 minutes (square) and 35-40 minutes (round) or until cake tests done. Cool for 10 minutes; remove from pans to wire racks to cool completely. In a small mixing bowl, combine butter and reserved syrup. Gradually add sugar; beat until light and fluffy, about 2 minutes. Place square cake diagonally on a 20-in. x 15-in. covered board. Cut round cake in half. Frost cut sides; place frosted sides against the top two sides of square cake, forming a heart. Frost sides and top of cake. Decorate with red-hots if desired. **Yield:** 12-16 servings.

Cherry Puddles Cake

(Pictured on page 136)

This lovely, distinctive cake is a satisfying treat. The "puddle" of cherries in each slice makes it special.
—Shirley Kidd, New London, Minnesota

✓ Uses less fat, sugar or salt. Includes Nutritional Analysis and Diabetic Exchanges.

1/2 cup butter *or* margarine, softened
1 cup sugar
1/2 cup buttermilk
Egg substitute equivalent to 4 eggs
1 tablespoon lemon juice
1 teaspoon vanilla extract
2 cups all-purpose flour
1 teaspoon baking soda
1 can (20 ounces) light cherry pie filling
Confectioners' sugar, optional

In a mixing bowl, cream butter and sugar. Beat in buttermilk, egg substitute, lemon juice and vanilla. Combine flour and baking soda; add to the creamed mixture. Pour into a 13-in. x 9-in. x 2-in. baking pan coated with nonstick cooking spray. Use a knife to divide batter into 24 rectangles; spoon a small amount of pie filling into the center of each. Bake at 350° for 35 minutes or until a toothpick inserted near the center comes out clean. Dust with confectioners' sugar if desired. **Yield:** 24 servings. **Nutritional Analysis:** One serving (prepared with margarine and without confectioners' sugar) equals 134 calories, 123 mg sodium, trace cholesterol, 21 gm carbohydrate, 3 gm protein, 4 gm fat. **Diabetic Exchanges:** 1-1/2 starch, 1 fat.

Tiny Shortbread Tarts

These tasty little tarts are nice for a family—kids love having their own tiny pies. For company, I use a variety of fillings and arrange them on a pretty platter.
—Kim Marie Van Rheenen, Mendota, Illinois

1 cup butter *or* margarine, softened
1/2 cup confectioners' sugar
2 cups all-purpose flour

1 can (21 ounces) raspberry, cherry *or* strawberry pie filling

In a mixing bowl, cream butter and sugar. Add flour; mix well. Shape into 1-in. balls; press onto the bottom and up the sides of greased miniature muffin cups. Bake at 300° for 17-22 minutes. Cool for 15 minutes; carefully remove from pans. Spoon 1 teaspoon of pie filling into each tart. **Yield:** about 3 dozen.

Chocolate Raspberry Layer Cake

This recipe pulls together some of my favorite flavors. It's delicious, practically foolproof and looks beautiful. Impress dinner guests with this pretty cake.
—Robert Ulis, Alexandria, Virginia

1 package (18-1/4 ounces) yellow cake mix
1 cup (6 ounces) semisweet chocolate chips
2 tablespoons milk
1/2 to 1 teaspoon almond extract
1 carton (8 ounces) frozen whipped topping, thawed
1/3 cup raspberry jam *or* preserves

Bake cake according to package directions, using two greased and floured 9-in. round baking pans. Cool for 10 minutes; remove from pans to wire racks to cool completely. In a microwave or double boiler, melt chocolate chips; stir in milk and extract. Fold in whipped topping. Place one cake layer on a serving plate. Spread with raspberry jam. Top with second cake layer. Frost top and sides with chocolate topping. Store in the refrigerator. **Yield:** 8-10 servings.

Cherry Cheese Pizza

(Pictured above right and on page 136)

This dessert pizza is a great way to use cherries—my family likes it better than cherry pie. Each bite just melts in your mouth. People who sample it rave about this "sweet" pizza. When my neighbor tried a piece, she couldn't stop saying "Mmm..." the entire time she was eating.
—Elaine Darbyshire
Golden, British Columbia

1 cup all-purpose flour
1/8 teaspoon baking powder
1/4 cup cold butter *or* margarine
2 tablespoons shortening
3 to 4 tablespoons water
1 package (8 ounces) cream cheese, softened
1/2 cup sugar

2 eggs
1 teaspoon vanilla extract
1/3 cup chopped pecans *or* almonds

TOPPING:

2-1/2 cups fresh *or* frozen pitted tart cherries *or* 1 can (15 *or* 16 ounces) pitted tart cherries
1/3 cup sugar
2 tablespoons cornstarch
1 tablespoon butter *or* margarine
1/8 teaspoon almond extract
1/8 teaspoon red food coloring
Whipped cream and fresh mint, optional

In a bowl, combine flour and baking powder; cut in butter and shortening until mixture resembles coarse crumbs. Gradually add water, tossing with a fork until dough forms a ball. Roll out into a 14-in. circle. Place on an ungreased 12-in. pizza pan. Flute edges to form a rim; prick bottom of crust. Bake at 350° for 15 minutes. In a mixing bowl, beat cream cheese and sugar until smooth. Beat in eggs and vanilla. Stir in nuts. Spread over crust. Bake 10 minutes longer. Cool. Drain cherries, reserving 1/3 cup juice. Set the cherries and juice aside. In a saucepan, combine sugar and cornstarch; stir in reserved juice until smooth. Add cherries. Cook and stir over medium heat until mixture comes to a boil. Cook and stir 2 minutes longer. Remove from the heat; stir in butter, extract and food coloring. Cool to room temperature; spread over cream cheese layer. Garnish with whipped cream and mint if desired. **Yield:** 10-12 slices.

Tin Roof Fudge Pie

(Pictured above and on page 136)

This delectable pie makes a great hostess gift for a holiday get-together or a wonderful ending to a meal for company. —*Cynthia Kolberg, Syracuse, Indiana*

2 squares (1 ounce *each*) semisweet baking chocolate
1 tablespoon butter (no substitutes)
1 pastry shell (9 inches), baked
PEANUT LAYER:
20 caramels
1/3 cup whipping cream
1-1/2 cups salted peanuts
CHOCOLATE LAYER:
8 squares (1 ounce *each*) semisweet baking chocolate
2 tablespoons butter (no substitutes)
1 cup whipping cream
2 teaspoons vanilla extract
Whipped cream and salted peanuts, optional
TOPPING:
3 caramels
5 teaspoons whipping cream
1 tablespoon butter (no substitutes)

In a microwave or double boiler, melt chocolate and butter. Spread onto the bottom and up the sides of crust; refrigerate until the chocolate is set. In a saucepan over low heat, melt caramels and cream, stirring frequently until smooth. Remove from the heat; stir in peanuts. Spoon into pie shell; refrigerate. In a small saucepan over low heat, melt chocolate and butter. Remove from the heat; let stand 15 minutes. Meanwhile, in a mixing bowl, beat cream and vanilla until soft peaks form. Carefully fold a third of the whipped cream into the chocolate mixture; fold in the remaining whipped cream. Spread over peanut layer; refrigerate until set. Garnish with whipped cream and peanuts if desired. In a small saucepan over low heat, melt caramels, cream and butter. Drizzle over pie. Refrigerate until serving. **Yield:** 8-10 servings.

Cranberry Snack Cake

I remember scrambling to write this recipe down while listening to a radio call-in show. The way they described it made it sound irresistible. I was pleased when it tasted as good as it sounded. —*Vicki Raatz Waterloo, Wisconsin*

1/2 cup butter *or* margarine, softened
1 cup sugar
2 eggs
1 teaspoon vanilla extract
1-1/2 cups all-purpose flour
2 teaspoons baking powder
1/2 teaspoon salt
3/4 cup milk
1-1/2 cups fresh *or* frozen cranberries, chopped
TOPPING:
1-1/2 cups miniature marshmallows
1/2 cup packed brown sugar
1/2 cup chopped pecans
2 tablespoons butter *or* margarine, melted

In a mixing bowl, cream butter and sugar. Beat in eggs and vanilla. Combine flour, baking powder and salt; add to creamed mixture alternately with milk. Stir in cranberries. Pour into a greased 13-in. x 9-in. x 2-in. baking pan. Sprinkle with marshmallows; lightly press into batter. Sprinkle with the brown sugar and pecans. Drizzle with butter. Bake at 350° for 35-40 minutes or until a toothpick inserted near the center comes out clean. **Yield:** 12 servings.

Chocolate Zucchini Roll

I created this moist cake roll to use my garden zucchini. The combination of chocolate and zucchini is fantastic! —*Victoria Zmarzley-Hahn Northampton, Pennsylvania*

3 eggs
1 teaspoon vanilla extract
1 cup all-purpose flour
3/4 cup sugar

1/2 cup baking cocoa
1 teaspoon baking soda
1 teaspoon ground cinnamon
1/4 teaspoon salt
1 cup shredded peeled zucchini

FILLING:

1 package (8 ounces) cream cheese, softened
1/4 cup butter *or* margarine, softened
2 teaspoons vanilla extract
1 cup confectioners' sugar
Additional confectioners' sugar

In a mixing bowl, beat eggs and vanilla. Combine flour, sugar, cocoa, baking soda, cinnamon and salt; add to egg mixture and mix well. Stir in zucchini. Spread into a greased and waxed paper-lined 15-in. x 10-in. x 1-in. baking pan. Bake at 350° for 15-20 minutes or until cake springs back when lightly touched. Turn onto a linen towel dusted with confectioners' sugar. Peel off waxed paper. Roll up, jelly-roll style, starting with a short side. Cool on a wire rack. In a mixing bowl, beat cream cheese, butter and vanilla until fluffy. Beat in confectioners' sugar. Unroll cake; spread filling to within 1 in. of edges. Roll up again; dust with confectioners' sugar. Chill until serving. **Yield:** 10 servings.

Tart Cherry Pie

My aunt and I are diabetic. We both enjoy this yummy, fruity pie...and our friends even request this dessert when they come to visit. —Bonnie Johnson DeKalb, Illinois

✓ Uses less fat, sugar or salt. Includes Nutritional Analysis and Diabetic Exchanges.

2 cans (15 *or* 16 ounces *each*) pitted tart cherries
1 package (.8 ounce) cook-and-serve sugar-free vanilla pudding mix
1 package (.3 ounce) sugar-free cherry gelatin
Artificial sweetener equivalent to 4 teaspoons sugar
1 pastry shell (9 inches), baked

Drain cherries, reserving juice; set cherries aside. In a saucepan, combine cherry juice and dry pudding mix. Cook and stir until mixture comes to a boil and is thickened and bubbly. Remove from the heat; stir in gelatin powder and sweetener until dissolved. Stir in the cherries; transfer to pastry shell. Cool completely. Store in the refrigerator. **Yield:** 8 servings. **Nutritional Analysis:** One serving equals 176 calories, 293 mg sodium, 0 cholesterol, 24 gm carbohydrate, 3 gm protein, 8 gm fat. **Diabetic Exchanges:** 1 starch, 1/2 fruit, 1/2 fat.

Sunny Coconut Cake

(Pictured below)

I've been making this easy cake for over 15 years and get many requests for the recipe. —Annette Buckner Charlotte, North Carolina

2 cups (16 ounces) sour cream
2 cups sugar
1/4 cup orange juice
1 package (14 ounces) flaked coconut
1 package (18-1/4 ounces) yellow cake mix
1 package (3 ounces) orange gelatin
1 cup water
1/3 cup vegetable oil
2 eggs
1 cup whipping cream
1 can (11 ounces) mandarin oranges, well drained

In a mixing bowl, combine sour cream, sugar and orange juice. Beat in coconut. Cover and refrigerate. In another mixing bowl, combine dry cake mix, gelatin powder, water, oil and eggs; mix well. Pour into two greased and floured 9-in. round cake pans. Bake at 350° for 30-35 minutes or until cakes test done. Cool for 10 minutes; remove from pans to wire racks to cool completely. Split cakes in half. Set aside 1 cup of the coconut filling; spread remaining filling between cake layers. Refrigerate. Beat cream until stiff peaks form; fold into reserved filling. Frost top and sides of cake; garnish with oranges. Refrigerate until serving. **Yield:** 12-16 servings.

Fruitcake Is Festive and Fun

FOR fruitcake fans, the holidays would not be complete without this time-tested treat.

Chocolate Chip Fruitcake

(Pictured below)

Chocolate chips tempt even those who don't care for fruitcake to try this one. By mixing up a few ingredients, you can make this festive dessert in no time.
—Ruth Peterson, Jenison, Michigan

3 eggs
1 cup sugar
1-1/2 cups all-purpose flour
1-1/2 teaspoons baking powder
1/4 teaspoon salt
2 cups coarsely chopped pecans
1 cup chopped dates
1 cup halved candied cherries
2/3 cup semisweet chocolate chips

In a mixing bowl, beat eggs and sugar. Combine flour, baking powder and salt; add to sugar mixture

TRADITIONAL TREATS come in a tasty variety of types, such as Southern Fruitcake, Miniature Fruitcakes and Chocolate Chip Fruitcake (shown above, clockwise from upper right).

and mix well. Fold in pecans, dates, cherries and chocolate chips. Pour into a greased 9-in. x 5-in. x 3-in. loaf pan. Bake at 325° for 1-1/4 to 1-1/2 hours or until golden brown and a toothpick inserted near the center comes out clean. Cool for 10 minutes; remove from pan to a wire rack to cool completely. **Yield:** 1 loaf.

Miniature Fruitcakes

(Pictured at left)

I've been using this recipe for 40 years, and it never fails to please. The serving-size cakes make great gifts.
—Ruth Burrus, Zionsville, Indiana

3/4 cup sugar
1/4 cup all-purpose flour
1/2 teaspoon baking powder
1/8 teaspoon salt
1-1/2 cups chopped walnuts
1 cup chopped dates
3/4 cup chopped mixed candied fruit (about 4 ounces)
2 eggs, *separated*
1/2 teaspoon vanilla extract
Halved candied cherries

In a bowl, combine the first seven ingredients. Combine egg yolks and vanilla; stir into dry ingredients. In a small mixing bowl, beat egg whites until stiff peaks form; fold into batter. Fill greased and floured muffin cups two-thirds full. Cover the muffin tin tightly with heavy-duty aluminum foil. Bake at 275° for 1 hour. Uncover; top each fruitcake with cherries. Bake 5 minutes longer or until a toothpick inserted near the center comes out clean. Cool for 5 minutes. Run a knife around the edges of each cup; remove to a wire rack to cool completely. **Yield:** 1 dozen.

Southern Fruitcake

(Pictured at left)

I've never found anyone who doesn't like this lovely fruitcake. The recipe makes two loaves—one to keep and one to share.
—Ruth Marie Lyons Boulder, Colorado

4 cups chopped pecans
1-3/4 cups chopped candied pineapple
1-1/2 cups chopped dried peaches *or* apricots
1-1/2 cups golden raisins
2 cups all-purpose flour, *divided*
1 cup butter *or* margarine, softened
1 cup packed brown sugar
5 eggs
1 cup peach *or* apricot nectar, *divided*
1/2 cup honey
1/4 cup milk
1-1/2 teaspoons ground cinnamon
3/4 teaspoon baking powder
1/2 teaspoon salt
1/2 teaspoon ground allspice

Grease and flour two 9-in. x 5-in. x 3-in. loaf pans. Line the bottoms with waxed paper; grease and flour the paper. Set aside. Combine the pecans, pineapple, peaches, raisins and 1/2 cup flour; set aside. In a mixing bowl, cream butter and brown sugar; add the eggs, one at a time, beating well after each addition. Add 1/2 cup peach nectar, honey and milk; beat well (mixture will appear curdled). Combine cinnamon, baking powder, salt, allspice and remaining flour; add to the creamed mixture and mix well. Add pecan mixture; stir well. Pour into prepared pans. Bake at 325° for 1-1/2 hours or until a toothpick inserted near the center comes out clean. Cool for 10 minutes. With a skewer, poke holes in the loaves. Spoon remaining nectar over loaves. Let stand for 10 minutes; remove from pans to a wire rack to cool completely. Wrap tightly and store in a cool place. Slice and bring to room temperature before serving. **Yield:** 2 loaves.

No-Bake Fruitcake

Because this fruitcake doesn't need to be baked, you can keep your oven free for other holiday baking.
—Joy Maynard, St. Ignatius, Montana

1 can (5 ounces) evaporated milk
1/3 cup orange juice concentrate
2 cups miniature marshmallows
1 package (13-1/2 ounces) graham cracker crumbs (4 cups)
1 cup raisins
1 cup chopped mixed candied fruit
1 cup chopped walnuts
3/4 cup chopped dates
1/4 cup halved candied cherries
1 teaspoon ground cinnamon
1 teaspoon ground nutmeg
1/2 teaspoon ground cloves

Line a 9-in. x 5-in. x 3-in. loaf pan with waxed paper; coat the paper with nonstick cooking spray. Set aside. In a saucepan, combine milk and orange juice concentrate. Add marshmallows; cook and stir until marshmallows are melted and mixture is smooth. Remove from the heat. Stir in remaining ingredients; mix well. Pat into prepared pan. Cover and refrigerate for at least 8 hours. **Yield:** 1 loaf.

JUST DESSERTS. Go for the goodies with sweet ideas like Mint Brownies and Lemon Meringue Torte (shown above).

Mint Brownie Pie

(Pictured above and on back cover)

When I served this treat to my family on St. Patrick's Day, it was an instant success. The cool creamy filling goes well with the rich chocolate crust.
—Karen Hayes, Conneaut Lake, Pennsylvania

- **6 tablespoons butter (no substitutes)**
- **2 squares (1 ounce *each*) unsweetened chocolate**
- **1 cup sugar**
- **2 eggs, beaten**
- **1/2 teaspoon vanilla extract**
- **1/2 cup all-purpose flour**

FILLING:

- **1 package (8 ounces) cream cheese, softened**
- **3/4 cup sugar**
- **1/2 teaspoon peppermint extract**
- **Green food coloring, optional**
- **1 carton (8 ounces) frozen whipped topping, thawed**
- **1/4 cup semisweet chocolate chips, melted**
- **Additional whipped topping and chocolate chips, optional**

In a saucepan, melt butter and chocolate. Stir in sugar until well blended. Add eggs and vanilla; mix well. Stir in flour until well blended. Pour into a greased 9-in. springform pan. Bake at 350° for 18-20 minutes or until a toothpick inserted near the center comes out clean. Cool on a wire rack. In a mixing bowl, beat cream cheese and sugar until smooth. Add extract and food coloring if desired; mix well. Fold in whipped topping. Spread evenly over brownie layer. Cover and refrigerate for at least 1 hour. Remove sides of pan just before serving. Melt chocolate chips; drizzle over the top. Garnish with whipped topping and chocolate chips if desired. **Yield:** 8 servings.

Lemon Meringue Torte

(Pictured at left and on back cover)

I copied this recipe from a notebook that my grandmother compiled as a teenager. Its old-fashioned goodness has stood the test of time.
—Sue Gronholz
Columbus, Wisconsin

- **1/2 cup shortening**
- **1/2 cup sugar**
- **4 egg yolks**
- **6 tablespoons milk**
- **1 cup all-purpose flour**
- **1 teaspoon baking powder**

FILLING:

- **1 cup sugar**
- **3 tablespoons cornstarch**
- **1 cup cold water**
- **2 egg yolks, beaten**
- **1 tablespoon butter *or* margarine**
- **3 tablespoons lemon juice**
- **1 tablespoon grated lemon peel**

TOPPING:
- **6 egg whites**
- **3/4 cup sugar**
- **2 teaspoons ground cinnamon**
- **1 cup slivered almonds**

In a mixing bowl, cream shortening and sugar. Beat in egg yolks and milk. Combine flour and baking powder; add to the creamed mixture and mix well. Spread into a greased 13-in. x 9-in. x 2-in. baking pan. Bake at 350° for 15 minutes or until a toothpick inserted near the center comes out clean. In a saucepan, combine sugar and cornstarch; stir in water until smooth. Bring to a boil over medium heat; cook and stir for 1 minute. Remove from the heat. Stir a small amount into egg yolks; return all to pan. Cook over medium heat for 2 minutes. Remove from the heat. Add butter, lemon juice and peel; set aside. In a small mixing bowl, beat the egg whites until soft peaks form. Gradually add sugar, beating until stiff peaks form. Beat in cinnamon. Fold in almonds. Spread hot filling over the crust. Spread topping over filling. Bake at 350° for 15 minutes or until lightly browned. Cool on a wire rack. Store in the refrigerator. **Yield:** 16 servings.

Brownie Snack Cake

Even if you're on a restricted diet, you can have your cake and eat it, too, with this luscious, easy-to-prepare chocolate dessert. *—Gessica Brown Rochester, Indiana*

 Uses less fat, sugar or salt. Includes Nutritional Analysis and Diabetic Exchanges.

- **4 egg whites**
- **1/4 cup vegetable oil**
- **2 teaspoons vanilla extract**
- **1/2 cup all-purpose flour**
- **1/2 cup sugar**
- **1/2 cup packed brown sugar**
- **1/2 cup baking cocoa**
- **1/2 teaspoon baking powder**
- **Confectioners' sugar**

In a mixing bowl, beat egg whites until foamy. Add oil and vanilla. Combine flour, sugars, cocoa and baking powder; gradually stir into the egg mixture. Transfer to an 8-in. square baking pan coated with nonstick cooking spray. Bake at 350° for 15-20 minutes or until the center is set. Cool on a wire rack. Dust with confectioners' sugar. **Yield:** 16 servings. **Nutritional Analysis:** One serving equals 106 calories, 32 mg sodium, 0 cholesterol, 18 gm carbohydrate, 2 gm protein, 4 gm fat. **Diabetic Exchanges:** 1 starch, 1 fat.

'I Wish I Had That Recipe...'

FROM Bismarck, Missouri, Dawn Mangan writes, "What I remember most about a wonderful lunch at The Elsah Landing Restaurant near my hometown of Alton, Illinois is the Ozark Mountain Berry Pie I had for dessert.

Contacting owner Helen Crafton, we learned that after operating for 23 years at Elsah, Illinois on the Mississippi, she moved her restaurant 4 miles upriver to a larger site in Grafton. There she continues to delight patrons with a made-from-scratch menu, including the pie Dawn recalls.

"The recipe for Ozark Mountain Pie was sent to us by a woman who dined with us and said her aunt had a recipe that we should use," relates Helen. "It's one of our most popular desserts."

The Elsah Landing Restaurant, at 420 E. Main St. in Grafton, is open 11:30 a.m. to 7:30 p.m. Tuesday through Sunday and from 11:30 a.m. to 4 p.m. on federal holiday Mondays. Phone: 1-618/786-7687.

Ozark Mountain Berry Pie

- **1-1/2 cups sugar**
- **4 tablespoons plus 1-1/2 teaspoons cornstarch**
- **3/4 cup cold water**
- **3 tablespoons lemon juice**
- **3 cups fresh blueberries**
- **1 cup fresh raspberries**
- **1 cup fresh blackberries**
- **Pastry for double-crust pie (9 inches)**

In a saucepan, combine sugar and cornstarch. Stir in water and lemon juice until smooth. Add berries; stir gently. Bring to a boil over medium heat; cook and stir for 2 minutes or until thickened and bubbly. Remove from the heat; cool. Line a 9-in. pie plate with the bottom pastry. Add filling. Roll out remaining pastry; make a lattice crust. Seal and flute edges. Cover edges loosely with foil. Bake at 400° for 10 minutes. Reduce heat to 350°. Remove foil; bake 40-50 minutes longer or until crust is golden brown and filling is bubbly. Cool completely. **Yield:** 6-8 servings.

Peanut Butter Pie

(Pictured below)

I entered this pie in our county fair, and it was selected Grand Champion! Who can resist a tempting chocolate crumb crust and a creamy filling with big peanut butter taste? Be prepared to take home an empty pan when you serve this pie. —*Doris Doherty, Albany, Oregon*

CRUST:
1-1/4 cups chocolate cookie crumbs (20 cookies)
1/4 cup sugar
1/4 cup butter *or* margarine, melted
FILLING:
1 package (8 ounces) cream cheese, softened
1 cup creamy peanut butter
1 cup sugar
1 tablespoon butter *or* margarine, softened
1 teaspoon vanilla extract
1 cup whipping cream, whipped
Grated chocolate *or* chocolate cookie crumbs, optional

Combine crust ingredients; press into a 9-in. pie plate. Bake at 375° for 10 minutes. Cool. In a mixing bowl, beat cream cheese, peanut butter, sugar, butter and vanilla until smooth. Fold in whipped cream. Gently spoon into crust. Garnish with chocolate or cookie crumbs if desired. Refrigerate. **Yield:** 8-10 servings.

White Chocolate Berry Pie

When strawberries are in season, I make this pretty pie. There are fresh berries in each luscious bite. —*Connie Laux, Englewood, Ohio*

5 squares (1 ounce *each*) white baking chocolate, *divided*
2 tablespoons milk
1 package (3 ounces) cream cheese, softened
1/3 cup confectioners' sugar
1 teaspoon grated orange peel
1 cup whipping cream, whipped
1 graham cracker crust (9 inches)
2 cups sliced fresh strawberries

In a microwave or double boiler, melt four squares of chocolate with milk. Cool to room temperature. Meanwhile, beat cream cheese and sugar in a mixing bowl until smooth. Beat in orange peel and melted chocolate. Fold in whipped cream. Spread into crust. Arrange strawberries on top. Melt remaining chocolate; drizzle over berries. Refrigerate for at least 1 hour. Store in the refrigerator. **Yield:** 8 servings.

Pretty Pineapple Torte

For delightful fare with tropical flair, pineapple is perfect all year long. In this beautiful dessert, it stars in both the cake and filling. It's creamy and just slightly sweet. —*Iola Egle, McCook, Nebraska*

1/2 cup butter *or* margarine, softened
1 cup sugar, *divided*
3 eggs, *separated*
1 can (20 ounces) crushed pineapple
1 teaspoon vanilla extract
2-1/2 cups cake flour
2 teaspoons baking powder
1/2 teaspoon baking soda
1/2 teaspoon salt
FILLING:
1-1/2 cups whipping cream
1/4 cup confectioners' sugar
1/2 teaspoon almond extract
2 tablespoons slivered almonds, toasted

In a large mixing bowl, cream butter and 3/4 cup sugar. Beat in egg yolks. Drain pineapple, reserving 2/3 cup juice (discard remaining juice or save for another use). In a bowl, combine juice, 3/4 cup pineapple and vanilla (set remaining pineapple aside for the filling). Combine dry ingredients; add to the creamed mixture alternately with the pineapple mixture. In a small mixing bowl, beat egg whites until soft peaks form. Add remaining sugar, 1 tablespoon at a time, beating until stiff peaks form. Fold a fourth of the egg whites into batter; fold in remaining egg whites. Spoon into two greased and floured 9-in. round cake pans. Bake at 350° for 28-32 minutes or until cake springs back when lightly touched. Cool for 10 minutes; remove from pans to wire racks to cool completely. For filling, beat the cream, sugar and extract in a mixing bowl until stiff peaks form. Fold in reserved pineapple. Split each cake layer in half horizontally. Spread about 3/4 cup filling between each layer; spread remaining filling over the top. Sprinkle with almonds. **Yield:** 10-12 servings.

Homemade Angel Food Cake

This tall old-fashioned cake is just slightly sweet. Whipped cream and a hint of chocolate assure each slice is extra delightful. *—Joan Schroeder, Pinedale, Wyoming*

1 cup cake flour
1 cup confectioners' sugar
1-1/2 cups egg whites (about 12)
1 teaspoon cream of tartar
Pinch salt
1 teaspoon vanilla extract
1-1/4 cups sugar
FROSTING:
1 plain milk chocolate candy bar (7 ounces)
2 cups whipping cream
3 tablespoons confectioners' sugar
1 teaspoon vanilla extract
Chocolate shavings, optional

Sift flour and confectioners' sugar together twice; set aside. In a mixing bowl, beat egg whites, cream of tartar and salt on medium speed until soft peaks form. Add vanilla. Gradually beat in sugar, about 2 tablespoons at a time, until stiff peaks form, scraping bowl occasionally. Gradually fold in flour mixture, about 1/2 cup at a time. Pour into an ungreased 10-in. tube pan. Bake at 325° for 50-60 minutes or until lightly browned and entire top appears dry. Immediately invert cake pan onto a wire rack; cool completely, about 1 hour. For frosting, melt the candy bar in a microwave or double boiler; cool for 5 minutes. In a mixing bowl, beat cream and sugar until stiff peaks form; stir in vanilla. Fold in melted chocolate. Run a knife around sides of cake and remove to a serving plate; frost top and sides. Garnish with chocolate shavings if desired. Store in the refrigerator. **Yield:** 12-16 servings.

Candy Apple Pie

(Pictured above)

This is the only apple pie my husband will eat, but that's all right since he makes it as often as I do. Like a combination of apple and pecan pie, it's a sweet treat that usually tops off our holiday meals year-round. *—Cindy Kleweno, Burlington, Colorado*

6 cups thinly sliced peeled baking apples
2 tablespoons lime juice
3/4 cup sugar
1/4 cup all-purpose flour
1/2 teaspoon ground cinnamon *or* nutmeg
1/4 teaspoon salt
Pastry for double-crust pie (9 inches)
2 tablespoons butter *or* margarine
TOPPING:
1/4 cup butter *or* margarine
1/2 cup packed brown sugar
2 tablespoons whipping cream
1/2 cup chopped pecans

In a large bowl, toss apples with lime juice. Combine dry ingredients; add to the apples and toss lightly. Place bottom pastry in a 9-in. pie plate; fill with apple mixture. Dot with butter. Cover with top crust. Flute edges high; cut steam vents. Bake at 400° for 40-45 minutes or until golden brown and apples are tender. Meanwhile, for topping, melt butter in a small saucepan. Stir in brown sugar and cream; bring to a boil, stirring constantly. Remove from the heat and stir in pecans. Pour over top crust. Return to the oven for 3-4 minutes or until bubbly. Serve warm. **Yield:** 8 servings.

TEMPTING TASTES. Strawberry Meringue Cake and Cool Lime Pie (shown above) are sensational summer desserts.

Strawberry Meringue Cake

(Pictured above and on page 136)

Guests says "Wow!" when I present this torte. Mashed berries add flavor and color to the cream filling.
—Dorothy Anderson, Ottawa, Kansas

- **1 package (18-1/4 ounces) yellow cake mix**
- **1-1/3 cups orange juice**
- **4 eggs, *separated***
- **1-1/2 teaspoons grated orange peel**
- **1/4 teaspoon cream of tartar**
- **1 cup plus 1/4 cup sugar, *divided***
- **2 cups whipping cream**
- **2 pints fresh strawberries, *divided***

In a mixing bowl, combine dry cake mix, orange juice, egg yolks and orange peel. Beat on medium speed for 4 minutes. Pour into two greased and floured 9-in. round baking pans; set aside. In a mixing bowl, beat egg whites and cream of tartar on medium speed until foamy. Gradually beat in 1 cup sugar, a tablespoon at a time, on high until stiff glossy peaks form and sugar is dissolved. Spread the meringue evenly over cake batter. Bake at 350° for 35 minutes or until meringue is lightly browned. Cool in pans on wire racks (meringue will crack). Beat cream until stiff peaks form. Mash 1/2 cup of strawberries with remaining sugar; fold into whipped cream. Loosen edges of cakes from pans with a knife. Using two large spatulas, carefully remove one cake to a serving platter, meringue side up. Carefully spread with about two-thirds of the cream mixture. Slice the remaining berries; arrange half over cream mixture. Repeat layers. Store in the refrigerator. **Yield:** 12-16 servings.

Cool Lime Pie

(Pictured at left and on page 136)

This delightfully sweet-tart dessert is pretty to set on the table and so quick and easy to make.
—Waydella Hart, Parsons, Kansas

- **1 package (8 ounces) cream cheese, softened**
- **1 can (14 ounces) sweetened condensed milk**
- **6 ounces limeade concentrate**
- **4 drops green food coloring, optional**
- **1 carton (8 ounces) frozen whipped topping, thawed, *divided***
- **1 graham cracker crust (9 inches)**
- **1 kiwifruit, peeled and sliced**
- **Mandarin oranges and chopped pistachios, optional**

In a mixing bowl, beat cream cheese and milk until smooth. Add limeade and food coloring if desired. Fold in half of the whipped topping. Pour into crust. Cover and refrigerate for 2 hours. Garnish with kiwi, remaining whipped topping, and oranges and pistachios if desired. **Yield:** 6-8 servings.

Creamy Pineapple Pie

Friends at the medical clinic where I work as a com-

puter operator often ask me for the recipe for this pie. You can use either fresh or canned fruit to sample this refreshing treat. It's one of my special favorites.
—Bonnie Sandlin, Lakeland, Florida

1/4 cup sugar
3 tablespoons cornstarch
1-1/3 cups pineapple juice
1 egg yolk
2 cups fresh pineapple chunks (1/2-inch pieces)
1 pastry shell (9 inches), baked
1/4 cup flaked coconut, toasted

In a saucepan, combine sugar and cornstarch. Add pineapple juice; bring to a boil, stirring occasionally. Boil for 2 minutes. In a small bowl, beat egg yolk; stir in 1/4 cup of the hot mixture. Return all to pan; cook and stir for 1 minute. Remove from the heat; stir in pineapple. Pour into crust. Chill for 2 hours or until firm. Store in the refrigerator. Sprinkle with coconut just before serving. **Yield:** 6-8 servings. **Editor's Note:** Canned pineapple can be substituted for fresh. Use one 20-ounce can and one 8-ounce can of pineapple tidbits. Drain, reserving juice. Add additional pineapple juice if necessary to equal 1-1/3 cups. Prepare recipe as directed.

Applesauce Loaf Cake

Slices of this moist old-fashioned cake hold up well in a lunch bag. Kids of all ages will love it.
—Pamela Kelley, Downey, California

1-1/2 cups unsweetened applesauce
1 egg
1 cup sugar
2 tablespoons butter *or* margarine, softened
1 teaspoon vanilla extract
2 cups all-purpose flour
2 teaspoons baking soda
1/2 teaspoon ground cinnamon
1/4 teaspoon ground cloves
1/4 teaspoon ground nutmeg
1 cup raisins
1 cup chopped walnuts

In a mixing bowl, combine the first five ingredients. Combine flour, baking soda, cinnamon, cloves and nutmeg. Add to applesauce mixture; mix well. Stir in the raisins and walnuts. Pour into two greased 8-in. x 4-in. x 2-in. loaf pans. Bake at 350° for 45-55 minutes or until a toothpick inserted near the center comes out clean. Cool for 10 minutes before removing from pans to wire racks. **Yield:** 12-16 servings.

Sweet Potato Layer Cake

A true Southern classic, this cake is a hit at church functions and bake sales. I always get requests for the recipe. —Christy Shepard, Marion, North Carolina

1-1/2 cups vegetable oil
2 cups sugar
4 eggs, *separated*
1-1/2 cups finely shredded uncooked sweet potato (about 1 medium)
1/4 cup hot water
1 teaspoon vanilla extract
2-1/2 cups cake flour
3 teaspoons baking powder
1 teaspoon ground cinnamon
1 teaspoon ground nutmeg
1/4 teaspoon salt
1 cup chopped pecans

FROSTING:

1/2 cup butter *or* margarine
1-1/3 cups sugar
2 cans (5 ounces *each*) evaporated milk
4 egg yolks, beaten
2-2/3 cups flaked coconut
1 cup chopped pecans
2 teaspoons vanilla extract

In a mixing bowl, beat oil and sugar. Add egg yolks, one at a time, beating well after each addition. Add sweet potato, water and vanilla; mix well. In a small mixing bowl, beat egg whites until stiff; fold into sweet potato mixture. Combine flour, baking powder, cinnamon, nutmeg and salt; add to potato mixture. Stir in pecans. Pour into three greased 9-in. round cake pans. Bake at 350° for 22-27 minutes or until a toothpick inserted near the center comes out clean. Cool 10 minutes before removing to wire racks. For frosting, melt butter in a saucepan; whisk in sugar, milk and egg yolks until smooth. Cook and stir over medium heat for 10-12 minutes or until thickened and bubbly. Remove from the heat; stir in coconut, pecans and vanilla. Cool slightly. Place one cake layer on a serving plate; spread with a third of the frosting. Repeat layers. **Yield:** 10-12 servings.

We've Got You Covered

The more airtight a cake storage container, the longer the cake will stay fresh and moist. To ensure that your cake stays moist, cut an apple in half and put it in the storage container with the cake. If a cake becomes too dry, turn it into crumbs for topping fresh fruit, pudding or ice cream.

Pumpkin Chiffon Pie

(Pictured below)

Even those on restricted diets should be able to enjoy a good piece of pie once in a while. This creamy, wonderful dessert is a treat for the whole family. Folks are shocked to discover it's sugar-free and low in fat. —Marijean Ackers, Riverside, California

 Uses less fat, sugar or salt. Includes Nutritional Analysis and Diabetic Exchanges.

2-3/4 cups cold skim milk
2 packages (1.5 ounces *each*) instant sugar-free vanilla pudding mix
1 can (15 ounces) solid-pack pumpkin
1 teaspoon ground cinnamon
1/2 teaspoon ground ginger
1/4 teaspoon ground cloves
1 reduced-fat graham cracker crust (9 inches)
Light frozen whipped topping and additional cinnamon, optional

In a mixing bowl, combine the milk and pudding mix. Beat for 1 minute (the mixture will be thick). Add pumpkin and spices; beat 1 minute longer. Pour into pie crust. Cover and refrigerate for 2 hours or until firm. If desired, garnish with whipped topping and sprinkle with cinnamon. **Yield:** 8 servings. **Nutritional Analysis:** One serving (without garnish) equals 217 calories, 684 mg sodium, 1 mg cholesterol, 42 gm carbohydrate, 4 gm protein, 3 gm fat. **Diabetic Exchanges:** 2-1/2 starch, 1/2 fat.

German Chocolate Sauerkraut Cake

People who compliment me on this chocolaty treat are surprised to learn it's a sauerkraut cake. —Patricia Kile, Greentown, Pennsylvania

3/4 cup butter *or* margarine, softened
1-1/2 cups sugar
3 eggs
1 teaspoon vanilla extract
2 cups all-purpose flour
3/4 cup baking cocoa
1 teaspoon baking soda
1 teaspoon baking powder
1/4 teaspoon salt
1 cup water
1 cup sauerkraut, rinsed, drained, squeezed dry and finely chopped
2/3 cup flaked coconut
1/2 cup finely chopped pecans

FILLING/FROSTING:

2 cups (12 ounces) semisweet chocolate chips, melted
2/3 cup mayonnaise*
2/3 cup flaked coconut, *divided*
2/3 cup chopped pecans, *divided*

In a mixing bowl, cream butter and sugar. Add eggs, one at a time, beating well after each addition. Beat in vanilla. Combine dry ingredients; add to creamed mixture alternately with water. Stir in sauerkraut, coconut and pecans. Pour into three greased and floured 9-in. round baking pans. Bake at 350° for 20-24 minutes or until a toothpick inserted near the center comes out clean. Cool for 10 minutes before removing from pans to wire racks; cool completely. In a bowl, combine melted chocolate and mayonnaise. Set aside 1-1/4 cups for frosting. To the remaining chocolate mixture, add half of the coconut and pecans; spread between cake layers. Spread reserved chocolate mixture over top and sides of cake. Combine remaining coconut and pecans; press onto sides of cake. Store in the refrigerator. Slice with a serrated knife. **Yield:** 12-14 servings. ***Editor's Note:** Light or fat-free mayonnaise may not be substituted for regular mayonnaise.

Clove Apple Cake

This warm, spicy and sweet cake is a wonderful dessert

or coffee-break snack, especially topped with the creamy custard sauce. —*Kim Marie Van Rheenen Mendota, Illinois*

6 tablespoons butter *or* margarine, softened
3/4 cup sugar
1 teaspoon ground cloves
2 eggs
1-1/3 cups all-purpose flour
1 teaspoon baking powder
1/2 cup milk
1-1/2 cups chopped peeled tart apples
CUSTARD SAUCE:
1/4 cup sugar
2 tablespoons all-purpose flour
2 cups milk
1 egg, beaten
3 tablespoons butter *or* margarine, softened
1/2 teaspoon vanilla extract
Additional ground cloves, optional

In a mixing bowl, cream butter, sugar and cloves. Add eggs, one at a time, beating well after each addition. Combine flour and baking powder; add to creamed mixture alternately with milk. Fold in apples. Transfer to a greased and floured 9-in. round baking pan. Bake at 375° for 35-40 minutes or until a toothpick inserted near the center comes out clean. Cool on a wire rack. Meanwhile, in a saucepan, combine sugar, flour and milk until smooth. Bring to a boil over medium-high heat; cook and stir for 2 minutes or until thickened and bubbly. Remove from the heat. Stir a small amount into egg; return all to pan. Bring to a gentle boil. Reduce heat; cook and stir for 2 minutes. Remove from the heat; whisk in butter and vanilla. Serve over warm cake. Sprinkle with ground cloves if desired. **Yield:** 6-8 servings.

Packable Chocolate Chip Cake

Kids and adults like this moist cake dotted with chocolate chips. —*Barbara Hofstede, Waukesha, Wisconsin*

1 box (18-1/2 ounces) yellow cake mix with pudding
1 cup (8 ounces) sour cream
1/2 cup vegetable oil
1/4 cup water
4 eggs, lightly beaten
1 to 1-1/2 cups semisweet chocolate chips
Confectioners' sugar

In a mixing bowl, combine cake mix, sour cream, oil, water and eggs. Beat for 2 minutes. Fold in chocolate chips. Pour into a greased 10-in. fluted tube pan. Bake at 350° for 45-50 minutes or until cake tests done. Cool in pan for 20 minutes before removing to a wire rack. Just before serving, dust with confectioners' sugar. **Yield:** 12-16 servings.

Peach Berry Pie

(Pictured above)

I won a state fair pie contest with this pretty lattice-topped entry. It features a fresh-tasting trio of fruits. —*Maxine Griggs, Sedalia, Missouri*

1-1/2 cups sugar
1/4 cup all-purpose flour
2 tablespoons cornstarch
1/2 teaspoon salt
1/2 teaspoon ground nutmeg
1-3/4 cups sliced peeled fresh *or* frozen peaches, thawed and drained
3/4 cup fresh *or* frozen blueberries
3/4 cup fresh *or* frozen cranberries
1 teaspoon vanilla extract
Pastry for double-crust pie (9 inches)
1 tablespoon butter *or* margarine

In a large bowl, combine sugar, flour, cornstarch, salt and nutmeg. Add fruit and vanilla; toss to mix. Let stand for 15 minutes, stirring occasionally. Line a 9-in. pie plate with bottom pastry; add filling. Dot with butter. Roll out remaining pastry; make a lattice crust. Seal and flute edges. Bake at 375° for 50-55 minutes or until crust is golden brown and filling is bubbly. Cool on a wire rack. **Yield:** 6-8 servings.

Banana Squares

(Pictured above)

When we were first married, my husband was in the Navy. Stationed in Puerto Rico, we had banana trees growing in our yard, so I found ways to use dozens of ripe bananas at a time. These banana squares freeze well. —Susan Miller, Raleigh, North Carolina

2 eggs, *separated*
2/3 cup shortening
1-1/2 cups sugar
1 cup mashed ripe bananas (2 to 3 medium)
1-1/2 cups all-purpose flour
1 teaspoon baking soda
1/4 cup sour milk*
1/2 teaspoon vanilla extract
1/2 cup chopped walnuts, optional
Whipped cream and sliced bananas, optional

In a small mixing bowl, beat egg whites until soft peaks form; set aside. In a large mixing bowl, cream shortening and sugar. Beat in egg yolks; mix well. Add bananas. Combine flour and baking soda; add to creamed mixture alternately with milk, beating well after each addition. Add vanilla. Fold in egg whites. Fold in nuts if desired. Pour into a greased 13-in. x 9-in. x 2-in. baking pan. Bake at 350° for 45-50 minutes. Cool on a wire rack. If desired, garnish with a dollop of whipped cream and a few banana slices. **Yield:** 12-16 servings. ***Editor's Note:** To sour milk, place 1 teaspoon white vinegar in a measuring cup. Add enough milk to equal 1/4 cup.

Gooseberry Meringue Pie

This pie has a creamy filling dotted with tangy gooseberries. It's a dessert that draws compliments every time I serve it. —Mary Hand, Cleveland, Missouri

2 cups canned, fresh *or* frozen gooseberries
2 tablespoons water
1-1/2 cups sugar, *divided*
3 tablespoons cornstarch
1 cup milk
2 eggs, *separated*
1 pastry shell (9 inches), baked

In a covered saucepan over medium heat, cook gooseberries and water for 3-4 minutes or until tender. Stir in 3/4 cup of sugar; set aside. In another saucepan, combine 1/2 cup sugar and cornstarch. Gradually add milk until smooth; bring to a boil. Cook and stir over medium-high heat until thickened. Reduce heat; cook and stir 2 minutes longer. Remove from the heat. In a bowl, beat egg yolks. Gradually whisk a small amount of hot filling into yolks; return all to the pan. Bring to a gentle boil; cook and stir for 2 minutes. Remove from the heat; stir in gooseberry mixture. Pour into pastry shell. In a small mixing bowl, beat egg whites until soft peaks form. Gradually add remaining sugar, beating on high until stiff peaks form. Spread evenly over hot filling, sealing meringue to crust. Bake at 350° for 10-15 minutes or until golden. Store leftovers in the refrigerator. **Yield:** 6-8 servings.

Sugarless Applesauce Cake

My mother-in-law is a diabetic, so I made this cake for her birthday. —Kay Hale, Doniphan, Missouri

✓ Uses less fat, sugar or salt. Includes Nutritional Analysis and Diabetic Exchanges.

1 cup raisins
1 cup diced dried fruit
2 cups water
2 cups all-purpose flour
1 teaspoon baking soda
1/2 teaspoon salt
1/2 teaspoon ground nutmeg
1-1/2 teaspoons ground cinnamon
Egg substitute equivalent to 2 eggs
1 cup unsweetened applesauce
2 tablespoons liquid sweetener
3/4 cup vegetable oil

1 teaspoon vanilla extract
1/2 cup chopped nuts

Combine raisins, fruit and water in a saucepan; cook, uncovered, until water is evaporated and fruit is soft. Set aside to cool. Meanwhile, in a mixing bowl, combine flour, baking soda, salt, nutmeg and cinnamon. In another bowl, combine egg substitute, applesauce, sweetener, oil and vanilla. Add nuts and reserved fruit mixture. Stir into dry ingredients and blend thoroughly. Pour into a greased 10-in. fluted tube pan. Bake at 350° for 35-40 minutes or until the cake tests done. **Yield:** 32 servings. **Nutritional Analysis:** One serving equals 125 calories, 60 mg sodium, 0 mg cholesterol, 15 gm carbohydrate, 2 gm protein, 7 gm fat. **Diabetic Exchanges:** 1 fat, 1/2 starch, 1/2 fruit.

Zucchini Fudge Cake

Even those who don't care for zucchini will love it baked inside this luscious chocolaty cake.
—Robert Keith, Rochester, Minnesota

1 cup butter *or* margarine, softened
2-1/2 cups sugar
4 eggs
2 teaspoons vanilla extract
3 cups all-purpose flour
1/2 cup baking cocoa
2 teaspoons baking powder
1 teaspoon baking soda
3/4 teaspoon salt
1 cup buttermilk
3 cups shredded zucchini
3-1/2 cups prepared chocolate frosting

In a mixing bowl, cream butter and sugar. Add the eggs, one at a time, beating well after each addition. Beat in vanilla. Combine flour, cocoa, baking powder, baking soda and salt; add to the creamed mixture alternately with buttermilk. Stir in zucchini. Pour into three greased and floured 9-in. round baking pans. Bake at 350° for 25-30 minutes or until cakes test done. Cool for 10 minutes; remove from pans to wire racks to cool completely. Frost between layers and top and sides of cake. **Yield:** 12-14 servings.

Cinnamon-Apple Angel Food Cake

(Pictured at right)

This heavenly dessert is as light as a feather and melts in your mouth. The cinnamon-apple glaze is delightful. *—Marlys Benning, Wellsburg, Iowa*

1-1/2 cups egg whites (about 12 eggs)
1-1/2 teaspoons cream of tartar
1/4 teaspoon salt
1 cup sugar
1 teaspoon vanilla extract
1/2 teaspoon almond extract
1-1/2 cups confectioners' sugar
1 cup cake flour

GLAZE:

1/3 cup butter *or* margarine
2 cups confectioners' sugar
1/2 teaspoon ground cinnamon
3 to 4 tablespoons apple juice *or* cider

In a mixing bowl, beat egg whites, cream of tartar and salt on medium speed until soft peaks form. Add sugar, 2 tablespoons at a time, beating well after each addition; beat until smooth and glossy and stiff peaks form. Add extracts on low speed. Combine confectioners' sugar and flour; gently fold into egg mixture. Pour into an ungreased 10-in. tube pan. Bake on the lowest rack at 375° for 35-40 minutes or until top crust is golden brown and cracks feel dry. Immediately invert cake in pan to cool completely. Loosen sides of cake from pan and remove. For glaze, melt butter in a saucepan. Stir in the confectioners' sugar and cinnamon. Add apple juice slowly until glaze is thin enough to drizzle. Drizzle over cake. **Yield:** 12-16 servings.

Just Desserts

Folks will save room for dessert when these luscious cheesecakes, ice cream treats, candies and more are the flavorful finale.

FINISHING TOUCH. Clockwise from upper left: Honey Pineapple Sherbet (p. 168), Banana Split Supreme (p. 174), Cranberry Cheesecake and Chocolate Chip Cookie Dough Cheesecake (p. 170), Apple Danish Cheesecake (p. 162) and Tiny Cherry Cheesecakes (p. 169).

Chocolate Truffle Cheesecake

(Pictured above)

If you delight in the taste of chocolate, then this is the cheesecake for you. Every creamy bite melts in your mouth. It's so impressive yet not difficult to prepare—I whip up this dessert each time I want a yummy treat for my family, friends or co-workers. —Mary Jones Cumberland, Maine

1-1/2 cups chocolate wafer crumbs
2 tablespoons sugar
1/4 cup butter *or* margarine, melted
FILLING:
1/4 cup semisweet chocolate chips
1/4 cup whipping cream
3 packages (8 ounces *each*) cream cheese, softened
1 cup sugar
1/3 cup baking cocoa
3 eggs
1 teaspoon vanilla extract
TOPPING:
1-1/2 cups semisweet chocolate chips
1/4 cup whipping cream
1 teaspoon vanilla extract
Whipped cream and miniature chocolate kisses, optional

In a small bowl, combine cookie crumbs and sugar; stir in butter. Press onto the bottom and 1-1/2 in. up the sides of a greased 9-in. springform pan. Bake at 350° for 10 minutes. Cool on a wire rack. Reduce heat to 325°. In a saucepan over low heat, melt chocolate chips; stir until smooth. Remove from the heat; add cream and mix well. Set aside. In a mixing bowl, beat cream cheese and sugar until smooth. Add cocoa and beat well. Add eggs; beat on low just until combined. Stir in vanilla and reserved chocolate mixture just until blended. Pour over crust. Bake for 45-50 minutes or until center is almost set. For topping, melt chocolate chips in a saucepan over low heat, stirring until smooth. Remove from the heat. Stir in cream and vanilla; mix well. Spread over filling. Refrigerate overnight. Carefully run a knife around edge of pan to loosen. Remove sides of pan. Just before serving, garnish with whipped cream and miniature chocolate kisses if desired. **Yield:** 12 servings.

Rocky Road Fudge

Ever since my granddaughter Heather was little, she loved to work with me in the kitchen. We both enjoy making this fudge. She likes the variety of ingredients we can add, and I like that it's quick and easy to make. —Judy Bolton, Alpine, Utah

2 cups semisweet *or* milk chocolate chips
1 cup miniature marshmallows
1/2 cup crisp rice cereal
1/2 cup chopped walnuts
1/2 cup butterscotch chips, flaked coconut *or* raisins, optional

In a large microwave-safe bowl, melt chocolate chips on high for 1-1/2 minutes; stir. Microwave 30-40 seconds longer or until smooth. Blend in the marshmallows, cereal and walnuts. If desired, add butterscotch chips, coconut or raisins. Spread into a buttered foil-lined 8-in. square pan. Chill until firm. Lift out of the pan and remove the foil; cut into squares. **Yield:** about 1 pound. **Editor's Note:** This recipe was tested in an 850-watt microwave.

Say "Cheesecake"!

Disguise any cracks on top of your homemade cheesecake with slightly sweetened sour cream or whipped cream, assorted fresh berries or your favorite fruit jam or pie filling. You should only slice a chilled cheesecake. But for maximum flavor, allow the slices to stand at room temperature for 15 to 30 minutes before serving.

Chocolate Eclair Dessert

My father, who's diabetic, loves chocolate and baked goods. Our whole family can enjoy this beautiful mouth-watering dessert. —Owen Jack Hiatt Colorado Springs, Colorado

✓ Uses less fat, sugar or salt. Includes Nutritional Analysis and Diabetic Exchanges.

1 cup water
1/2 cup margarine
1 cup all-purpose flour
4 eggs
1 package (1.5 ounces) instant sugar-free vanilla pudding mix
2-3/4 cups skim milk
1 package (8 ounces) light cream cheese, softened
1/2 cup light chocolate syrup

In a saucepan, bring water and margarine to a boil, stirring constantly until margarine is melted. Reduce heat to low; add the flour. Stir vigorously with a wooden spoon until mixture leaves sides of pan and forms a smooth ball. Remove from the heat. Add eggs, one at a time, beating well after each addition until the batter becomes smooth. Spread into a greased and floured 13-in. x 9-in. x 2-in. baking pan. Bake at 400° for 30 minutes or until puffed and golden. Immediately remove from pan and cut in half horizontally. Cool completely. For filling, beat the pudding mix, milk and cream cheese in a mixing bowl until smooth. Just before serving, place the bottom eclair layer on a serving platter; cover with filling. Replace top layer and drizzle with chocolate syrup. **Yield:** 15 servings. **Nutritional Analysis:** One serving equals 175 calories, 312 mg sodium, 65 mg cholesterol, 15 gm carbohydrate, 6 gm protein, 10 gm fat. **Diabetic Exchanges:** 2 fat, 1 starch.

Tangy Lemon Cheesecake

(Pictured at right)

This dessert gets added spark from a gingersnap crust and a luscious lemon sauce. The mix of sweet and tart is unexpected and delightful. I came up with the recipe based on several others I encountered on a trip to California. —Pam Persons, Towanda, Kansas

2-1/2 cups crushed gingersnaps (about 40 cookies)
1/3 cup butter *or* margarine, melted

FILLING:

3 packages (8 ounces *each*) cream cheese, softened
1 cup sugar
3 eggs
1 tablespoon lemon juice
1 tablespoon vanilla extract

SAUCE:

1/2 cup sugar
2 tablespoons cornstarch
3/4 cup water
2 tablespoons butter *or* margarine
1/4 cup lemon juice
1 tablespoon grated lemon peel

In a small bowl, combine cookie crumbs and butter; mix well. Press onto the bottom and 2 in. up the sides of a greased 9-in. springform pan; set aside. In a mixing bowl, beat cream cheese and sugar until smooth. Add eggs; beat on low just until combined. Add lemon juice and vanilla; beat just until blended. Pour into crust. Bake at 350° for 35-40 minutes or until center is almost set. Cool on a wire rack for 10 minutes. Carefully run a knife around the edge of pan to loosen; cool 1 hour longer. In a saucepan, combine sugar and cornstarch. Stir in water until smooth; bring to a boil. Reduce heat; cook and stir over medium heat for 2 minutes or until thickened. Remove from the heat; stir in butter, lemon juice and peel. Refrigerate cheesecake and sauce overnight. Serve sauce over cheesecake. **Yield:** 12 servings.

Tropical Cheesecake

(Pictured below)

I don't bake many sweet items, but I like to put together this cheesecake for parties. The colorful fruit topping is refreshing, and the coconut gives each slice a delicious tropical taste. It looks pretty as part of a buffet. —Shawntel Kemp, Pickens, Oklahoma

1 cup flaked coconut
1/4 cup chopped almonds
2 tablespoons butter *or* margarine, melted

FILLING:
2 packages (8 ounces *each*) cream cheese, softened
1 cup sugar
3 tablespoons cornstarch
3 eggs
1 cup (8 ounces) sour cream
3 tablespoons lemon juice
2 teaspoons vanilla extract
1/4 teaspoon almond extract

TOPPING:
1/3 cup apricot preserves
1/2 cup pineapple tidbits
2 to 4 kiwifruit, peeled, sliced and halved
1/4 to 3/4 cup flaked coconut, toasted

In a small bowl, combine coconut and almonds; stir in butter. Press onto the bottom of a greased 9-in. springform pan. Bake at 350° for 10 minutes. Cool on a wire rack. In a mixing bowl, beat cream cheese and sugar until smooth. Add cornstarch and beat well. Add eggs; beat on low just until combined. Add sour cream, lemon juice and extracts; beat just until blended. Pour over crust. Bake at 350° for 45-50 minutes or until center is almost set. Cool on a wire rack for 1 hour. Refrigerate overnight. Remove sides of pan. In a small saucepan, heat preserves, stirring to break up any apricot pieces. Arrange the pineapple and kiwi on top of cheesecake. Brush preserves over fruit and on sides of cheesecake. Press coconut onto the sides of the cheesecake. Chill until serving. **Yield:** 10-12 servings.

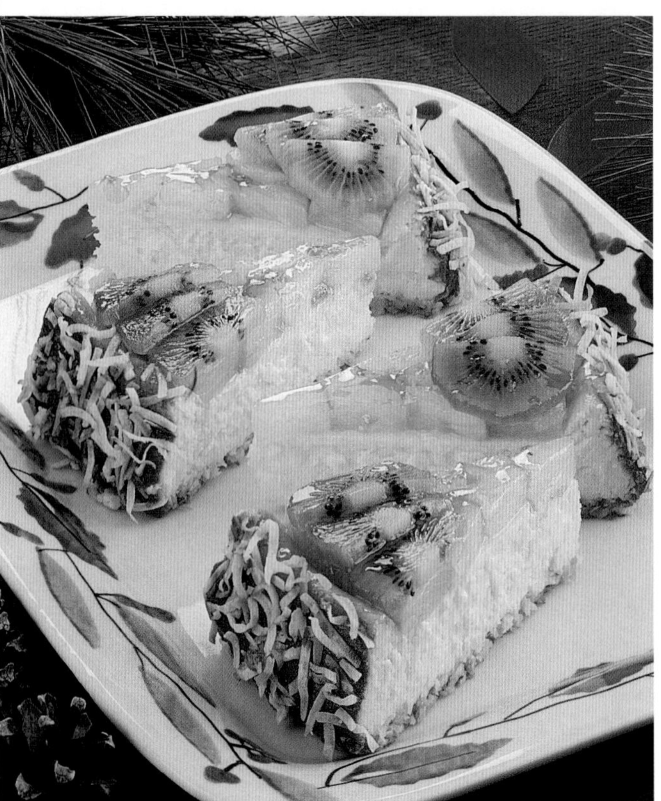

Strawberry Cheesecake Trifle

For a fantastic finale, this trifle makes any meal a special one. Because it is best made ahead so the flavors can blend, there's no last-minute fuss.
—Marnie Stoughton, Glenburnie, Ontario

2 pints fresh strawberries, sliced
1 cup sugar, *divided*
2 packages (8 ounces *each*) cream cheese, softened
3 tablespoons orange juice
3 cups whipping cream, whipped
1 loaf (10-3/4 ounces) frozen pound cake, thawed and cut into 1/2-inch cubes
3 squares (1 ounce *each*) semisweet chocolate, grated
Chocolate curls and additional strawberries, optional

In a bowl, toss strawberries with 1/2 cup sugar; set aside. In a mixing bowl, beat cream cheese, orange juice and remaining sugar until smooth. Fold in the whipped cream; set aside. Drain strawberries, reserving the juice; set the berries aside. Gently toss cake cubes with reserved juice. Place half of the cake in a 4-qt. trifle dish or serving bowl. Top with a third of the cream cheese mixture, half of the strawberries and half of the grated chocolate. Repeat layers. Top with remaining cream cheese mixture. Garnish with chocolate curls and strawberries if desired. Cover and refrigerate for at least 4 hours. **Yield:** 14-16 servings.

Cran-Apple Crisp

In this version of the ever-popular apple crisp, cranberries are the featured fruit. Topped with a scoop of ice cream, this fresh-from-oven dessert will earn you rave reviews. —Valerie Jones, Portland, Maine

4 medium tart apples, peeled and chopped
2 cups fresh *or* frozen cranberries
1 cup sugar
1-1/2 teaspoons lemon juice
1-1/2 cups quick-cooking oats
1 cup chopped walnuts
1/2 cup butter *or* margarine, melted
1/3 cup packed brown sugar
Vanilla ice cream, optional

Combine apples and cranberries in a greased 11-in. x 7-in. x 2-in. baking dish. Sprinkle with sugar and lemon juice. Toss oats, walnuts, butter and sugar; sprinkle over fruit. Bake at 325° for 1 hour or until golden brown. Serve warm with ice cream if desired. **Yield:** 8 servings.

Pineapple Cobbler

I think of our trip to Hawaii every time I taste this favorite dessert. It's a quick-and-easy cobbler made with juicy fresh pineapple. —*Aljene Wendling, Seattle, Washington*

1 cup sugar
1/3 cup biscuit/baking mix
1 teaspoon grated lemon peel
4 cups fresh pineapple chunks
TOPPING:
3/4 cup biscuit/baking mix
2/3 cup sugar
1 egg, beaten
1/4 cup butter *or* margarine, melted
Vanilla ice cream, optional

In a bowl, combine sugar, biscuit mix and lemon peel; stir in pineapple. Pour into a greased 9-in. square baking dish. Combine the biscuit mix, sugar and egg; sprinkle over the top. Drizzle with butter. Bake at 350° for 40-45 minutes or until browned. Serve warm or cold with ice cream if desired. **Yield:** 9 servings.

Fluffy Pistachio Dessert

(Pictured above right)

This creamy, light sweet torte is one of my family's favorites, even with the low-fat and low-sugar ingredients. —*Christine Strouf, St. Nazianz, Wisconsin*

✓ Uses less fat, sugar or salt. Includes Nutritional Analysis and Diabetic Exchanges.

1/2 cup reduced-fat margarine (70% vegetable oil spread), softened

1 cup all-purpose flour
1/2 cup confectioners' sugar
1/2 cup chopped walnuts
FIRST LAYER:
1 package (8 ounces) fat-free cream cheese, softened
1 cup (8 ounces) nonfat sour cream
1 carton (8 ounces) frozen light whipped topping, thawed
SECOND LAYER:
3 cups cold skim milk
2 packages (1 ounce *each*) sugar-free fat-free instant pistachio pudding mix
TOPPING:
1 carton (8 ounces) frozen light whipped topping, thawed
2 tablespoons ground walnuts

In a mixing bowl, cream the margarine. Add flour and sugar; blend until crumbly. Stir in walnuts. Press onto the bottom of a 13-in. x 9-in. x 2-in. baking dish coated with nonstick cooking spray. Bake at 375° for 10-12 minutes or until set. Cool. In a mixing bowl, beat cream cheese and sour cream. Fold in whipped topping. Spread over the crust. In another mixing bowl, combine milk and pudding mixes; beat on low speed for 2 minutes. Spread over first layer. Carefully spread whipped topping over second layer. Sprinkle with walnuts. Refrigerate for at least 1 hour. **Yield:** 24 servings. **Nutritional Analysis:** One serving equals 153 calories, 206 mg sodium, 2 mg cholesterol, 17 gm carbohydrate, 4 gm protein, 6 gm fat. **Diabetic Exchanges:** 1-1/2 starch, 1 fat.

Apple Danish Cheesecake

(Pictured above and on page 156)

As a teacher, I've collected many recipes. The one for this delightful cheesecake has traveled with me to several schools. —Ann Wandler, Camrose, Alberta

- **1 cup all-purpose flour**
- **1/2 cup ground almonds**
- **1/4 cup sugar**
- **1/2 cup cold butter *or* margarine**
- **1/4 teaspoon almond extract**

FILLING:

- **1 package (8 ounces) cream cheese, softened**
- **1/4 cup sugar**
- **1/4 teaspoon cream of tartar**
- **1 egg**

TOPPING:

- **1/3 cup packed brown sugar**
- **1 tablespoon all-purpose flour**
- **1 teaspoon ground cinnamon**
- **4 cups thinly sliced peeled tart apples**
- **1/3 cup slivered almonds**

In a small bowl, combine flour, almonds and sugar; cut in butter until crumbly. Add extract. Shape dough into a ball; place between two sheets of waxed paper. Roll out into a 10-in. circle. Transfer to a greased 9-in. springform pan; gently press dough against the bottom and up the sides of pan. Refrigerate for 30 minutes. In a mixing bowl, beat cream cheese, sugar and cream of tartar until smooth. Add egg; beat on low just until combined. Pour over crust. In a bowl, combine brown sugar, flour and cinnamon. Add apples and stir until coated. Spoon over the filling. Sprinkle with almonds. Bake at 350° for 40-45 minutes or until golden brown. Cool on a wire rack for 10 minutes. Carefully run a knife around edge of pan to loosen; cool 1 hour longer. Refrigerate overnight. Remove sides of pan. **Yield:** 8-10 servings.

Chocolate Peanut Butter Bars

My daughter won first place in a contest with this candy, which I make at Christmastime. It melts in your mouth. —Mary Esther Holloway, Bowerston, Ohio

- **1 jar (18 ounces) creamy peanut butter**
- **3 cups sugar**
- **1 cup light corn syrup**
- **1/2 cup water**
- **1-1/2 pounds milk chocolate confectionery coating***

Place peanut butter in a large greased heatproof bowl and set aside. In a large heavy saucepan, combine sugar, corn syrup and water. Cook and stir over low heat until sugar is dissolved; bring to a full rolling boil. Boil, stirring constantly, until a candy thermometer reads 290° (soft-crack stage). Pour hot syrup over peanut butter; stir quickly until blended. Pour onto a well-buttered baking sheet; cover with a piece of buttered waxed paper. Roll mixture into a 14-in. x 12-in. rectangle. While warm, cut into 1-1/2-in. x 1-in. bars using a buttered pizza cutter or knife. Cool completely. Melt confectionery coating; dip bars and place on waxed paper to harden. **Yield:** 6 dozen. ***Editor's Note:** Confectionery coating is found in the baking section of most grocery stores. It is sometimes called candy coating and is often sold in bulk packages of 1 to 1-1/2 pounds.

Candy Caution

You should check your candy thermometer each time you make candy. To do this, simply place the thermometer in a saucepan of boiling water and wait for several minutes. If the thermometer reads 212° in boiling water, it's accurate. If it rises above 212° or doesn't reach 212°, add or subtract the difference to the temperature called for in the recipe you're making.

Anise Hard Candy

I like to wrap pieces of this candy in plastic wrap to share with friends. —Bea Aubry, Dubuque, Iowa

2 cups sugar
1 cup light corn syrup
1 cup water
2 teaspoons anise extract *or* 1 teaspoon anise oil
6 to 9 drops red food coloring

In large heavy saucepan, combine sugar, corn syrup and water. Bring to a boil over medium heat, stirring occasionally. Cover and cook for 3 minutes or until sugar is dissolved. Uncover; cook on medium-high heat, without stirring, until a candy thermometer reads 300° (hard-crack stage). Remove from heat; stir in extract and food coloring (keep face away from mixture as the aroma will be very strong). Pour into a buttered 13-in. x 9-in. x 2-in. pan. When cooled slightly but not hardened, cut into 1-in. squares. Cool completely. Store in an airtight container. **Yield:** about 8-1/2 dozen.

Peanut Pralines

I have several great peanut recipes...but these pralines are heavenly. —Belinda Brown, Wedowee, Alabama

2-1/2 cups sugar
1 cup buttermilk
1 cup butter (no substitutes)
2 tablespoons peanut butter
1 tablespoon vanilla extract
1/2 teaspoon baking soda
2-1/2 cups dry roasted peanuts

In a saucepan, combine the sugar, buttermilk and butter. Cook and stir over low heat until butter is melted and sugar is dissolved. Cook over medium heat until a candy thermometer reads 234°-240° (soft-ball stage), stirring occasionally. Add peanut butter, vanilla, baking soda and peanuts; stir rapidly until the mixture is thickened and creamy. Drop quickly by tablespoonfuls onto waxed paper-lined or lightly buttered baking sheets, shaping into patties. Let stand until cool and set. Store in an airtight container. **Yield:** about 2-1/2 pounds.

Spumoni Loaf

I found this recipe years ago when I was teaching home economics. —Donna Hanson, Lusk, Wyoming

1 cup milk
1 teaspoon vanilla extract
2 jars (7 ounces *each*) marshmallow creme
4 plain milk chocolate candy bars (1.55 ounces *each*), chopped
1/2 cup chopped almonds
1/2 cup chopped maraschino cherries
2 cups whipping cream, whipped

In a saucepan, combine milk and vanilla; stir in marshmallow creme. Cook and stir over low heat until smooth. Cool. Stir in candy bars, almonds and cherries. Fold in whipped cream. Transfer to an ungreased 9-in. x 5-in. x 3-in. loaf pan. Cover and freeze for at least 4 hours. Remove from the freezer 10 minutes before serving. Unmold and slice. **Yield:** 10-12 servings.

Sugared Peanut Clusters

(Pictured below)

I made these nuts for my aunt's birthday, and everybody loved them. I've also given them as Christmas gifts. —Gail McClantoc, Sweet Water, Alabama

1-1/2 cups sugar
1/2 cup brewed coffee
1 tablespoon light corn syrup
1 teaspoon ground cinnamon
1 teaspoon vanilla extract
1 jar (16 ounces) dry roasted peanuts

In a heavy saucepan, combine the first four ingredients. Bring to a boil over medium heat, stirring occasionally. Cook until a candy thermometer reads 234°-240° (soft-ball stage). Remove from heat; stir in vanilla. Add peanuts; stir quickly. Pour onto two buttered baking sheets. Quickly separate into small clumps with two forks. Cool completely. Store in an airtight container. **Yield:** 6 cups.

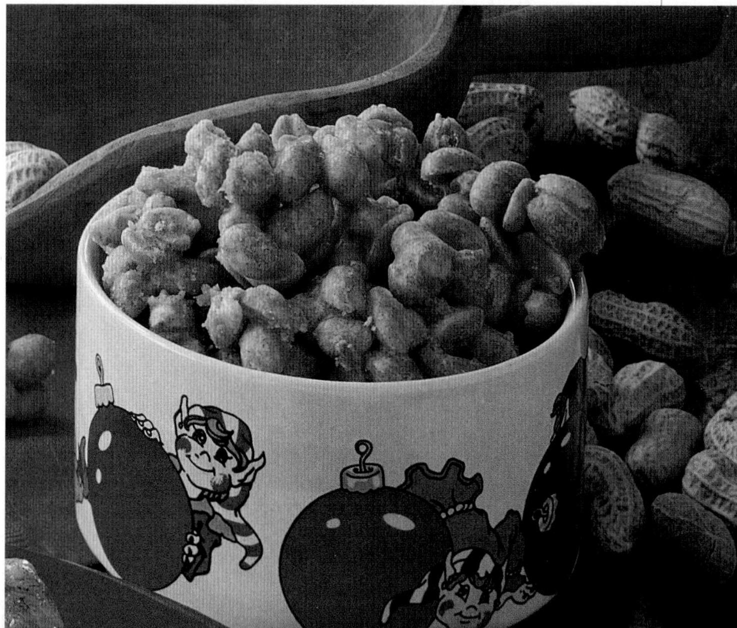

Lemon Trifle

(Pictured below)

The rich lemony filling and fresh berries in this tempting trifle make it as tasty as it is beautiful. I like to serve it in a clear glass dish.—Pat Stevens, Granbury, Texas

1 can (14 ounces) sweetened condensed milk
1 carton (8 ounces) lemon yogurt
1/3 cup lemon juice
2 teaspoons grated lemon peel
2 cups whipped topping
1 angel food cake (10 inches), cut into 1-inch cubes
2 cups fresh raspberries
1/2 cup flaked coconut, toasted
Fresh mint, optional

In a bowl, combine the first four ingredients. Fold in whipped topping. Place half of the cake cubes in a trifle bowl or 2-qt. serving bowl. Top with half of the lemon mixture. Repeat layers. Top with raspberries. Garnish with coconut and mint if desired. **Yield:** 14 servings.

Pear Crisp Cups

Canned pears get new appeal when made into individual dessert cups. These yummy treats are no fuss to prepare, and my kids love the crunchy brown sugar, cinnamon and almond topping. —Marilyn Kutzli Preston, Iowa

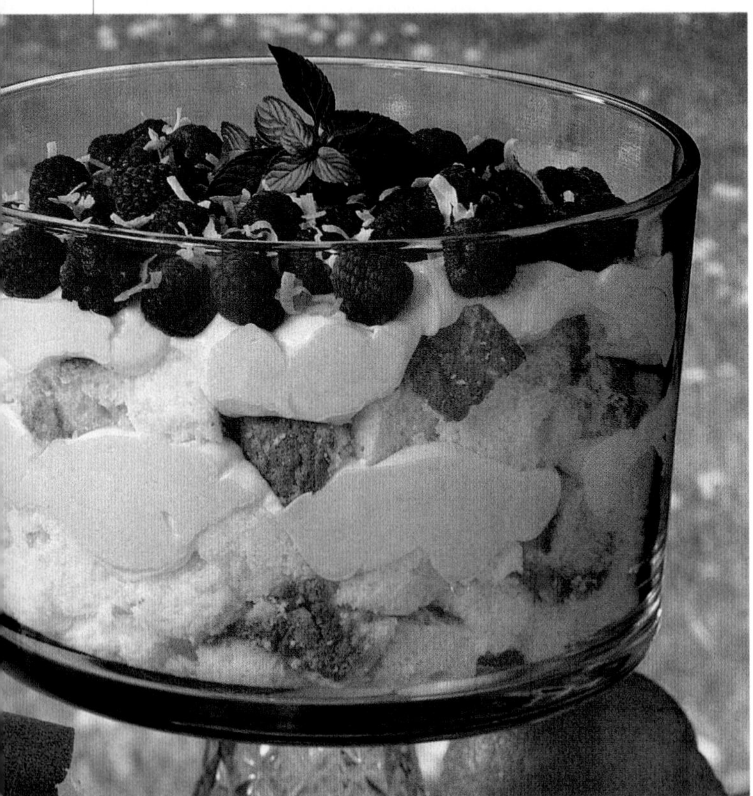

1 can (16 ounces) sliced pears
1/4 cup all-purpose flour
1/4 cup whole wheat flour
2 tablespoons brown sugar
1/2 teaspoon grated lemon peel
1/4 teaspoon ground cinnamon
3 tablespoons cold butter *or* margarine
1/4 cup finely chopped almonds, optional

Drain pears, reserving juice. Divide the pears among six greased 6-oz. custard cups. Spoon 1 tablespoon reserved juice into each cup. (Discard remaining juice or save for another use.) In a bowl, combine the flours, brown sugar, lemon peel and cinnamon; cut in butter until crumbly. Stir in almonds if desired. Sprinkle over pears. Bake at 350° for 20 minutes or until golden brown. **Yield:** 6 servings.

Creamy Rhubarb Dessert

Rhubarb gives a burst of tangy flavor to this dessert. Sometimes I'll add strawberries to the rhubarb layer. —Carol Forcum, Marion, Illinois

1/2 cup cold butter *or* margarine
1-1/2 cups all-purpose flour
1/2 cup chopped pecans
RHUBARB LAYER:
4 cups sliced rhubarb
1/2 cup sugar
2 tablespoons all-purpose flour
CHEESECAKE LAYER:
2 packages (8 ounces *each*) cream cheese, softened
1/2 cup sugar
1 teaspoon vanilla extract
3 eggs
TOPPING:
1-1/2 cups (12 ounces) sour cream
3 tablespoons sugar
1 teaspoon vanilla extract
Additional chopped pecans, optional

In a bowl, cut butter into flour until mixture resembles coarse crumbs; stir in pecans. Press into an ungreased 13-in. x 9-in. x 2-in. baking pan. Bake at 350° for 15 minutes. Combine rhubarb, sugar and flour; spoon over the crust. Bake for 15 minutes. Meanwhile, in a mixing bowl, beat cream cheese, sugar and vanilla until fluffy. Add eggs, one at a time, beating well after each addition. Pour over hot rhubarb layer. Bake for 30 minutes. Combine sour cream, sugar and vanilla; spread over hot cheesecake. Cool on a wire rack for 1 hour. Refrigerate overnight. Sprinkle with additional pecans if desired. **Yield:** 14-16 servings.

Lemonade Angel Fluff

I highly recommend this fluffy refreshing dessert. Surprisingly, it gets its creaminess from whipped evaporated milk. —*Katherine Stallwood Kennewick, Washington*

1 cup evaporated milk
2 envelopes unflavored gelatin
1 cup cold water
1/2 cup sugar
3/4 cup pink lemonade concentrate
Red food coloring, optional
4 cups angel food cake cubes

Pour milk into a small metal mixing bowl; place mixer beaters in the bowl. Cover and chill for at least 2 hours. In a saucepan, sprinkle gelatin over cold water; let stand for 2 minutes. Stir in sugar; heat until the sugar and gelatin are dissolved. Remove from the heat; stir in lemonade concentrate and food coloring if desired. Cover and chill until slightly thickened. Gradually add to chilled milk; beat until light and fluffy. Fold in cake cubes. Pour into an 8-in. x 4-in. x 2-in. loaf pan coated with nonstick cooking spray. Cover and chill for at least 2 hours. Remove from pan; cut into eight slices. **Yield:** 8 servings.

Family-Favorite Cheesecake

(Pictured above right)

This fluffy, delicate cheesecake has been a family favorite for almost 20 years. A friend gave me the recipe back when I was single. I've shared it at many gatherings over the years and have even started baking it for our friends instead of Christmas cookies. —*Esther Wappner, Mansfield, Ohio*

2-1/2 cups graham cracker crumbs (about 40 squares)
1/3 cup sugar
1/2 teaspoon ground cinnamon
1/2 cup butter *or* margarine, melted
FILLING:
3 packages (8 ounces *each*) cream cheese, softened
1-1/2 cups sugar
1 teaspoon vanilla extract
4 eggs, *separated*

TOPPING:
1/2 cup sour cream
2 tablespoons sugar
1/2 teaspoon vanilla extract
1/2 cup whipping cream, whipped

In a small bowl, combine the cracker crumbs, sugar and cinnamon; stir in butter. Press onto the bottom and 2 in. up the sides of a greased 9-in. springform pan. Bake at 350° for 5 minutes. Cool on a wire rack. Reduce heat to 325°. In a mixing bowl, beat cream cheese, sugar and vanilla until smooth. Add egg yolks; beat on low just until combined. In a small mixing bowl, beat egg whites until soft peaks form; fold into cream cheese mixture. Pour over crust. Bake for 1 hour or until center is almost set. Cool on a wire rack for 10 minutes. Carefully run a knife around edge of pan to loosen; cool 1 hour longer. Refrigerate until completely cooled. Combine the sour cream, sugar and vanilla; fold in whipped cream. Spread over the cheesecake. Refrigerate overnight. Remove sides of pan. **Yield:** 12 servings.

Simple Separation

A funnel makes quick work of separating an egg. Crack the egg into a funnel over a bowl. The yolk stays in the funnel while the white slips into the bowl.

Peanut Butter Cheesecake

(Pictured above)

The first time I served this cheesecake, my friends all went wild over it. They were surprised when I told them the crust is made of pretzels. The pairing of sweet and salty and creamy and crunchy, plus peanut butter and chocolate, left everyone asking for another slice.
—Lois Brooks, Newark, Delaware

1-1/2 cups crushed pretzels
1/3 cup butter *or* margarine, melted
FILLING:
5 packages (8 ounces *each*) cream cheese, softened
1-1/2 cups sugar
3/4 cup creamy peanut butter
2 teaspoons vanilla extract
3 eggs
1 cup peanut butter chips
1 cup semisweet chocolate chips
TOPPING:
1 cup (8 ounces) sour cream
3 tablespoons creamy peanut butter
1/2 cup sugar
1/2 cup finely chopped unsalted peanuts

In a small bowl, combine pretzels and butter. Press onto the bottom and 1 in. up the sides of a greased 10-in. springform pan. Bake at 350° for 5 minutes. Cool on a wire rack. In a mixing bowl, beat cream cheese and sugar until smooth. Add peanut butter and vanilla; mix well. Add eggs; beat on low just until combined. Stir in the chips. Pour over the crust. Bake at 350° for 50-55 minutes or until the center is almost set. Cool on a wire rack for 15 minutes (leave the oven on). Meanwhile, in a mixing bowl, combine sour cream, peanut butter and sugar; spread over filling. Sprinkle with nuts. Return to the oven for 5 minutes. Cool on a wire rack for 10 minutes. Carefully run a knife around the edge of the pan to loosen; cool 1 hour longer. Refrigerate overnight. Remove sides of pan. **Yield:** 12-14 servings.

Delightful Strawberry Dessert

My area is known for its strawberries, so I prepare this delicious and easy treat often. It always gets raves and prompts recipe requests.
—Lynne Wilhelm
West Hill, Ontario

3 egg whites
1-1/2 cups sugar, *divided*
3/4 teaspoon cream of tartar
1/2 cup crushed saltines (about 15 crackers)
1/2 cup flaked coconut
1/2 cup chopped pecans
2 cups whipping cream
1/2 teaspoon unflavored gelatin
1 quart fresh strawberries, sliced

In a mixing bowl, beat egg whites until soft peaks form. Gradually add 1 cup sugar and cream of tartar, beating until stiff peaks form. Gently fold in cracker crumbs, coconut and pecans. Spread onto the bottom and up the sides of a 9-in. pie plate. Bake at 375° for 20-22 minutes or until lightly browned. Cool completely. In a mixing bowl, beat cream, gelatin and remaining sugar until stiff peaks form. Fold in strawberries; pour into shell. Refrigerate for 2 hours. **Yield:** 10-12 servings.

Ice Cream Crunch

Settle in with a slice of this easy dessert, which is a summertime favorite in my home. It's a cool, crunchy and chewy make-ahead treat.
—Carol Seybert
Willmar, Minnesota

1/2 cup butter *or* margarine
1/2 cup packed brown sugar

3 cups crisp rice cereal
2 cups flaked coconut
1 cup chopped mixed nuts
1/2 gallon vanilla ice cream, softened

In a saucepan over medium heat, cook butter and brown sugar until butter is melted and sugar is dissolved. In a large bowl, combine cereal, coconut and nuts; add sugar mixture and stir until coated. Press half into a greased 13-in. x 9-in. x 2-in. baking pan. Spread ice cream over crust. Top with remaining cereal mixture. Freeze until firm. **Yield:** 12-16 servings.

Strawberry Peach Melba

(Pictured below right)

I get "oohs" and "aahs" when setting out this cool, fruity dessert. It combines my three favorites—peaches, strawberries and ice cream. It's so simple I can assemble it for company after we all finish the main course. —Marion Karlin, Waterloo, Iowa

3 cups fresh *or* frozen whole strawberries
1 cup confectioners' sugar
1/4 cup water
1 teaspoon lemon juice
2 teaspoons cornstarch
1 tablespoon cold water
1 teaspoon vanilla extract
4 slices or scoops vanilla ice cream
1 can (15 ounces) sliced peaches, drained
Whipped topping

In a saucepan, mash strawberries; add sugar, water and lemon juice. Cook and stir until mixture comes to a boil. Combine the cornstarch and cold water until smooth; stir into the strawberry mixture. Cook and stir for 2 minutes or until thickened and bubbly. Remove from the heat; stir in vanilla. Strain to remove the pulp. Place the pan in an ice-water bath to cool, stirring occasionally. Serve the strawberry sauce over ice cream; top with peaches and whipped topping. **Yield:** 4 servings.

Chocolate Cream Dessert

Our daughter and her boyfriend are both on restricted diets, so they appreciate having this yummy dessert for birthdays and other gatherings. We all enjoy it! —Ronald Scorse, Snowflake, Arizona

✓ Uses less fat, sugar or salt. Includes Nutritional Analysis and Diabetic Exchanges.

1/4 cup cold margarine
1 cup all-purpose flour
1 package (8 ounces) light cream cheese, softened
Artificial sweetener equivalent to 2 tablespoons sugar
1 carton (8 ounces) frozen light whipped topping, thawed, *divided*
1-1/2 cups cold skim milk
1 package (1.4 ounces) instant sugar-free chocolate pudding mix

In a bowl, cut margarine into flour until crumbly. Press into an 11-in. x 7-in. x 2-in. baking dish coated with nonstick cooking spray. Bake at 350° for 15-18 minutes or until lightly browned. Cool completely. In a mixing bowl, beat cream cheese and sweetener until smooth. Fold in half of the whipped topping. Carefully spread over the crust. In a mixing bowl, combine milk and pudding mix. Beat on low speed for 2 minutes. Let stand for 2-3 minutes. Spread over the cream cheese layer. Top with the remaining whipped topping. **Yield:** 15 servings. **Nutritional Analysis:** One serving equals 134 calories, 184 mg sodium, 6 mg cholesterol, 14 gm carbohydrate, 4 gm protein, 6 gm fat. **Diabetic Exchanges:** 1-1/2 fat, 1 starch.

Honey Pineapple Sherbet

(Pictured below and on page 156)

Tart and fruity, this wonderfully light and frosty dessert is a delight for the eyes and taste buds, especially in the heat of summer. I love its sunny yellow color and the juicy bits of pineapple. —Marsha Ransom South Haven, Michigan

✓ Uses less fat, sugar or salt. Includes Nutritional Analysis and Diabetic Exchanges.

2 cans (8 ounces *each*) unsweetened crushed pineapple
1/2 cup honey
2 cartons (8 ounces *each*) plain nonfat yogurt
1 teaspoon vanilla extract
Fresh raspberries and mint, optional

Drain pineapple, reserving the juice; set pineapple aside. In a saucepan, combine honey and pineapple juice. Bring to a boil, stirring several times. Reduce heat; simmer, uncovered, for 5 minutes. Cool completely. Stir in yogurt, vanilla and pineapple. Pour into a 9-in. square freezer-proof dish. Cover and freeze for 2 hours, stirring every 30 minutes or until slushy. Transfer to a mixing bowl; beat for 1-2 minutes. Return to pan; cover and freeze until firm. Remove from the freezer 10-15 minutes before serving. Garnish with raspberries and mint if desired. **Yield:** 8 servings. **Nutritional Analysis:** One 1/2-cup serving (without garnish) equals 116 calories, 45 mg sodium, 1 mg cholesterol, 27 gm carbohydrate, 4 gm protein, trace fat. **Diabetic Exchanges:** 1 starch, 1 fruit.

Coconut Cream Eggs

The filling of these homemade chocolate Easter eggs is wonderfully creamy and not too sweet. —Janet Galasso, Lehighton, Pennsylvania

1 package (8 ounces) cream cheese, softened
1 tablespoon butter (no substitutes), softened
4 cups confectioners' sugar
1 cup flaked coconut
2 cups (12 ounces) semisweet chocolate chips
1 tablespoon shortening

In a mixing bowl, beat cream cheese and butter until smooth. Add confectioners' sugar and coconut. Refrigerate for 1-1/2 hours or until easy to handle. Using hands dusted with confectioners' sugar, mold rounded tablespoonfuls of coconut mixture into egg shapes. Place on a waxed paper-lined baking sheet. Freeze for 2 hours or until slightly firm. In a microwave or double boiler, melt chocolate chips and shortening. Remove eggs from the freezer a few at a time; dip into chocolate mixture until completely coated. Return to waxed paper; chill until hardened. Store in the refrigerator. **Yield:** 3 dozen.

Rhubarb Rumble

I first tried this fruity, refreshing dessert at a potluck and loved it. Only after requesting the recipe did I learn it was sugar-free. —Charla Sackmann Glidden, Iowa

✓ Uses less fat, sugar or salt. Includes Nutritional Analysis and Diabetic Exchanges.

3 cups chopped rhubarb
1 package (.3 ounce) sugar-free strawberry gelatin
1-1/2 cups cold skim milk
1 package (1 ounce) instant sugar-free vanilla pudding mix
1 reduced-fat graham cracker crust (8 inches)

Place rhubarb in a microwave-safe bowl; cover and microwave on high for 6-8 minutes or until rhubarb is softened, stirring every 2 minutes. Stir in the gelatin until dissolved; cool completely. In a mixing bowl, combine milk and pudding mix; beat on low speed for 2 minutes. Fold into rhubarb mixture. Spoon into crust. Cover and refrigerate until firm. **Yield:** 8 servings. **Nutritional Analysis:** One serving equals 134 calories, 160 mg sodium, 1 mg cholesterol, 23 gm carbohydrate, 3 gm protein, 3 gm fat. **Diabetic Exchanges:** 1 starch, 1/2 fruit, 1/2 fat. **Editor's Note:** This recipe was tested in an 850-watt microwave.

Toffee Mocha Dessert

Simple angel food cake takes on richness and the bold flavors of coffee and chocolate in this special treat. —*Jean Ecos, Waukesha, Wisconsin*

- **1 angel food cake (8 inches), cut into 1-inch cubes**
- **3/4 cup strong brewed coffee, cooled**
- **1 package (8 ounces) cream cheese, softened**
- **1/2 cup chocolate syrup**
- **2 to 4 tablespoons sugar**
- **2 cups whipped topping**
- **2 Heath bars (1.4 ounces *each*), crushed**
- **Additional Heath bars, optional**

Place cake cubes in an ungreased 13-in. x 9-in. x 2-in. dish. Add coffee and toss lightly. In a mixing bowl, combine cream cheese, chocolate syrup and sugar until blended. Fold in the whipped topping. Spread over cake. Sprinkle with crushed Heath bars. Cover and refrigerate for at least 1 hour. Garnish with additional Heath bars if desired. **Yield:** 16-20 servings.

Tiny Cherry Cheesecakes

(Pictured above right and on page 156)

I prepare these mini cheesecakes every Christmas and for many weddings. I've received countless compliments and recipe requests. When I send these along in my husband's lunch, I have to be sure to pack extras because the men he works with love them, too. —*Janice Hertlein, Esterhazy, Saskatchewan*

- **1 cup all-purpose flour**
- **1/3 cup sugar**
- **1/4 cup baking cocoa**
- **1/2 cup cold butter *or* margarine**
- **2 tablespoons cold water**

FILLING:

- **2 packages (3 ounces *each*) cream cheese, softened**
- **1/4 cup sugar**
- **2 tablespoons milk**
- **1 teaspoon vanilla extract**
- **1 egg**
- **1 can (21 ounces) cherry *or* strawberry pie filling**

In a small bowl, combine flour, sugar and cocoa; cut in butter until crumbly. Gradually add water, tossing with a fork until dough forms a ball. Shape into 24 balls. Place in greased miniature muffin cups; press dough onto the bottom and up the sides of each cup. In a mixing bowl, beat cream cheese and sugar until smooth. Beat in milk and vanilla. Add egg; beat on low just until combined. Spoon about 1 tablespoonful into each cup. Bake at 325° for 15-18 minutes or until set. Cool on a wire rack for 30 minutes. Carefully remove from pans to cool completely. Top with pie filling. Store in the refrigerator. **Yield:** 2 dozen.

Honey Hints

Liquid honey can be stored for up to 1 year at room temperature in an airtight container in a dry place. Honey shouldn't be refrigerated.

When measuring honey, lightly grease the measuring cup so all of the honey easily slides out.

CHEESECAKE CELEBRATION. Serving Cranberry Cheesecake or Chocolate Chip Cookie Dough Cheesecake is a "slice" of life!

Chocolate Chip Cookie Dough Cheesecake

(Pictured above and on page 156)

I created this recipe to combine two of my all-time favorites—cheesecake for the grown-up in me and chocolate chip cookie dough for the little girl in me. Sour cream offsets the sweetness and adds a nice tang. Everyone who tries this scrumptious treat loves it.

—Julie Craig, Jackson, Wisconsin

1-3/4 cups crushed chocolate chip cookies *or* chocolate wafer crumbs
1/4 cup sugar
1/3 cup butter *or* margarine, melted

FILLING:
3 packages (8 ounces *each*) cream cheese, softened
1 cup sugar
3 eggs
1 cup (8 ounces) sour cream
1/2 teaspoon vanilla extract

COOKIE DOUGH:
1/4 cup butter *or* margarine, softened
1/4 cup sugar
1/4 cup packed brown sugar
1 tablespoon water
1 teaspoon vanilla extract
1/2 cup all-purpose flour
1-1/2 cups miniature semisweet chocolate chips, *divided*

In a small bowl, combine cookie crumbs and sugar; stir in butter. Press onto the bottom and 1 in. up the sides of a greased 9-in. springform pan; set aside. In a mixing bowl, beat cream cheese and sugar until smooth. Add eggs; beat on low just until combined. Add sour cream and vanilla; beat just until blended. Pour over crust; set aside. In another mixing bowl, cream butter and sugars on medium speed for 3 minutes. Add water and vanilla. Gradually add flour. Stir in 1 cup chocolate chips. Drop dough by teaspoonfuls over filling, gently pushing dough below surface (dough should be completely covered by filling). Bake at 350° for 45-55 minutes or until center is almost set. Cool on a wire rack for 10 minutes. Carefully run a knife around edge of pan to loosen; cool 1 hour longer. Refrigerate overnight; remove sides of pan. Sprinkle with remaining chips. **Yield:** 12-14 servings.

Cranberry Cheesecake

(Pictured at left and on page 156)

The holidays wouldn't be the same without cranberries and eggnog. This lovely cheesecake is a perfect Christmas dinner finale. Set it out at the start of the meal to remind folks to save room for dessert.

—Nancy Zimmerman
Cape May Court House, New Jersey

1 cup sugar
2 tablespoons cornstarch
1 cup cranberry juice
1-1/2 cups fresh *or* frozen cranberries

CRUST:
1 cup graham cracker crumbs (about 14 squares)
3 tablespoons sugar
3 tablespoons butter *or* margarine, melted

FILLING:

- **4 packages (8 ounces *each*) cream cheese, softened**
- **1 cup sugar**
- **3 tablespoons all-purpose flour**
- **4 eggs**
- **1 cup eggnog***
- **1 tablespoon vanilla extract**

In a saucepan, combine the first four ingredients; bring to a boil. Reduce heat; cook and stir over medium heat for 2 minutes. Remove from the heat; set aside. In a small bowl, combine cracker crumbs and sugar; stir in butter. Press onto the bottom of a greased 9-in. springform pan. Bake at 325° for 10 minutes. Cool on a wire rack. In a mixing bowl, beat cream cheese and sugar until smooth. Add flour and beat well. Add eggs; beat on low just until combined. Add eggnog and vanilla; beat just until blended. Pour two-thirds of the filling over crust. Top with half of the cranberry mixture (cover and chill remaining cranberry mixture). Carefully spoon remaining filling on top. Bake at 325° for 60-70 minutes or until center is almost set. Cool on a wire rack for 10 minutes. Carefully run a knife around edge of pan to loosen; cool 1 hour longer. Refrigerate overnight. Remove sides of pan. Spoon the remaining cranberry mixture over cheesecake. **Yield:** 12 servings. ***Editor's Note:** This recipe was tested with commercially prepared eggnog.

Frosty Angel Torte

This flavorful dessert looks like you fussed but is so easy to make. It's a nice cool treat to serve guests on a hot summer day. —*Blanche Whytsell*
Arnoldsburg, West Virginia

- **1 loaf (10-1/2 ounces) angel food cake**
- **1 pint vanilla ice cream**
- **1 package (10 ounces) frozen sweetened sliced strawberries, thawed and drained**
- **1 can (8 ounces) crushed unsweetened pineapple, drained**
- **1 cup miniature marshmallows**
- **1/2 cup chopped pecans, *divided***
- **1 carton (8 ounces) frozen whipped topping, thawed**

Slice cake in half horizontally. Cut ice cream into slices to fit cake; place on bottom cake layer. Replace the top. Combine strawberries, pineapple, marshmallows and 1/4 cup pecans; fold in whipped topping. Spread over top and sides of cake. Sprinkle with remaining pecans. Freeze for at least 2 hours. Slice and serve frozen. **Yield:** 10 servings.

'I Wish I Had That Recipe...'

"DINING at Vincent Guerithault on Camelbac in Phoenix, I tasted White Chocolate Truffles," relates Gloria Nolan of Peoria, Arizona.

"I'd like the recipe so I could try making these delectable candies myself."

Chef and owner Vincent Guerithault was happy to share the how-to. "These truffles are very easy!" he relates. "I came up with the recipe more than 13 years ago when I opened my restaurant. They are included on a plate of sweets we serve to patrons at the end of their meal."

A native of France and an acclaimed chef, Vincent mixes the California style of an open kitchen and a mesquite grill with the feel of a French bistro.

Located at 3930 E. Camelback Rd., Vincent Guerithault on Camelback is open for lunch 11:30 a.m. to 2:30 p.m. weekdays and for dinner 6 to 10:30 p.m. nightly (5:30 p.m. on Saturdays). For reservations, call 1-602/224-0225.

White Chocolate Truffles

- **18 ounces white confectionery coating,* cut into pieces**
- **9 tablespoons butter (no substitutes)**
- **2 tablespoons whipping cream**
- **1/4 cup confectioners' sugar**
- **Additional confectioners' sugar**

In a microwave or double boiler, melt confectionery coating, butter and cream over low heat until smooth, stirring frequently. Stir in sugar. (If mixture separates, beat with a mixer for 30 seconds.) Pour into an 8-in. square pan. Chill for 20 minutes or until slightly hardened. Using a melon baller or spoon, scoop out and shape into 1-in. balls. Roll in sugar. Store in an airtight container in the refrigerator. **Yield:** about 5 dozen. ***Editor's Note:** White confectionery coating is found in the baking section of most grocery stores. It is sometimes labeled "almond bark" or "candy coating" and often sold in bulk packages of 1 to 1-1/2 pounds.

S'more Cheesecake

(Pictured below)

This luscious dessert is just as wonderfully tasty as the campfire snack that inspired it. It's a great way to savor a summer classic anytime of year.
—Robin Andrews, Cary, North Carolina

2-1/4 cups graham cracker crumbs (about 36 squares)
1/3 cup sugar
1/2 cup butter *or* margarine, melted

FILLING:
2 packages (8 ounces *each*) cream cheese, softened
1 can (14 ounces) sweetened condensed milk
2 teaspoons vanilla extract
3 eggs
1 cup miniature semisweet chocolate chips
1 cup miniature marshmallows

TOPPING:
1 cup miniature marshmallows
1/2 cup semisweet chocolate chips
1 tablespoon shortening

In a small bowl, combine cracker crumbs and sugar; stir in butter. Press onto the bottom and 1-3/4 in. up the sides of a greased 10-in. springform pan; set aside. In a mixing bowl, beat cream cheese, milk and vanilla until smooth. Add eggs; beat on low just until combined. Stir in chocolate chips and marshmallows. Pour over crust. Bake at 325° for 40-45 minutes or until center is almost set. Sprinkle with marshmallows. Bake 4-6 minutes longer or until marshmallows are puffed. Meanwhile, melt chocolate chips and shortening; stir until smooth. Drizzle over marshmallows. Cool on a wire rack for 10 minutes. Carefully run a knife around edge of pan to loosen; cool 1 hour longer. Refrigerate overnight. Remove sides of pan. **Yield:** 12 servings.

Apple Tart

My family prefers this wonderful tart over traditional apple pie. *—Marilyn Begres, Dexter, Michigan*

1 cup sugar, *divided*
2 tablespoons all-purpose flour
1/2 teaspoon ground cinnamon
6 medium baking apples, peeled and thinly sliced
1 tablespoon butter *or* margarine
Pastry for single-crust pie

In a small skillet, heat 3/4 cup sugar, stirring constantly until it is liquefied and just golden. Remove from the heat and quickly pour into a 10-in. pie plate; set aside. In a small bowl, combine the flour, cinnamon and remaining sugar. Arrange half of the apples in a single layer in a circular pattern in pie plate. Sprinkle with half of the sugar mixture. Arrange half of the remaining apples in a circular pattern over sugar; sprinkle with the remaining sugar mixture. Place remaining apples over all, keeping the top as level as possible. Dot with butter. Roll out pastry to 9 in.; place over apples, pressing gently to completely cover. Do not flute. Bake at 400° for 50 minutes or until golden brown and apples are tender. As soon as tart comes out of the oven, carefully invert onto a large serving plate and remove pie plate. Cool. **Yield:** 8 servings.

Mocha Souffles

Anytime I want a special treat just for my husband, Al, and me, I make these souffles.
—Andrea Thomas, Gaithersburg, Maryland

✓ Uses less fat, sugar or salt. Includes Nutritional Analysis and Diabetic Exchanges.

1/2 teaspoon plus 6 tablespoons sugar, *divided*
3 tablespoons baking cocoa
1 tablespoon cornstarch
1/2 teaspoon instant coffee granules
1/2 cup milk
1/2 teaspoon vanilla extract

2 egg whites
1/4 teaspoon cream of tartar

Coat two 12-oz. souffle dishes with nonstick cooking spray and sprinkle each with 1/4 teaspoon of sugar; set aside. In a saucepan, combine the cocoa, 2 tablespoons of sugar, cornstarch and coffee granules. Gradually stir in milk. Bring to a boil; cook and stir for 2 minutes or until thickened. Remove from the heat; stir in vanilla and set aside. In a small mixing bowl, beat egg whites and cream of tartar until foamy. Beat in remaining sugar until stiff peaks form. Gently fold into mocha mixture. Pour into prepared dishes. Place in a shallow pan; add 1 in. of hot water to pan. Bake, uncovered, at 350° for 25 minutes or until tops feel firm when lightly touched. Serve immediately. **Yield:** 2 servings. **Nutritional Analysis:** One serving (prepared with skim milk) equals 221 calories, 89 mg sodium, 1 mg cholesterol, 49 gm carbohydrate, 7 gm protein, 1 gm fat. **Diabetic Exchanges:** 2 fruit, 1 starch, 1/2 lean meat.

State Fair Cream Puffs

The Wisconsin Bakers Association has served these treats at our state fair since 1924. They're real crowd pleasers. —Ruth Jungbluth, Dodgeville, Wisconsin

1 cup water
1/2 cup butter (no substitutes)
1 cup all-purpose flour
1/4 teaspoon salt
4 eggs
2 tablespoons milk
1 egg yolk, lightly beaten
2 cups whipping cream
1/4 cup confectioners' sugar
1/2 teaspoon vanilla extract
Additional confectioners' sugar

In a saucepan over medium heat, bring water and butter to a boil. Add flour and salt all at once; stir until a smooth ball forms. Remove from the heat; let stand for 5 minutes. Add eggs, one at a time, beating well after each addition. Beat until smooth. Drop by 1/4 cupfuls 3 in. apart onto greased baking sheets. Combine milk and egg yolk; brush over puffs. Bake at 400° for 35 minutes or until golden brown. Remove to wire racks. Immediately cut a slit in each for steam to escape; cool. In a mixing bowl, whip cream until soft peaks form. Gradually add sugar and vanilla, beating until almost stiff. Split puffs; remove soft dough. Add filling; replace tops. Dust with confectioners' sugar. Refrigerate until serving. **Yield:** 10 servings.

Frozen Chocolate Cheesecake Tart

(Pictured above)

I first made this irresistible dessert for some dinner guests. They were overwhelmed by its rich flavor and appearance. My husband commented that it was the best dessert he'd ever eaten in his whole life. —Heather Bennett, Dunbar, West Virginia

2-1/4 cups crushed chocolate cream-filled sandwich cookies (about 22 cookies)
1/3 cup butter *or* margarine, melted
FILLING:
2 packages (8 ounces *each*) cream cheese, softened
1/3 cup confectioners' sugar
1/3 cup whipping cream
1 teaspoon vanilla extract
3 cups vanilla chips, melted and cooled
1/2 cup miniature semisweet chocolate chips
Chocolate curls, optional

In a small bowl, combine cookie crumbs and butter. Press onto the bottom and up the sides of a greased 9-in. fluted tart pan with a removable bottom. Cover; place in freezer, being careful not to push up on the removable pan bottom. Freeze for at least 1 hour. In a mixing bowl, beat the cream cheese and sugar until smooth. Add cream, vanilla and melted vanilla chips; beat for 3 minutes. Stir in chocolate chips; pour over crust. Cover and freeze for 8 hours or overnight. Uncover and refrigerate 3-4 hours before serving. Garnish with chocolate curls if desired. Refrigerate leftovers. **Yield:** 12 servings.

Banana Split Supreme

(Pictured above and on page 156)

This lovely and delightful dessert has the classic flavor of a banana split. It's a cool, creamy treat with no last-minute fuss since you just pull it from the freezer. It always solicits praise from our big family.
—Marye Franzen, Gothenburg, Nebraska

3/4 cup butter *or* margarine, *divided*
2 cups confectioners' sugar
1 cup evaporated milk
3/4 cup semisweet chocolate chips
24 cream-filled chocolate sandwich cookies, crushed
3 to 4 medium firm bananas, cut into 1/2-inch slices
2 quarts vanilla ice cream, softened, *divided*
1 can (20 ounces) crushed pineapple, drained
1 jar (10 ounces) maraschino cherries, drained and halved
3/4 cup chopped pecans
Whipped topping, optional

In a saucepan, combine 1/2 cup of butter, sugar, milk and chocolate chips. Bring to a boil over medium heat; boil and stir for 8 minutes. Remove from the heat and cool completely. Meanwhile, melt the remaining butter; toss with cookie crumbs. Press into a greased 13-in. x 9-in. x 2-in. pan. Freeze for 15 minutes. Arrange banana slices over crust; spread with 1 quart of ice cream. Top with 1 cup of chocolate sauce. Freeze for 1 hour. Refrigerate remaining chocolate sauce. Spread the remaining ice cream over dessert; top with pineapple, cherries and pecans. Cover and freeze for several hours or overnight. Remove from the freezer 10 minutes before serving. Reheat the chocolate sauce. Cut dessert into squares; serve with chocolate sauce and whipped topping if desired. **Yield:** 12-15 servings.

Chocolate Spiders

Turn your kitchen into a "web site" by preparing a batch of these creepy candy spiders. Kids of all ages will delight in sampling—and helping to put together—these simple-to-fix treats.
—Sandi Pichon
Slidell, Louisiana

8 squares (1 ounce *each*) semisweet chocolate
2 cups miniature marshmallows
Black *or* red shoestring licorice
24 small round candy-coated milk chocolate balls (such as Hersheys or Sixlets)

In a microwave-safe bowl, heat chocolate for 2 minutes at 50% power, stirring after 1 minute. Stir until melted; let stand for 5 minutes. Stir in marshmallows. Drop by tablespoonfuls onto a waxed paper-lined baking sheet. Cut licorice into 2-in. pieces; press eight pieces into each mound for legs. Press two chocolate balls into each for eyes. Refrigerate until firm, about 20 minutes. **Yield:** 2 dozen. **Editor's Note:** This recipe was tested in an 850-watt microwave.

Peeling Peaches

To easily peel a peach, dip it into boiling water for 20 to 30 seconds. Remove it with a slotted spoon and immediately immerse into a bowl of ice water. Peel the skin off with a paring knife, working from the stem to the bottom of the peach. If the skin doesn't easily peel off, repeat the process.

Butter-Crunch Topping

It's nice to keep this crisp, golden mixture on hand to top pudding or pie filling over ice cream. I got this handy dessert idea from a neighbor.
—Ellen Benninger, Greenville, Pennsylvania

1 cup all-purpose flour
1/4 cup packed brown sugar
1/2 cup cold butter *or* margarine
1/2 cup flaked coconut
1/2 cup coarsely chopped nuts
Vanilla ice cream
Warmed apple pie filling

In a small bowl, combine the flour and brown sugar; cut in butter until mixture resembles coarse crumbs. Add coconut and nuts. Spread in a greased 15-in. x 10-in. x 1-in. baking pan. Bake at 400° for 10-15 minutes or until golden brown, stirring occasionally. Cool. Store in the refrigerator. Top ice cream with apple pie filling; sprinkle with topping. **Yield:** 3 cups.

Peach Gelatin Dessert

When peaches are in season, we enjoy their sweet, fresh flavor in this low-calorie dessert.
—Elizabeth Hunter, Prosperity, South Carolina

 Uses less fat, sugar or salt. Includes Nutritional Analysis and Diabetic Exchanges.

1 can (20 ounces) unsweetened crushed pineapple, undrained
1 cup water
1 package (6 ounces) peach gelatin
4 tablespoons sugar, *divided*
2 cups chopped peeled fresh peaches
1 cup buttermilk
1 carton (12 ounces) frozen whipped topping, thawed

In a saucepan, combine pineapple, water, gelatin powder and 2 tablespoons sugar. Cook and stir over medium heat just until mixture comes to a boil. Pour into a large bowl. Refrigerate until mixture begins to thicken, about 45 minutes. In a bowl, combine peaches, buttermilk and remaining sugar; fold in whipped topping. Fold into gelatin mixture. Pour into a 13-in. x 9-in. x 2-in. dish. Refrigerate until firm. **Yield:** 12-14 servings. **Nutritional Analysis:** One 3/4-cup serving (prepared with sugar-free orange gelatin and light whipped topping) equals 118 calories, 49 mg sodium, 1 mg cholesterol, 18 gm carbohydrate, 2 gm protein, 4 gm fat. **Diabetic Exchanges:** 1 fruit, 1 fat.

'I Wish I Had That Recipe...'

A GREAT dessert is the Strawberry Napoleon at Something Special Bakery and Tea Room here in Farmington, New Mexico," says Brenda Schrag.

Owner Dean Barns relates, "I 'constructed' this elegant and popular creation 6 years ago, and my wife, Deci, embellished it into a work of art."

Something Special Bakery and Tea Room, at 116 N. Auburn Ave., is open Monday through Friday, 7 a.m. to 2 p.m. Phone: 1-505/325-8183.

Strawberry Napoleon

1 package (17-1/4 ounces) frozen puff pastry sheets, thawed
3/4 cup sugar
2 tablespoons cornstarch
1/4 teaspoon salt
1-1/2 cups milk
3 egg yolks, beaten
1 tablespoon butter *or* margarine
3 teaspoons vanilla extract
TOPPING:
2 cups whipping cream
1/2 cup confectioners' sugar
1 teaspoon vanilla extract
3 pints fresh strawberries, sliced
Additional confectioners' sugar

On a lightly floured surface, roll out each pastry sheet to a 9-in. square. Place on ungreased baking sheets. Bake at 350° for 30 minutes or until golden brown. Meanwhile, in a saucepan, combine sugar, cornstarch and salt. Gradually add milk until smooth. Bring to a boil; cook and stir for 2 minutes or until thickened and bubbly. Remove from the heat. Stir a small amount into egg yolks; return all to pan. Bring to a gentle boil; cook and stir for 2 minutes. Remove from the heat; stir in butter and vanilla. Pour custard into a bowl; cover surface with plastic wrap and chill. In a mixing bowl, beat cream, sugar and vanilla until soft peaks form. Place one pastry square on a serving platter. Top with custard, strawberries, sweetened whipped cream and second pastry. Dust with confectioners' sugar. Refrigerate leftovers. **Yield:** 12 servings.

Cran-Apple Crumble

(Pictured below)

A toasted almond streusel topping makes this fruity dessert extra delicious. It's great for the holidays.
—Billie Moss, El Sobrante, California

1 cup orange juice
1 cup sugar, *divided*
4 teaspoons grated orange peel
1 package (12 ounces) fresh *or* frozen cranberries, thawed
2 tablespoons butter *or* margarine
2 tablespoons maple syrup
2 tablespoons honey
5 medium tart apples, peeled and cut into 1/2-inch slices
2 tablespoons quick-cooking tapioca

TOPPING:
1-1/2 cups all-purpose flour
3/4 cup packed brown sugar
1-1/2 teaspoons ground cinnamon
1/2 teaspoon ground nutmeg
1/2 cup cold butter *or* margarine
3 tablespoons almond paste
1 cup slivered almonds, toasted

In a saucepan, combine orange juice, 3/4 cup of sugar and orange peel; mix well. Bring to a boil. Reduce heat; simmer, uncovered, for 5 minutes, stirring occasionally. Add cranberries; simmer, uncovered, for 8-10 minutes or until berries begin to pop. Remove from the heat. Melt butter in a large saucepan. Stir in syrup, honey and remaining sugar. Add apples; cook over medium heat for 5 minutes. Remove from the heat; stir in cranberry mixture. Sprinkle with tapioca; mix gently. Let stand 15 minutes. Transfer to a greased 13-in. x 9-in. x 2-in. baking dish. For topping, combine the flour, brown sugar, cinnamon and nutmeg in a bowl; cut in butter and almond paste until mixture resembles coarse crumbs. Sprinkle crumb mixture and almonds over cranberry mixture (pan will be full). Bake at 400° for 15-20 minutes or until bubbly around the edges. **Yield:** 12-15 servings.

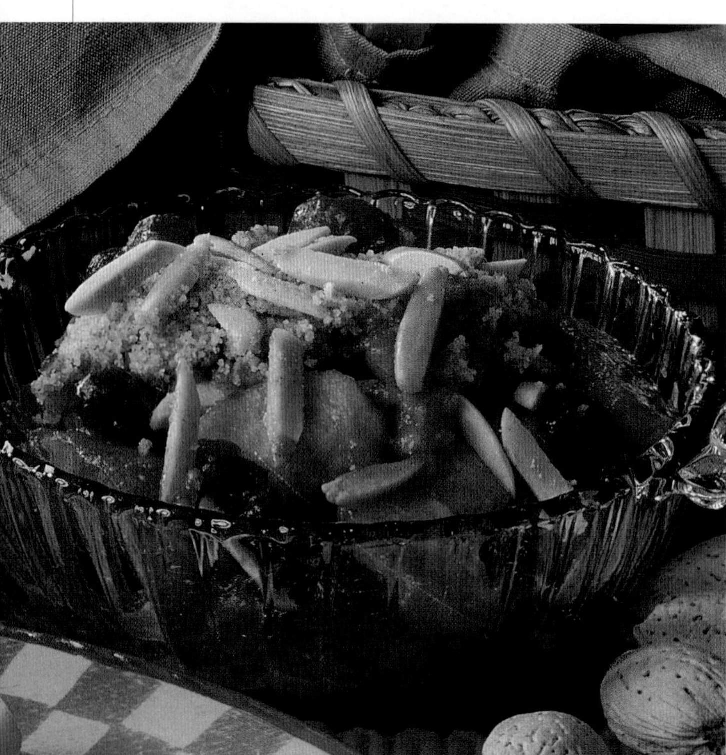

Spiced Walnut Sauce

For a deliciously different topping for ice cream, pancakes and waffles, try this thick, rich sauce. It's the perfect blend of spice and walnut flavors.
—Myra Innes, Auburn, Kansas

1 cup packed brown sugar
1/2 cup water
1 teaspoon ground cinnamon
2 to 4 whole cloves
1/2 cup chopped walnuts

In a saucepan, combine brown sugar, water, cinnamon and cloves. Bring to a boil; cook for 5 minutes, stirring frequently. Remove from the heat; discard cloves. Stir in walnuts. Cool. Serve over ice cream, pancakes or waffles. Store in the refrigerator. **Yield:** 1 cup.

Chocolate Bread Pudding

My father loved chocolate, so if we weren't having this dessert, we'd have homemade chocolate ice cream or chocolate cake.
—Jackie Atwood, Lincoln, Nebraska

1/4 cup butter *or* margarine
2 cups milk
3 tablespoons baking cocoa
4-1/2 cups cubed day-old bread (about 9 slices)
1 cup flaked coconut, *divided*
3/4 cup sugar
2 eggs, beaten
1 teaspoon vanilla extract
1/4 teaspoon salt
Whipped cream and grated chocolate, optional

In a large saucepan, heat butter and milk until butter is melted; stir in cocoa. Remove from the heat and set aside. Toss bread and 3/4 cup coconut; place in a greased 1-1/2-qt. shallow baking dish. Add sugar, eggs, vanilla and salt to milk mixture;

mix well. Pour over the bread. Sprinkle with the remaining coconut. Place baking dish in a 13-in. x 9-in. x 2-in. pan in oven; add 1 in. of water to pan. Bake at 350° for 50-55 minutes or until a knife inserted near the center comes out clean. Serve warm or cold; if desired, garnish with whipped cream and grated chocolate. **Yield:** 6-8 servings.

Peach Crumble

Old-fashioned, delicious and easy to make describes this yummy dessert. It's wonderful served with ice cream. —Nancy Horsburgh, Everett, Ontario

6 cups sliced peeled ripe peaches
1/4 cup packed brown sugar
3 tablespoons all-purpose flour
1 teaspoon lemon juice
1/2 teaspoon grated lemon peel
1/2 teaspoon ground cinnamon
TOPPING:
1 cup all-purpose flour
1 cup sugar
1 teaspoon baking powder
1/4 teaspoon salt
1/4 teaspoon ground nutmeg
1 egg, beaten
1/2 cup butter *or* margarine, melted and cooled
Vanilla ice cream, optional

Place peaches in a greased shallow 2-1/2-qt. baking dish. Combine brown sugar, flour, lemon juice, peel and cinnamon; sprinkle over the peaches. In a bowl, combine flour, sugar, baking powder, salt and nutmeg. Stir in egg until the mixture resembles coarse crumbs. Sprinkle over the peaches. Pour butter evenly over topping. Bake at 375° for 35-40 minutes. Serve with ice cream if desired. **Yield:** 10-12 servings.

Paul's Pumpkin Patch Pudding

This recipe originated with Donna Esh, whose husband, John, is the manager at the restaurant my brother Jim and I operate. I reworked it slightly and named it after our dad. —John Smucker, Bird-in-Hand, Pennsylvania

2-1/2 cups graham cracker crumbs (about 40 squares)
1/3 cup sugar
1/2 cup butter *or* margarine, melted
CREAM CHEESE LAYER:
1 package (8 ounces) cream cheese, softened
3/4 cup sugar
2 eggs
PUMPKIN FILLING:
1 tablespoon unflavored gelatin
1/4 cup cold water
6 egg yolks
3 cups cooked *or* canned pumpkin
1-1/4 cups sugar, *divided*
1 cup milk
1 tablespoon ground cinnamon
1 teaspoon salt
1 cup whipping cream
1 teaspoon vanilla extract
Additional whipped cream, optional

Combine the first three ingredients; press into a 13-in. x 9-in. x 2-in. baking pan; set aside. In a mixing bowl, beat the cream cheese, sugar and eggs until blended; pour over crust. Bake at 350° for 15 minutes or until set. Cool on a wire rack for 1 hour. Soften gelatin in cold water; set aside. In a small mixing bowl, beat egg yolks until thick and lemon-colored; set aside. In a saucepan, combine pumpkin, 1 cup of sugar, milk, cinnamon and salt; bring to a boil. Boil for 2 minutes. Stir 1 cup hot pumpkin mixture into yolks; return all to pan. Bring to a gentle boil; cook and stir for 2 minutes. Remove from the heat; stir in softened gelatin. Set pan in ice water and stir until mixture reaches room temperature, about 5 minutes. In another mixing bowl, beat cream until soft peaks form; gradually add vanilla and remaining sugar. Beat until stiff peaks form. Fold into pumpkin mixture. Pour over cream cheese layer. Refrigerate for 2 hours. Serve with whipped cream if desired. **Yield:** 12-15 servings.

Easy Chocolate Ice Cream

If your family's anything like mine, chances are chocolate's high on their list of favorite flavors. So you'll savor this easy recipe. Serve it alone or with an assortment of toppings. —Sharon Skildum, Maple Grove, Minnesota

2 cups half-and-half cream
1-1/2 cups sugar
1/2 cup baking cocoa
1 teaspoon vanilla extract
2 cups whipping cream

Combine half-and-half, sugar, cocoa and vanilla in a blender; process on low until smooth. Stir in whipping cream. Freeze in an ice cream freezer according to manufacturer's directions. **Yield:** 1-1/2 quarts.

RIVAL
CROCK•POT
STONEWARE SLOW COOKER
Off
Low
High

Potluck Pleasers

Whether you're cooking for 10 or 100, you can rely on these large-quantity recipes. They come from experienced cooks, so they're guaranteed to satisfy your hungry brood.

COOKING FOR A CROWD. Clockwise from upper left: Rainbow Pasta Salad (p. 192), Chicken Nut Puffs (p. 192), No-Bake Chocolate Mallow Dessert (p. 188), Potluck Pan Rolls (p. 186) and Slow-Cooked Chicken and Stuffing (p. 194).

Icy Holiday Punch

(Pictured above)

It's easy and convenient to prepare the base of this slushy punch ahead. Its rosy color makes it so pretty for Christmas. I've also made it with apricot gelatin for a bridal shower. This fun beverage makes any occasion a bit more special. —Margaret Matson
Metamora, Illinois

1 package (6 ounces) cherry gelatin
3/4 cup sugar
2 cups boiling water
1 can (46 ounces) pineapple juice
6 cups cold water
2 liters ginger ale, chilled

In a 4-qt. freezer-proof container, dissolve gelatin and sugar in boiling water. Stir in pineapple juice and cold water. Cover and freeze overnight. Remove from the freezer 2 hours before serving. Place in a punch bowl; stir in ginger ale just before serving. **Yield:** 32-36 servings (5-3/4 quarts).

Crumb-Topped Mushrooms

A crunchy golden topping contrasts nicely with the creamy mushroom mixture. Mushroom lovers help themselves to generous servings of this comforting casserole. With only five ingredients, it couldn't be easier to prepare. —Clara Honeyager
Mukwonago, Wisconsin

2 packages (12 ounces *each*) butter-flavored crackers, crushed, *divided*
1 cup butter *or* margarine, melted
4-1/2 pounds fresh mushrooms, thickly sliced
3 cups whipping cream
1 teaspoon paprika

Toss 3 cups of cracker crumbs with butter; set aside. Divide half of the mushrooms between three greased 13-in. x 9-in. x 2-in. baking dishes. Sprinkle with unbuttered crumbs; top with remaining mushrooms. Pour cream over all. Sprinkle with buttered crumbs and paprika. Bake, uncovered, at 350° for 30-35 minutes or until golden brown. **Yield:** 50-60 servings.

Stroganoff for a Crowd

This economical, enjoyable entree is perfect when serving a crowd. I've also served it with mashed potatoes with successful results. —Ada Lower
Minot, North Dakota

20 pounds ground beef
5 large onions, chopped
7 cans (26 ounces *each*) condensed cream of mushroom soup, undiluted
3 quarts milk
1/2 cup Worcestershire sauce
3 tablespoons garlic powder
2 tablespoons salt
1 tablespoon pepper
1 teaspoon paprika
5 pints sour cream
Hot cooked noodles

In several large stockpots, cook beef and onions until beef is browned; drain. Combine soup, milk, Worcestershire sauce, garlic powder, salt, pepper and paprika; add to beef mixture. Bring to a boil; reduce heat. Just before serving, stir in sour cream; heat through but do not boil. Serve over noodles. **Yield:** 70 (1-cup) servings.

Storing Unused Onions

If you use only part of an onion, leave the skin on the unused portion to keep it fresh, wrap it tightly in plastic wrap and refrigerate. Once cut, an onion should be used within 5 days.

Gingerbread with Amber Cream

This gingerbread has just the right amount of spices and bakes up nice and moist. Topping individual servings with flavored whipped cream turns this into an extra-special dessert. —*Ann Le Duc Gloversville, New York*

1 cup shortening
1 cup sugar
4 eggs
2 cups molasses
2 cups water
4-2/3 cups all-purpose flour
2 teaspoons *each* baking powder, baking soda, salt, ground cinnamon and ginger
1 teaspoon ground cloves
AMBER CREAM:
2 cups whipping cream
2/3 cup packed brown sugar
1/2 teaspoon vanilla extract

In a mixing bowl, cream shortening and sugar until fluffy. Add the eggs, one at a time, beating well after each addition. Combine molasses and water. Combine dry ingredients; add to creamed mixture alternately with molasses mixture, beating well after each addition. Pour into two greased 13-in. x 9-in. x 2-in. baking pans. Bake at 350° for 30-35 minutes or until a toothpick inserted near the center comes out clean. In a small mixing bowl, combine cream, brown sugar and vanilla; chill for at least 1 hour. Whip until stiff peaks form. Serve with the gingerbread. **Yield:** 24-32 servings.

Raspberry Lemonade

This crisp, tart beverage is a real thirst-quencher on a hot day. Pretty enough to serve at a bridal shower and refreshing enough to pour at a picnic, it's a fun change from iced tea or regular lemonade. —*Dorothy Jennings, Waterloo, Iowa*

2 cans (12 ounces *each*) frozen lemonade concentrate, thawed
2 packages (10 ounces *each*) frozen sweetened raspberries, partially thawed
2 to 4 tablespoons sugar
2 liters club soda, chilled
Ice cubes

In a blender, combine the lemonade concentrate, raspberries and sugar. Cover and process until blended. Strain to remove seeds. In a 4-1/2-qt. container, combine raspberry mixture, club soda and ice cubes; mix well. Serve immediately. **Yield:** 3-1/2 quarts.

Mom's Portable Beef

(Pictured below)

This delicious beef makes great sandwiches for a picnic, party or camping trip. The meat has a tempting from-scratch flavor that beats deli cold cuts. My family has savored these sandwiches for many years. —*Lorene Sinclair, Belleville, Ontario*

1 can (14-1/2 ounces) beef broth
1 medium onion, chopped
1/4 cup cider *or* red wine vinegar
2 tablespoons minced fresh parsley
1 bay leaf
1 tablespoon mixed pickling spices
1/2 teaspoon dried marjoram
1/2 teaspoon dried savory
1/2 teaspoon salt
1/4 teaspoon pepper
1 eye of round roast (about 3 pounds)
12 to 14 sandwich rolls, split
Lettuce, tomato and onion, optional

In a Dutch oven, combine the first 10 ingredients; add roast. Cover and bake at 325° for 1-1/2 hours or until meat is tender. Remove the roast and cool completely. Meanwhile, skim fat and strain cooking juices. Thinly slice the beef. Serve on rolls with warmed juices and lettuce, tomato and onion if desired. **Yield:** 12-14 servings.

Overnight Fruit Salad

(Pictured below)

I first tasted this rich salad at my wedding reception almost 40 years ago. The ladies who did the cooking wouldn't share the recipe at the time, but I eventually got it. I've made it for many meals...and our daughters copied the recipe when they married.
—Eileen Duffeck, Lena, Wisconsin

- **3 eggs, beaten**
- **1/4 cup sugar**
- **1/4 cup vinegar**
- **2 tablespoons butter *or* margarine**
- **2 cups green grapes**
- **2 cups miniature marshmallows**
- **1 can (20 ounces) pineapple chunks, drained**
- **1 can (15 ounces) mandarin oranges, drained**
- **2 medium firm bananas, sliced**
- **2 cups whipping cream, whipped**
- **1/2 cup chopped pecans**

In a double boiler over medium heat, cook and stir eggs, sugar and vinegar until mixture is thickened and reaches 160°. Remove from the heat; stir in butter. Cool. In a large serving bowl, combine grapes, marshmallows, pineapple, oranges and bananas; add cooled dressing and stir to coat. Refrigerate for 4 hours or overnight. Just before serving, fold in whipped cream and pecans. **Yield:** 12-16 servings.

Meaty Chili

This recipe—from our church cookbook—makes the best chili bar none. The secret ingredients are sugar and bay leaf. *—Sue Norem, Ellsworth, Iowa*

- **10 pounds ground beef**
- **5 large onions, chopped**
- **5 quarts tomato juice**
- **4 cups water**
- **5 cans (16 ounces *each*) kidney beans, rinsed and drained**
- **1/3 cup sugar**
- **1/2 to 2/3 cup chili powder**
- **1 tablespoon salt**
- **1 bunch celery with leaves**
- **5 garlic cloves, peeled**
- **3 bay leaves**

In several large soup kettles, cook beef and onions over medium heat until meat is no longer pink; drain. Add the tomato juice, water, beans, sugar, chili powder and salt. Cut leaves off celery and set aside. Chop celery and add to soup. Chop celery leaves; place in cheesecloth with the garlic and bay leaves. Tie with string and place in soup. Bring to a boil; reduce heat. Cover and simmer for 1-1/2 to 2 hours. Remove spice bag before serving. **Yield:** about 45 (1-cup) servings.

Chunky Oatmeal Cookies

Dotted with M&M's, these cookies are sure to satisfy adults and kids alike. I first made these to serve at a housewarming party.
—Donna Borth, Lowell, Michigan

- **12 eggs**
- **1 package (32 ounces) brown sugar**
- **4 cups sugar**
- **2 cups butter *or* margarine, softened**
- **18 cups old-fashioned oats**
- **3 jars (1 pound *each*) peanut butter**
- **1/4 cup ground cinnamon**
- **1/4 cup vanilla extract**
- **8 teaspoons baking soda**
- **3 cups (18 ounces) semisweet chocolate chips**
- **1 package (16 ounces) M&M's**

In mixing bowls, combine eggs and sugars. Add butter; mix well. Add oats. Add the peanut butter, cinnamon, vanilla and baking soda; mix well. Stir in chocolate chips and M&M's. Drop by rounded tablespoonfuls 2 in. apart onto ungreased baking sheets. Flatten if desired. Bake at 350° for 12-14 minutes or until set. **Yield:** 24 dozen. **Editor's Note:** These cookies do not contain flour.

Corn Bread for a Crowd

These sunny squares are a terrific accompaniment for chili or any savory dish with gravy or sauce.
—Samuel Warnock, Union, Ohio

3-1/2 cups cornmeal
2-1/2 cups all-purpose flour
2 tablespoons baking powder
1-1/2 teaspoons baking soda
1-1/2 teaspoons salt
4 eggs
3 cups buttermilk
1 cup vegetable oil

In a large bowl, combine cornmeal, flour, baking powder, baking soda and salt. Combine eggs, buttermilk and oil; stir into dry ingredients just until moistened. Pour into a greased 13-in. x 9-in. x 2-in. baking pan and a greased 9-in. square baking pan. Bake at 425° for 20-25 minutes or until a toothpick inserted near the center comes out clean. Serve warm. **Yield:** 30-36 servings.

Pepper Salad Dressing

This dressing is a zippy salad topper that's creamy and rich. It's so simple to mix up a big batch of this hearty dressing. I give bottles as gifts. —Sue Braunschweig Delafield, Wisconsin

6 quarts mayonnaise
2 quarts half-and-half cream
3/4 cup coarsely ground pepper
1/3 cup thinly sliced green onions
1/4 cup salt
2 tablespoons white pepper
2 tablespoons hot pepper sauce
1 tablespoon Worcestershire sauce

Combine all ingredients in a large bowl; mix well. Transfer to jars or bottles; refrigerate. **Yield:** about 2 gallons.

Turkey Stir-Fry Supper

(Pictured above right)

Tempting turkey is combined with rice, crisp colorful vegetables and a mild sauce in this meal-in-one entree. I share it at many gatherings and get compliments in return. —Mavis Diment, Marcus, Iowa

✓ Uses less fat, sugar or salt. Includes Nutritional Analysis and Diabetic Exchanges.

2-1/4 pounds boneless skinless turkey breast
2 tablespoons vegetable oil

3/4 cup uncooked long grain rice
2 cans (14-1/2 ounces *each*) chicken broth, *divided*
5 tablespoons soy sauce
2 garlic cloves, minced
1/2 teaspoon ground ginger
1/4 teaspoon pepper
1 package (10 ounces) frozen broccoli spears, thawed
1 pound carrots, thinly sliced
3 bunches green onions, sliced
3 tablespoons cornstarch
1 can (14 ounces) bean sprouts, drained

Cut turkey into 2-in. strips. In a Dutch oven or wok, stir-fry turkey in batches in oil for 5-7 minutes or until juices run clear. Set turkey aside. Add rice, 3-1/2 cups broth, soy sauce, garlic, ginger and pepper to pan; bring to a boil. Reduce heat; cover and simmer for 15 minutes or until rice is tender. Cut broccoli into 3-in. pieces. Add broccoli, carrots and onions to rice mixture; simmer for 3-5 minutes. Combine cornstarch and remaining broth; add to pan. Bring to a boil; cook and stir for 2 minutes. Stir in turkey and bean sprouts; heat through. **Yield:** 14 servings. **Nutritional Analysis:** One 1-cup serving (prepared with low-sodium broth and light soy sauce) equals 233 calories, 345 mg sodium, 46 mg cholesterol, 19 gm carbohydrate, 22 gm protein, 8 gm fat. **Diabetic Exchanges:** 2 meat, 1 starch, 1 vegetable.

Cream-Filled Cupcakes

(Pictured above)

Folks who enjoy homemade chocolate cupcakes are even more impressed when they bite into these treats and find a fluffy cream filling. These are great in a lunch box or on a buffet table. —*Edie DeSpain Logan, Utah*

3 cups all-purpose flour
2 cups sugar
1/3 cup baking cocoa
2 teaspoons baking soda
1 teaspoon salt
2 eggs
1 cup milk
1 cup vegetable oil
1 cup water
1 teaspoon vanilla extract

FILLING:

1/4 cup butter *or* margarine, softened
1/4 cup shortening
2 cups confectioners' sugar
3 tablespoons milk
1 teaspoon vanilla extract
Pinch salt
Chocolate frosting

In a mixing bowl, combine the first five ingredients. Add eggs, milk, oil, water and vanilla. Beat until smooth, about 2 minutes. Fill *paper-lined* muffin cups half full. Bake at 375° for 15-20 minutes or until a toothpick inserted near the center comes out clean. Remove from pans to wire racks to cool completely. In a mixing bowl, combine butter, shortening, confectioners' sugar, milk, vanilla and salt; beat until fluffy, about 5 minutes. Insert a very small tip into a pastry or plastic bag; fill with cream filling. Push the tip through the bottom of paper liner to fill each cupcake. Frost tops with chocolate frosting. **Yield:** 3 dozen.

Coney Dogs for a Crowd

Dress up plain hot dogs by topping them with this slightly sweet meat sauce. They're a lot more filling, and everyone comments on their great flavor. —*Betty Ann Miller, Holmesville, Ohio*

2 pounds ground beef
2 celery ribs, chopped
1 medium onion, chopped
1/4 cup packed brown sugar
1/4 cup cornstarch
1 teaspoon salt
1/4 teaspoon pepper
1 bottle (32 ounces) ketchup
2 cups tomato juice
4 packages (1 pound *each*) hot dogs
32 to 40 hot dog buns, split

In a large saucepan, cook beef, celery and onion until meat is no longer pink; drain. Combine the brown sugar, cornstarch, salt and pepper; stir into beef mixture. Add ketchup and tomato juice. Bring to a boil; boil and stir for 2 minutes. Reduce heat; simmer, uncovered, for 15-20 minutes. Cook hot dogs according to package directions; place on buns. Top each with about 1/4 cup beef mixture. **Yield:** 32-40 servings.

Smoky Beans

I first made these savory beans for a large gathering years ago. The combination of three different types of beans, bacon and mini smoked sausages is unbeatable. —*Pat Turner, Seneca, South Carolina*

3 pounds sliced bacon, diced
3 medium sweet onions, chopped
6 cans (28 ounces *each*) baked beans, undrained

- 6 cans (16 ounces each) kidney beans, rinsed and drained
- 6 cans (15-1/2 ounces *each*) butter beans, rinsed and drained
- 3 pounds miniature fully cooked smoked sausage links, cut into thirds
- 3 cups packed brown sugar
- 1-1/2 cups ketchup
- 1-1/2 cups vinegar
- 1 tablespoon garlic powder
- 1 tablespoon ground mustard

In a large Dutch oven, cook the bacon until crisp. Drain, reserving 3 tablespoons drippings. Set bacon aside. In the drippings, saute onions until tender. Combine beans, sausage, bacon and onions. Combine the remaining ingredients; add to bean mixture and mix well. Pour into four greased 13-in. x 9-in. x 2-in. baking dishes. Bake, uncovered, at 350° for 45-55 minutes or until heated through. **Yield:** 90-95 servings.

Peanut Cake Bars

The librarian at my son's high school brought these bars in as a treat for her helpers one day. He enjoyed them so much he requested the recipe and has made them many times since. The whole family loves the blend of chocolate and peanuts. —*Pam Clayton Brownsboro, Texas*

- 1 package (18-1/4 ounces) chocolate cake mix
- 1/2 cup water
- 1/3 cup butter *or* margarine, softened
- 1 egg

TOPPING:

- 3 cups miniature marshmallows
- 1 package (10 ounces) peanut butter chips
- 2/3 cup light corn syrup
- 1/4 cup butter *or* margarine
- 2 teaspoons vanilla extract
- 2 cups crisp rice cereal
- 2 cups salted peanuts

In a bowl, combine dry cake mix, water, butter and egg until blended. Press into a greased 15-in. x 10-in. x 1-in. baking pan. Bake at 350° for 13-16 minutes or until a toothpick inserted near the center comes out clean. Sprinkle with marshmallows. Bake 2 minutes longer. Cool. In a saucepan, combine peanut butter chips, corn syrup, butter and vanilla. Cook over low heat until melted; stir until smooth. Remove from the heat; stir in cereal and peanuts. Spoon over marshmallows. Cool before cutting. **Yield:** about 3 dozen.

Garden Bean Salad

(Pictured below)

A colorful blend of hearty beans and crunchy vegetables is what brings folks back for seconds after they try this salad. It never fails to spark compliments and recipe requests. —*Mildred Sherrer, Bay City, Texas*

- 2 cans (16 ounces *each*) kidney beans, rinsed and drained
- 2 cans (15 ounces *each*) garbanzo beans, rinsed and drained
- 2 medium carrots, grated
- 1 small cucumber, peeled, seeded and diced
- 1 small zucchini, diced
- 5 medium radishes, sliced
- 2/3 cup olive *or* vegetable oil
- 1/3 cup cider *or* red wine vinegar
- 1 teaspoon Italian seasoning
- 1/2 teaspoon salt
- 1/2 teaspoon garlic powder
- 1/2 teaspoon onion powder
- 1/2 cup shredded Swiss cheese

In a bowl, combine the first six ingredients. In a small bowl, combine the oil, vinegar, Italian seasoning, salt, garlic powder and onion powder; mix well. Pour over vegetable mixture and toss to coat. Cover and refrigerate for at least 2 hours. Top with cheese. Serve with a slotted spoon. **Yield:** 18-20 servings.

Potluck Pan Rolls

(Pictured below and on page 178)

The appealing homemade yeast-bread flavor of these golden rolls is unbeatable. Soft and light, they're great alongside any entree. Folks are disappointed if I don't bring them to potluck dinners. —Carol Mead Los Alamos, New Mexico

✓ Uses less fat, sugar or salt. Includes Nutritional Analysis and Diabetic Exchanges.

1 package (1/4 ounce) active dry yeast
1/3 cup plus 1 teaspoon sugar, *divided*
1-1/2 cups warm water (110° to 115°), *divided*
1/2 cup butter *or* margarine, melted
2 eggs
1/4 cup instant nonfat dry milk powder
1-1/4 teaspoons salt
5-1/2 to 6 cups all-purpose flour

In a mixing bowl, dissolve yeast and 1 teaspoon sugar in 1/2 cup water. Add butter, eggs, milk powder, salt, 3 cups flour and remaining sugar and water. Beat on medium speed for 3 minutes or until smooth. Stir in enough remaining flour to form a soft dough. Turn onto a floured surface; knead until smooth and elastic, about 6-8 minutes. Place in a greased bowl, turning once to grease top. Cover and let rise in a warm place until doubled, about 1-1/2 hours. Punch dough down. Divide into 27 pieces; shape into balls. Place 18 balls in a greased 13-in. x 9-in. x 2-in. baking pan and remaining balls in a greased 9-in. square baking pan. Cover and let rise until doubled, about 45 minutes. Bake at 375° for 17-20 minutes or until golden brown. Cool on wire racks. **Yield:** 27 rolls. **Nutritional Analysis:** One roll (prepared with margarine) equals 142 calories, 156 mg sodium, 16 mg cholesterol, 23 gm carbohydrate, 4 gm protein, 4 gm fat. **Diabetic Exchanges:** 1-1/2 starch, 1 fat.

Milk Chocolate Bundt Cake

Try this recipe for a moist mild chocolate cake that cuts cleanly and doesn't need frosting. This scrumptious snack cake travels very well, so it's a snap to share anywhere. —Sharan Williams, Spanish Fork, Utah

1 milk chocolate candy bar (7 ounces)
1/2 cup chocolate syrup
1 cup butter *or* margarine, softened
1-1/2 cups sugar
4 eggs
1 teaspoon vanilla extract
2-3/4 cups all-purpose flour
1/2 teaspoon salt
1/2 teaspoon baking soda
1 cup buttermilk
Confectioners' sugar, optional

In a saucepan, heat the candy bar and chocolate syrup over low heat until melted; set aside to cool. In a mixing bowl, cream butter and sugar. Add eggs, one at a time, beating well after each addition. Stir in chocolate mixture and vanilla. Combine flour, salt and baking soda; add to creamed mixture alternately with buttermilk. Pour into a greased and floured 10-in. fluted tube pan. Bake at 350° for 65-70 minutes or until a toothpick inserted near the center comes out clean. Cool in pan on a wire rack for 15 minutes. Remove from pan and cool completely. Dust with confectioners' sugar if desired. **Yield:** 12-14 servings.

Oven-Fried Potatoes

These tasty potatoes are a family favorite. They're easy to make and take to potlucks. We enjoy them as part of a hearty breakfast or alongside meat for supper. They're better than plain baked potatoes. —Delores Billings, Koksilah, British Columbia

12 medium potatoes, peeled and cubed
1/4 cup grated Parmesan cheese

2 teaspoons salt
1 teaspoon garlic powder
1 teaspoon paprika
1/2 teaspoon pepper
1/3 cup vegetable oil

Place potatoes in two large resealable plastic bags. Combine the Parmesan cheese and seasonings; add to potatoes and shake to coat. Pour oil into two 15-in. x 10-in. x 1-in. baking pans; pour potatoes into pans. Bake, uncovered, at 375° for 40-50 minutes or until tender. **Yield:** 12-14 servings.

Five-Cheese Lasagna

I prepared this for a Cub Scout banquet. It was easy since there was nothing to do at the last minute but cut and serve. It was a big success. —Todd Newman La Porte, Texas

6 packages (16 ounces *each*) lasagna noodles
10 pounds bulk Italian sausage
10 medium onions, chopped
30 garlic cloves, minced
11 cans (29 ounces *each*) tomato sauce
2/3 cup dried basil
3 tablespoons ground nutmeg
2 tablespoons fennel seed, crushed
1 tablespoon salt
1 tablespoon pepper
6 cartons (32 ounces *each*) ricotta cheese
10 pounds shredded mozzarella cheese
4 cartons (8 ounces *each*) grated Parmesan cheese
5 blocks (5 ounces *each*) Romano cheese, grated
10 packages (6 ounces *each*) sliced provolone cheese, cut into strips
1 cup minced fresh parsley

Cook noodles in boiling water for 5 minutes; rinse in cold water and drain. Cook sausage, onions and garlic until meat is no longer pink; drain. Add the tomato sauce and seasonings; bring to a boil. Reduce heat; simmer, uncovered, for 50-60 minutes. Grease ten 13-in. x 9-in. x 2-in. baking dishes. In each dish, layer about 1-1/2 cups tomato sauce, four noodles, about 1-1/4 cups ricotta, 1-1/2 cups mozzarella, about 1/3 cup Parmesan, 1/4 cup Romano and three slices provolone. Repeat layers. Top with four noodles, about 1-1/2 cups of tomato sauce, 1 cup mozzarella and about 1 tablespoon parsley. Bake, uncovered, at 375° for 40-50 minutes or until browned and bubbly. Let stand 10-15 minutes before serving. **Yield:** 120-150 servings.

Creamy Frozen Fruit Cups

(Pictured above)

I love to prepare these cool, fluffy fruit cups to give a refreshing boost to many meals. They've been well-received at family gatherings and summer barbecues. There's no last-minute fuss since you make them well in advance. —Karen Hatcher, St. Amant, Louisiana

1 package (8 ounces) cream cheese, softened
1/2 cup sugar
1 jar (10 ounces) maraschino cherries, drained
1 can (11 ounces) mandarin oranges, drained
1 can (8 ounces) crushed pineapple, drained
1/2 cup chopped pecans
1 carton (8 ounces) frozen whipped topping, thawed
Fresh mint, optional

In a mixing bowl, beat the cream cheese and sugar until fluffy. Halve 9 cherries; chop the remaining cherries. Set aside halved cherries and 18 oranges for garnish. Add pineapple, pecans and chopped cherries to cream cheese mixture. Fold in whipped topping and remaining oranges. Line muffin cups with paper or foil liners. Spoon fruit mixture into cups; garnish with reserved cherries and oranges. Freeze until firm. Remove from the freezer 10 minutes before serving. Top with mint if desired. **Yield:** 1-1/2 dozen.

Raspberry Crumb Cake

(Pictured above)

A cake spiced with cinnamon and mace, a yummy filling featuring raspberries and a crunchy almond topping assure this tempting treat will brighten any buffet. Its delicious homemade goodness will bring folks back for seconds. —*Pat Habiger Spearville, Kansas*

2/3 cup sugar
1/4 cup cornstarch
3/4 cup water
2 cups fresh *or* frozen unsweetened raspberries
1 tablespoon lemon juice

CRUST:

3 cups all-purpose flour
1 cup sugar
1 tablespoon baking powder
1 teaspoon salt
1 teaspoon ground cinnamon
1/4 teaspoon ground mace
1 cup cold butter *or* margarine
2 eggs
1 cup milk
1 teaspoon vanilla extract

TOPPING:

1/2 cup all-purpose flour
1/2 cup sugar
1/4 cup cold butter *or* margarine
1/4 cup sliced almonds

In a saucepan, combine sugar, cornstarch, water and raspberries. Bring to a boil over medium heat; boil for 5 minutes or until thickened, stirring constantly. Remove from the heat; stir in lemon juice. Cool. Meanwhile, in a bowl, combine the first six crust ingredients. Cut in butter until mixture resembles coarse crumbs. Beat eggs, milk and vanilla; add to crumb mixture and mix well. Spread two-thirds of the mixture into a greased 13-in. x 9-in. x 2-in. baking dish. Spoon raspberry filling over crust to within 1 in. of the edges. Top with the remaining crust mixture. For topping, combine flour and sugar; cut in butter until crumbly. Stir in almonds. Sprinkle over the top. Bake at 350° for 50-55 minutes or until lightly browned. **Yield:** 12-16 servings.

No-Bake Chocolate Mallow Dessert

(Pictured on page 178)

Since the 1960's, whenever I've asked my family what dessert I should fix, this is what they've requested. It has a light texture and also a tempting pale chocolate color and is not overly sweet. It's a delightful treat. —*Laurine Muhle, Lake Park, Minnesota*

3 cups crushed vanilla wafers
2/3 cup butter *or* margarine, melted
1/4 cup sugar
1/2 teaspoon ground cinnamon

FILLING:

1 milk chocolate candy bar (7 ounces), plain *or* with almonds, broken into pieces
1 package (10 ounces) large marshmallows
1 cup milk
2 cups whipping cream, whipped
1/2 teaspoon vanilla extract
Sliced almonds, toasted, optional

In a bowl, combine wafer crumbs, butter, sugar and cinnamon; mix well. Set aside 1/3 cup for topping. Press remaining crumb mixture into a greased 13-in. x 9-in. x 2-in. pan; refrigerate until firm. In a saucepan, heat the candy bar, marshmallows and milk over medium-low heat until chocolate and marshmallows are melted, stirring often. Remove from the heat; cool to room temperature. Fold in whipped cream and vanilla; pour over crust. Chill for 3-4 hours. Sprinkle with reserved crumb mixture and almonds if desired. **Yield:** 12-16 servings.

Chocolate Coconut Nests

These nests look and taste fancy but have only three ingredients. They've been very popular with our girls and their friends over the years. You can substitute any flavor ice cream for the mint chocolate chip.
—Claire Hudson, South Wales, New York

2 packages (14 ounces *each*) flaked coconut
1-1/3 cups semisweet chocolate chips, melted
3 quarts mint chocolate chip ice cream

In a bowl, toss coconut and chocolate until well blended. On baking sheets covered with waxed paper, shape about 1/3 cupfuls into 2-1/2-in. nests. Chill until firm. Just before serving, top each nest with 1/2 cup of ice cream. **Yield:** 24 servings.

Potluck Meatballs

I've found that these mini meatballs make a hearty, "can't-miss" appetizer year-round. They are always well-received at a potluck, and the only "utensil" I need to supply is toothpicks. They also make a good entree over noodles.
—Debbie Jones
Hollywood, Maryland

1 egg, beaten
2/3 cup soft bread crumbs
1/2 cup grated onion
1 teaspoon salt
1/2 teaspoon ground allspice
1/4 teaspoon pepper
1 pound ground beef
1 tablespoon cornstarch
1 can (10-1/2 ounces) condensed beef consomme, undiluted

In a bowl, combine the first six ingredients; add beef and mix well. Shape into 1-1/4-in. balls. In a skillet over medium heat, brown meatballs; drain. Transfer to a greased 1-1/2-qt. baking dish. Combine the cornstarch and consomme until smooth; add to skillet. Bring to a boil, stirring to loosen browned bits from pan. Boil for 2 minutes or until thickened. Pour over the meatballs. Bake, uncovered, at 350° for 50-60 minutes or until no longer pink. **Yield:** 2-1/2 dozen.

Ham and Cheese Puff

(Pictured at right)

This recipe is an absolute winner for brunch, lunch or whatever. People really seem to go for the big chunks of ham combined with the flavors of mustard and cheese. Since it's assembled the night before, it is a great make-ahead potluck dish.
—Nina Clark
Wareham, Massachusetts

2 loaves (1 pound *each*) Italian bread, cut into 1-inch cubes
6 cups cubed fully cooked ham
1-1/2 pounds Monterey Jack *or* Muenster cheese, cubed
1 medium onion, chopped
1/4 cup butter *or* margarine
16 eggs
7 cups milk
1/2 cup prepared mustard

Toss bread, ham and cheese; divide between two greased 13-in. x 9-in. x 2-in. baking dishes. In a skillet, saute onion in butter until tender; transfer to a bowl. Add eggs, milk and mustard; mix well. Pour over the bread mixture. Cover and refrigerate overnight. Remove from the refrigerator 30 minutes before baking. Bake, uncovered, at 350° for 55-65 minutes or until a knife inserted near the center comes out clean. Serve immediately. **Yield:** 24-30 servings.

Sausage Sandwich Squares

(Pictured below)

As Sunday school teachers, my husband and I often host youth groups, so I dreamed up this "handy" recipe to feed hungry teenagers. They loved this pizza-like sandwich and still request it when they visit.
—Mary Merrill, Bloomingdale, Ohio

3 to 3-1/2 cups all-purpose flour
1 package (1/4 ounce) active dry yeast
1/2 teaspoon salt
1-1/3 cups warm water (120° to 130°)
1 pound bulk Italian sausage
1 medium sweet red pepper, diced
1 medium green pepper, diced
1 large onion, diced
4 cups (16 ounces) shredded mozzarella cheese
1 egg
1 tablespoon water
2 tablespoons grated Parmesan cheese
2 tablespoons minced fresh parsley
1/2 teaspoon dried oregano
1/8 teaspoon garlic powder

In a bowl, combine 2 cups flour, yeast and salt. Add warm water; mix well. Add enough remaining flour to form a firm dough. Turn onto a floured surface; knead until smooth and elastic, about 6 minutes. Place in a greased bowl, turning once to grease top. Cover and let rise in a warm place until doubled, about 50 minutes. In a skillet, cook sausage until no longer pink; remove with a slotted spoon and set aside. In the drippings, saute peppers and onion until tender; drain. Press half of the dough onto the bottom and 1/2 in. up the sides of a greased 15-in. x 10-in. x 1-in. baking pan. Spread sausage evenly over the crust. Top with peppers and onion. Sprinkle with mozzarella cheese. Roll out remaining dough to fit pan; place over cheese and seal the edges. In a small bowl, beat egg and water. Add remaining ingredients; mix well. Brush over dough. Cut slits in top. Bake at 400° for 20-25 minutes or until golden brown. Cut into squares. **Yield:** 12-15 servings.

Smoky Spareribs

These ribs bake up tender and flavorful, coated with a simple-to-make sauce. Folks agree they're finger-lickin' good.
—Lornetta Kaminski, St. Benedict, Saskatchewan

100 pounds pork spareribs, cut into serving-size pieces
8 bottles (42 ounces *each*) barbecue sauce
4 cans (20 ounces *each*) crushed pineapple, undrained
5 pounds brown sugar
1 to 2 bottles (4 ounces *each*) liquid smoke

Place the ribs in large roasting pans. Cover and bake at 350° for 1 hour; drain. Bake 15-30 minutes longer or until almost tender. Meanwhile, in a kettle, combine the barbecue sauce, pineapple, brown sugar and liquid smoke; cook and stir until the sugar is dissolved. Drain ribs; pour sauce over ribs. Bake, uncovered, for 15-20 minutes or until tender. **Yield:** 100 servings.

Sunflower Slaw

This salad is a favorite at church suppers. It deliciously combines a tangy dressing with crisp cabbage, slivered almonds, sunflower kernels and ramen noodles. This dish pairs nicely with many entrees.
—Betty Thompson, St. Charles, Missouri

6 packages (3 ounces *each*) ramen noodles
2 packages (2-1/4 ounces *each*) slivered almonds

1-1/3 cups sunflower kernels
1/2 cup butter *or* margarine, melted
3-1/2 cups vegetable oil
2 cups vinegar
2 cups sugar
1/2 cup soy sauce
2 teaspoons salt
10 pounds cabbage, shredded

Break noodles into small pieces (save seasoning envelopes for another use). Place noodles, almonds and sunflower kernels in a 15-in. x 10-in. x 1-in. baking pan. Drizzle with butter; mix well. Bake at 350° for 8-10 minutes or until lightly browned, stirring several times; set aside. Combine oil, vinegar, sugar, soy sauce and salt; toss with cabbage. Cover and refrigerate for at least 1 hour. Stir in noodle mixture just before serving. Serve with a slotted spoon. **Yield:** 66 (3/4-cup) servings.

Citrus Iced Tea

I catered for 5 years, and this was by far my most-requested beverage recipe. Fresh citrus juice makes it special. It's a refreshing change from ordinary iced tea. —Marcia Porch, Winter Park, Florida

3 quarts water
8 whole cloves
10 individual tea bags
2-1/2 cups sugar
1 can (46 ounces) unsweetened pineapple juice
Juice of 7 lemons
Juice of 6 oranges
Ice cubes

In a large kettle, bring water and cloves to a boil. Reduce heat; simmer, uncovered, for 10 minutes. Remove from the heat; add the tea bags. Steep for 5 minutes. Discard tea bags and cloves. Stir in sugar and juices. Serve over ice. **Yield:** 24 (3/4-cup) servings.

Peanut Butter Caramel Bars

(Pictured above right)

When my husband, Bob, and our three sons sit down to dinner, they ask, "What's for dessert?" I have a happy group of guys when I report that these rich bars are on the menu. They're chock-full of yummy ingredients. —Lee Ann Karnowski, Stevens Point, Wisconsin

1 package (18-1/4 ounces) yellow cake mix
1/2 cup butter *or* margarine, softened
1 egg
20 miniature peanut butter cups, chopped
2 tablespoons cornstarch
1 jar (12-1/4 ounces) caramel ice cream topping
1/4 cup peanut butter
1/2 cup salted peanuts

TOPPING:
1 can (16 ounces) milk chocolate frosting
1/2 cup chopped salted peanuts

In a mixing bowl, combine the dry cake mix, butter and egg; beat until no longer crumbly, about 3 minutes. Stir in the peanut butter cups. Press into a greased 13-in. x 9-in. x 2-in. baking pan. Bake at 350° for 18-22 minutes or until lightly browned. Meanwhile, in a saucepan, combine the cornstarch, caramel topping and peanut butter until smooth. Cook over low heat, stirring occasionally, until mixture comes to a boil, about 25 minutes. Cook and stir 1-2 minutes longer. Remove from the heat; stir in peanuts. Spread evenly over warm crust. Bake 6-7 minutes longer or until almost set. Cool completely on a wire rack. Spread with frosting; sprinkle with peanuts. Refrigerate for at least 1 hour before cutting. Store in the refrigerator. **Yield:** about 3 dozen.

Chicken Nut Puffs

(Pictured on page 178)

Of the many items I set out when hosting parties, these savory puffs are the first to get snapped up. People enjoy the zippy flavor. —*Jo Groth, Plainfield, Iowa*

1-1/2 cups finely chopped cooked chicken
1/3 cup chopped almonds, toasted
1 cup chicken broth
1/2 cup vegetable oil
2 teaspoons Worcestershire sauce
1 tablespoon dried parsley flakes
1 teaspoon seasoned salt
1/2 to 1 teaspoon celery seed
1/8 teaspoon cayenne pepper
1 cup all-purpose flour
4 eggs

Combine the chicken and almonds; set aside. In a large saucepan, combine the next seven ingredients; bring to a boil. Add flour all at once; stir until a smooth ball forms. Remove from the heat; let stand for 5 minutes. Add eggs, one at a time, beating well after each. Beat until smooth. Stir in chicken and almonds. Drop by heaping teaspoonfuls onto greased baking sheets. Bake at 450° for 12-14 minutes or until golden brown. Serve warm. **Yield:** about 6 dozen.

Rainbow Pasta Salad

(Pictured above and on page 178)

This refreshing, colorful salad is my mother's recipe. It features an uncommon but tempting mixture of vegetables. Mother always cooks with wonderful flair, and everything she makes is delicious as well as lovely on the table. —*Barbara Carlucci, Orange Park, Florida*

1 package (16 ounces) tricolor spiral pasta
2 cups broccoli florets
1 cup chopped carrots
1/2 cup chopped tomato
1/2 cup chopped cucumber
1/4 cup chopped onion
1 can (15-1/4 ounces) whole kernel corn, drained
1 jar (6-1/2 ounces) marinated artichoke hearts, drained and halved
1 bottle (8 ounces) Italian salad dressing

Cook the pasta according to package directions; drain and rinse in cold water. Place in a large bowl; add remaining ingredients and toss to coat. Cover and refrigerate for 2 hours or overnight. **Yield:** 12-14 servings.

Beefy Vegetable Soup

With a mild-tasting tomato-based broth and lots of colorful vegetables, this savory soup is always a real crowd-pleaser. —*Linda Yutzy, Middlefield, Ohio*

12 cups diced peeled potatoes
12 cups frozen sliced carrots
12 cups frozen peas
12 cups frozen lima beans
12 cups frozen cut green beans
9 cups diced celery
1 package (16 ounces) small shell macaroni
4 quarts tomato sauce
2 cans (32 ounces *each*) chicken broth
10 pounds ground beef
2 pounds ground turkey
4 cups diced onions
3 tablespoons salt
2 tablespoons dried basil
1-1/2 teaspoons pepper

In an 8-gal. kettle, combine the first seven ingredients. Add water to cover. Add tomato sauce and broth. In another large kettle, cook beef, turkey and onions until meat is no longer pink; drain. Add to vegetable mixture. Stir in salt, basil and pepper; bring to a boil. Reduce heat; cover and simmer for 1-1/2 hours or until celery is tender. **Yield:** 120 (1-cup) servings.

Chicken Supreme with Gravy

A group of friends and I have shared countless recipes through the years. This dish never fails to satisfy.
—Bernice Hartje, Cavalier, North Dakota

1-1/2 celery stalks, diced (about 6 cups)
6 medium onions, diced (about 4 cups)
1 pound butter *or* margarine
3 loaves (1-1/2 pounds *each*) white bread
3 tablespoons rubbed sage
3 tablespoons salt
1 tablespoon baking powder
2 teaspoons pepper
12 eggs
9 cups milk
24 cups diced cooked chicken (about 6 chickens)
3 cans (14-1/2 ounces *each*) chicken broth
GRAVY:
8 cans (10-3/4 ounces *each*) condensed creamy chicken mushroom soup, undiluted
9 to 10 cups water

In a large skillet, saute celery and onions in butter. Break bread into small pieces into a large bowl. Add sage, salt, baking powder and pepper; toss to coat. Add celery and onions; mix well. Beat eggs and milk; add to bread mixture. Divide half of the chicken in four 13-in. x 9-in. x 2-in. greased baking pans. Cover with half of the bread mixture. Repeat layers. Pour broth into each pan. Cover and bake at 300° for 1 hour and 45 minutes or until broth is absorbed; uncover and bake 15 minutes more. For gravy, combine the soup and water in a large saucepan; mix well. Simmer about 10 minutes. Serve with the chicken dish. **Yield:** 70-80 servings.

Poppy Seed Fruit Dressing

(Pictured at right)

This tasty topper has subtle peach flavor and a pretty tint to match. It draws "oohs" and "aahs".
—Ruby Williams, Bogalusa, Louisiana

✓ Uses less fat, sugar or salt. Includes Nutritional Analysis and Diabetic Exchanges.

1 large peach, peeled and sliced
1/4 cup sugar
1/4 cup apple juice
2 tablespoons cider vinegar
2 teaspoons chopped onion
1/2 teaspoon ground mustard
1/4 teaspoon salt
1 tablespoon vegetable oil
1 tablespoon poppy seeds
1 large orange, peeled and sectioned
1 small pineapple, peeled and cut into wedges
1 small cantaloupe, cut into balls *or* cubes
2 cups strawberries *or* blueberries
1 cup blackberries
1 cup seedless grapes
1 medium unpeeled red apple, sliced
2 medium kiwifruit, peeled and sliced

Place the peach in a blender; cover and process until smooth. Add sugar, apple juice, vinegar, onion, mustard and salt. Cover and process for 10-15 seconds. Slowly add oil; process 1 minute longer. Stir in poppy seeds. Arrange fruit on a large platter; serve with dressing. **Yield:** 22 servings. **Nutritional Analysis:** One serving with 2 teaspoons dressing (prepared with artificial sweetener equivalent to 1/4 cup sugar and unsweetened apple juice) equals 58 calories, 30 mg sodium, 0 cholesterol, 13 gm carbohydrate, 1 gm protein, 1 gm fat. **Diabetic Exchange:** 1 fruit.

Slow-Cooked Chicken and Stuffing

(Pictured below and on page 178)

Prepared in a slow cooker, this tasty, no-fuss main dish has a flavorful blend of seasonings and the irresistible duo of tender chicken and moist stuffing. It's nice enough for the holidays and easy enough to fix year-round. —Angie Marquart, New Washington, Ohio

2-1/2 cups chicken broth
1 cup butter *or* margarine
1/2 cup chopped onion
1/2 cup chopped celery
1 can (4 ounces) mushroom stems and pieces, drained
1/4 cup dried parsley flakes
1-1/2 teaspoons rubbed sage
1 teaspoon poultry seasoning
1 teaspoon salt
1/2 teaspoon pepper
12 cups day-old bread cubes (1/2-inch pieces)
2 eggs
1 can (10-3/4 ounces) condensed cream of chicken soup, undiluted
5 to 6 cups cubed cooked chicken

In a saucepan, combine the first 10 ingredients. Simmer for 10 minutes; remove from the heat. Place bread cubes in a large bowl. Combine eggs and soup; stir into broth mixture until smooth. Pour over bread; toss well. In a 5-qt. slow cooker, layer half of the dressing and chicken; repeat layers. Cover and cook on low for 4-1/2 to 5 hours or until a meat thermometer inserted into stuffing reads 160°. **Yield:** 14-16 servings.

Soft White Bread

I feed 70 people at church every Wednesday. A good oven-fresh bread like this helps fill folks up and stretches the main dish. —Awynne Thurstenson Siloam Springs, Arkansas

11 to 11-1/2 cups all-purpose flour
6 tablespoons sugar
1/3 cup nonfat dry milk powder
3 packages (1/4 ounce *each*) active dry yeast
1 tablespoon salt
4 cups water
1/2 cup butter *or* margarine

In a mixing bowl, combine 5 cups flour, sugar, dry milk powder, yeast and salt. In a saucepan, heat water and butter to 120°-130° (butter does not need to melt). Add to flour mixture. Beat on low speed until moistened; beat on medium for 3 minutes. Add enough remaining flour to form a soft dough. Turn onto a floured surface; knead until smooth and elastic, about 6-8 minutes. Place in a greased bowl, turning once to grease top. Cover and let rise in a warm place until doubled, about 1 hour. Punch dough down. Divide into thirds; shape into loaves. Place in greased 8-in. x 4-in. x 2-in. loaf pans. Cover and let rise until doubled, about 45 minutes. Bake at 350° for 25-30 minutes or until golden brown. Remove from pans to wire racks. **Yield:** 3 loaves.

Apple Spice Cake Trifle

We like this cake because it's economical, looks elegant and tastes delicious. Our friends enjoy it. —Nora Lee Ingle, Swan, Iowa

1 package (18-1/4 ounces) spice cake mix
1-1/4 cups cinnamon applesauce
3 eggs
1/3 cup vegetable oil
1 can (21 ounces) apple pie filling
1 tablespoon butter *or* margarine

7 teaspoons ground cinnamon, *divided*
3 cups cold milk
1 package (5.1 ounces) instant vanilla pudding mix
1 envelope whipped topping mix
1 carton (12 ounces) frozen whipped topping, thawed
1/2 cup chopped walnuts
1/4 cup English toffee bits *or* almond brickle chips

In a mixing bowl, combine dry cake mix, applesauce, eggs and oil; beat on medium speed for 2 minutes. Pour into a greased 13-in. x 9-in. x 2-in. baking pan. Bake at 350° for 35-40 minutes or until a toothpick inserted near the center comes out clean. Cool on a wire rack. In a saucepan, cook pie filling, butter and 1 teaspoon cinnamon until butter is melted; stir until well blended. Cool. In a mixing bowl, combine milk, pudding mix, topping mix and remaining cinnamon. Beat on high until thickened, about 5 minutes. Let stand 5 minutes. Spread a third of the topping in a 6-qt. bowl. Cut cake into cubes; place half over topping. Top with half of the fruit mixture, walnuts and pudding mixture. Repeat layers, ending with remaining topping mixture. Sprinkle with toffee bits. Cover and chill for at least 2 hours. **Yield:** 20-24 servings.

Cranberry Oatmeal Cookies

(Pictured above right)

Dotted with cranberries, orange peel and vanilla chips, these cookies are so colorful and fun to eat. They look lovely on a dessert tray. *—Pat Habiger, Spearville, Kansas*

1 cup butter *or* margarine, softened
1-1/2 cups sugar
2 eggs
1 teaspoon vanilla extract
2 cups all-purpose flour
1 teaspoon baking powder
1/2 teaspoon salt
1/4 teaspoon baking soda
2 cups quick-cooking oats
1 cup raisins
1 cup coarsely chopped fresh *or* frozen cranberries
1 tablespoon grated orange peel
1 package (12 ounces) vanilla chips

In a mixing bowl, cream butter and sugar. Add eggs, one at a time, beating well after each addition. Beat in vanilla. Combine flour, baking powder, salt and baking soda; add to the creamed mixture. Stir in oats, raisins, cranberries and orange peel. Stir in vanilla chips. Drop by rounded teaspoonfuls 2 in. apart onto greased baking sheets. Bake at 375° for 10-12 minutes or until edges are lightly browned. Cool on wire racks. **Yield:** 6 dozen.

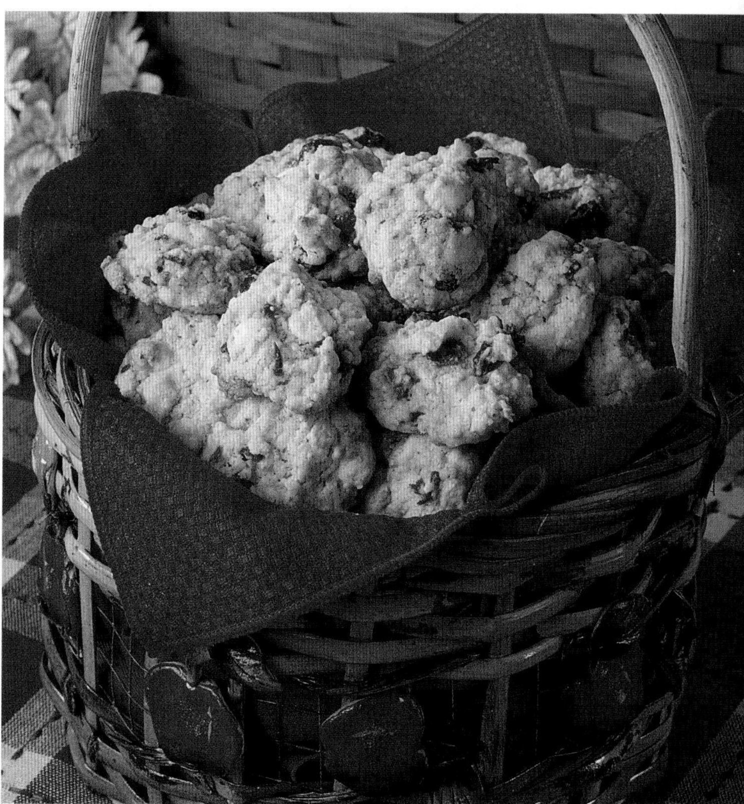

Escalloped Potatoes

These creamy potatoes add down-home goodness to any potluck supper. *—Bernice Hartje, Cavalier, North Dakota*

25 to 30 pounds red potatoes, sliced
1 pound butter *or* margarine
2 cups all-purpose flour
2-1/2 teaspoons salt
2-1/2 teaspoons pepper
2-1/2 quarts milk
2-1/2 quarts whipping cream
4 medium onions, sliced

Cover potatoes with cold water and refrigerate overnight. In a large kettle, melt butter; add flour, salt and pepper. Cook until thickened, stirring constantly. Gradually add milk and cream. Cook and stir until thickened and bubbly. Drain potatoes; place in eight 3-qt. baking pans. Add onions. Pour the sauce over and stir gently. Cover and bake at 300° for 2 hours and 15 minutes. Uncover and bake 15 minutes longer. **Yield:** 70-80 servings.

Favorite Apple Salad

(Pictured above)

A friend gave us this refreshing recipe, which immediately became a family favorite, especially with my mother and mother-in-law. For many meals, I'll prepare this crisp, colorful dish in place of an ordinary green salad. —*Sharon Bielmyer*
Holtwood, Pennsylvania

✓ Uses less fat, sugar or salt. Includes Nutritional Analysis and Diabetic Exchanges.

- **1 can (20 ounces) unsweetened pineapple chunks**
- **1/4 cup butter *or* margarine**
- **1/4 cup sugar**
- **1 tablespoon lemon juice**
- **2 tablespoons cornstarch**
- **2 tablespoons cold water**
- **1 cup mayonnaise**
- **8 cups chopped tart apples**
- **2 cups green grapes**
- **2 teaspoons poppy seeds**
- **3/4 cup chopped pecans, toasted**

Drain pineapple, reserving juice; set pineapple aside. Place juice in a saucepan; add butter, sugar and lemon juice. Bring to a boil. Combine cornstarch and cold water until smooth; add to the saucepan, stirring constantly. Return to a boil; cook and stir for 2 minutes. Chill. Stir in mayonnaise. In a large bowl, combine pineapple, apples, grapes, poppy seeds and cooked dressing. Fold in pecans just before serving. **Yield:** 14 servings. **Nutritional Analysis:** One 3/4-cup serving (prepared with margarine and fat-free mayonnaise) equals 170 calories, 159 mg sodium, 0 cholesterol, 26 gm carbohydrate, 1 gm protein, 8 gm fat. **Diabetic Exchanges:** 1-1/2 fruit, 1-1/2 fat.

Tapioca Pudding

Cooking for a crowd doesn't mean you have to prepare foods in a frazzle. This dessert should be made the night before. —*Bernice Hartje*
Cavalier, North Dakota

- **4 packages (3 ounces *each*) tapioca pudding mix**
- **4 cups milk**
- **1 carton (16 ounces) frozen whipped topping, thawed**
- **2 cans (22 ounces *each*) lemon pie filling**
- **1 package (10-1/2 ounces) colored *or* white miniature marshmallows**
- **4 cans (17 ounces *each*) fruit cocktail, drained**
- **4 cans (15 ounces *each*) mandarin oranges, drained**
- **1 can (20 ounces) crushed pineapple, drained**

In a large saucepan, cook pudding and milk according to package directions; cool. In a large bowl, fold whipped topping into pie filling. Add the remaining ingredients; stir gently. Fold in pudding. Refrigerate overnight. **Yield:** 70-80 servings.

Proven Potluck Tips

When hosting a potluck, ask guests to bring 1 or 2 cups of their favorite salad ingredient. You provide the lettuce, and everyone can enjoy a great tossed salad with very little work.

Making meat loaf for a crowd? Score across the top of the raw meat in the loaf pan where each serving is to be sliced. After the meat loaf is baked, there's no question about the size of servings.

Coleslaw in a Bag

You can easily transport this fresh-tasting salad to a picnic in a cooler. Prepare it days in advance to save time. —*Alice Baker, Woodstock, Illinois*

2 large carrots, shredded
1 small head cabbage, shredded
1 medium green pepper, chopped
1 small onion, chopped
DRESSING:
1 cup (8 ounces) sour cream
1/2 cup mayonnaise *or* salad dressing
2 tablespoons vinegar
2 tablespoons sugar
2 teaspoons celery seed
1/2 to 1 teaspoon lemon juice
1/4 to 1/2 teaspoon grated lemon peel
1/2 teaspoon salt
1/4 teaspoon pepper

In a large plastic bag, toss the carrots, cabbage, green pepper and onion. In a bowl, combine all dressing ingredients. Pour into bag; toss. Chill until serving. **Yield:** 15-20 servings.

Mushroom Green Bean Casserole

(Pictured at right)

The fresh mushrooms, sliced water chestnuts and slivered almonds make this casserole special.
—*Pat Richter, Lake Placid, Florida*

1 pound fresh mushrooms, sliced
1 large onion, chopped
1/2 cup butter *or* margarine
1/4 cup all-purpose flour
1 cup half-and-half cream
1 jar (16 ounces) process cheese sauce
2 teaspoons soy sauce
1/2 teaspoon pepper
1/8 teaspoon hot pepper sauce
1 can (8 ounces) sliced water chestnuts, drained
2 packages (16 ounces *each*) frozen French-style green beans, thawed, drained
Slivered almonds

In a skillet, saute mushrooms and onion in butter. Stir in flour until blended. Gradually stir in cream. Bring to a boil; cook and stir for 2 minutes. Stir in cheese sauce, soy sauce, pepper and hot pepper sauce until cheese is melted. Remove from the heat; stir in water chestnuts. Place beans in an ungreased 3-qt. baking dish. Pour cheese mixture over top. Sprinkle with almonds. Bake, uncovered, at 375° for 25-30 minutes or until bubbly. **Yield:** 14-16 servings.

Clam Chowder for 60

When we had "Soup Day" at my mobile home park a few years ago, I brought along a large kettle of this creamy soup. Folks were bowled over by its terrific taste. —*Gretchen Draeger, Santa Cruz, California*

30 cans (6-1/2 ounces *each*) minced clams
8 cups diced onions
1-1/2 pounds butter *or* margarine
2 cups all-purpose flour
3 quarts milk
3 bunches celery, sliced
3 cups minced fresh parsley
12 pounds potatoes, peeled and cubed
3 pounds sharp cheddar cheese, shredded
Salt and pepper to taste

Drain and rinse clams, reserving juice; set aside. In a large kettle, saute onions in butter until tender. Add flour; stir to form a smooth paste. Gradually add the milk, stirring constantly until slightly thickened (do not boil). Add celery, parsley and potatoes; cook until tender, about 45 minutes. Add the clams and cheese; cook until cheese is melted and soup is heated through. Add reserved clam juice and salt and pepper. **Yield:** 60 servings (15 quarts).

Cooking for One or Two

These perfectly portioned menus—featuring mouth-watering main dishes, side dishes, desserts and more—yield smaller servings that are big on taste.

SMALLER SERVINGS. Clockwise from upper left: Spiced Apple Bagel and Individual Quiche (page 200); Breaded Pork Chops, Parmesan Baked Tomatoes and Italian-Style Rice (pages 206 and 207); Meat Loaf for One, Tomato Zucchini Salad and Creamy Scalloped Potatoes (pages 204 and 205); Chicken Caesar Salad and Blueberry Cake Cups (page 208).

Singling Out Good Food

RECIPES that serve only one can have as much appeal as those that feed a bunch. The delightful duo pictured at right makes a mighty good meal for one. (You'll find more singular sensations on the following pages.)

Individual Quiche is suggested by Laura Stoltzfus of New Holland, Pennsylvania. "This filling and flavorful dish requires only a minimal amount of preparation," she says. "Don't limit this egg dish to breakfast," suggests Laura. "It also makes a delicious light lunch or dinner."

Angela Sansom of New York, New York has created lots of single-serving specialties like her Spiced Apple Bagel. "Raisins, cinnamon and apples transform a simple bagel into a hot, filling morning meal," Angela assures. "Or try it as a hearty midday snack."

As a treat for himself, Richard Ward from Three Rivers, Michigan likes to make Aunt Betty's Jelly Crepes almost every Sunday. "My Aunt Betty made these for me when I was a boy," Richard reports. "They're so simple to make and taste so good I've been eating them ever since."

Individual Quiche

1/4 cup bulk pork sausage
1 egg
1/3 cup milk
Dash *each* salt, pepper and ground mustard
1 slice bread, crust removed
1 green onion, sliced
1 tablespoon shredded cheddar cheese

In a small skillet, brown sausage; drain. In a small bowl, beat egg, milk, salt, pepper and mustard; set aside. Cube bread; place in a greased 8-oz. custard cup. Top with sausage and onion. Pour egg mixture over top. Sprinkle with cheese. Bake, uncovered, at 350° for 25-30 minutes or until a knife inserted near the center comes out clean. **Yield:** 1 serving.

Spiced Apple Bagel

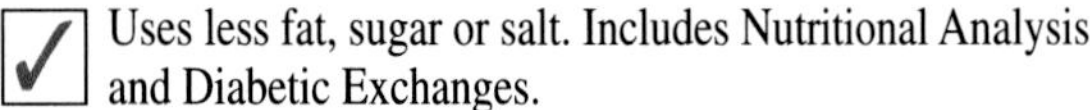

✓ Uses less fat, sugar or salt. Includes Nutritional Analysis and Diabetic Exchanges.

3 tablespoons cream cheese, softened

1 honey-wheat *or* plain bagel, split
3 tablespoons chopped apple
4 teaspoons raisins
1 teaspoon brown sugar
1/4 teaspoon ground cinnamon
1/8 teaspoon ground nutmeg

Spread cream cheese on bagel halves. Top with apple and raisins. Combine brown sugar, cinnamon and nutmeg; sprinkle over the top. Place on a baking sheet; broil 6-8 in. from the heat for 2-3 minutes or until hot and bubbly. **Yield:** 1 serving. **Nutritional Analysis:** One serving (prepared with honey-wheat bagel and fat-free cream cheese)

equals 255 calories, 513 mg sodium, 3 mg cholesterol, 51 gm carbohydrate, 13 gm protein, 2 gm fat. **Diabetic Exchanges:** 2 starch, 1 fruit, 1 lean meat.

Aunt Betty's Jelly Crepes

(Not pictured)

2 eggs
3/4 cup milk
1/8 teaspoon salt
1/2 cup all-purpose flour
Butter *or* margarine, softened
Strawberry *or* grape jelly
Confectioners' sugar

In a small bowl, whisk eggs, milk and salt. Add flour; beat until smooth. Melt 1 teaspoon butter in a 10-in. nonstick skillet. Pour 1/4 cup batter into center of skillet; lift and turn pan to cover bottom. Cook until lightly browned; turn and brown the other side. Remove and keep warm. Repeat with remaining batter, adding butter to skillet as needed. Spread crepes with butter and jelly; roll up. Dust with confectioners' sugar. Serve immediately. **Yield:** 3 crepes.

PUT SPRING'S first fresh vegetables to good use by preparing this producc-packcd mcal. It's a super sin gle-serving supper that will have you celebrating the season's arrival.

Joan Nichols of Sarnia, Ontario suggests Mushroom-Orange Chop as a small main dish that's big on flavor. "Marmalade in the sauce gives the moist pork chop a tasty tang I really enjoy," she remarks. "And the sunflower kernels add a delightful crunch."

A plain baked potato will seem boring after you've tried a Loaded Potato. The recipe was created by Jill Werle of Saskatoon, Saskatchewan back when she was single. "This stuffed potato goes great with any meat. Or it can even be a satisfying quick lunch all by itself," informs Jill.

What springtime meal would be complete without fresh-from-the-garden asparagus? "The recipe for Sesame Asparagus turns a super spring vegetable into a more special one," says Marshall, Illinois cook Violet Beard. "It's nice to treat myself to a 'fancy' side dish with very little work."

Mushroom-Orange Chop

1 butterfly pork chop (3/4 inch thick)
2 teaspoons vegetable oil
2 green onions, thinly sliced
2 fresh mushrooms, chopped
1 garlic clove, minced
2 tablespoons orange marmalade
1 teaspoon soy sauce
1 tablespoon sunflower kernels, optional

In a skillet over medium heat, brown pork chop in oil on both sides. Continue cooking until a meat thermometer reads 160°-170°, about 6 minutes. Remove and keep warm. In the same skillet, saute onions, mushrooms and garlic until tender. Add marmalade and soy sauce; cook and stir until heated through. Pour over chop. Sprinkle with sunflower kernels if desired. **Yield:** 1 serving.

Loaded Potato

✓ Uses less fat, sugar or salt. Includes Nutritional Analysis and Diabetic Exchanges.

1/2 cup small-curd cottage cheese
2 tablespoons shredded cheddar cheese
2 tablespoons chopped tomato
1 tablespoon chopped green pepper
1 tablespoon chopped green onion
1 hot baked potato

In a bowl, combine the cottage cheese, cheddar cheese, tomato, green pepper and onion. With a sharp knife, cut an X in the top of the potato; fluff pulp with a fork. Top with cottage cheese mixture. Serve immediately. **Yield:** 1 serving. **Nutritional Analysis:** One serving (prepared with fat-free cottage cheese and fat-free cheddar cheese) equals 245 calories, 563 mg sodium, 11 mg cholesterol, 38 gm carbohydrate, 22 gm protein, trace fat. **Diabetic Exchanges:** 3 very lean meat, 2 starch, 1 vegetable.

Sesame Asparagus

☑ Uses less fat, sugar or salt. Includes Nutritional Analysis and Diabetic Exchanges.

6 fresh asparagus spears, trimmed
1/4 teaspoon salt, optional
1 teaspoon butter *or* margarine, melted
1 teaspoon lemon juice
3/4 teaspoon sesame seeds, toasted

Place asparagus in a skillet; sprinkle with salt. Add 1/2 in. of water; bring to a boil. Reduce heat; cover and simmer until crisp-tender, about 4 minutes. Combine butter, lemon juice and sesame seeds. Drain asparagus; drizzle with butter mixture. **Yield:** 1 serving. **Nutritional Analysis:** One serving (prepared with margarine and without salt) equals 71 calories, 47 mg sodium, 0 cholesterol, 5 gm carbohydrate, 3 gm protein, 5 gm fat. **Diabetic Exchanges:** 1 vegetable, 1 fat.

THINK you can't make a hearty meat-and-potatoes meal just because you're cooking for one? Well, think again!

The down-home dinner featured here is made up of satisfying single servings that won't fill the fridge with leftovers.

Lynne Oberst-Bishop of Dorris, California suggests Meat Loaf for One. "When I dine alone, I often fix myself this hearty, flavorful mixture," Lynne says. "Combining meat, bread and a vegetable, it can be a complete meal."

You will enjoy Creamy Scalloped Potatoes without days of leftovers using the recipe shared by Dawn Fagerstrom of Warren, Minnesota.

"It makes a small quantity but still has old-fashioned goodness," Dawn assures. "These tender potatoes taste great with any main dish, but I especially like them with meat loaf."

Lettuce, tomato, zucchini and a homemade dressing make a super salad for one using the recipe from Dorothy Pritchett of Wills Point, Texas.

"Tomato Zucchini Salad is more special than a plain green salad and hardly any fuss to put together," Dorothy remarks.

Meat Loaf for One

1 egg, beaten
1/4 cup frozen corn, thawed
1/4 cup seasoned bread crumbs
1 teaspoon Dijon mustard
1/8 teaspoon dried thyme
4 ounces ground beef
2 ounces bulk pork sausage
1 to 2 tablespoons ketchup

In a bowl, combine the egg, corn, bread crumbs, mustard and thyme. Add meat and mix well. Shape into a 5-in. x 3-in. loaf. Place in an ungreased shallow baking pan. Bake, uncovered, at 350° for 15 minutes. Drizzle with ketchup. Bake 20 minutes longer or until meat is no longer pink and a meat thermometer reads 160°. **Yield:** 1 serving.

Creamy Scalloped Potatoes

3-1/2 teaspoons butter *or* margarine, *divided*
1 tablespoon all-purpose flour
1/4 teaspoon salt
Dash pepper
3/4 cup milk
1 cup sliced peeled potatoes
1 tablespoon finely chopped onion

In a saucepan over medium heat, melt 3 teaspoons of butter. Stir in flour, salt and pepper until smooth. Gradually add milk. Bring to a boil; cook and stir for 2 minutes or until thickened and bubbly. Place half of the potatoes in a greased 2-cup baking dish; top with the onion and half of the sauce. Layer with remaining potatoes and sauce. Dot with remaining butter. Cover and bake at 350° for 30 minutes. Uncover; bake 30-40 minutes longer or until the potatoes are tender. **Yield:** 1 serving.

Tomato Zucchini Salad

✓ Uses less fat, sugar or salt. Includes Nutritional Analysis and Diabetic Exchanges.

1 cup torn salad greens
1/2 small tomato, cut into wedges
1/4 cup thinly sliced zucchini
1 tablespoon mayonnaise
1 tablespoon French salad dressing
1 teaspoon wheat germ, toasted
1/4 teaspoon sugar
1/4 teaspoon vinegar

Combine greens, tomato and zucchini. Combine remaining ingredients; drizzle over salad. **Yield:** 1 serving. **Nutritional Analysis:** One serving (prepared with light mayonnaise and fat-free salad dressing) equals 107 calories, 279 mg sodium, 0 cholesterol, 14 gm carbohydrate, 2 gm protein, 6 gm fat. **Diabetic Exchanges:** 1 vegetable, 1 fat, 1/2 starch.

Cooking for 'Just the Two of Us'

WHEN it's just a couple at the table, it can be tricky finding perfectly portioned dishes. So, here and on the following pages, we provide recipes that are just right for serving two people.

Breaded Pork Chops, a baked entree that's ideal for chilly days, comes from Sally Fausch of Dunnellon, Florida. After one bite, however, Sally's husband started requesting these satisfying chops year-round.

"I came up with this recipe to serve something a little different for just my husband and me," Sally relates. "We love the combination of barbecue sauce, lemon-pepper seasoning and Parmesan cheese on these moist pork chops."

Parmesan Baked Tomatoes are suggested by Joy Beck of Cincinnati, Ohio. "Tomatoes are my husband Tom's favorite food," says Joy. "This dish is quick, tasty and one we both enjoy. The flavor of juicy tomatoes topped with Parmesan cheese and seasoned bread crumbs is scrumptious."

While living for 4-1/2 years in Milan, Italy with husband Leon, Kathryn Manwiller of Wyomissing, Pennsylvania picked up the recipe for Italian-Style Rice.

"Since it contains very little spice, this simple side dish is good for folks who can't eat spicy food," Kathryn reports.

Breaded Pork Chops

1 egg
1 tablespoon barbecue sauce
1/3 cup dry bread crumbs
2 teaspoons grated Parmesan cheese
1/4 teaspoon dried oregano
1/8 to 1/4 teaspoon lemon-pepper seasoning
1/8 teaspoon onion salt
2 bone-in pork chops (3/4 inch thick)

In a bowl, combine egg and barbecue sauce; mix well. In another bowl, combine bread crumbs, cheese, oregano, lemon-pepper and salt. Dip chops in egg mixture, then coat with bread crumb mixture. Place in a greased 8-in. square baking dish. Cover and refrigerate for 2 hours. Bake, uncovered, at 325° for 1 hour or until juices run clear. **Yield:** 2 servings.

Parmesan Baked Tomatoes

1 can (14-1/2 ounces) whole tomatoes, drained and quartered
2 tablespoons seasoned bread crumbs
1/4 to 1/2 teaspoon Italian seasoning
1/4 teaspoon garlic salt
2 tablespoons shredded Parmesan cheese
1 tablespoon butter *or* margarine

Place the tomatoes in a greased 1-qt. baking dish. Combine bread crumbs, Italian seasoning and

garlic salt; sprinkle over the tomatoes. Top with Parmesan cheese; dot with butter. Bake, uncovered, at 325° for 15-20 minutes or until lightly browned. **Yield:** 2-3 servings.

Italian-Style Rice

1 tablespoon chopped onion
1 tablespoon butter *or* margarine
1/3 cup uncooked long grain rice
1-1/4 cups chicken broth
Dash ground turmeric
1/4 cup shredded Parmesan cheese

In a saucepan, saute onion in butter until tender. Add rice; cook over medium heat for 2 minutes, stirring constantly. Stir in broth and turmeric; bring to a boil. Reduce heat; cover and simmer for 20-25 minutes or until liquid is absorbed. Stir in cheese. **Yield:** 2 servings.

TAKE THE WORK out of paring down large-quantity recipes with these recipes perfectly portioned for those days when cooking for just the two of you.

Chicken Caesar Salad, a refreshing main dish, is from Kay Andersen of Bear, Delaware. "It looks and tastes fancy but couldn't be easier to make," relates Kay. "It's my husband's favorite dinner."

Simple and fruity Blueberry Cake Cups are suggested by Suzanne McKinley of Lyons, Georgia.

Judi Brinegar of Liberty, North Carolina recommends crunchy, tangy Veggie Rice Salad. "It's a great use for leftover rice and quick to prepare," says Judi.

Writes Opal Hinson from her home in Lubbock, Texas, "Comforting Banana Pudding's a terrific small-quantity alternative to banana cream pie."

Chicken Caesar Salad

✓ Uses less fat, sugar or salt. Includes Nutritional Analysis and Diabetic Exchanges.

2 boneless skinless chicken breast halves (1/2 pound)
2 teaspoons olive *or* vegetable oil
1/8 teaspoon dried basil
1/8 teaspoon dried oregano
1/4 teaspoon garlic salt, optional
1/4 teaspoon pepper
1/4 teaspoon paprika
4 cups torn romaine
1 small tomato, thinly sliced
Caesar salad dressing
Caesar salad croutons, optional

Brush chicken with oil. Combine basil, oregano, garlic salt if desired, pepper and paprika; sprinkle over chicken. Grill, uncovered, over medium-low heat for 12-15 minutes or until juices run clear, turning several times. Arrange romaine and tomato on plates. Cut chicken into strips; place on top. Drizzle with dressing. Sprinkle with croutons if desired. **Yield:** 2 servings. **Nutritional Analysis:** One serving (prepared without garlic salt and croutons and with 2 tablespoons fat-free salad dressing) equals 219 calories, 467 mg sodium, 73 mg cholesterol, 6 gm carbohydrate, 29 gm protein, 8 gm fat. **Diabetic Exchanges:** 3-1/2 very lean meat, 1 vegetable, 1 fat.

Blueberry Cake Cups

1/4 cup all-purpose flour
1/4 cup sugar
1/2 teaspoon baking powder
Dash salt
1/4 cup milk

1 tablespoon butter *or* margarine, melted
1 cup blueberries, *divided*

In a bowl, combine flour, sugar, baking powder and salt. Stir in milk and butter just until moistened. Divide half of the berries between two greased 10-oz. custard cups. Top with the batter and remaining berries. Bake at 375° for 25-30 minutes or until golden brown. Serve warm. **Yield:** 2 servings.

Veggie Rice Salad

(Not pictured)

1 cup cooked rice
1/3 cup shredded carrot
1/4 cup diced celery

1/4 cup diced green pepper
1 jar (2 ounces) diced pimientos, drained
1 green onion, thinly sliced
2 tablespoons vegetable oil
2 tablespoons cider *or* red wine vinegar
1/2 teaspoon sugar
Salt and pepper to taste

In a bowl, combine the first six ingredients. In a jar with a tight-fitting lid, combine oil, vinegar, sugar, salt and pepper; shake well. Pour over salad and toss. Chill until serving. **Yield:** 2 servings.

Comforting Banana Pudding

(Not pictured)

1 cup sugar
1 tablespoon cornstarch
1-1/2 cups milk
1 egg, beaten
1/4 teaspoon vanilla extract
8 vanilla wafers
1 large firm banana, sliced

In a saucepan, combine the sugar and cornstarch; gradually stir in milk until smooth. Cook and stir over medium-high heat until thickened and bubbly. Reduce heat; cook and stir 2 minutes longer. Remove from the heat. Stir 1 cup hot mixture into egg; return all to the pan and bring to a gentle boil. Remove from the heat; stir in vanilla. Refrigerate for 15 minutes. Layer vanilla wafers and banana slices in parfait glasses or bowls. Top with pudding. **Yield:** 2 servings.

SATISFY TASTE BUDS with this smaller-serving meal that yields finger-lickin'-good flavor.

The recipe for Braised Short Ribs was developed by Maureen DeGarmo of Concord, California. "My husband, who is a rather selective eater, devoured these tender beef ribs in their tangy herb sauce," Maureen relates. "It's a special main dish for two."

Ruby Williams of Bogalusa, Louisiana sometimes cooks for her great-grandson Derek. "Being a teenager, he has developed his own tastes and doesn't always care for the same things I do," admits Ruby, a widow. "But Pecan Green Beans is a tasty vegetable dish we both enjoy."

Crusty Dinner Biscuits, suggested by Sharon McClatchey from Muskogee, Oklahoma, bake up with golden crusty outsides and moist and tender insides.

For a deliciously different treat, try Orange Cobbler. Margery Bryan of Royal City, Washington shares the recipe and informs, "Orange marmalade is a sweet and tangy base for this cobbler."

Braised Short Ribs

6 tablespoons water
6 tablespoons olive *or* vegetable oil, *divided*
4 teaspoons Dijon mustard
4 teaspoons cider *or* red wine vinegar
4 teaspoons dried basil
4 teaspoons dried thyme
1 tablespoon dried rosemary, crushed
1/4 teaspoon pepper
6 to 8 boneless beef short ribs (about 1-1/2 pounds)
1 can (8 ounces) tomato sauce

In a small bowl, combine water, 2 tablespoons oil, mustard, vinegar and seasonings; mix well. Place the ribs in a large resealable plastic bag or shallow glass container. Set aside half of the marinade. Pour remaining marinade over ribs; turn to coat. Cover and refrigerate for several hours. Drain, discarding marinade. Transfer ribs to a greased shallow 1-qt. baking dish. Combine tomato sauce and reserved marinade; pour over ribs. Cover and bake at 350° for 1-1/2 hours or until the meat is tender. **Yield:** 2 servings.

Pecan Green Beans

1-1/2 cups cut fresh green beans
2 tablespoons chopped pecans
1 tablespoon butter *or* margarine
1/4 teaspoon salt
1/8 teaspoon pepper

Place beans in a saucepan and cover with water; bring to a boil. Cook, uncovered, for 8-10 minutes or until crisp-tender. Meanwhile, in a skillet, saute pecans in butter for 3 minutes or until golden brown. Drain beans; add to skillet. Sprinkle with salt and pepper; toss to coat. **Yield:** 2 servings.

Crusty Dinner Biscuits

1 cup all-purpose flour
1 teaspoon baking powder
1/2 teaspoon salt
1/2 cup milk
1 tablespoon vegetable oil
Half-and-half cream *or* milk, optional
Butter *and/or* honey

In a bowl, combine the flour, baking powder and salt. Combine milk and oil; pour over the dry ingredients and stir just until moistened. Turn onto a floured surface; knead 5-6 times. Roll out to 1/2-in. thickness; cut with a floured 2-in. biscuit cutter. Place on a greased baking sheet. Brush tops with cream if desired. Bake at 425° for 13-15 minutes or until golden brown. Serve warm with butter and/or honey. **Yield:** 6 biscuits.

Orange Cobbler

(Not pictured)

2 tablespoons sugar
1 tablespoon cornstarch
1/2 cup water
1/4 cup orange marmalade
2 tablespoons orange juice concentrate
2 teaspoons butter *or* margarine
1/2 cup biscuit/baking mix
Dash ground nutmeg
3 tablespoons milk
Vanilla ice cream

In a small saucepan, combine the sugar and cornstarch. Stir in water, marmalade and orange juice concentrate. Cook and stir over medium-low heat until thickened. Stir in butter until melted. Pour into a greased 1-qt. baking dish. In a small bowl, combine biscuit mix and nutmeg; stir in milk just until moistened. Drop dough by tablespoonfuls over orange mixture. Bake, uncovered, at 400° for 20-25 minutes or until topping is golden brown. Serve warm with ice cream. **Yield:** 2 servings.

'My Mom's Best Meal'

Six cooks recall special times when they prepare the same favorite meals their moms often served.

FONDLY REMEMBERED FOODS include, clockwise from upper left: Memorable Holiday Meal (p. 234), Heartfelt Fare (p. 230), Flavorful Fish Dinner (p. 222) and Country-Style Menu (p. 226).

After working hard on the farm each Saturday morning, we looked forward to this home-style menu featuring a hearty meatball stew.

By Teresa Ingebrand, Perham, Minnesota

GROWING UP on a farm, we never were afforded the luxury of sleeping in on Saturday mornings. Instead, they meant a lot of hard work both inside and out.

But one thing all seven of us looked forward to was this fit-for-a-king midday meal prepared by Mom (Odilia Riestenberg, above, of Elizabeth, Minnesota).

Her Meatball Stew was a favorite main dish at our house, especially during the cold winter months. We delighted in the aroma of the stew simmering on the stove as we came in for dinner. Mom liked that it was simple to prepare and that it satisfied all of our hearty appetites.

Sweet and tangy, Mom's Coleslaw went so well with the stew. It can be made in advance, giving you more time to complete other chores around the house or cook up another treat in the kitchen.

Like most cooks of her day, Mom was always looking for ways to use up leftovers. Older bread was never thrown away…it got recycled into Quick Garlic Toast. It never seemed like a leftover to us—we thought it was a special treat!

We didn't have dessert at every meal, but when Mom asked for suggestions, Chocolate Marshmallow Cake is what we usually requested. It was very difficult to stop at one piece.

Now Mom and Dad are semi-retired (I don't think farmers ever really retire). Mom grows flowers for dried floral arrangements, and she still invites us to dinner once in a while.

I learned most of what I know about cooking from her. As a homemaker with three children, I frequently turn to Mom's recipes like these. We hope your family will enjoy them, too.

PICTURED AT LEFT: Meatball Stew, Mom's Coleslaw, Quick Garlic Toast and Chocolate Marshmallow Cake (recipes are on the next page).

Meatball Stew

The combination of tender meatballs plus potatoes, carrots and pearl onions in a golden gravy really hit the spot on chilly days after we'd worked up an appetite doing our morning chores. Mom served it with pride for Saturday dinners when I was growing up on the farm.

1 egg, beaten
1 cup soft bread crumbs
1/4 cup finely chopped onion
1 teaspoon salt
1 teaspoon dried marjoram
1/2 teaspoon dried thyme
1-1/2 pounds ground beef
2 tablespoons vegetable oil
2 cans (14-1/2 ounces *each*) beef broth
2 cans (10-3/4 ounces *each*) condensed golden mushroom soup, undiluted
4 medium potatoes, peeled and quartered
4 medium carrots, cut into chunks
1 jar (16 ounces) whole pearl onions, drained
1/4 cup minced fresh parsley

In a bowl, combine egg, bread crumbs, chopped onion, salt, marjoram and thyme. Add beef and mix well. Shape into 48 meatballs. In a Dutch oven, brown meatballs in oil; drain. Add broth, soup, potatoes, carrots and pearl onions; bring to a boil. Reduce heat; simmer for 30 minutes or until the vegetables are tender. Sprinkle with parsley. **Yield:** 8 servings.

Mom's Coleslaw

Year-round, our family always goes for this crisp, refreshing salad. With a tangy vinegar and oil dressing, it has wonderful homemade flavor. When Mom made it years ago for our family of seven, it was rare to have leftovers.

1 large head cabbage, shredded
2 medium carrots, shredded
1 teaspoon celery seed
1 cup vegetable oil
1 cup sugar
1/2 cup vinegar
1 teaspoon salt
1 teaspoon ground mustard
1 medium onion, quartered

In a large bowl, toss cabbage, carrots and celery seed. Place the remaining ingredients in a blender or food processor; cover and process until combined. Pour over cabbage mixture and toss to coat. Cover and refrigerate for at least 2 hours. Serve with a slotted spoon. **Yield:** 10-12 servings.

Quick Garlic Toast

Mom knew how to easily round out a meal with this crisp, cheesy garlic toast. We gobbled it up when she served it alongside slaw or salad...and used it to soak up gravy from her stew, too.

1/3 cup butter *or* margarine, softened
12 slices bread
1/2 teaspoon garlic salt
3 tablespoons grated Parmesan cheese

Spread butter on one side of each slice of bread. Cut each slice in half; place plain side down on a baking sheet. Sprinkle with garlic salt and Parmesan cheese. Broil 4 in. from the heat for 1-2 minutes or until lightly browned. **Yield:** 12 slices.

Chocolate Marshmallow Cake

When Mom wanted to treat us to something special, she made this awesome dessert. We could never resist the tender chocolate cake, the fluffy marshmallow layer or the fudge topping.

1/2 cup butter (no substitutes)
2 squares (1 ounce *each*) unsweetened chocolate
1 cup all-purpose flour
1/2 teaspoon baking powder
1/4 teaspoon baking soda
1/4 teaspoon salt
2 eggs
1 cup sugar
1/2 cup unsweetened applesauce
1 teaspoon vanilla extract
1 package (10-1/2 ounces) miniature marshmallows, *divided*

GLAZE:

1/2 cup sugar
2 tablespoons milk
2 tablespoons butter
1/4 cup semisweet chocolate chips

In a microwave or double boiler, melt butter and chocolate; cool for 10 minutes. Combine the flour, baking powder, baking soda and salt; set aside. In a mixing bowl, beat eggs, sugar, applesauce and vanilla. Stir in chocolate mixture. Add dry ingredients; mix well. Pour into a greased 13-in. x 9-in. x 2-in. baking pan. Bake at 350° for 20-30 minutes or until cake tests done. Set aside 1/2 cup marshmallows for glaze. Sprinkle remaining marshmallows over cake. Return to the oven for 2 minutes or until marshmallows are softened. In a saucepan, combine sugar, milk and butter. Bring to a boil; boil for 1-1/2 minutes. Remove from the heat; stir in chocolate chips and reserved marshmallows until melted. Quickly drizzle over the cake (glaze will harden as it cools). **Yield:** 12-16 servings.

Marvelous Marshmallows

To keep marshmallows from turning hard, store them in the freezer. If marshmallows are already hard, tightly seal them in a plastic bag with a few slices of fresh white bread and let stand for 3 days. They'll be like fresh.

Every summer, family members and friends look forward to a barbecue that features different foods from around the world.

By Jennifer McQuillan, Jacksonville, Florida

MY MOM is an adventurous cook who loves to entertain. Since Dad was in the Air Force, they've both done a lot of traveling over the years. Mom (Carol Stickney, above, of Sparta, New Jersey) picked up plenty of great recipes along the way.

This family-favorite meal combines some of those delicious recipes.

Curried Beef Kabobs is a colorful main dish that Mom came across while Dad was stationed in Turkey in the 1970's. She enrolled in a cooking class while living there, and learned to fix many new dishes, including these zesty kabobs.

That's also where she got the recipe for Salsa Green Beans. Everyone who tries them agrees they're very fresh-tasting and nicely seasoned.

Years later, Mom discovered Mushroom Pasta Pilaf. She knew that savory dish featuring mushrooms, onions and pasta would pair perfectly with the kabobs.

Whenever she serves this menu, Mom usually includes light and fruity Frozen Hawaiian Pie. It's chockfull of tasty things like pineapple, maraschino cherries and walnuts.

Each summer, she and Dad like to host a barbecue that features this meal (the kabobs can be grilled rather than broiled). Family members and friends look forward to the party months in advance...Uncle Bob starts inquiring about it as early as April!

My brother, James, says he still lives at home because he loves Mom's cooking so much. My husband, Patrick, and I live far away from my parents, so we don't get to enjoy Mom's meals on a regular basis. But I try to duplicate terrific ones like this using her recipes.

PICTURED AT LEFT: Curried Beef Kabobs, Salsa Green Beans, Mushroom Pasta Pilaf and Frozen Hawaiian Pie (recipes are on the next page).

Curried Beef Kabobs

A tongue-tingling marinade gives delightful flavor to the tender chunks of beef in this main dish. My mother prepares these kabobs for guests often since they're so colorful and popular.

2/3 cup olive *or* vegetable oil
1/2 cup beef broth
1/2 cup lemon juice
2 garlic cloves, minced
2 teaspoons curry powder
2 teaspoons salt
4 bay leaves
16 whole peppercorns
2 pounds beef tenderloin, cut into 1-1/4-inch cubes
2 large green peppers, cut into 1-1/2-inch pieces
3 medium tomatoes, cut into wedges
3 medium onions, cut into wedges

In a large resealable plastic bag or shallow glass dish, combine the first eight ingredients; mix well. Remove 2/3 cup for basting; refrigerate. Add beef to remaining marinade; turn to coat. Cover and refrigerate for 8 hours or overnight. Drain and discard the marinade. On metal or soaked bamboo skewers, alternate beef, green peppers, tomatoes and onions. Place on a greased rack in a broiler pan; broil 5 in. from the heat for 3 minutes on each side. Baste with reserved marinade. Continue broiling, turning and basting for 8-10 minutes or until meat reaches desired doneness (for rare, a meat thermometer should read 140°; medium, 160°; well-done, 170°). **Yield:** 8 servings.

Mushroom Pasta Pilaf

This simmered side dish is an excellent complement to Mom's shish kabobs or any beef main dish. Tiny pieces of pasta pick up bold seasoning from mushrooms, onion and Worcestershire sauce.

1 small onion, chopped
1/4 cup butter *or* margarine
1-1/3 cups uncooked ring, orzo *or* other small pasta
1 can (10-1/2 ounces) beef consomme, undiluted
1 cup water
1 can (7 ounces) mushroom stems and pieces, undrained
1 tablespoon Worcestershire sauce
1 teaspoon salt
1/4 teaspoon soy sauce
Dash pepper

In a large skillet, saute onion in butter until tender. Add remaining ingredients; bring to a boil. Reduce heat; cover and simmer for 20 minutes or until the pasta is tender and the liquid is absorbed. **Yield:** 6-8 servings.

Salsa Green Beans

This simple treatment is a wonderful way of dressing up plain green beans. Maybe the reason I really enjoy this vegetable is because Mom has been fixing it this way since I was a little girl. Onions, salsa and garlic add just the right amount of zip.

4 cups fresh *or* frozen cut green beans
2 small onions, chopped
1/4 cup butter *or* margarine
3 medium tomatoes, cut into wedges
2 tablespoons salsa
1 garlic clove, minced
1/4 to 1/2 teaspoon salt

In a saucepan, cover beans with water; bring to a boil. Cook, uncovered, for 8-10 minutes or until crisp-tender. Meanwhile, in a skillet, saute onions in butter until tender. Drain beans. Add the tomatoes, salsa, garlic, salt and onions; heat through. **Yield:** 6-8 servings.

Frozen Hawaiian Pie

Cool summer pies are one of Mom's specialties. This version offers pineapple, maraschino cherries and walnuts that are folded into a fluffy filling. It's an easy yet tempting no-bake dessert.

1 can (14 ounces) sweetened condensed milk
1 carton (12 ounces) frozen whipped topping, thawed
1 can (20 ounces) crushed pineapple, drained
1/2 cup chopped walnuts
1/2 cup chopped maraschino cherries
2 tablespoons lemon juice
2 graham cracker crusts (9 inches)
Fresh mint and additional walnuts and maraschino cherries

In a bowl, combine milk and whipped topping. Gently fold in pineapple, nuts, cherries and lemon juice. Pour into the crusts. Freeze until firm, about 4 hours. Remove from the freezer 20 minutes before serving. Garnish with mint, nuts and cherries. **Yield:** 2 pies (6-8 servings each).

Compliments on her own meals are credited to Mom—a welcoming cook who draws folks into the best spot in the house...the kitchen.

By Lisa Kivirist, Browntown, Wisconsin

WHEN GUESTS in our home compliment me on a great meal, I share some of the credit with my mom (Aelita Kivirist, above, of Glenview, Illinois). She's my inspiration in the kitchen.

I could put together a cookbook of all Mom's recipes we enjoy, but this savory and satisfying meal is my personal favorite.

When my husband, John Ivanko, and I visit my parents, Mom often prepares her light and flaky Lemon Grilled Salmon.

In the 1950's, Mom emigrated from Latvia, where dill is a very popular seasoning. It certainly tastes wonderful on this salmon. We savor every bite.

Cottage Cheese Spinach Salad is a unique take-off on a traditional spinach salad. Everyone who tries it comments on the unusual (and pleasing!) combination of ingredients.

Herbed Oven Potatoes have a delightful onion and herb flavor. These seasoned potatoes are easy to make since there's no peeling required. I'm always sure to help myself to a big serving.

We all save room for a big slice of Frozen Mocha Torte. It's surprisingly simple to make and never lasts long at gatherings.

Mom has a talent for making guests feel welcome. She's warm and cheerful as she dances around the kitchen putting the finishing touches on a meal.

She laughs when everyone crowds around the counter as she works instead of sitting in comfortable living room chairs just a few steps away.

They've discovered what I've known for many years—the best spot in the house is the kitchen when Mom's cooking.

PICTURED AT LEFT: Lemon Grilled Salmon, Cottage Cheese Spinach Salad, Herbed Oven Potatoes and Frozen Mocha Torte (recipes are on the next page).

Lemon Grilled Salmon

Mom proudly serves this tender, flaky fish to family and guests. A savory marinade that includes dill gives the salmon mouth-watering flavor. Since it can be grilled or broiled, we enjoy it year-round.

✓ Uses less fat, sugar or salt. Includes Nutritional Analysis and Diabetic Exchanges.

- **2 teaspoons snipped fresh dill *or* 3/4 teaspoon dill weed**
- **1/2 teaspoon lemon-pepper seasoning**
- **1/2 teaspoon salt, optional**
- **1/4 teaspoon garlic powder**
- **1 salmon fillet (1-1/2 pounds)**
- **1/4 cup packed brown sugar**
- **3 tablespoons chicken broth**
- **3 tablespoons vegetable oil**
- **3 tablespoons soy sauce**
- **3 tablespoons finely chopped green onions**
- **1 small lemon, thinly sliced**
- **2 onion slices, separated into rings**

Sprinkle dill, lemon-pepper, salt if desired and garlic powder over salmon. Place in a large resealable plastic bag or shallow glass container. Combine the brown sugar, broth, oil, soy sauce and green onions; pour over the salmon. Cover and refrigerate for 1 hour, turning once. Drain and discard marinade. Place salmon skin side down on grill over medium heat; arrange lemon and onion slices over the top. Cover and cook for 15-20 minutes or until fish flakes easily with a fork. **Yield:** 6 servings. **Nutritional Analysis:** One serving (prepared with salt-free lemon-pepper seasoning and light soy sauce and without salt) equals 199 calories, 181 mg sodium, 68 mg cholesterol, 7 gm carbohydrate, 22 gm protein, 9 gm fat. **Diabetic Exchanges:** 3 lean meat, 1 vegetable. **Editor's Note:** Salmon can be broiled instead of grilled. Place the fillet on a greased broiler pan. Broil 3-4 in. from the heat for 6-8 minutes or until fish flakes easily with a fork.

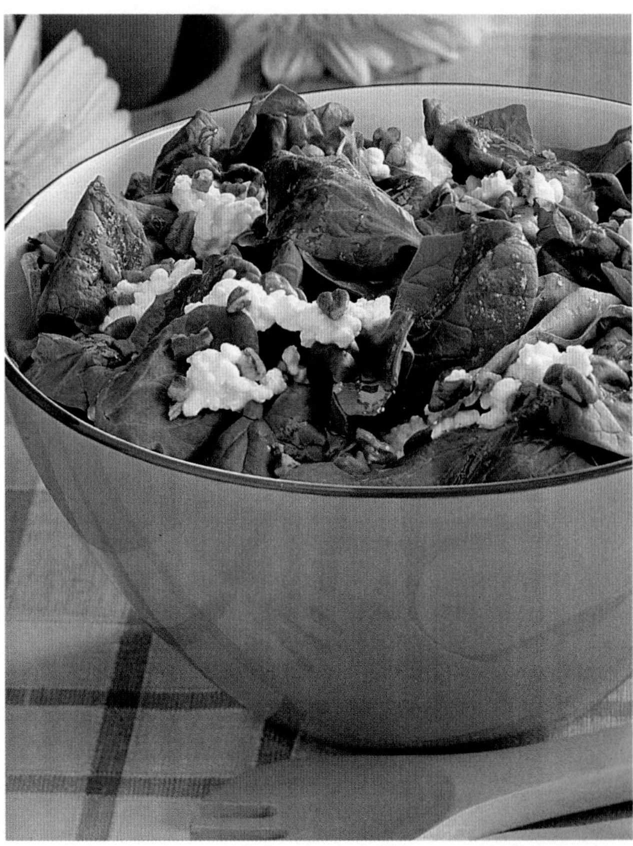

Cottage Cheese Spinach Salad

Even folks who don't care for spinach enjoy this distinctive salad. The creamy dressing is a bit sweet, and cottage cheese assures that this dish is extra hearty and satisfying.

- **1 package (10 ounces) fresh spinach, torn**
- **1 carton (12 ounces) small-curd cottage cheese**
- **1/2 cup chopped pecans, toasted**
- **1/2 cup sugar**
- **3 tablespoons vinegar**
- **2 teaspoons prepared horseradish**
- **1/2 teaspoon salt**
- **1/2 teaspoon ground mustard**

In a large serving bowl, layer half of the spinach, cottage cheese and pecans. Repeat layers. In a small bowl, combine the remaining ingredients. Drizzle over salad and toss to coat. Serve immediately. **Yield:** 10 servings.

Herbed Oven Potatoes

Mom loves to use the fresh new potatoes my husband, John, and I share from our garden for this yummy recipe. The well-seasoned potato chunks are an excellent side dish for fish, poultry or meat. It's easy to make since there's no peeling required.

1/2 cup olive *or* vegetable oil
1/4 cup butter *or* margarine, melted
1 envelope onion soup mix
1 teaspoon dried thyme
1 teaspoon dried marjoram
1/4 teaspoon pepper
2 pounds red potatoes, quartered
Minced fresh parsley

In a shallow bowl, combine the first six ingredients. Add potatoes, a few at a time; toss to coat. Place in a single layer in a greased 15-in. x 10-in. x 1-in. baking pan. Drizzle with remaining oil mixture. Bake, uncovered, at 450° for 50-55 minutes or until tender, stirring occasionally. Sprinkle with parsley. **Yield:** 6 servings.

Frozen Mocha Torte

For an easy, make-ahead dessert that's elegant and luscious, try this recipe that Mom has used for years. The perfect blend of mocha and chocolate is in each cool refreshing slice. It never lasts long in the freezer.

1-1/4 cups chocolate wafer crumbs (about 24 wafers), *divided*
1/4 cup sugar
1/4 cup butter *or* margarine, melted
1 package (8 ounces) cream cheese, softened
1 can (14 ounces) sweetened condensed milk
2/3 cup chocolate syrup
2 tablespoons instant coffee granules
1 tablespoon hot water
1 cup whipping cream, whipped
Chocolate-covered coffee beans, optional

Combine 1 cup wafer crumbs, sugar and butter. Press onto the bottom and 1 in. up the sides of a greased 9-in. springform pan; set aside. In a mixing bowl, beat cream cheese, milk and chocolate syrup until smooth. Dissolve coffee granules in hot water; add to cream cheese mixture. Fold in whipped cream. Pour over the crust. Sprinkle with remaining crumbs. Cover and freeze for 8 hours or overnight. Uncover and remove from the freezer 10-15 minutes before serving. Garnish with coffee beans if desired. **Yield:** 10-12 servings.

Mom patiently taught this cook and her three sisters the importance of preparing and serving well-balanced and delicious meals.

By Alyson Armstrong, Parkersburg, West Virginia

AFTER MOVING away from home, I quickly came to appreciate all the effort my mom (Jane Forshey, above, of St. Clairsville, Ohio) put into providing us with well-balanced and delicious meals.

With a family of six, we each had our favorite foods. But all of us requested this country-style meal whenever we had guests coming for dinner.

Everyone enjoys Mom's tangy Miniature Ham Loaves and creamy Cheese Potato Puff. The enticing aroma while these are baking always draws people into the kitchen.

Whoever tries the puff agrees that it's the lightest, fluffiest, tastiest potato dish they've ever tasted.

Accordion Rye Rolls warm from the oven are also wonderful. Any extra effort in making these fresh rolls is worth it.

Our favorite part of the meal is when Mom brings out dessert—Bavarian Apple Torte. This rich cheesecake topped with tender apple slices is a fitting way to end a mouth-watering meal.

These recipes are convenient, too, since much of the preparation can be done a day in advance. This is important if you enjoy visiting with your guests as much as Mom does.

My three sisters and I have learned a lot of important things from Mom over the years.

Besides patiently teaching us to prepare and serve good meals, she and our father, Jim, guided us in Christian living and good work ethics, and demonstrated a strong, loving marriage.

I hope you enjoy this scrumptious meal. Good food is an important part of our lifestyle, and my mom serves only the best.

PICTURED AT LEFT: Miniature Ham Loaves, Cheese Potato Puff, Accordion Rye Rolls and Bavarian Apple Torte (recipes are on the next page).

Miniature Ham Loaves

When there's a special dinner coming, Mom will usually prepare these scrumptious loaves several days in advance and freeze them. Then she only needs to bake them before dinner. We all anticipate their wonderful aroma and flavor.

2 eggs
1 cup evaporated milk
1-1/2 cups graham cracker crumbs (about 22 squares)
1-1/4 pounds ground fully cooked ham
1-1/4 pounds bulk pork sausage
1 can (10-3/4 ounces) condensed tomato soup, undiluted
1 cup plus 2 tablespoons packed brown sugar
1/3 cup vinegar
1 teaspoon ground mustard

In a bowl, combine eggs, milk and cracker crumbs; mix well. Add ham and sausage. Shape 1/2 cupfuls into individual loaves. Place in a greased 13-in. x 9-in. x 2-in. baking dish. Combine the soup, brown sugar, vinegar and mustard; mix well. Pour over loaves. Bake, uncovered, at 350° for 1 hour, basting after 30 minutes. **Yield:** 12-14 servings.

Cheese Potato Puff

These fluffy potatoes can be made a day ahead and refrigerated until ready to bake. This dish is Mom's specialty, and we all especially love the part along the edge of the casserole dish that gets golden brown.

12 medium potatoes, peeled and cubed
2 cups (8 ounces) shredded cheddar *or* Swiss cheese, *divided*
1-1/4 cups milk
1/3 cup butter *or* margarine, softened
1 to 2 teaspoons salt
2 eggs, beaten

Place the potatoes in a saucepan and cover with water; cover and bring to a boil. Cook until tender, about 15-20 minutes. Drain and mash. Add 1-3/4 cups cheese, milk, butter and salt; cook and stir over low heat until the cheese and butter are melted. Fold in eggs. Spread into a greased 13-in. x 9-in. x 2-in. baking dish. Bake, uncovered, at 350° for 25-30 minutes. Sprinkle with the remaining cheese. Bake 5 minutes longer or until golden brown. **Yield:** 12-14 servings.

Accordion Rye Rolls

These rolls will make anyone like rye bread. Even though Mom fixes the dough a day ahead, she bakes them right before serving so they're hot and fresh.

2 packages (1/4 ounce *each*) active dry yeast

1/2 cup warm water (110° to 115°)
1-1/2 cups warm milk (110° to 115°)
1/4 cup molasses
4 tablespoons butter *or* margarine, softened, *divided*
1 tablespoon sugar
1 tablespoon plus 1/2 teaspoon salt, *divided*
3 to 3-1/2 cups all-purpose flour
2-1/2 cups rye flour
Vegetable oil
1 egg white
2 teaspoons caraway seeds

In a mixing bowl, dissolve yeast in water. Add milk, molasses, 2 tablespoons butter, sugar and 1 tablespoon salt. Add 2 cups all-purpose flour; beat until smooth. Add rye flour and enough remaining all-purpose flour to form a soft dough. Turn onto a floured surface; knead until smooth and elastic, about 6-8 minutes. Place in a greased bowl, turning once to grease top. Let stand for 20 minutes. Divide dough into four portions. On a lightly floured surface, roll each portion into a 14-in. x 6-in. rectangle. Brush with remaining butter. With the blunt edge of a knife, make creases in dough at 2-in. intervals, beginning at a short side. Fold dough accordion-style back and forth along creased lines. Cut folded dough into 1-in. pieces. Place each piece cut side down in a greased muffin cup. Brush with oil. Cover loosely with plastic wrap. Refrigerate for 4-24 hours. When ready to bake, uncover and let stand at room temperature for 10 minutes. In a small mixing bowl, beat egg white until stiff peaks form; brush over dough. Sprinkle with caraway seeds and remaining salt. Bake at 375° for 20-25 minutes or until lightly browned. **Yield:** 2 dozen.

Bavarian Apple Torte

This rich, creamy torte has always been one of my favorite autumn desserts. Mom uses the freshest apples from a local orchard and bakes this treat until the apples are crisp-tender. It tastes as good as it looks.

3/4 cup butter *or* margarine, softened
1/2 cup sugar
1-1/2 cups all-purpose flour
1/2 teaspoon vanilla extract

FILLING:

2 packages (8 ounces *each*) cream cheese, softened
1/4 cup sugar
2 eggs
3/4 teaspoon vanilla extract

TOPPING:

3 cups thinly sliced peeled tart apples
1/2 cup sugar
1 teaspoon ground cinnamon

Combine the first four ingredients. Press onto the bottom of an ungreased 9-in. springform pan. In a mixing bowl, beat cream cheese and sugar. Add eggs and vanilla; mix well. Pour over the crust. Combine topping ingredients; spoon over filling. Bake at 350° for 55-65 minutes or until the center is set. Cool on a wire rack. Store in the refrigerator. Cut into wedges with a serrated knife. **Yield:** 12-14 servings. **Editor's Note:** Even a tight-fitting springform pan may leak. To prevent drips, place the pan on a baking sheet in the oven.

When Mom prepared a meal for her family and friends, it wasn't considered a chore. It was a labor of love.

By Linda McGinty, Parma, Ohio

FOR my mom (Edythe Wagy, above, of Winter Haven, Florida), preparing an evening meal for our family was not a chore, but a labor of love.

In those days, she was a real homemaker. She not only loved to sew, cook and bake, she also strived to make our home a warm inviting place.

Sunday mornings were extra nice since Mom would make a batch of homemade fritters or pecan rolls. All of my friends would beg to sleep overnight on Saturday so they could indulge in the scrumptious breakfast pastries.

Mom also hosted many large gatherings when my two brothers and I were growing up. Everyone looked forward to a satisfying main dish like her flavorful So-Tender Swiss Steak.

Fork-tender pieces of beef topped with a rich, thick gravy over hot cooked noodles made everyone's mouth water.

Side dishes, like her Cauliflower Casserole and Strawberry Pear Gelatin, were both comforting and extra-special at the same time.

A blend of cheeses, crushed cornflakes and garden-fresh peppers dress up plain cauliflower, while the addition of cream cheese makes the gelatin salad smooth and creamy.

But the thing family and friends most eagerly anticipated was dessert, which Mom always made from scratch. Mom's Chocolate Cake, with its delicate chocolate flavor and fluffy frosting, is a wonderful end to any special-occasion or weekday meal.

Although Mom and Dad are not as active as they used to be, Mom still prepares one of our favorites whenever we visit. After all, the kitchen is still her favorite room in the house.

PICTURED AT LEFT: So-Tender Swiss Steak, Cauliflower Casserole, Strawberry Pear Gelatin and Mom's Chocolate Cake (recipes are on the next page).

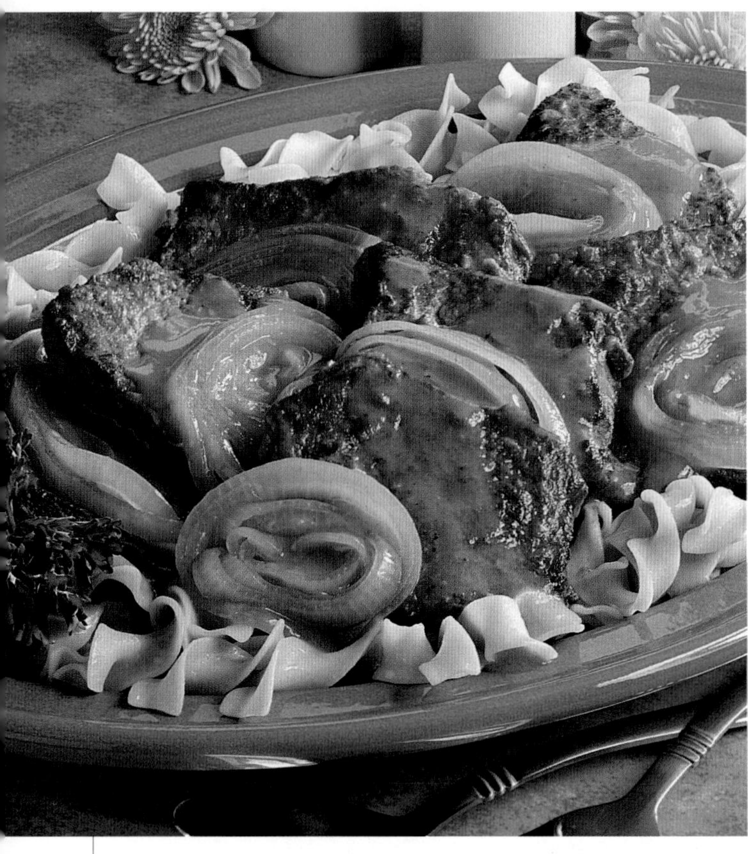

So-Tender Swiss Steak

This Swiss steak with rich, meaty gravy was an often-requested main dish around our house when I was growing up. Mom took pride in preparing scrumptious, hearty meals like this for our family and guests.

1/4 cup all-purpose flour
1/2 teaspoon salt
1/4 teaspoon pepper
2 pounds round steak, cut into serving-size pieces
2 tablespoons vegetable oil
1 medium onion, thinly sliced
2 cups water
2 tablespoons Worcestershire sauce

GRAVY:

1/4 cup all-purpose flour
1/4 teaspoon salt
1/8 teaspoon pepper
1-1/4 cups beef broth *or* water
Hot cooked noodles *or* mashed potatoes, optional

In a shallow bowl, combine flour, salt and pepper. Dredge steak, a few pieces at a time. Pound with a mallet to tenderize. In a Dutch oven, brown steak in oil on all sides. Arrange onion slices between layers of meat. Add water and Worcestershire sauce. Cover and bake at 325° for 2 to 2-1/2 hours or until meat is very tender. Remove to a serving platter and keep warm. In a small bowl, combine flour, salt, pepper and broth until smooth; stir into the pan juices. Bring to a boil over medium heat; cook and stir for 2 minutes. Serve steak and gravy over noodles or mashed potatoes if desired. **Yield:** 8 servings.

Cauliflower Casserole

To dress up cauliflower, Mom used a delightful mixture of a cheesy sauce, bright red and green pepper pieces and crushed cornflakes. We enjoyed this casserole so much that leftovers were rare.

1 medium head cauliflower, broken into florets
1 cup (8 ounces) sour cream
1 cup (4 ounces) shredded cheddar cheese
1/2 cup crushed cornflakes
1/4 cup chopped green pepper
1/4 cup chopped sweet red pepper
1 teaspoon salt
1/4 cup grated Parmesan cheese
Paprika

Place cauliflower and a small amount of water in a saucepan; cover and cook for 5 minutes or until crisp-tender. Drain. Combine cauliflower, sour cream, cheddar cheese, cornflakes, peppers and salt; transfer to a greased 2-qt. baking dish. Sprinkle with Parmesan cheese and paprika. Bake, uncovered, at 325° for 30-35 minutes or until heated through. **Yield:** 6-8 servings.

Strawberry Pear Gelatin

Mom had a way of making every dish she served just a little more special. A good example is this fluffy salad. It's both fruity and refreshing.

1 can (29 ounces) pears
1 package (6 ounces) strawberry gelatin
1 package (8 ounces) cream cheese, cubed
1 carton (8 ounces) frozen whipped topping, thawed
Mandarin oranges, optional

Drain pears, reserving juice. Chop pears and set aside. Add water to the juice to measure 3 cups. Place in a saucepan; bring to a boil. Transfer to a large bowl. Add gelatin and stir until dissolved. Whisk in cream cheese until smooth. Refrigerate until slightly thickened. Whisk in whipped topping until smooth. Add chopped pears. Transfer to a 13-in. x 9-in. x 2-in. dish. Cover and refrigerate until firm. Cut into squares. Garnish with mandarin oranges if desired. **Yield:** 12-16 servings.

Mom's Chocolate Cake

Over the years, Mom has become known for wonderful from-scratch desserts like this old-fashioned chocolate cake topped with a yummy, rich frosting. It was difficult, but my brothers and I would always manage to save room for dessert.

2 squares (1 ounce *each*) unsweetened chocolate, broken into pieces
1/2 cup boiling water
1/2 cup shortening
2 cups packed brown sugar
2 eggs, *separated*
2 cups sifted cake flour
2 teaspoons baking powder
1/2 teaspoon baking soda
1/2 teaspoon salt
1/2 cup buttermilk *or* sour milk*
1/2 cup water
1/2 cup chopped walnuts
1 teaspoon vanilla extract
COCOA FROSTING:
6 tablespoons butter *or* margarine, softened
3-1/2 cups confectioners' sugar
1/2 cup baking cocoa
1-1/2 teaspoons vanilla extract
Pinch salt
4 to 6 tablespoons milk

In a small bowl, stir chocolate in boiling water until melted; set aside to cool, about 10 minutes. In a mixing bowl, cream shortening and brown sugar. Beat in egg yolks and chocolate mixture. Combine flour, baking powder, baking soda and salt; add to creamed mixture alternately with buttermilk. Gradually beat in water, nuts and vanilla. In a small mixing bowl, beat egg whites until soft peaks form; fold into batter. Pour into a greased 13-in. x 9-in. x 2-in. baking pan. Bake at 350° for 35-40 minutes or until a toothpick inserted near the center comes out clean. Cool on a wire rack. In a mixing bowl, cream butter. Combine confectioners' sugar and cocoa; gradually add to butter with vanilla, salt and enough milk to achieve desired spreading consistency. Frost cake. **Yield:** 12-15 servings. ***Editor's Note:** To sour milk, place 1-1/2 teaspoons white vinegar in a measuring cup. Add milk to equal 1/2 cup.

She re-creates special childhood Christmas dinners by cooking up old-fashioned foods that are reminiscent of times spent in a cozy kitchen with two grandmas.

By Chere Bell, Colorado Springs, Colorado

WHEN I was growing up, my great-grandma, Bertha Morgan, was like a mother to me. My mom was ill, so I was raised for many years by both Grandma and Great-Grandma.

Grandma worked outside the home, so I spent a lot of time with Great-Grandma, who took care of the house and did most of the cooking.

Whenever anyone visited, she'd say, "Sit down—you look hungry." Then she'd get busy fixing them something to eat.

For the holidays, Great-Grandma cooked up a storm. At Christmas, the house smelled heavenly. She was raised on a farm and cooked everything from scratch—I don't remember ever seeing her use a written recipe.

Over the years, I've re-created those memorable Christmas dinners based on what I learned working in the kitchen with my grandmas.

Cranberry-Stuffed Chicken is a mouth-watering main dish. The tart cranberries make the stuffing extra-special. Everyone relishes the moist meat and tempting stuffing.

For wonderful old-fashioned flavor, we enjoy Wilted Curly Endive. Vinegar and bacon make it a savory warm salad.

Christmas Rice has a wonderful flavor. And it looks festive with red and green pepper mixed in. It's the perfect light side dish for the big holiday meal.

To top off this delicious dinner, we have Honey Baked Apples. They're sweet and tender—a real treat topped with ice cream. The wonderful aroma as they bake beckons people to the kitchen.

I always think of Great-Grandma when I fix this meal for my husband, our four children and their families during the holidays.

PICTURED AT LEFT: Cranberry-Stuffed Chicken, Wilted Curly Endive, Christmas Rice and Honey Baked Apples (recipes are on the next page).

Cranberry-Stuffed Chicken

For the holidays or any Sunday dinner, I suggest this delightful main dish. My great-grandma used to roast this chicken for our family, and now I do the same for our nine grandchildren.

- **1 cup chopped celery**
- **1 cup chopped onion**
- **2/3 cup dried cranberries**
- **1/2 cup plus 2 tablespoons butter *or* margarine, *divided***
- **1 garlic clove, minced**
- **3 cups herb-seasoned stuffing croutons**
- **1 cup corn bread stuffing *or* crumbled corn bread**
- **1-1/2 to 2 cups chicken broth**
- **1 roasting chicken (5 to 7 pounds)**
- **1/2 teaspoon salt**
- **1/2 teaspoon pepper**
- **1/4 teaspoon poultry seasoning**
- **1/4 teaspoon rubbed sage**

In a skillet, saute celery, onion and cranberries in 1/2 cup of butter until tender. Stir in garlic, stuffing and enough broth to moisten; set aside. Place chicken with breast side up on a rack in a roasting pan. Combine salt, pepper, poultry seasoning and sage; sprinkle over inside and outside of chicken. Loosely stuff with cranberry mixture. Melt remaining butter; brush over chicken. Bake, uncovered, at 350° for 2-1/2 to 3 hours or until juices run clear and a meat thermometer reads 180° for the chicken and 165° for the stuffing, basting occasionally. **Yield:** 6-8 servings. **Editor's Note:** Stuffing may be baked separately in a greased 1-1/2-qt. baking dish. Cover and bake at 350° for 40 minutes.

Wilted Curly Endive

This warm salad is a deliciously different way to serve lettuce. Unlike other wilted versions, this one is not sweet. Vinegar and bacon give it old-fashioned savory goodness.

- **12 bacon strips, diced**
- **3 medium bunches curly endive**
- **4 quarts water**
- **2-1/4 teaspoons salt, *divided***
- **2 to 3 tablespoons cider vinegar**
- **3 tablespoons finely chopped onion**
- **1/4 teaspoon pepper**

Cook the bacon until crisp; remove with a slotted spoon to paper towels to drain. Reserve 3 tablespoons drippings. Cut or tear endive from center stalk; discard the stalks. In a large saucepan or Dutch oven, bring water and 1-1/2 teaspoons salt to a boil. Add endive; cover and cook for 3 minutes. Drain. Stir in bacon, reserved drippings, vinegar, onion, pepper and remaining salt; mix well. Serve immediately. **Yield:** 6 servings.

Christmas Rice

My family has enjoyed this delicious rice dish for many years. With chopped red and green peppers, it's both fresh-tasting and festive-looking.

✓ Uses less fat, sugar or salt. Includes Nutritional Analysis and Diabetic Exchanges.

1/2 cup finely chopped onion
3 celery ribs, finely chopped
1/2 medium sweet red pepper, chopped
1/2 medium green pepper, chopped
1 tablespoon butter *or* margarine
2 cups chicken broth
2 cups uncooked instant rice
1/2 teaspoon salt, optional
1/4 teaspoon pepper

In a skillet, saute onion, celery and peppers in butter over medium heat for 2 minutes or until crisp-tender. Remove from the heat; set aside. In a saucepan, bring broth to a full boil. Remove from the heat. Quickly stir in rice, celery mixture, salt if desired and pepper. Cover and let stand for 6-7 minutes. Stir before serving. **Yield:** 6 servings. **Nutritional Analysis:** One 1/2-cup serving (prepared with margarine and low-sodium broth and without salt) equals 152 calories, 44 mg sodium, trace cholesterol, 30 gm carbohydrate, 3 gm protein, 2 gm fat. **Diabetic Exchanges:** 1-1/2 starch, 1 vegetable, 1/2 fat.

Honey Baked Apples

These tender apples smell so good while they're in the oven—and taste even better. We enjoy the golden raisins inside and the soothing taste of honey. They're a yummy change from the cinnamon and sugar seasoning traditionally used with apples.

2-1/4 cups water
3/4 cup packed brown sugar
3 tablespoons honey
6 large tart apples
1 cup golden raisins
Vanilla ice cream, optional

In a saucepan, bring water, brown sugar and honey to a boil. Remove from the heat. Core apples and peel the top third of each. Place in an ungreased 9-in. baking dish. Fill apples with raisins; sprinkle any remaining raisins into pan. Pour sugar syrup over apples. Bake, uncovered, at 350° for 1 hour or until tender, basting occasionally. Serve with ice cream if desired. **Yield:** 6 servings.

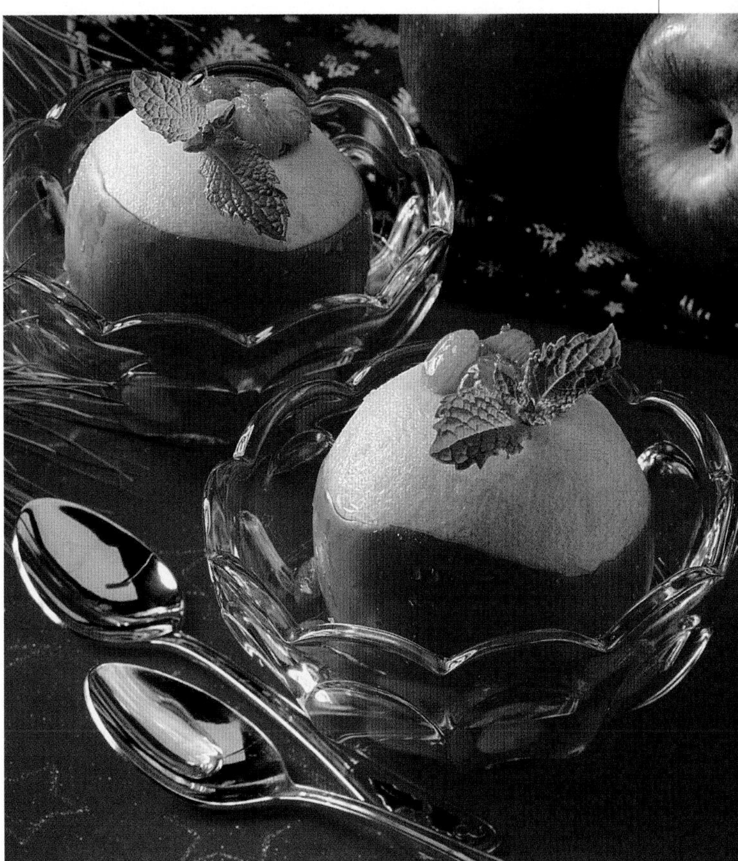

Stuffing Stretcher

Turn leftover stuffing into a succulent new side dish. To 1-1/2 cups stuffing, add 2 eggs, 1/4 cup milk and 1/2 cup flour to form a dough. Divide dough and shape into patties, then fry in a small amount of oil. They're delicious!

Editors' Meals

***Taste of Home* magazine is edited by 1,000 cooks across North America. On the following pages, you'll "meet" six of those cooks who share a family-pleasing meal.**

FAMILY FAVORITES. Clockwise from upper left: Fuss-Free Fare (p. 248), Savory Seafood Supper (p. 256), Traditional Sunday Dinner (p. 260) and Treasured Family Recipes (p. 252).

A fragrant roast is in the oven...the rest of her delightful dinner is already prepared... and she's ready to relish Christmas Day with her family!

By Audrey Thibodeau, Gilbert, Arizona

I LOOK FORWARD to having a relaxed Christmas—thanks to a mostly make-ahead dinner.

My husband, Roger, and I often celebrate at home with a few of our children and grandchildren. (We have two daughters and three sons, 10 grandchildren and one great-grandson.)

The rosemary gives off a wonderful aroma while the Rosemary Pork Roast is cooking. This is an herb I use often in breads, cookies and vegetables. Sometimes I'll use fresh rosemary sprigs and bright red crab apples to garnish the roast.

Fancy Baked Potatoes have long been my favorite way to prepare double-baked potatoes for guests. They can be made the day before and kept in the refrigerator. (It's best to remove them from the fridge a half hour before reheating.)

This recipe saves the hassle of mashing potatoes at the last minute. I'll add pimientos as a colorful touch for my holiday dinner.

Apple Sweet Potato Bake is another delicious do-ahead dish I often depend on.

Cranberry Shiver has just the right tart flavor after a rich dinner. You can make it well ahead, since it will keep up to a month in the freezer.

Of course, there's always a tray of Christmas cookies to pass. Holly Berry Cookies star in my assortment, and I make extra to give as gifts. Spicy and fruity, they're holiday-special!

I also serve a green vegetable or crunchy salad and hot rolls or biscuits for our Christmas repast. It's a gratifying meal, but one that I can manage quite easily and still have time to enjoy with my family.

Perhaps you'll want to put some of my make-ahead holiday recipes to the test!

PICTURED AT LEFT: Rosemary Pork Roast, Fancy Baked Potatoes, Apple Sweet Potato Bake, Cranberry Shiver and Holly Berry Cookies (recipes are on the next page).

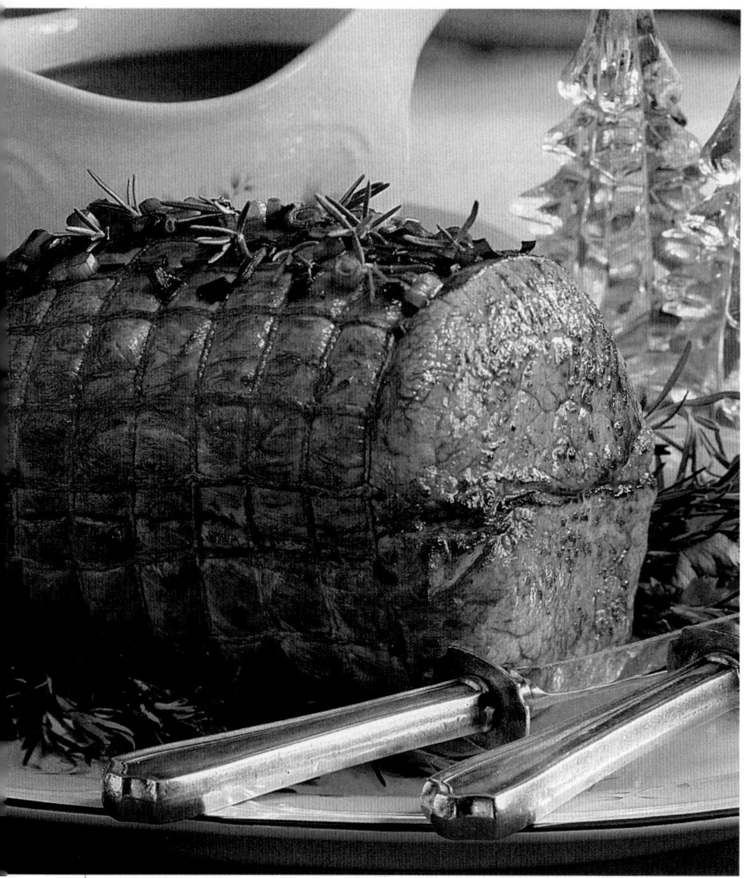

Rosemary Pork Roast

Tender and full of flavor, this lovely roast is an impressive main dish for a Christmas dinner.

Uses less fat, sugar or salt. Includes Nutritional Analysis and Diabetic Exchanges.

- **1 boneless pork loin roast (3 to 3-1/2 pounds)**
- **1/2 cup chopped green onions**
- **2-1/4 cups chicken broth, *divided***
- **1/4 cup cider *or* red wine vinegar**
- **2 tablespoons olive *or* vegetable oil**
- **4 garlic cloves, minced**
- **1 tablespoon minced fresh rosemary *or* 1 teaspoon dried rosemary, crushed**
- **1/4 teaspoon pepper**
- **1 teaspoon salt, optional**
- **2 tablespoons cornstarch**
- **1/4 cup cold water**

Place roast in a large resealable plastic bag or glass container. Combine onions, 1/4 cup broth, vinegar, oil, garlic, rosemary and pepper; pour over roast. Cover and refrigerate for 4-8 hours, turning occasionally. Remove roast and place with fat side up in an ungreased shallow roasting pan. Combine marinade with remaining broth; pour over roast. Sprinkle with salt if desired. Bake, uncovered, at 350° for 2 to 2-1/2 hours or until a meat thermometer reads 160°-170°. Remove roast to a warm serving platter; let stand for 10 minutes before slicing. Meanwhile, skim fat from pan juices. Combine cornstarch and water until smooth; stir into juices. Bring to a boil over medium heat; boil and stir for 2 minutes. Serve with the roast. **Yield:** 8 servings. **Nutritional Analysis:** One serving (prepared with low-sodium broth and without salt) equals 305 calories, 117 mg sodium, 102 mg cholesterol, 4 gm carbohydrate, 36 gm protein, 15 gm fat. **Diabetic Exchanges:** 5 lean meat, 1 vegetable.

Fancy Baked Potatoes

(Pictured on page 241)

I can't count the times I've turned to this tried-and-true recipe when company is coming.

- **4 large baking potatoes**
- **Vegetable oil**
- **2 tablespoons butter *or* margarine**
- **1/2 cup sour cream**
- **1/4 cup milk**
- **1/2 teaspoon salt**
- **1/4 teaspoon pepper**
- **1 jar (2 ounces) diced pimientos, drained, *divided***
- **2 tablespoons minced chives, *divided***

Rub potatoes with oil; place in a shallow baking pan. Bake at 400° for 1 hour or until tender. Cool. Cut in half lengthwise. Scoop out pulp, leaving a 1/4-in. shell; set shells aside. In a mixing bowl, combine pulp, butter, sour cream and milk; beat until creamy. Stir in salt, pepper and half of the pimientos and chives. Spoon or pipe filling into shells. Return to the baking pan. Bake at 350° for 35-40 minutes or until lightly browned. Sprinkle with the remaining pimientos and chives. **Yield:** 8 servings.

Apple Sweet Potato Bake

(Pictured on page 241)

Grandmother always served sweet potatoes and apples with pork, so I know she'd approve of this dish I created to combine the two.

- **3 cups sliced peeled cooked sweet potatoes**
- **3 cups sliced peeled tart apples (about 2 large)**

3/4 cup packed brown sugar
3/4 teaspoon ground nutmeg
1/4 teaspoon ground allspice
1/4 teaspoon salt
Dash pepper
3 tablespoons butter *or* margarine

In a greased 1-1/2-qt. baking dish, layer half of the sweet potatoes and apples. Combine brown sugar, nutmeg, allspice, salt and pepper; sprinkle half over apples. Dot with half of the butter. Repeat layers. Cover and bake at 350° for 15 minutes. Baste with pan juices. Bake, uncovered, 15 minutes longer or until the apples are tender. **Yield:** 8 servings.

Holly Berry Cookies

(Pictured on page 240)

These festive filled cookies are the all-time favorites of my family. Back when our children were small, we began baking them the day after Halloween and put them in the freezer.

2 cups all-purpose flour
1 cup sugar
1 teaspoon ground cinnamon
3/4 teaspoon baking powder
1/4 teaspoon salt
1/2 cup cold butter (no substitutes)
1 egg
1/4 cup milk
2/3 cup seedless raspberry jam
GLAZE:
2 cups confectioners' sugar
2 tablespoons milk
1/2 teaspoon vanilla extract
Red-hot candies
Green food coloring

In a large bowl, combine the first five ingredients. Cut in butter until the mixture resembles coarse crumbs. In a small bowl, beat egg and milk. Add to crumb mixture just until moistened. Cover and refrigerate for 1 hour or until dough is easy to handle. On a lightly floured surface, roll out dough to 1/8-in. thickness. Cut with a 2-in. round cookie cutter. Place on ungreased baking sheets. Bake at 375° for 8-10 minutes or until edges are lightly browned. Cool on wire racks. Spread jam on half of the cookies; top each with another cookie. In a small mixing bowl, combine sugar, milk and vanilla until smooth; spread over cookies. Decorate with red-hots before glaze is set. Let dry. Using a small new paintbrush and green food coloring, paint holly leaves on cookies. **Yield:** 2 dozen.

Cranberry Shiver

Cool and refreshing, this pretty dessert is delightfully sweet-tart. You can make it ahead.

✓ Uses less fat, sugar or salt. Includes Nutritional Analysis and Diabetic Exchanges.

1 package (12 ounces) fresh *or* frozen cranberries
3 cups water, *divided*
1-3/4 cups sugar
1/4 cup lemon juice
1 teaspoon grated orange peel
Fresh mint, optional

In a saucepan, bring the cranberries and 2 cups of water to a boil. Reduce heat; simmer for 5 minutes. Press through a strainer to remove skins; discard skins. To the juice, add sugar, lemon juice, orange peel and remaining water; mix well. Pour into an 8-in. square pan. Cover and freeze until ice begins to form around the edges of the pan, about 1-1/2 hours; stir. Freeze until mushy, about 30 minutes. Spoon into a freezer container; cover and freeze. Remove from the freezer 20 minutes before serving. Scoop into small dishes; garnish with mint if desired. **Yield:** 10 servings. **Nutritional Analysis:** One 1/2-cup serving equals 154 calories, 1 mg sodium, 0 cholesterol, 40 gm carbohydrate, trace protein, trace fat. **Diabetic Exchange:** 2-1/2 fruit.

This newlywed is not new to the kitchen! Her company-pleasing menu has broad appeal and is well-suited to special occasions like Valentine's Day.

By Christy Freeman, Central Point, Oregon

HAVING people over for dinner and not sure of their tastes? You can't go wrong with pasta, bread, salad and chocolate! This is also a favorite special-occasion meal my husband, Allen, and I enjoy for Valentine's Day and other holidays.

My Make-Ahead Spinach Manicotti is prepared the night before, which really makes things easier the next day. I created this recipe after a friend told me she'd made lasagna without cooking the noodles first. I figured I could probably do the same with manicotti. After many attempts at adapting the ingredients, I finally got the recipe just right.

The easiest way to stuff the shells, I've found, is to use a pastry bag with a large tip. Place all the filling in the bag at once, since it can get a little messy trying to refill the bag.

I have my mother to thank for the terrific Blue Cheese Salad Dressing. She combined two different dressing recipes to come up with it, and I think she hit the nail on the head.

Crusty French Bread is an old reliable recipe I use often. I found it in a tattered recipe book that Mom was going to throw away.

There's no need to knead the dough for these crunchy loaves. Diagonal cuts and a little cornmeal sprinkled over the tops give them a nice appearance.

If you asked Allen to name his favorite dessert, he'd quickly say Heavenly Chocolate Mousse. This treat is rich, creamy and oh-so-chocolaty!

Let me assure you, this recipe is really not too difficult—and it's definitely worth the effort.

When company's due in your home, why not make this Italian-style meal?

PICTURED AT LEFT: Make-Ahead Spinach Manicotti, Blue Cheese Salad Dressing, Crusty French Bread and Heavenly Chocolate Mousse (recipes are on the next page).

Make-Ahead Spinach Manicotti

This is my favorite recipe when company's coming. It's prepared the night before, plus the manicotti is stuffed uncooked, making it even more convenient.

1 carton (15 ounces) ricotta cheese
1 package (10 ounces) frozen chopped spinach, thawed and squeezed dry
1-1/2 cups (6 ounces) shredded mozzarella cheese, *divided*
3/4 cup shredded Parmesan cheese, *divided*
1 egg
2 teaspoons minced fresh parsley
1/2 teaspoon onion powder
1/2 teaspoon pepper
1/8 teaspoon garlic powder
2 jars (28 ounces *each*) spaghetti sauce with meat
1-1/2 cups water
1 package (8 ounces) manicotti shells

In a large bowl, combine ricotta, spinach, 1 cup mozzarella, 1/4 cup Parmesan, egg, parsley, onion powder, pepper and garlic powder. Combine the spaghetti sauce and water; spread 1 cup sauce in an ungreased 13-in. x 9-in. x 2-in. baking dish. Stuff uncooked manicotti with spinach mixture; arrange over sauce. Pour remaining sauce over manicotti. Sprinkle with remaining mozzarella and Parmesan. Cover and refrigerate overnight. Remove from the refrigerator 30 minutes before baking. Bake, uncovered, at 350° for 40-50 minutes or until heated through. **Yield:** 6-8 servings.

Blue Cheese Salad Dressing

This distinctively flavored dressing makes a great accompaniment to a mix of fresh salad greens. The thick, creamy dressing does double duty at our house—I often serve it as a dip with fresh vegetables. Either way, it's delicious!

2 cups mayonnaise
1 cup (8 ounces) sour cream
1/4 cup cider *or* white wine vinegar
1/4 cup minced fresh parsley
1 garlic clove, crushed
1/2 teaspoon ground mustard
1/2 teaspoon salt
1/4 teaspoon pepper
4 ounces crumbled blue cheese
Torn salad greens

Place the first nine ingredients in a blender; cover and process until smooth. Store in the refrigerator. Serve over salad greens. **Yield:** 3 cups.

Crusty French Bread

I love to treat guests to these golden brown, crusty loaves. Don't hesitate to try this recipe even if you are not an accomplished bread baker—there's no kneading required!

✓ Uses less fat, sugar or salt. Includes Nutritional Analysis and Diabetic Exchanges.

1 package (1/4 ounce) active dry yeast
1-1/2 cups warm water (110° to 115°), *divided*
1 tablespoon sugar
2 teaspoons salt
1 tablespoon shortening, melted
4 cups all-purpose flour
Cornmeal

In a mixing bowl, dissolve yeast in 1/2 cup water. Add sugar, salt, shortening and remaining water; stir until dissolved. Add flour and stir until smooth (do not knead). Cover and let rise in a warm place for 1 hour or until doubled. Turn onto a floured surface. Divide in half; let rest for 10 minutes. Roll each half into a 10-in. x 8-in. rectangle. Roll up from a long side; pinch to seal. Place seam side down on greased baking sheets sprinkled with cornmeal. Sprinkle the tops with cornmeal. Cover and let rise until doubled, about 45 minutes. With a sharp knife, make five diagonal cuts across the top of each loaf. Bake at 400° for 20-30 minutes or until lightly browned. Cool on wire racks. **Yield:** 2 loaves (10 slices each). **Nutritional Analysis:** One slice equals 100 calories, 233 mg sodium, 0 cholesterol, 20 gm carbohydrate, 3 gm protein, 1 gm fat. **Diabetic Exchange:** 1-1/2 starch.

Heavenly Chocolate Mousse

"Heaven on a spoon" is how one friend describes this chocolaty dessert. My husband, Allen, rates it best of all the special treats I've made. The filling can also be used for a pie.

8 squares (1 ounce *each*) semisweet baking chocolate, coarsely chopped
1/2 cup water, *divided*
2 tablespoons butter (no substitutes)
3 egg yolks
2 tablespoons sugar
1-1/4 cups whipping cream, whipped

In a microwave or double boiler, heat chocolate, 1/4 cup water and butter until the chocolate and butter are melted. Cool for 10 minutes. In a small heavy saucepan, whisk egg yolks, sugar and remaining water. Cook and stir over low heat until mixture reaches 160°, about 1-2 minutes. Remove from the heat; whisk in chocolate mixture. Set saucepan in ice and stir until cooled, about 5-10 minutes. Fold in whipped cream. Spoon into dessert dishes. Refrigerate for 4 hours or overnight. **Yield:** 6-8 servings.

Tending her flock doesn't keep this busy country cook from serving up a savory meal to family and friends...a slow cooker's her secret!

By Sandra McKenzie, Braham, Minnesota

DURING SPRING, when farm work, tending the sheep and gardening limit my time in the kitchen, I serve this memorable and manageable meal.

My husband, Dale, and I enjoy lamb, so I've experimented with different ways to prepare it. Liking my slow cooker's convenience, I put some chops in the pot along with seasonings I felt go well with lamb.

Slow-Cooked Lamb Chops are simple to prepare, and the recipe really highlights the flavor of the meat. Tender and delicious, the chops never fail to bring compliments.

For the Parmesan Potato Rounds, I like to use my own crisp white, red or gold potatoes and onions from the garden. The Parmesan cheese, pepper and garlic powder baked on the potato slices give them a great flavor.

People are pleasantly surprised by the hint of sweetness in Buttery Mint Carrots. While looking for new ways to use an abundance of carrots, I tried this minty variation. They complement lamb nicely.

Ginger, one of my favorite spices, plays a lead role in my Gingered Lime Gelatin. To save time, I make the pretty mold the day before serving.

We enjoy cheesecakes for any occasion. A cupboard full of homemade wild red raspberry jam prompted me to experiment, and the result was Raspberry Swirl Cheesecake Pie—a delectable and colorful spring dessert.

I remove the pie from the refrigerator about half an hour before serving. This short warm-up brings out the full cheesecake flavor.

I'm delighted to share my favorite springtime meal. Hope you enjoy it, too!

PICTURED AT LEFT: Slow-Cooked Lamb Chops, Parmesan Potato Rounds, Buttery Mint Carrots, Gingered Lime Gelatin and Raspberry Swirl Cheesecake Pie (recipes are on the next page).

Slow-Cooked Lamb Chops

Chops are without a doubt the cut of lamb we like best. I usually simmer them on low for hours in a slow cooker. The aroma is irresistible, and they come out so tender they practically melt in your mouth!

1 medium onion, sliced
1 teaspoon dried oregano
1/2 teaspoon dried thyme
1/2 teaspoon garlic powder
1/4 teaspoon salt
1/8 teaspoon pepper
8 loin lamb chops (about 1-3/4 pounds)
2 garlic cloves, minced

Place onion in a slow cooker. Combine oregano, thyme, garlic powder, salt and pepper; rub over the lamb chops. Place chops over onion. Top with garlic. Cover and cook on low for 4-6 hours or until the meat is tender. **Yield:** 4 servings.

Buttery Mint Carrots

(Pictured on page 249)

I reworked an old recipe to blend mint (traditionally a complement to lamb) with buttery-sweet carrots. This quick way of dressing up carrots makes a colorful accompaniment for other meats as well.

1 cup water
1/4 teaspoon salt
6 medium carrots, julienned
2 tablespoons butter *or* margarine
1 to 2 tablespoons confectioners' sugar
1-1/2 teaspoons minced fresh mint *or* 1/2 teaspoon dried mint flakes

In a saucepan, bring water and salt to a boil. Add carrots; cook until crisp-tender, about 8 minutes. Drain and set aside. In the same saucepan, melt butter. Stir in the sugar and mint until blended. Return carrots to pan; cook and stir for 2-3 minutes or until carrots are tender and evenly coated. **Yield:** 4 servings.

Parmesan Potato Rounds

These pretty cheese-coated potato slices go very well with lamb chops. It's the first recipe I turn to when I have potatoes and onions ready in the garden.

4 medium red potatoes, thinly sliced
1 small onion, thinly sliced and separated into rings
3 tablespoons butter *or* margarine, melted
1/4 cup grated Parmesan cheese
1/4 teaspoon salt
1/8 teaspoon pepper
1/8 teaspoon garlic powder

Place half of the potatoes in a greased 2-qt. or 11-in. x 7-in. x 2-in. baking dish. Top with onion and remaining potatoes; drizzle with butter. Sprinkle with Parmesan cheese, salt, pepper and garlic pow-

der. Bake, uncovered, at 450° for 25-30 minutes or until the potatoes are golden brown and tender. **Yield:** 4 servings.

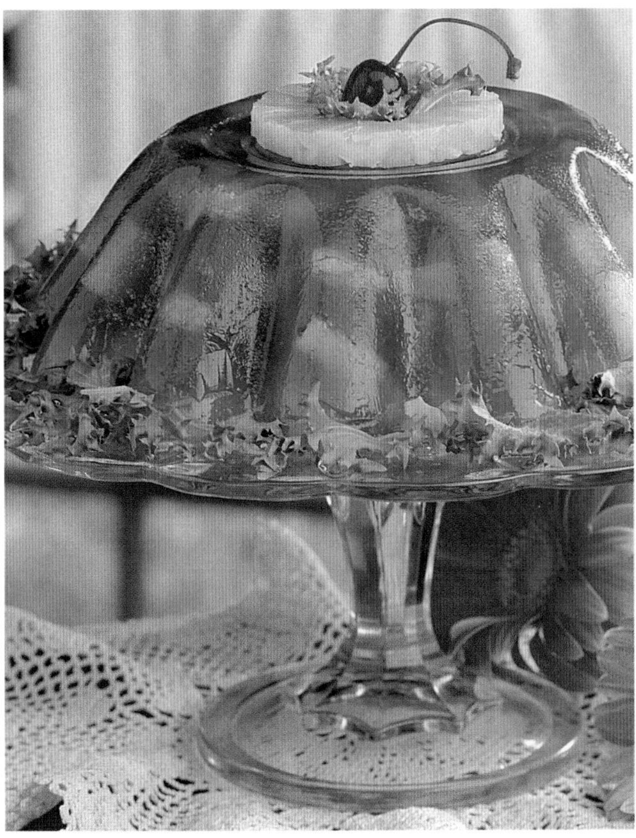

Gingered Lime Gelatin

This recipe calls for ginger ale in place of cold water, which gives the salad a "tingly" taste and heightens the ginger flavor.

✓ Uses less fat, sugar or salt. Includes Nutritional Analysis and Diabetic Exchanges.

1 can (20 ounces) pineapple tidbits
1 package (6 ounces) lime gelatin
1-1/2 cups boiling water
1 cup ginger ale, chilled
1/4 teaspoon ground ginger

Drain pineapple, reserving juice; set the pineapple aside. In a bowl, dissolve the gelatin in water. Stir in ginger ale, ginger and the reserved juice. Chill until syrupy, about 45 minutes. Fold in the pineapple. Transfer to a 6-cup mold coated with nonstick cooking spray. Refrigerate until firm. Unmold onto a serving platter. **Yield:** 12 servings. **Nutritional Analysis:** One serving (prepared with unsweetened pineapple, sugar-free gelatin and diet ginger ale) equals 21 calories, 37 mg sodium, 0 cholesterol, 4 gm carbohydrate, 1 gm protein, trace fat. **Diabetic Exchange:** Free food.

Raspberry Swirl Cheesecake Pie

I use jam made from plentiful wild raspberries on our farm to give this pretty dessert its marbled effect. While the cheesecake refrigerates overnight, its flavors blend beautifully.

Pastry for single-crust pie (9 inches)
2 packages (8 ounces *each*) cream cheese, softened
1/2 cup sugar
1/2 teaspoon vanilla extract
2 eggs
3 tablespoons raspberry jam
Whipped topping, optional

Line unpricked pastry shell with a double thickness of heavy-duty foil. Bake at 450° for 5 minutes; remove foil. Bake 5 minutes longer. Remove from the oven; reduce heat to 350°. In a mixing bowl, beat the cream cheese, sugar and vanilla until smooth. Add eggs, beating on low speed just until combined. Pour into pastry shell. Stir jam; drizzle over the filling. Cut through filling with a knife to swirl the jam. Bake for 25-30 minutes or until center is almost set. Cool on a wire rack for 1 hour. Refrigerate overnight. Let stand at room temperature for 30 minutes before slicing. If desired, pipe whipped topping around pie. **Yield:** 6-8 servings.

From a treasury of family-endorsed dishes, this practiced cook compiles a dinner that's lip-smacking good from start to finish.

By Grace Yaskovic, Branchville, New Jersey

WE OFTEN have a houseful of hungry people! My husband, Tom, and I love to have relatives over for birthdays and holidays.

On such occasions, I frequently serve this crowd-pleasing meal. Successful time and time again, it's a menu I can always count on.

I like to start with an appetizer, and everyone loves fresh-tasting Cucumber Pita Wedges.

Chicken and Garlic Potatoes is a hearty dish my in-laws have served at gatherings for many years.

My father-in-law generally prepares the entree with assorted chicken pieces and sometimes throws in a sweet potato or two. I prefer to use chicken breasts with the bone in (for added moistness) and good old russet potatoes. The seasonings heighten the flavor.

My Rosemary Carrots are low in fat with a nice light flavor and healthy crunch. If I have any red peppers on hand, I'll add some strips for even more color. You can cut the carrots into coins or julienne them for a fancier look.

I can hardly think of a special occasion or holiday meal on my side of the family when we didn't have Orange-Onion Lettuce Salad. The poppy seed dressing is just sweet enough to enhance the mixture of lettuce, oranges and red onions.

Another treasured recipe is Old-Fashioned Apple Crisp—every bite is bursting with goodness. The crumbly oat topping is made with brown sugar, cinnamon and a touch of allspice. It's yummy!

Guests often call this a comforting meal, and everyone agrees it's delectable. I give it high points for versatility—it's nice enough for company, and the recipes are easy enough that I don't hesitate to fix them for just the family.

PICTURED AT LEFT: Cucumber Pita Wedges, Chicken and Garlic Potatoes, Rosemary Carrots, Orange-Onion Lettuce Salad and Old-Fashioned Apple Crisp (recipes are on the next page).

Chicken and Garlic Potatoes

Originally my father-in-law's invention, this home-style oven entree is one we never tire of. I've made a few improvisations to suit the next generation's tastes.

 Uses less fat, sugar or salt. Includes Nutritional Analysis and Diabetic Exchanges.

4 medium potatoes, peeled and sliced
1 large onion, cut into small wedges
6 bone-in skinless chicken breast halves (4 pounds)
1 teaspoon dried tarragon
1 teaspoon rubbed sage
1 teaspoon salt, optional
1/2 teaspoon pepper
1 whole garlic bulb
3 tablespoons olive *or* vegetable oil

Place potatoes and onion in a greased 13-in. x 9-in. x 2-in. baking dish. Top with chicken. Combine tarragon, sage, salt if desired and pepper; sprinkle over chicken. Cut the top off the garlic bulb (the end that comes to a closed point) so each clove is exposed. Place cut side up in the baking dish. Drizzle oil over garlic and chicken. Cover and bake at 350° for 60 minutes. Uncover and bake 10-15 minutes longer or until chicken juices run clear and garlic is soft. Transfer chicken to a serving platter and keep warm. Cool garlic for 5 minutes; gently squeeze into a bowl and lightly mash. Toss garlic with potatoes and onion; arrange around chicken. **Yield:** 6 servings. **Nutritional Analysis:** One serving (prepared without salt) equals 281 calories, 70 mg sodium, 73 mg cholesterol, 18 gm carbohydrate, 29 gm protein, 10 gm fat. **Diabetic Exchanges:** 3 lean meat, 1 starch, 1/2 vegetable.

Rosemary Carrots

My husband and I cook with many different kinds of herbs and have found rosemary to be delightful with these colorful and fresh-tasting carrots.

1-1/2 pounds carrots, sliced
1 tablespoon olive *or* vegetable oil
1/2 cup diced green pepper
1 teaspoon dried rosemary, crushed
1/2 teaspoon salt
1/4 teaspoon coarsely ground pepper

In a skillet, cook and stir carrots in oil for 10-12 minutes or until crisp-tender. Add green pepper; cook and stir for 5 minutes until carrots and green pepper are tender. Sprinkle with rosemary, salt and pepper; heat through. **Yield:** 4-6 servings.

Cucumber Pita Wedges

(Pictured on page 253)

I first tasted these delicious snacks at a friend's house. Of the finger foods she served, this platter was the first to empty.

1 package (8 ounces) cream cheese, softened
2 tablespoons Italian salad dressing mix
4 whole pita breads
1 to 2 medium cucumbers, peeled and cut into 1/8-inch slices
Lemon-pepper seasoning

In a mixing bowl, beat cream cheese and salad dressing mix until combined. Split pita breads in half, forming two circles. Spread cream cheese mixture over pita circles; cut each into six wedges. Top with cucumbers. Sprinkle with lemon-pepper. **Yield:** 4 dozen.

Orange-Onion Lettuce Salad

A pleasant poppy seed dressing, sweet citrus sections, tangy red onion slices and mild lettuce blend deliciously in this pretty salad.

2 heads Bibb lettuce, torn
3 medium navel oranges, peeled and sectioned
1 small red onion, sliced and separated into rings
1/4 cup vegetable oil
2 tablespoons vinegar
2 teaspoons sugar
2 teaspoons poppy seeds
1/8 teaspoon salt
Dash pepper

Arrange lettuce on six salad plates. Top with oranges and onion rings. In a small bowl, combine the oil, vinegar, sugar, poppy seeds, salt and pepper. Drizzle over salads; serve immediately. **Yield:** 6 servings.

Old-Fashioned Apple Crisp

Now young adults, our children say this dessert is "awesome" with ice cream. Everyone who takes a bite nods in agreement! Nostalgic, comforting, luscious—call it what you will, this is one of those simple, old-time treats that never goes out of style.

4 cups sliced peeled tart apples (about 3 medium)
3/4 cup packed brown sugar
1/2 cup all-purpose flour
1/2 cup rolled oats
1 teaspoon ground cinnamon
1/4 to 1/2 teaspoon ground allspice
1/3 cup cold butter *or* margarine
Vanilla ice cream, optional

Place the apples in a greased 8-in. square baking dish. In a bowl, combine brown sugar, flour, oats, cinnamon and allspice; cut in butter until crumbly. Sprinkle over apples. Bake at 375° for 30-35 minutes or until apples are tender. Serve warm with ice cream if desired. **Yield:** 4-6 servings.

Autumn flavors from her seaside location are reflected in a distinctive menu that landlubbers will also savor.

By Debbie Terenzini, Lusby, Maryland

SEAFOOD is plentiful where I live, so my favorite fall meal celebrates the harvest of the sea as well as the land. Sunshine along with the bright yellows and oranges of the autumn leaves create the perfect background for this bountiful menu.

Classic Crab Cakes are a local favorite I learned how to make from a cook at a restaurant I owned for several years. I sometimes shape the patties ahead of time, wrap them individually in plastic wrap and pack them into zipper freezer bags. Later, I can defrost and cook as many as needed.

This entree can easily be transformed into an appetizer. I place cooked crab cakes on English muffin halves, cut these in quarters, top with shredded cheddar cheese and broil for 2 to 3 minutes.

Grandma's Popovers were a frequent Sunday dinner treat when I was growing up. Served warm with butter and honey, the light, golden popovers melt in your mouth!

Unique and delicious, Sauerkraut Apple Salad is my variation on a recipe a friend of mine brought back from Chelsea, England. Apples add a fresh crunch and sweet flavor.

I created the recipe for Spiced Cider years ago on a chilly fall New England day. My son, Roman, and I still enjoy this tangy, warming beverage whenever he's home during autumn or for the holidays.

Everyone "oohs" and "aahs" about my fancy-looking Frozen Mud Pie. But this yummy dessert is one of the easiest I make. Chocolate syrup swirled through the ice cream filling makes this treat especially appealing.

Sharing my favorite fall meal has been a pleasure. Try it soon—you're sure to harvest a bushel of compliments!

PICTURED AT LEFT: Classic Crab Cakes, Grandma's Popovers, Sauerkraut Apple Salad, Spiced Cider and Frozen Mud Pie (recipes are on the next page).

Classic Crab Cakes

This region is known for good seafood, and crab cakes are a traditional favorite. I learned to make them from a chef in a restaurant where they were a best-seller. The crabmeat's sweet and mild flavor is sparked by the blend of other ingredients.

- **1 pound canned *or* cooked crabmeat, flaked and cartilage removed (about 2 cups)**
- **2 to 2-1/2 cups soft bread crumbs**
- **1 egg, beaten**
- **3/4 cup mayonnaise**
- **1/3 cup *each* chopped celery, green pepper and onion**
- **1 tablespoon seafood seasoning**
- **1 tablespoon minced fresh parsley**
- **2 teaspoons lemon juice**
- **1 teaspoon Worcestershire sauce**
- **1 teaspoon prepared mustard**
- **1/4 teaspoon pepper**
- **1/8 teaspoon hot pepper sauce**
- **2 to 4 tablespoons vegetable oil**
- **Lemon slices, optional**

In a bowl, combine crab, bread crumbs, egg, mayonnaise, vegetables and seasonings. Shape into eight patties. Broil patties or cook in a skillet in oil for 4 minutes on each side or until golden brown. Serve with lemon if desired. **Yield:** 8 servings.

Sauerkraut Apple Salad

Guests say this salad is crisp, delicious, different and surprising! That's because of the unusual combination of ingredients, including sauerkraut, apple, onion and dill pickles. See if you agree.

- **1 can (27 ounces) sauerkraut, rinsed and drained**
- **1 medium tart apple, peeled and chopped**
- **1 small onion, chopped**
- **3/4 cup chopped dill pickle**
- **3 tablespoons lemon juice**
- **1 tablespoon sugar**
- **1 tablespoon dried basil**
- **1 tablespoon dill weed**
- **1 tablespoon dried parsley flakes**
- **1 teaspoon salt**
- **1/4 cup vegetable oil**

In a bowl, combine the first 10 ingredients. Drizzle with oil; toss to coat. Cover and refrigerate for at least 2 hours before serving. **Yield:** 8 servings.

Grandma's Popovers

Still warm from the oven, popovers are always a fun accompaniment to a homey meal. I was raised on these —my grandmother often made them for our Sunday dinners. The recipe could not be simpler.

- **1 cup all-purpose flour**

1/8 teaspoon salt
3 eggs
1 cup milk

In a bowl, combine flour and salt. Combine eggs and milk; whisk into the dry ingredients just until blended. Using two 12-cup muffin tins, grease and flour five alternating cups of one tin and four cups of the second tin; fill two-thirds full with batter. Fill the empty cups two-thirds full with water. Bake at 450° for 15 minutes. Reduce heat to 350° (do not open oven door). Bake 15 minutes longer or until deep golden brown (do not underbake). **Yield:** 9 popovers.

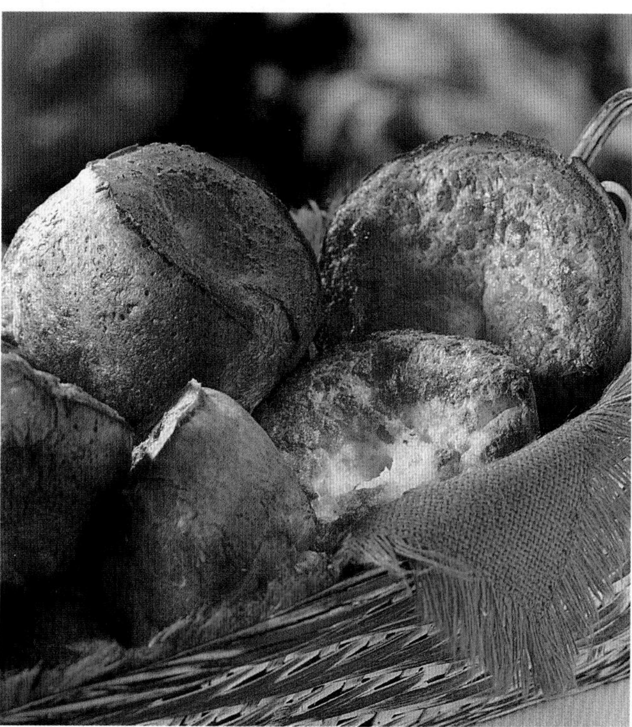

Spiced Cider

(Pictured on page 257)

I first concocted this beverage years ago for my son on a chilly fall New England day. Now he's grown and in the Navy, but he still enjoys this tangy cider whenever he's home for a visit.

2 quarts apple cider
1/2 cup packed brown sugar
3 cinnamon sticks (3 inches)
1/2 to 1 teaspoon ground allspice
1/8 teaspoon salt
1/8 teaspoon ground nutmeg
Additional cinnamon sticks, optional

In a large saucepan, combine the first six ingredients; bring to a boil. Reduce heat; cover and simmer for 20 minutes. Discard cinnamon sticks. Use additional cinnamon sticks for stirrers if desired. **Yield:** 8-10 servings (about 2 quarts).

Frozen Mud Pie

Here's one of those "looks like you fussed" desserts that is so easy it's become a standard for me. I love the mocha version, but pure chocolate lovers may prefer using chocolate chip ice cream. The cookie crust is a snap to make.

1-1/2 cups crushed cream-filled chocolate sandwich cookies (about 15)
1-1/2 teaspoons sugar, optional
1/4 cup butter *or* margarine, melted
2 pints chocolate chip *or* coffee ice cream, softened
1/4 cup chocolate syrup, *divided*
Additional cream-filled chocolate sandwich cookies, optional

In a bowl, combine cookie crumbs and sugar if desired. Stir in butter. Press onto the bottom and up the sides of an ungreased 9-in. pie plate. Refrigerate for 30 minutes. Spoon 1 pint of ice cream into crust. Drizzle with half of the chocolate syrup; swirl with a knife. Carefully top with the remaining ice cream. Drizzle with remaining syrup; swirl with a knife. Cover and freeze until firm. Remove from the freezer 10-15 minutes before serving. Garnish with whole cookies if desired. **Yield:** 8 servings.

Her three-generation Sunday dinners are making memories as the family gathers for delicious food like this fall feast.

By Bertha Johnson, Indianapolis, Indiana

SUNDAY DINNER after church is a long-standing tradition in our family. Our four sons and their families have a standing invitation to join my husband, Granville (his nickname's "Buster"), and me for the noon meal.

When autumn arrives with the harvest of pumpkins and other offerings, this is a well-loved Sunday menu at Grandma's.

Autumn Pork Chops are special but not time-consuming. This skillet entree simmers for just an hour, and the fruit sauce is easy to make. Its combination of prunes, apricots and cider is delightful with the chops.

Our grandchildren think you can't have a meal without macaroni and cheese. My creamy Deluxe Macaroni 'n' Cheese meets the approval of everyone at the table. Put together ahead of time, the dish is ready for the oven after church.

It bakes along with Butternut Squash Bake, another make-ahead dish that's so appealing. We first tasted this recipe when visiting my brother in Huntsville, Alabama several years ago.

It was a big hit and has become one of my preferred ways to fix winter squash. I put it together the night before or early Sunday morning. Later, I let it return to room temperature after removing it from the refrigerator and bake as directed.

Also perfect for my time frame is Make-Ahead Lettuce Salad. This favorite is made up of crispy lettuce, fresh colorful vegetables and a tangy dressing.

The recipe for Streusel Pumpkin Pie was sent to me by a very dear friend. Since she shared it, I've never made another kind of pumpkin pie. A nutty crust and streusel topping make it unique.

I just love to cook and have everyone enjoy what they are eating. This menu has been a Sunday success at our house. We hope your family will like it, too.

PICTURED AT LEFT: Autumn Pork Chops, Deluxe Macaroni 'n' Cheese, Butternut Squash Bake, Make-Ahead Lettuce Salad and Streusel Pumpkin Pie (recipes are on the next page).

Autumn Pork Chops

A delicious fruit sauce makes this easy pork chop dish Sunday-special. It's an autumn favorite when the children and grandchildren gather at our place for dinner after church. The chops simmer to a wonderful tenderness in just an hour.

6 loin pork chops (1/2 inch thick)
1 tablespoon butter *or* margarine
12 dried apricots
6 dried pitted prunes
1-1/2 cups apple cider *or* juice
1 tablespoon sugar
1 teaspoon salt
1/4 teaspoon curry powder
2 tablespoons cornstarch
2 tablespoons cold water

In a large skillet, brown pork chops in butter for 1-2 minutes on each side. Arrange the apricots and prunes over pork. Combine the cider, sugar, salt and curry; pour over fruit. Cover and simmer for 1 hour. Remove pork and fruit and keep warm. Combine cornstarch and water until smooth; add to pan juices. Bring to a boil; cook and stir for 2 minutes or until thickened. Serve with the pork chops and fruit. **Yield:** 6 servings.

Butternut Squash Bake

For a side dish with special harvesttime appeal, you can't go wrong with this savory squash bake. It's creamy, comforting and looks so delectable, thanks to the rich yellow butternut squash and golden crumb topping.

1 small butternut squash, peeled, seeded and cubed (about 2 cups)
1/2 cup mayonnaise*
1/2 cup finely chopped onion
1 egg, lightly beaten
1 teaspoon sugar
Salt and pepper to taste
1/4 cup crushed saltines (about 8 crackers)
2 tablespoons grated Parmesan cheese
1 tablespoon butter *or* margarine, melted

Place squash in a saucepan and cover with water; bring to a boil. Reduce heat; cover and simmer for 20-25 minutes or until very tender. Drain well and place in a large bowl; mash squash. In another bowl, combine the mayonnaise, onion, egg, sugar, salt and pepper; add to squash and mix well. Transfer to a greased 1-qt. baking dish. Combine cracker crumbs, cheese and butter; sprinkle over top. Bake, uncovered, at 350° for 30-40 minutes or until heated through and top is golden brown. **Yield:** 6 servings. ***Editor's Note:** Light or fat-free mayonnaise may not be substituted for regular mayonnaise.

Deluxe Macaroni 'n' Cheese

(Pictured on page 261)

Our six grandchildren, who don't think a meal is complete without macaroni and cheese, love this creamy version featuring cheddar and cottage cheese.

2 cups small-curd cottage cheese
1 cup (8 ounces) sour cream
1 egg, lightly beaten
3/4 teaspoon salt
Garlic salt and pepper to taste
2 cups (8 ounces) shredded sharp cheddar cheese
1 package (7 ounces) elbow macaroni, cooked and drained
Paprika, optional

In a large bowl, combine the cottage cheese, sour cream, egg, salt, garlic salt and pepper. Add cheddar cheese; mix well. Add macaroni and stir until coated. Transfer to a greased 2-1/2-qt. baking dish. Bake, uncovered, at 350° for 25-30 minutes or until heated through. Sprinkle with paprika if desired. **Yield:** 8-10 servings.

Make-Ahead Lettuce Salad

"Make-ahead" is a magic word when you're planning a hearty meal and trying to minimize last-minute preparation. If you serve it in a glass bowl, be sure to bring the salad to the table before tossing so everyone can see the pretty layers.

 Uses less fat, sugar or salt. Includes Nutritional Analysis and Diabetic Exchanges.

1 head iceberg lettuce, torn
1 large onion, chopped
1/2 cup chopped celery
1/2 cup chopped green pepper
1 can (8 ounces) sliced water chestnuts, drained
1 package (10 ounces) frozen peas, thawed
2 cups mayonnaise
1 tablespoon sugar
1/4 cup shredded Parmesan cheese
4 bacon strips, cooked and crumbled, optional

In a 6-qt. bowl, layer half of the lettuce, onion, celery, green pepper, water chestnuts and peas. Combine mayonnaise and sugar; spread half over the salad. Repeat layers. Sprinkle with cheese and bacon if desired. Cover and refrigerate for 12-24 hours. **Yield:** 14-16 servings. **Nutritional Analysis:** One 1-cup serving (prepared with fat-free mayonnaise and nonfat Parmesan cheese topping and without bacon) equals 54 calories, 262 mg sodium, trace cholesterol, 11 gm carbohydrate, 2 gm protein, trace fat. **Diabetic Exchanges:** 1/2 starch, 1/2 vegetable.

Streusel Pumpkin Pie

Basic pumpkin pie is good, but we think this dressed-up version is even better. Plenty of pecans add a nutty crunch to the pastry and the yummy streusel topping. It's perfect any time you want something special.

2 cups all-purpose flour
1/4 cup finely chopped pecans
1 teaspoon salt
2/3 cup plus 1 tablespoon vegetable shortening
4 to 5 tablespoons water

FILLING:
1 can (30 ounces) pumpkin pie mix
1 can (14 ounces) sweetened condensed milk
1 egg, lightly beaten

STREUSEL TOPPING:
1/2 cup packed brown sugar
1/4 cup all-purpose flour
1/4 cup chopped pecans
1/2 teaspoon ground cinnamon
3 tablespoons cold butter *or* margarine

In a bowl, combine flour, pecans and salt; cut in shortening until crumbly. Gradually add water, tossing with a fork until a ball forms. Divide dough in half. Roll out each portion to fit a 9-in. pie plate; place pastry in pie plates. Flute edges and set aside. Combine pie mix, milk and egg; pour into pastry shells. For topping, combine sugar, flour, pecans and cinnamon in a small bowl; cut in butter until crumbly. Sprinkle over filling. Cover edges loosely with foil. Bake at 375° for 40-45 minutes or until a knife inserted near the center comes out clean. Cool on a wire rack for 2 hours. Refrigerate until serving. **Yield:** 2 pies (6-8 servings each).

Meals in Minutes

Mix and match these rapid recipes to make countless meals that go from start to finish in less than 30 minutes.

SPEEDY SOLUTIONS. Clockwise from upper left: Turn Ho-Hum Hamburgers into Easy Italian Entree (p. 272), Soup-and-Sandwich Duo Always Delights (p. 268), Take Stock in Festive No-Fuss Feast (p. 266) and Hearty Ham Dinner's Ready in a Hurry (p. 270).

Take Stock in Festive No-Fuss Feast

WITH CARDS to send, a tree to trim and presents to wrap, who has time to spend hours in the kitchen during the holiday season? This satisfying quick meal may be just the gift to give yourself and your family!

The complete-meal menu here is made up of favorite recipes shared by three great cooks and combined in our test kitchen. You can have everything ready to serve in just half an hour.

Chicken Crescent Wreath is an impressive-looking main dish that's a snap to prepare. "Even when my cooking time is limited, I can still serve this delicious wreath," says Marlene Denissen of Maplewood, Minnesota. "The red pepper and green broccoli add a festive touch."

Parmesan Buttered Rice is recommended by Rose Marie Dama of Waco, Texas. "The flavorful and simple butter, Parmesan cheese and parsley topping gives plain rice a tasty twist the whole family enjoys," Rose Marie assures.

"Cherry Cream Parfaits are lovely and special desserts that look fussy but are really easy to fix," assures Jeannette Mack of Rushville, New York. "I've also made them using other pie fillings like strawberry, raspberry and blueberry."

Chicken Crescent Wreath

2 tubes (8 ounces *each*) refrigerated crescent rolls
1 cup (4 ounces) shredded Co-Jack cheese
2/3 cup condensed cream of chicken soup, undiluted
1/2 cup chopped fresh broccoli
1/2 cup chopped sweet red pepper
1/4 cup chopped water chestnuts
1 can (5 ounces) white chicken, drained *or* 3/4 cup cubed cooked chicken
2 tablespoons chopped onion

Arrange the crescent rolls on a 12-in. pizza pan, forming a ring with pointed ends facing the outer edge of pan and wide ends overlapping. Combine the remaining ingredients; spoon over wide ends of rolls. Fold points over filling and tuck under wide ends (filling will be visible). Bake at 375° for 20-25 minutes or until golden brown. **Yield:** 6-8 servings.

Parmesan Buttered Rice

3 cups water
1-1/2 cups uncooked long grain rice
1/2 cup butter (no substitutes)
1-1/2 cups grated Parmesan cheese
1 tablespoon minced fresh parsley

In a large saucepan, bring water to a boil; stir in rice. Reduce heat to low; cover and cook for 20 minutes or until tender. Meanwhile, in a skillet over medium heat, melt the butter until browned. Place rice in a serving dish and sprinkle with Parmesan cheese. Pour butter over rice; cover and let stand for 2-3 minutes. Sprinkle with parsley. **Yield:** 6-8 servings.

Cherry Cream Parfaits

1 cup whipping cream
3 tablespoons sugar
1 teaspoon vanilla extract
Dash salt
1 cup (8 ounces) sour cream
1 can (21 ounces) cherry pie filling, *divided*

In a mixing bowl, whip cream until soft peaks form. Gradually add sugar, vanilla and salt; beat until stiff peaks form. Fold in sour cream. Set aside six cherries from pie filling. Spoon half of the remaining pie filling into parfait glasses; top with half of the cream mixture. Repeat layers. Top with reserved cherries. **Yield:** 6 servings.

Rapid Recipes with Rice

Cooked rice can be stored in the refrigerator for up to 1 week and in the freezer for up to 6 months. So you can cook rice in double batches to have some on hand for making quick meals.

Leftovers make great fried rice. Just saute in a small amount of oil with chopped green onions or mushrooms. Or combine leftover rice, sliced bananas and a can of crushed pineapple for an easy dessert.

Soup-and-Sandwich Duo Always Delights

THE CLASSIC combination of soup and a sandwich makes a comforting and versatile meal. It's a dynamite duo that busy cooks across the country can turn to time and time again.

The soup and sandwich meal here is made up of family favorites from three great cooks. You can have everything ready to serve in only 30 minutes.

Cheeseburger Loaf is a satisfying quick main dish that Brenda Rohlman remembers her mom making years ago. "I sometimes use spaghetti sauce with mozzarella cheese or picante sauce with Monterey Jack cheese to vary the taste," says this Kingman, Kansas cook.

Zesty Potato Soup is suggested by Marsha Benda of Round Rock, Texas, who informs, "This creamy soup has a delightful zip that sparks recipe requests. Folks love the combination of potatoes, cheese and green chilies. It's a nice change of pace from regular potato soup."

Butterscotch Pecan Cookies have a rich buttery flavor. "No one will guess they started from convenient cake and pudding mixes," assures Betty Janway of Ruston, Louisiana. "I make a batch even when I do have time to spare."

Cheeseburger Loaf

1 pound ground beef
1/4 cup chopped onion
1 can (10-3/4 ounces) condensed tomato soup, undiluted
1/2 teaspoon garlic salt
1/4 teaspoon salt
1/4 teaspoon pepper
1 loaf (1 pound) French bread
1 tablespoon butter *or* margarine, softened
8 ounces process American *or* Mexican-flavored cheese, sliced

In a saucepan over medium heat, cook beef and onion until meat is no longer pink; drain. Add soup, garlic salt, salt and pepper; simmer for 5-10 minutes. Meanwhile, slice the top third off the bread. Hollow out bottom half of loaf, leaving a 3/4-in. shell (discard removed bread or save for another use). Spread butter on cut side of bread. Place loaf on a baking sheet and broil until lightly browned. Spoon beef mixture into shell; arrange cheese slices on top. Broil until cheese is melted, about 2-3 minutes. Replace bread top. **Yield:** 6-8 servings.

Zesty Potato Soup

4 large potatoes, peeled and cubed
2 cups water
1 teaspoon dried minced onion
1 garlic clove, minced
1/2 teaspoon salt
1/4 teaspoon pepper
1 cup milk
4 ounces process American cheese, cubed
1/3 cup chopped green chilies
2 tablespoons butter *or* margarine
1 tablespoon chicken bouillon granules
2 teaspoons minced fresh parsley

In a large saucepan, combine the potatoes, water, onion, garlic, salt and pepper; bring to a boil over medium heat. Reduce heat; cover and simmer for 15-20 minutes or until potatoes are tender. (Do not drain.) Mash potatoes in liquid until almost smooth. Add remaining ingredients; cook and stir until the cheese is melted. **Yield:** 6 servings.

Butterscotch Pecan Cookies

1 package (18-1/4 ounces) butter recipe cake mix*
1 package (3.4 ounces) instant butterscotch pudding mix
1/4 cup all-purpose flour
3/4 cup vegetable oil
1 egg
1 cup chopped pecans

In a mixing bowl, combine the first five ingredients and mix well. Stir in pecans (the dough will be crumbly). Roll tablespoonfuls into balls; place 2 in. apart on greased baking sheets. Bake at 350° for 10-12 minutes or until golden brown. Cool for 2 minutes; remove from pans to wire racks. **Yield:** 4 dozen. ***Editor's Note:** This recipe was tested with Pillsbury brand butter recipe cake mix.

Hearty Ham Dinner's Ready in a Hurry

FOR THOSE who love to cook, spending time in the kitchen preparing an elaborate meal is a joy. Still, there are some days when you need to pull together a satisfying meal in just minutes.

The fast and flavorful meal here is made up of tried-and-true favorites from three busy cooks. You can have everything on the table in just half an hour!

Hurry-Up Ham 'n' Noodles is a rich-tasting entree created by Lucille Howell of Portland, Oregon. "This basic hearty dish is ready to serve in almost the time it takes to cook the noodles," she says. "I make it often for luncheons and potlucks. Mostly I make it on days when I'm in a hurry to get something on the table."

Continues Lucille, "This stovetop specialty is a great way to use up leftover ham from Easter, Christmas or any other dinner."

Tangy Carrot Coins give a popular nutritious vegetable a new twist, remarks Lois Stephen from Mt. Morris, Michigan. "This colorful side dish is as easy to fix as plain carrots, but the light, creamy coating makes them extra yummy," she adds. "Even folks who don't usually care for carrots gobble them up in no time...then ask for more!"

Peachy Sundaes are a treat grandmother Betty Claycomb has enjoyed since she was a teenager. "Years ago, a friend worked at a fancy hotel where this deliciously different dessert was served," recalls this Alverton, Pennsylvania cook. "These sundaes are very simple to prepare but look and taste elegant."

Hurry-Up Ham 'n' Noodles

5 to 6 cups uncooked wide egg noodles
1/4 cup butter *or* margarine
1 cup whipping cream
1-1/2 cups julienned fully cooked ham
1/2 cup grated Parmesan cheese
1/4 cup thinly sliced green onions
1/4 teaspoon salt
1/8 teaspoon pepper

Cook noodles according to package directions. Meanwhile, in a skillet over medium heat, melt butter. Stir in cream. Bring to a boil; cook and stir for 2 minutes. Add ham, cheese, onions, salt and pepper; heat through. Drain noodles; add to ham mixture and heat through. **Yield:** 4 servings.

Tangy Carrot Coins

1 pound carrots, sliced
3 tablespoons butter *or* margarine
1 tablespoon brown sugar
1 tablespoon Dijon mustard
1/8 teaspoon salt

Place carrots in a saucepan. Add 1 in. of water; bring to a boil. Reduce heat; cover and simmer for 7-9 minutes or until crisp-tender. Drain. Add the butter, brown sugar, Dijon mustard and salt; cook and stir over medium heat for 1-2 minutes or until sauce is thickened and carrots are coated. **Yield:** 4 servings.

Peachy Sundaes

1 pint vanilla ice cream
1/2 to 1 cup peach preserves, warmed
1/4 cup chopped almonds, toasted
1/4 cup flaked coconut, toasted, optional

Divide ice cream among four individual dishes. Top with preserves; sprinkle with almonds and coconut if desired. **Yield:** 4 servings.

A Bunch of Carrot Tips

The best carrots are young and slender. Look for those that are firm and smooth; avoid any with cracks or that have begun to soften and wither.

If buying carrots with their greenery, make sure the leaves are moist and bright green. Carrot greens rob the roots of moisture and vitamins, so remove them as soon as you get home.

Store carrots in a plastic bag in the refrigerator for up to 2 weeks.

Turn Ho-Hum Hamburgers Into Easy Italian Entree

DRESS UP plain hamburgers with a few simple seasonings, and you have an easy Italian-style entree in a matter of minutes.

The savory, complete-menu here is made up of favorites from three great cooks and combined in our test kitchen. You can have everything ready to serve in only 30 minutes.

"Italian Hamburgers make a super supper that takes only minutes to prepare but still leaves the impression that I've spent time cooking," chuckles Ronda Lawson of Dublin, California.

Pepper Parmesan Beans, suggested by Marian Platt of Sequim, Washington, is a simple treatment that results in a colorful, flavorful and special side dish. "The garlic adds a savory zip, and the Parmesan cheese mixed in makes it both hearty and satisfying," Marian relates.

"Yogurt Berry Pies have just two ingredients in the filling, so they're a snap to assemble. Yet they look and taste like you fussed," says Dawn Fagerstrom of Warren, Minnesota. "Topped with fresh blueberries and raspberries, they're irresistible."

Italian Hamburgers

6 tablespoons dry bread crumbs
1/3 cup chopped onion
1/3 cup chopped green pepper
1 garlic clove, minced
3/4 teaspoon dried oregano
1/4 to 1/2 teaspoon salt
1/4 to 1/2 teaspoon pepper
1 pound ground beef
6 tablespoons grated Parmesan cheese, *divided*
1 can (15 ounces) tomato sauce
3/4 teaspoon Italian seasoning
Hot cooked spaghetti, optional

Combine the first seven ingredients. Add beef and 3 tablespoons of Parmesan cheese; mix well. Shape into six patties. In a skillet, brown patties for 2 minutes on each side. Combine the tomato sauce and Italian seasoning; pour over patties. Reduce heat; cover and simmer for 10-15 minutes or until meat is no longer pink. Sprinkle with remaining cheese. Serve patties and sauce over spaghetti if desired. **Yield:** 6 servings.

Pepper Parmesan Beans

1 large sweet red pepper, diced
1 small green pepper, diced
1/4 cup chopped onion
1 garlic clove, minced
1/4 cup olive *or* vegetable oil
1-1/2 pounds fresh green beans, cut into 2-inch pieces
1 tablespoon minced fresh basil *or* 1 teaspoon dried basil
1 teaspoon salt
1/3 to 1/2 cup shredded Parmesan cheese

In a large skillet, saute peppers, onion and garlic in oil until the vegetables are tender, about 3 minutes. Add beans, basil and salt; toss to coat. Cover and cook over medium-low heat for 7-8 minutes or until beans are crisp-tender. Stir in cheese; serve immediately. **Yield:** 6-8 servings.

Yogurt Berry Pies

1 carton (8 ounces) mixed berry yogurt *or* flavor of your choice
2 cups whipped topping
1 package (6 count) individual graham cracker tart shells
Blueberries and raspberries

In a bowl, stir the yogurt and whipped topping until combined. Spoon into tart shells. Cover and freeze for 20 minutes. Top with berries. **Yield:** 6 servings.

Hamburger Helpers

For juicier hamburgers, add 2 to 3 tablespoons of tomato juice to each pound of ground beef.

Dampen your hands with water while shaping hamburger patties so the meat won't stick to your fingers. Form patties using a light touch so meat mixture doesn't become too compact and produce tough, dense burgers.

When freezing hamburger patties, layer them between squares of plastic wrap for easier defrosting.

Summer Meal Adds Some Sizzle to Supper

SPICE UP your summer meal without turning up the heat in the kitchen. With this Southwestern-style meal, you'll be out of the kitchen in less than 30 minutes!

It's a complete-meal menu made up of favorites from three great cooks, combined in our test kitchen.

Chicken Quesadillas have an impressive look and taste without little preparation. "Leftover chicken gets Mexican flair from cumin in this fun main dish," says Linda Wetzel of Woodland Park, Colorado.

"Zippy Beans and Rice is a super side dish, and we also enjoy it as a light entree with corn bread and salad," relates Darlene Owen, Reedsport, Oregon.

Berry Pineapple Parfaits from Ruth Andrewson of Peck, Idaho are lovely and refreshing.

Chicken Quesadillas

2-1/2 cups shredded cooked chicken
2/3 cup salsa
1/3 cup sliced green onions
3/4 to 1 teaspoon ground cumin
1/2 teaspoon salt
1/2 teaspoon dried oregano
6 flour tortillas (8 inches)
1/4 cup butter *or* margarine, melted
2 cups (8 ounces) shredded Monterey Jack cheese
Sour cream and guacamole

In a skillet, combine the first six ingredients. Cook, uncovered, over medium heat for 10 minutes or until heated through, stirring occasionally. Brush one side of tortillas with butter. Spoon 1/3 cup chicken mixture over half of unbuttered side of each tortilla. Sprinkle with 1/3 cup cheese; fold plain side of tortilla over cheese. Place on a lightly greased baking sheet. Bake at 475° for 10 minutes or until crisp and golden brown. Cut into wedges; serve with sour cream and guacamole. **Yield:** 6 servings.

Zippy Beans and Rice

✓ Uses less fat, sugar or salt. Includes Nutritional Analysis and Diabetic Exchanges.

1 can (15 ounces) black beans, rinsed and drained
1 can (10 ounces) diced tomatoes and green chilies, undrained
1 cup frozen corn
3/4 cup water
1 medium jalapeno pepper, seeded and chopped*
1 teaspoon salt, optional
1 cup uncooked instant white *or* brown rice
1 green onion, sliced

In a skillet, combine the beans, tomatoes, corn, water, jalapeno and salt if desired. Bring to a boil; stir in rice. Cover and remove from the heat. Let stand for 5 minutes or until liquid is absorbed. Sprinkle with onion. **Yield:** 6 servings. **Nutritional Analysis:** One 3/4-cup serving (prepared with brown rice and without salt) equals 197 calories, 414 mg sodium, 0 cholesterol, 40 gm carbohydrate, 8 gm protein, 2 gm fat. **Diabetic Exchanges:** 2 starch, 1 vegetable, 1/2 fat. ***Editor's Note:** When cutting or seeding hot peppers, use rubber or plastic gloves to protect your hands. Avoid touching your face.

Berry Pineapple Parfaits

3 cups whole fresh strawberries
3 to 4 tablespoons sugar
12 scoops vanilla ice cream
1 can (8 ounces) crushed pineapple
Whipped topping

Reserve six strawberries for garnish. Slice the remaining strawberries and toss with sugar; let stand for 10 minutes. Spoon half of the sliced berries into six parfait glasses. Top with half of the ice cream and half of the pineapple. Repeat layers. Top with whipped topping and reserved strawberries. **Yield:** 6 servings.

Easy Equivalents

If you need 2 cups of shredded cooked chicken for a recipe, start with 3/4 pound boneless skinless chicken breasts or approximately 1-1/2 pounds bone-in chicken breasts.

From-Scratch 'Fast Food' Is Fit for Fall

ON THE GO with your kid's after-school practices and other fall activities? Forget the drive-thru—you can make satisfying fast food at home.

Ready to serve in just 30 minutes, the menu here combines recipes from three super cooks.

Skillet Pork Chops cook up moist and tender with a sauce seasoned with ginger and grape jelly. "We enjoyed this main dish while visiting our son and his family," recalls June Formanek of Belle Plain, Iowa. "It was so tasty I got the recipe from my daughter-in-law, Sandy."

Curried Celery and Apples is a delicious accompaniment for pork, suggested by Lois Miller of Bradenton, Florida. Curry powder adds a delightful zip.

Fluffy Fruit Salad, shared by Christine Halandras of Meeker, Colorado, is a simple refreshing salad. "I like this recipe since I can prepare it in advance when entertaining," Christina remarks. "Even people who don't care for cranberries usually like this treat."

Skillet Pork Chops

4 pork chops (1 inch thick)
1 tablespoon vegetable oil
1 medium onion, chopped
1 cup chicken broth
2 to 3 tablespoons grape jelly
1/4 teaspoon ground ginger
4-1/2 teaspoons cornstarch
3 tablespoons cold water
Hot cooked rice

In a skillet over medium heat, brown pork chops in oil; drain. Add onion; cook until tender. Pour broth around chops; bring to a boil. Reduce heat; cover and simmer for 12-16 minutes or until the meat is tender. Remove chops and keep warm. Stir jelly and ginger into broth. Combine cornstarch and water until smooth; add to broth. Bring to a boil; cook and stir for 2 minutes. Serve over pork chops and rice. **Yield:** 4 servings.

Curried Celery and Apples

2 cups thinly sliced celery
1 small onion, chopped
1/3 cup butter *or* margarine
1 medium tart apple, chopped
1 tablespoon all-purpose flour
1/2 to 1 teaspoon curry powder
1/2 teaspoon salt
1/8 teaspoon pepper

In a skillet, saute celery and onion in butter until crisp-tender, about 5 minutes. Stir in apple. Cover and simmer for 3 minutes. Sprinkle with flour, curry powder, salt and pepper. Cook for 2 minutes, stirring occasionally. Serve immediately. **Yield:** 4 servings.

Fluffy Fruit Salad

✓ Uses less fat, sugar or salt. Includes Nutritional Analysis and Diabetic Exchanges.

1 can (20 ounces) unsweetened pineapple tidbits, drained
1 can (16 ounces) whole-berry cranberry sauce
1 can (11 ounces) mandarin oranges, drained
1 carton (8 ounces) frozen whipped topping, thawed
1/2 to 1 teaspoon grated orange peel
Lettuce leaves, optional
1/2 cup pecan halves, toasted

In a bowl, combine pineapple, cranberry sauce and oranges. Fold in whipped topping and orange peel. Serve on lettuce if desired. Top with pecans just before serving. Store leftovers in the refrigerator. **Yield:** 14 servings. **Nutritional Analysis:** One 1/2-cup serving (prepared with light whipped topping) equals 138 calories, 10 mg sodium, 0 cholesterol, 23 gm carbohydrate, 1 gm protein, 5 gm fat. **Diabetic Exchanges:** 1-1/2 fruit, 1 fat.

Saving Citrus Peels

Before using oranges, lemons and limes, remove the peels with a vegetable peeler or citrus zester. (Be sure to avoid the white pith.) Store the peels in the freezer to use in a variety of recipes.

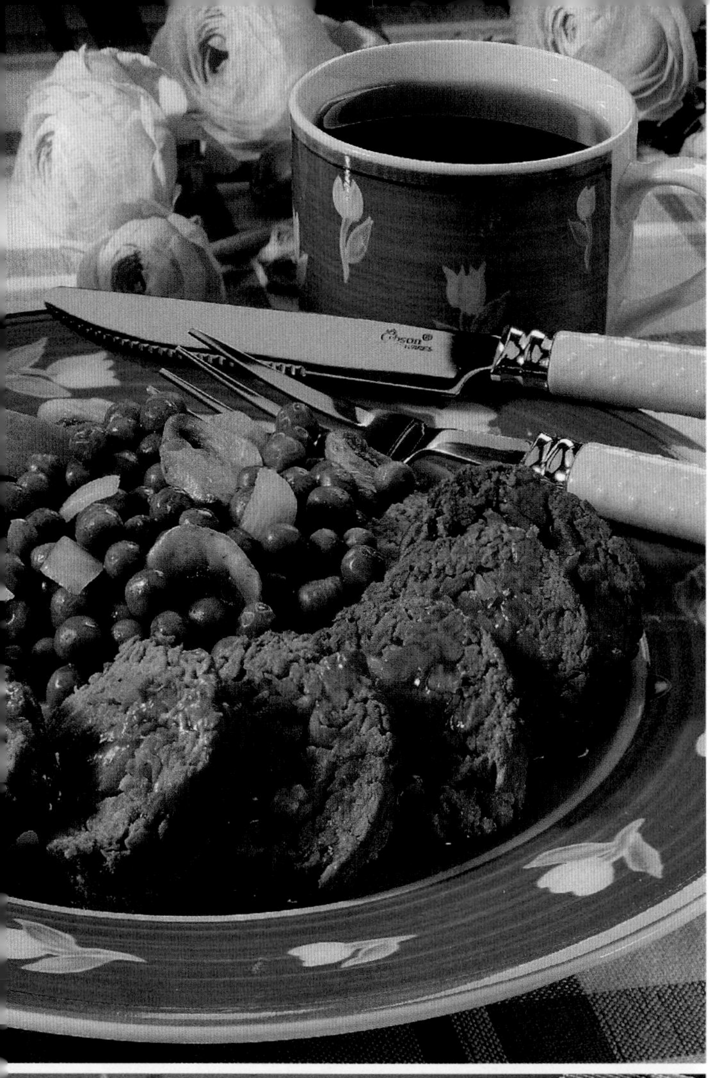

Meals on a Budget

With these six economical entrees, you can serve your family savory and satisfying meals for just pennies a person.

"CENT-SIBLE" EATING. Clockwise from upper left: Baked Omelet Roll, Eggnog Pancakes with Cranberry Sauce and Hot Fruit and Sausage (p. 280); Stuffed Cube Steaks, Sweet Peas and Mushrooms and Fresh Peach Cobbler (p. 288); Swiss Steak Supper, Whole Wheat Rolls and Chocolate Pudding Sundaes (p. 282); Upside-Down Meat Pie, Macaroni Medley Salad and Homemade Chocolate Syrup (p. 286).

Feed Your Family for $1.01 a Plate!

FEEDING your family a wholesome, hearty breakfast or brunch doesn't have to cost a bunch. This special penny-pinching early-morning menu comes from three great cooks who estimate the total cost at just $1.01 per setting.

Baked Omelet Roll is a deliciously different way to serve an omelet. It's a suggestion from Susan Hudon of Fort Wayne, Indiana.

The eggs bake in the oven, so you don't have to keep a constant eye on them like omelets made in a frying pan on the stove.

"Eggnog Pancakes with Cranberry Sauce are economical, quick and delicious," assures Iola Egle of McCook, Nebraska. "We love the subtle eggnog flavor and tangy cranberry topping," she says.

"These light and fluffy pancakes are especially good for a Christmas brunch. But my family enjoys them so much I make them year-round," continues Iola.

Hot Fruit and Sausage is a hearty dish sure to wake up taste buds. The recipe is shared by Marian Peterson of Wisconsin Rapids, Wisconsin.

"Pineapple, brown sugar and cinnamon make plain pork sausage links extra tasty," shares Marian. "And the banana slices really complement the sausage. This dish is super easy to prepare and makes any breakfast special."

Baked Omelet Roll

6 eggs
1 cup milk
1/2 cup all-purpose flour
1/2 teaspoon salt
1/4 teaspoon pepper
1 cup (4 ounces) shredded cheddar cheese

Place eggs and milk in a blender. Add flour, salt and pepper; cover and process until smooth. Pour into a greased 13-in. x 9-in. x 2-in. baking pan. Bake at 450° for 20 minutes or until eggs are set. Sprinkle with cheese. Roll up omelet in pan, starting with a short side. Place with seam side down on a serving platter. Cut into 1-in. slices. **Yield:** 6 servings.

Eggnog Pancakes With Cranberry Sauce

2 cups pancake mix
1 egg
1-1/2 cups eggnog*
1-1/2 teaspoons vanilla extract
Pinch ground nutmeg
1 can (16 ounces) whole-berry *or* jellied cranberry sauce

Place the pancake mix in a bowl. In another bowl, whisk egg, eggnog, vanilla and nutmeg; stir into pancake mix just until moistened. Pour batter by 1/3 cupfuls onto a lightly greased hot griddle; turn

when bubbles form on top of pancakes. Cook until second side is golden brown. Serve with cranberry sauce. **Yield:** 6 servings (12 pancakes). ***Editor's Note:** This recipe was tested with commercially prepared eggnog.

Hot Fruit and Sausage

1 package (12 ounces) uncooked pork sausage links
1 can (8 ounces) pineapple tidbits
2 tablespoons brown sugar
Pinch ground cinnamon
1 medium firm banana, sliced

In a skillet, cook sausage according to package directions; drain. Add pineapple, brown sugar and cinnamon; heat through. Stir in banana just before serving. **Yield:** 6 servings.

Banana Basics

Keep bananas at room temperature until they reach the desired ripeness. Then store in a sealed plastic bag in the refrigerator. The skin will darken but the flesh will remain unchanged for a few days.

Feed Your Family for $1.22 a Plate!

LOOKING to serve a steak dinner without breaking the bank? It's easy to assemble a low-budget menu for family and guests for just $1.22 per serving (including two rolls per person).

Swiss Steak Supper is a colorful, satisfying complete meal in one dish suggested by Dorothy Collins of Winnsboro, Texas.

Whole Wheat Rolls rise high and are a light, fluffy and slightly sweet accompaniment, assures Jennifer Martin of East Sebago, Maine.

The recipe for Chocolate Pudding Sundaes comes from Ruth Peterson of Jenison, Michigan. "This smooth pudding tastes great over ice cream," she says.

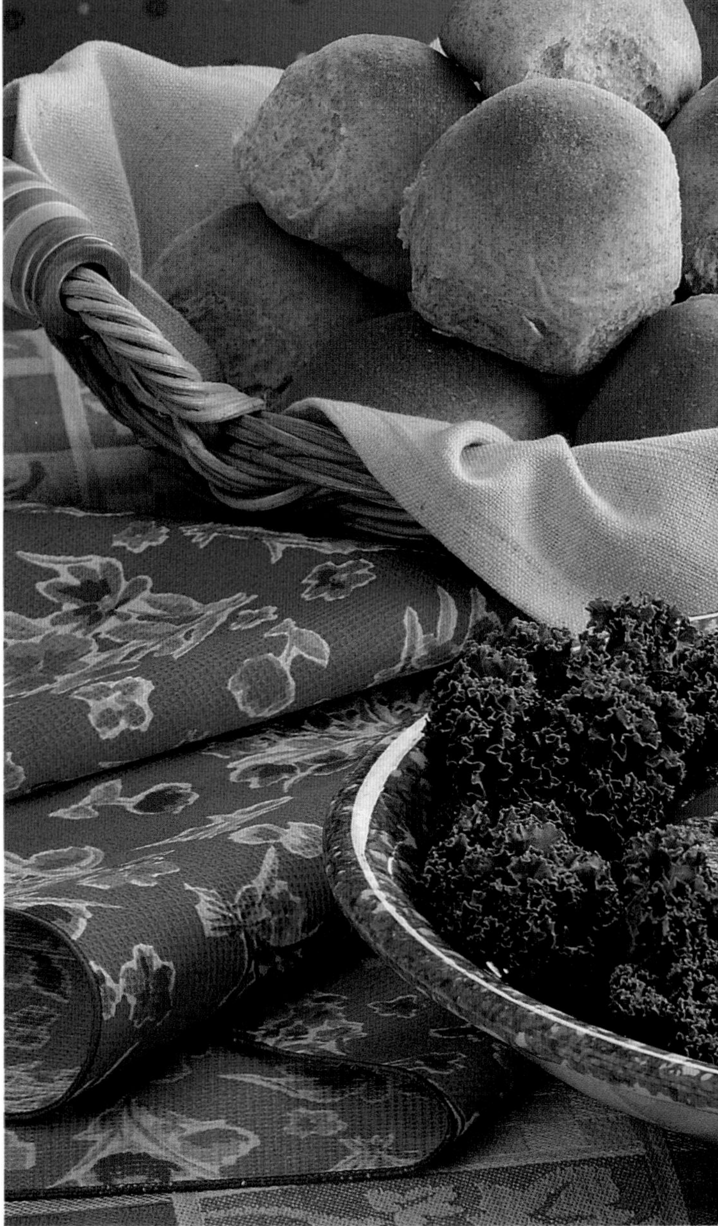

Swiss Steak Supper

1/4 cup all-purpose flour
1 teaspoon salt
1/4 teaspoon pepper
1-1/2 pounds round steak (1/2 inch thick), cut into serving-size pieces
1 tablespoon vegetable oil
1 can (28 ounces) diced tomatoes, undrained
1 medium onion, sliced
1 can (4 ounces) whole green chilies, drained
4 medium red potatoes (about 1 pound), peeled and quartered
4 carrots, cut into 2-inch chunks
2 tablespoons cornstarch
2 tablespoons water

In a large resealable plastic bag, combine flour, salt and pepper. Add steak and shake to coat. In a skillet over medium heat, brown steak in oil on both sides. Add tomatoes and onion. Place chilies over meat; bring to a boil. Reduce heat; cover and simmer for 30 minutes. Add potatoes and carrots. Cover and simmer for 70-80 minutes or until meat and vegetables are tender. Combine cornstarch and water until smooth; stir into skillet. Bring to a boil, stirring constantly until thickened and bubbly. **Yield:** 6 servings.

Whole Wheat Rolls

✓ Uses less fat, sugar or salt. Includes Nutritional Analysis and Diabetic Exchanges.

1-1/2 cups whole wheat flour
1/4 cup plus 2 tablespoons sugar
1 package (1/4 ounce) active dry yeast
1 teaspoon salt
1/2 cup milk
1/2 cup water
1/4 cup butter *or* margarine
1 egg
2 to 2-1/4 cups all-purpose flour
Additional vegetable oil, optional

In a mixing bowl, combine whole wheat flour, sugar, yeast and salt. In a saucepan, heat milk, water and butter to 120°-130°; add to flour mixture. Beat in egg. Beat on low speed for 1 minute; beat

on medium for 1 minute. Gradually stir in enough all-purpose flour to form a soft dough. Turn onto a floured surface and knead until smooth and elastic, about 6-8 minutes. Place in a greased bowl; turn once to grease top. Cover and let rise in a warm place until doubled, about 1-1/4 hours. Punch dough down; shape into 12 balls. Place in a greased 9-in. square baking pan. Cover and let rise until doubled, about 1 hour. Brush tops with oil if desired. Bake at 400° for 15-20 minutes or until golden brown. If necessary, cover with foil during the last 5 minutes to prevent overbrowning. Remove from pan and cool on a wire rack. **Yield:** 1 dozen. **Nutritional Analysis:** One roll (prepared with skim milk and margarine and without additional oil) equals 196 calories, 250 mg sodium, 18 mg cholesterol, 34 gm carbohydrate, 5 gm protein, 5 gm fat. **Diabetic Exchanges:** 2 starch, 1 fat.

Chocolate Pudding Sundaes

2/3 cup sugar
1/4 cup baking cocoa
3 tablespoons cornstarch
1/4 teaspoon salt
2-1/4 cups milk
2 tablespoons butter *or* margarine
1 teaspoon vanilla extract
3 cups vanilla ice cream

In a microwave-safe bowl, combine sugar, cocoa, cornstarch and salt. Gradually stir in milk until smooth. Microwave, uncovered, on high for 7-10 minutes, stirring every 2 minutes, until sauce comes to a boil. Stir in butter and vanilla. Serve warm over ice cream. Store leftovers in the refrigerator. **Yield:** 6 servings. **Editor's Note:** This recipe was tested in an 850-watt microwave.

Feed Your Family for 96¢ a Plate!

IT'S EASY to prepare an affordable turkey dinner that your family will gobble up in no time. This frugal yet flavorful meal is from three terrific cooks who estimate the total cost at just 96¢ per setting.

Turkey Tetrazzini is a tasty main dish and a great way to use leftover chicken or turkey, according to Sue Ross of Casa Grande, Arizona. "Everyone loves the spaghetti noodles mixed in," she says.

Lettuce with French Dressing is always a hit at the Mendota, Illinois home of Kim Marie Van Rheenen. "I got this recipe from my mother-in-law when my husband and I first started dating," Kim remembers. "Many years later, it's still our favorite salad."

Just to show that an inexpensive meal can still include dessert, Betty Speth of Vincennes, Indiana shares her recipe for Chewy Almond Cookies. "These old-fashioned cookies are often requested by my children and grandchildren," Betty states.

The unbaked cookie dough can be frozen (well wrapped) for up to 1 year. When ready to bake, remove from the freezer, let stand at room temperature for 15-30 minutes, slice and bake.

Turkey Tetrazzini

2 cups broken uncooked spaghetti (2-inch pieces)
1 chicken bouillon cube
3/4 cup boiling water
1 can (10-3/4 ounces) condensed cream of mushroom soup, undiluted
1/8 teaspoon celery salt
1/8 teaspoon pepper
1-1/2 cups cubed cooked turkey
1 small onion, finely chopped
2 tablespoons diced pimientos, drained
1-1/2 cups (6 ounces) shredded cheddar cheese, *divided*

Cook spaghetti according to package directions. Meanwhile, in a bowl, dissolve bouillon in water. Add soup, celery salt and pepper. Drain spaghetti; add to soup mixture. Stir in turkey, onion, pimientos and 1/2 cup of cheese. Transfer to a greased 8-in. square baking dish. Top with remaining cheese. Bake, uncovered, at 350° for 35-40 minutes or until heated through. **Yield:** 6 servings.

Lettuce with French Dressing

1/4 cup plus 2 tablespoons vegetable oil
1/4 cup sugar
2 tablespoons vinegar
2 tablespoons ketchup
1/8 teaspoon salt
Dash garlic powder
6 cups torn lettuce

Combine the vegetable oil, sugar, vinegar, ketchup, salt and garlic powder in a jar with a tight-fitting lid; shake well. Serve over lettuce. Refrigerate any leftover dressing. **Yield:** 6 servings (3/4 cup dressing).

Chewy Almond Cookies

3 tablespoons butter *or* margarine, softened
1 cup packed brown sugar
1 egg
1/4 teaspoon vanilla extract
1/4 teaspoon almond extract
1-1/2 cups all-purpose flour
1/4 teaspoon baking soda
1/4 teaspoon ground cinnamon
1/2 cup sliced almonds

In a mixing bowl, cream butter and brown sugar. Add egg and extracts; mix well. Combine flour, baking soda and cinnamon; gradually add to the creamed mixture and mix well. Shape into two 1-in. rolls; wrap each in plastic wrap. Refrigerate overnight. Unwrap; cut into 1/4-in. slices. Place 2 in. apart on greased baking sheets. Sprinkle with almonds. Bake at 350° for 7-10 minutes or until lightly browned. Cool for 2-3 minutes before removing to wire racks. **Yield:** 4-1/2 dozen.

Feed Your Family for $1.01 a Plate!

SERVING your family a "cent-sible" and savory supper is easy as pie! The great cooks who shared recipes for this frugal and filling meal estimate a total cost of just $1.01 per setting.

Upside-Down Meat Pie was sent by Jennifer Eilts of Central City, Nebraska. "Thanks to the yummy sloppy joe flavor, kids dig in...and adults do, too," Jennifer relates. "The recipe's been in my family for years."

Reports Vicky Linn of Corsicana, Texas, "Macaroni Medley Salad is so delicious, folks never believe it starts with packaged macaroni and cheese."

For a tasty low-cost treat, try sundaes made with Homemade Chocolate Syrup. The recipe comes from Greenfield, Iowa cook Sharon Mensing, who remarks, "I use this microwave recipe so often I have it memorized."

Upside-Down Meat Pie

1 pound ground beef
1/2 cup chopped celery
1/2 cup chopped onion
1/4 cup chopped green pepper
1 can (10-3/4 ounces) condensed tomato soup, undiluted
1 teaspoon prepared mustard
1-1/2 cups biscuit/baking mix
1/3 cup water
3 slices process American cheese, halved diagonally
Green pepper rings, optional

In a skillet over medium heat, cook beef, celery, onion and green pepper until the meat is no longer pink and vegetables are tender; drain. Stir in soup and mustard; mix well. Transfer to a greased 9-in. pie plate. In a bowl, combine the baking mix and water until a soft dough forms. Turn onto a lightly floured surface; roll into a 9-in. circle. Place over meat mixture. Bake at 425° for 20 minutes or until golden brown. Cool for 5 minutes. Run a knife around edge to loosen biscuit; invert onto a serving platter. Arrange cheese slices in a pinwheel pattern on top. Garnish with green pepper rings if desired. **Yield:** 6 servings.

Macaroni Medley Salad

1 package (7-1/4 ounces) macaroni and cheese
1/4 cup milk
1/4 cup butter *or* margarine
1/2 cup mayonnaise
2 tablespoons Dijon mustard
4 hard-cooked eggs, chopped
2 medium tomatoes, chopped
1 small cucumber, peeled and chopped
2 tablespoons chopped onion
1 dill pickle, chopped
1/2 teaspoon salt

1/8 teaspoon pepper

Prepare macaroni and cheese with milk and butter according to package directions. Place in a large bowl; cool for 15 minutes. Stir in mayonnaise and mustard. Fold in eggs, tomatoes, cucumber, onion, pickle, salt and pepper. Refrigerate until serving. **Yield:** 6 servings.

Homemade Chocolate Syrup

1/2 cup sugar
1 tablespoon baking cocoa
2-1/2 teaspoons cornstarch
1/2 cup water
2 teaspoons butter *or* margarine
1/2 teaspoon vanilla extract
1 quart vanilla ice cream

In a 1-qt. microwave-safe dish, combine the sugar, cocoa, cornstarch and water until smooth. Cover and microwave on high for 4 minutes or until the mixture boils, stirring twice. Stir in butter and vanilla until blended. Serve warm over ice cream. **Yield:** 6 servings. **Editor's Note:** This recipe was tested in an 850-watt microwave.

Feed Your Family for $1.46 a Plate!

WELCOME FOLKS into your home for some home country cooking that won't take you to the bank.

The comforting and cost-conscious meal here is from three terrific cooks who estimate the total cost at just $1.46 per setting.

"Stuffed Cube Steaks turn an inexpensive cut into a satisfying main dish," says great-grandmother Marie Reynolds of Gardner, Massachusetts.

Sweet Peas and Mushrooms, recommended by Wendy Masters of Grand Valley, Ontario, is a special yet simple vegetable dish.

Fresh Peach Cobbler uses late summer's delicious peaches. "I enjoy the nutmeg in this classic dessert," shares Pat Kinghorn of Morrill, Nebraska.

Stuffed Cube Steaks

8 cube steaks (about 2 pounds)
1-1/4 teaspoons salt, *divided*
1/4 teaspoon pepper
1/2 cup French salad dressing
1 cup shredded carrot
3/4 cup finely chopped onion
3/4 cup finely chopped celery
1/2 cup finely chopped green pepper
1/4 cup beef broth
2 tablespoons vegetable oil
1 tablespoon cornstarch
1/4 teaspoon browning sauce, optional

Pound steaks to 1/4-in. thickness. Sprinkle with 1 teaspoon salt and pepper. Place in a greased 13-in. x 9-in. x 2-in. baking dish. Spoon salad dressing over steaks. Cover and chill for 1 hour. In a saucepan, combine vegetables, broth and remaining salt. Cover and cook over medium heat for 6-8 minutes or until tender. Drain, reserving liquid. Spoon 1/4 cup vegetable mixture onto each steak; roll up and secure with toothpicks. In a large nonstick skillet, brown meat rolls in oil. Cover and simmer for 35-40 minutes or until meat is tender. Remove with a slotted spoon; keep warm. Combine the cornstarch and reserved cooking liquid until smooth; stir into pan drippings. Bring to a boil; cook and stir for 2 minutes. Add browning sauce if desired. Remove toothpicks from meat rolls; pour sauce over and serve immediately. **Yield:** 8 servings.

Sweet Peas and Mushrooms

2 packages (10 ounces *each*) frozen peas
2 cups sliced fresh mushrooms
1/2 cup chopped onion
1/4 cup butter *or* margarine
2 teaspoons sugar

1 teaspoon salt
Dash pepper

Cook peas according to package directions; drain. Meanwhile, in a skillet, saute mushrooms and onion in butter until onion is crisp-tender. Stir in sugar, salt, pepper and peas. Cover and cook until heated through. **Yield:** 8 servings.

Fresh Peach Cobbler

2 large peaches, peeled and sliced
1-1/2 cups sugar, *divided*
1/2 cup butter *or* margarine, melted
1 cup all-purpose flour
2 teaspoons baking powder
1/4 teaspoon salt
Dash ground nutmeg
3/4 cup milk

In a bowl, combine peaches and 3/4 cup sugar; set aside. Pour butter into an 8-in. square baking pan. In a bowl, combine flour, baking powder, salt, nutmeg and remaining sugar; stir in milk just until combined. Pour over butter. Top with the peaches. Bake at 375° for 45-50 minutes. **Yield:** 8 servings.

Feed Your Family for 75¢ a Plate!

WANT TO ADD spark to your supper without burning cash? The cooks who shared these tasty recipes estimate a total cost of just 75¢ per setting.

Chili Spaghetti is recommended by Pam Thompson of Girard, Illinois. "My husband often requested that his grandma make this dish," reveals Pam.

The recipe for Jalapeno Corn Bread comes from Anita LaRose. "We enjoy the combination of flavors in this golden corn bread," says this Benavides, Texas cook. "It's not dry or crumbly."

Chocolate Bundt Cake is a dessert from Lori Bennett's grandmother. "When I make this yummy, economical cake for my son and husband, it brings back many fond memories for me," she writes from her Greencastle, Indiana kitchen.

Chili Spaghetti

1 pound ground beef
1/2 cup chopped onion
2 garlic cloves, minced
3 cups tomato juice
1 can (16 ounces) kidney beans, rinsed and drained
6 ounces spaghetti, broken into 3-inch pieces
1 tablespoon Worcestershire sauce
2 to 3 teaspoons chili powder
1 teaspoon salt
1/2 teaspoon pepper

In a skillet over medium heat, cook beef, onion and garlic until meat is no longer pink; drain. Transfer to a greased 2-1/2-qt. baking dish; stir in the remaining ingredients. Cover and bake at 350° for 65-70 minutes or until spaghetti is just tender. Let stand, covered, for 10 minutes. **Yield:** 6 servings.

Jalapeno Corn Bread

1 cup cornmeal
1/2 cup shredded cheddar cheese
2 teaspoons baking powder
3/4 teaspoon salt
2 eggs, beaten
1 can (8-3/4 ounces) cream-style corn
1 cup buttermilk
1/4 cup vegetable oil
1 to 2 tablespoons minced fresh jalapeno peppers*

In a bowl, combine cornmeal, cheese, baking powder and salt. Combine the remaining ingredients; stir into cornmeal mixture just until moistened. Transfer to a greased 9-in. square baking pan. Bake at 350° for 1 hour or until a toothpick inserted near the center comes out clean. **Yield:** 9 servings. ***Editor's Note:** When cutting or seeding hot peppers,

use rubber or plastic gloves to protect your hands. Avoid touching your face.

Chocolate Bundt Cake

1 cup salad dressing*
1 cup water
2 teaspoons vanilla extract
2 cups all-purpose flour
1 cup sugar
2 tablespoons baking cocoa
2 teaspoons baking soda
1/4 teaspoon salt
Confectioners' sugar, optional

In a mixing bowl, combine salad dressing, water and vanilla. Combine the flour, sugar, cocoa, baking soda and salt. Add to salad dressing mixture and beat until mixed. Transfer to a greased and floured 10-in. fluted tube pan (pan will not be full). Bake at 350° for 35-40 minutes or until a toothpick inserted near the center comes out clean. Cool for 10 minutes; remove from pan to a wire rack. Dust with confectioners' sugar if desired. **Yield:** 12 servings. ***Editor's Note:** This recipe was tested using Miracle Whip brand salad dressing. Light or fat-free Miracle Whip may not be substituted for regular Miracle Whip.

Slam Dunk

Getting in the Theme of Things

With theme-related menus, decorating ideas and fun activities, these festive meals will make any get-together extra special.

CAUSE FOR CELEBRATION. Clockwise from upper left: Country Barnyard Buddies Party (p. 298), Winning Dinner Sparked by Games (p. 296), "Hoops" Fan Shows Spirited Colors (p. 294) and Reunion Fare with Patriotic Flair (p. 300).

'Hoops' Fan Shows Spirited Colors

By Sharon Landeen, Tucson, Arizona

TO CHEER on our favorite basketball team, the University of Arizona Wildcats, husband Don and I host a yearly party, inviting friends to come watch an out-of-town game on TV.

I decorate our whole house in the team colors, red and blue… and even our street sign is temporarily changed to "Wildcat Way".

Between 40 and 50 friends show up, so the menu must be a "grab and go" finger-food bonanza. The snack table holds annual favorites, including Slam Dunk Crab Dip, Sporty Sugar-Spice Nuts and my homemade Courtside Caramel Corn.

Folks like the curry in the zippy seafood dip, served with crackers and tortilla chips. The caramel corn, a family favorite, is a treat our children always request. Then there's the sweet and spicy nut mix—no one can stop at just one taste.

After trying a variety of desserts over the years, I've found that Butterscotch Basketball Cookies are the most popular. I use my gingerbread man cutter and then s-t-r-e-t-c-h the arms and legs into athletic positions before baking. "Suiting up" the players with icing can be a fun family project.

This casual menu is a slam dunk for the cook, since everything is easy to prepare ahead of time.

Why not plan a similar get-together to root for your home team? The crowd will love it!

Slam Dunk Crab Dip

The spirited crowd we invite is quick to dig in to this delectable dip.

1 package (8 ounces) cream cheese, softened
1/4 cup milk
1 package (8 ounces) imitation flaked crabmeat *or* 1 can (6 ounces) crabmeat, drained, flaked and cartilage removed
1/4 cup sliced green onions
1/4 cup chopped sweet red pepper
1 teaspoon curry powder
1/2 teaspoon garlic salt
Assorted crackers

In a mixing bowl, beat cream cheese and milk until smooth. Stir in the crab, onions, red pepper, curry powder and garlic salt. Refrigerate until serving. Serve with crackers. **Yield:** 3 cups.

Sporty Sugar-Spice Nuts

To save time on the day of the big party, I mix up a batch of these nuts days in advance.

3/4 cup sugar
3 tablespoons water
1 egg white, lightly beaten
1 teaspoon ground cinnamon
3/4 teaspoon salt
1/2 teaspoon ground cloves
1/4 teaspoon ground allspice
1/4 teaspoon ground nutmeg
2 cups pecan halves
1-1/2 cups whole unblanched almonds

In a large bowl, combine the first eight ingredients; mix well. Add nuts and stir until coated. Spread evenly in a greased 15-in. x 10-in. x 1-in. baking pan. Bake at 250° for 45 minutes or until golden brown, stirring every 15 minutes. Spread on a waxed paper-lined baking sheet to cool. Store in an airtight container. **Yield:** 3-1/2 cups.

Courtside Caramel Corn

I fill up a red tin sporting the University of Arizona logo with this sweet popcorn.

6 quarts popped popcorn
2 cups packed brown sugar
1 cup butter *or* margarine
1/2 cup corn syrup
1 teaspoon salt
1 tablespoon vanilla extract
1/2 teaspoon baking soda

Place popcorn in a large bowl and set aside. In a saucepan, combine brown sugar, butter, corn syrup and salt; bring to a boil over medium heat, stirring constantly. Boil for 5 minutes, stirring occasionally. Remove from the heat. Stir in vanilla and baking soda; mix well. Pour over popcorn and stir until well-coated. Pour into two greased 13-in. x 9-in. x 2-in. baking pans. Bake, uncovered, at 250° for 45 minutes, stirring every 15 minutes. Cool completely. Store in airtight containers or plastic bags. **Yield:** about 5-1/2 quarts.

Butterscotch Basketball Cookies

Nope, I didn't need a special basketball player cutter to shape these sporty cookies—the gingerbread men make the team!

1 cup butterscotch chips
1 cup butter (no substitutes), softened
1/2 cup sugar
1/2 cup packed brown sugar
1 egg
2 tablespoons milk
2 teaspoons vanilla extract
3 cups all-purpose flour
FROSTING:
3/4 cup shortening
1/4 cup water
2 tablespoons all-purpose flour
1-1/2 teaspoons vanilla extract
4 cups confectioners' sugar
Paste food coloring

In a microwave, melt butterscotch chips; cool for 10 minutes. In a mixing bowl, cream butter and sugars. Add egg, milk and vanilla; mix well. Beat in melted chips. Gradually add flour; mix well. Cover and refrigerate for 1 hour. On a floured surface, roll out dough to 1/4-in. thickness. Cut with a floured 4-1/2-in. gingerbread man cookie cutter and a 3-in. round cutter. Place 2 in. apart on greased baking sheets. Bake at 375° for 5-8 minutes or until edges are lightly browned. Cool for 1 minute; remove to wire racks to cool completely. For frosting, combine shortening, water, flour and vanilla in a mixing bowl; mix well. Gradually beat in sugar. Place 1 cup frosting in a plastic bag; cut a small hole in corner of bag. Pipe shirt and shorts on players. Fill in outline and smooth with a metal spatula. Tint 1/4 cup frosting black; place in a plastic bag. Pipe lines on round cookies to create basketballs; pipe hair, eyes and noses on players. Tint 1/4 cup frosting red; pipe a mouth on each player. Tint remaining frosting to match team colors of your choice; pipe around shirts and shorts and add a letter on shirts if desired. **Yield:** about 2 dozen.

Winning Dinner Sparked by Games

By Mina Dyck, Boissevain, Manitoba

THREE FRIENDS and I decided to get together regularly for dinner and an evening of fellowship. When it came to my turn to host, I planned a "cards and games" theme.

Invitations were printed on Yahtzee score sheets. Other well-known board and card games inspired my menu and decorations.

I made a tic-tac-toe tablecloth and set out checkerboard place mats and red napkins. Place cards were spelled in Scrabble letters.

As guests arrived, I poured Pictionary Punch—a sparkling blend with citrus and pineapple juices.

Scrabble Soup and Bingo Bread got our meal off to an appropriate start. The savory soup features alphabet macaroni, ground beef and vegetables. Warm golden loaves flavored with green onions, parsley and oregano were a wonderful accompaniment.

Meantime, baked ham and scalloped potatoes stayed warm in the oven for our main course.

For dessert, I baked a chessboard cake fit for a queen. And later, over cards, I served cappuccino and Card Trick Cookies—my favorite lemon cookie dough cut into hearts, diamonds, spades and clubs.

My guests figured that I had gone to a lot of work, but I assured them it was fun creating my theme meal.

Why not try your luck at this kind of party?

Pictionary Punch

This recipe goes a long way to satisfy the thirst of your guests. You can easily scale down the recipe when entertaining a smaller group.

1 cup sugar
1 cup water
3 cups *each* grapefruit, orange and pineapple juice
1/2 cup lemon juice
1/2 cup lime juice
2 liters ginger ale, chilled

In a saucepan, bring sugar and water to a boil; cook and stir for 2 minutes. Remove from the heat; cool. Pour into a large bowl; add juices. Cover and refrigerate. Stir in ginger ale just before serving. **Yield:** about 5 quarts.

Bingo Bread

This savory, delicious herb bread was a winner at my dinner! The pretty loaves get their deep golden color from whole wheat flour and eggs in the dough.

✓ Uses less fat, sugar or salt. Includes Nutritional Analysis and Diabetic Exchanges.

3-1/2 to 4 cups all-purpose flour
2 cups whole wheat flour
1/2 cup instant nonfat dry milk powder
1/4 cup sugar
1 package (1/4 ounce) active dry yeast
2 cups water
2 tablespoons vegetable oil
2 tablespoons butter *or* margarine
2 eggs, beaten
1/2 cup sliced green onions
3 tablespoons minced fresh parsley *or* 1 tablespoon dried parsley flakes
2 teaspoons dried oregano
1-1/2 teaspoons salt

In a mixing bowl, combine 1 cup all-purpose flour, whole wheat flour, milk powder, sugar and yeast. In a saucepan, heat water, oil and butter to 120°-130°; add to dry ingredients. Beat on medium for 3 minutes. Stir in eggs, onions, parsley, oregano, salt and enough remaining all-purpose flour to form a soft dough. Turn onto a floured surface; knead until smooth and elastic, about 6-8 minutes. Place in a greased bowl, turning once to grease top. Cover and let rise in a warm place until doubled, about 30 minutes. Punch dough down; divide in half. Shape into loaves; place in greased 9-in. x 5-in. x 3-in. loaf pans. Cover and let rise until doubled, about 30 minutes. Bake at 350° for 30-35 minutes. Remove from pans to wire racks. **Yield:** 2 loaves (16 slices each). **Nutritional Analysis:** One slice (prepared with margarine) equals 105 calories, 128 mg sodium, 13 mg cholesterol, 18 gm carbohydrate, 3 gm protein, 2 gm fat. **Diabetic Exchanges:** 1 starch, 1/2 fat.

Scrabble Soup

Many games involve letters, so I thought alphabet soup would be ideal to serve at my theme party.

1 pound ground beef
1 cup chopped onion
6 cups water
2 cans (14-1/2 ounces *each*) diced tomatoes, undrained
1 cup *each* chopped celery, carrot, turnip and potato
1 tablespoon dried parsley flakes
2 beef bouillon cubes
2 garlic cloves, minced
1 teaspoon dried oregano
1 teaspoon salt
1/2 teaspoon pepper
1/2 teaspoon dried basil
1/2 teaspoon Worcestershire sauce
1 cup uncooked alphabet macaroni

In a Dutch oven or soup kettle, cook beef and onion until meat is no longer pink; drain. Add water, vegetables and seasonings; bring to a boil. Reduce heat; simmer for 20 minutes or until the vegetables are crisp-tender. Add macaroni; simmer for 15 minutes or until the macaroni and vegetables are tender. **Yield:** 12 servings (3 quarts).

Card Trick Cookies

The dough is well "suited" for cutting out cookies in heart, spade, diamond and club shapes as late-night treats for card players.

1 cup butter (no substitutes), softened
1/2 cup sugar
1 to 2 tablespoons grated lemon peel
2 cups all-purpose flour

In a mixing bowl, cream the butter, sugar and lemon peel. Add flour; mix well. Cover and refrigerate until chilled, about 1 hour. Divide dough in half. Flatten each portion and roll out between two pieces of waxed paper to 1/4-in. thickness. Cut with 2-in. cookie cutters into desired shapes (such as hearts, spades, diamonds and clubs). Place 1 in. apart on ungreased baking sheets. Bake at 325° for 15-20 minutes or until cookies are lightly browned. Cool on wire racks. **Yield:** about 3 dozen.

Country Barnyard Buddies Party

By Kay Curtis, Guthrie, Oklahoma

ANIMALS are an important part of our family's life, so I had been thinking about a theme meal inspired by barnyard characters. The perfect opportunity came when we learned we'd be entertaining a missionary family with young children.

Our casual supper included Pigs in a Blanket, Farm Mouse Cookies, Cute Kitty Cookies plus other foods presented "country style".

Pigs in a Blanket are hot dogs that I wrap with cheese slices in yeast dough, then bake. They're easy for children to eat, and adults like them, too.

Peach halves took wing as little ducks. Our children helped cut heads, wings and webbed feet from construction paper.

Coloring book designs also inspired a chicken to guard the deviled eggs and a rabbit holding a carrot poised on the vegetable tray.

Transforming a favorite peanut butter cookie into Farm Mouse Cookies were peanut-half "ears" and licorice-string "tails". For the Cute Kitty Cookies, I used an oatmeal and chocolate cookie recipe.

It's easy to shape the dough to make ears. The "kitties" get their character from chocolate chip "eyes", a red-hot "nose" and licorice "whiskers".

My barnyard buffet was a big hit with young and old

alike. It's an easy theme meal you could adapt for a birthday or any lighthearted family gathering—even if you live in the city!

Pigs in a Blanket

Pigs in a Blanket were a natural choice for my farm animal theme meal. They are tasty, fun and handy to eat.

1 package (1/4 ounce) active dry yeast
1/3 cup plus 1 teaspoon sugar, *divided*
2/3 cup warm milk (110° to 115°)
1/3 cup warm water (110° to 115°)
1 egg, beaten
2 tablespoons plus 2 teaspoons shortening, melted
1 teaspoon salt
3-2/3 cups all-purpose flour
10 hot dogs
2 slices process American cheese

In a mixing bowl, dissolve yeast and 1 teaspoon sugar in milk and water; let stand for 5 minutes. Add egg, shortening, salt, remaining sugar and enough flour to form a soft dough. Turn onto a floured surface; knead until smooth and elastic, about 8-10 minutes. Place in a greased bowl, turning once to grease top. Cover and let rise in a warm place until doubled, about 1 hour. Cut a 1/4-in.-deep lengthwise slit in each hot dog. Cut cheese slices into five strips; place one strip in the slit of each hot dog. Punch dough down; divide into 10 portions. Roll each into a 5-in. x 2-1/2-in. rectangle and wrap around prepared hot dogs; pinch seam and ends to seal. Place seam side down on greased baking sheets; let rise for 30 minutes. Bake at 350° for 15-18 minutes or until golden brown. **Yield:** 10 servings.

Farm Mouse Cookies

Eeeek! The whimsical mice I made evoked shrieks of delight from the kids at our party. Peanut-half "ears" and licorice "tails" transformed these peanut butter cookies into country critters.

1 cup creamy peanut butter
1/2 cup butter *or* margarine, softened
1/2 cup sugar
1/2 cup packed brown sugar
1 egg
1 teaspoon vanilla extract
1-1/2 cups all-purpose flour
1/2 teaspoon baking soda
Peanut halves
Black shoestring licorice, cut into 2-1/2-inch pieces

In a mixing bowl, cream peanut butter, butter and sugars. Beat in egg and vanilla. Combine flour and baking soda; gradually add to creamed mixture. Cover and chill dough for 1 hour or overnight. Roll into 1-in. balls. Pinch one end, forming a teardrop shape. Place 2 in. apart on ungreased baking sheets; press to flatten. For ears, press two peanuts into each cookie near the pointed end. Using a toothpick, make a 1/2-in.-deep hole for the tail in the end opposite the ears. Bake at 350° for 8-10 minutes or until golden. While cookies are warm, insert licorice for tails. Cool on wire racks. **Yield:** 4 dozen.

Cute Kitty Cookies

An oatmeal cookie recipe proved "purr-fect" for cat cookies. Half of the dough is chocolate, which frames the playful faces. It was a game of cat and mouse to see what dessert plate would be emptied first!

1/2 cup butter *or* margarine, softened
1/4 cup shortening
1 cup sugar
2 eggs
1 teaspoon vanilla extract
2-1/4 cups all-purpose flour
3/4 teaspoon baking powder
1/2 teaspoon salt
1 cup quick-cooking oats
2 squares (1 ounce *each*) unsweetened chocolate, melted and cooled
Semisweet chocolate chips
Red-hot candies
Black shoestring licorice, cut into 1-1/2-inch pieces

In a mixing bowl, cream butter, shortening and sugar. Add eggs, one at a time, beating well after each addition. Beat in vanilla. Combine the flour, baking powder and salt; gradually add to the creamed mixture. Stir in oats. Divide dough in half. Add melted chocolate to one portion. Roll plain dough into an 8-in. log. Roll chocolate dough between waxed paper into an 8-in. square. Place log at one end of square; roll up. Wrap in plastic wrap; refrigerate for at least 3 hours. Cut into 1/4-in. slices. Place on ungreased baking sheets. To form ears, pinch two triangles on the top of each cookie. Bake at 350° for 8-10 minutes or until lightly browned. Immediately place two chocolate chips for eyes, a red-hot for the nose and six pieces of licorice on each for whiskers. Cool on wire racks. **Yield:** 3 dozen.

Reunion Fare with Patriotic Flair

By Jill Steiner, Hancock, Minnesota

SINCE our branch of the family is engaged in agriculture, we chose a "Country Cousins" theme for a reunion we hosted over the July Fourth weekend.

In keeping with our theme, we asked participants to dress comfortably in denim and wear a bandanna. My uncle really got into the spirit and wore his good ol' bib overalls!

Flags, patriotic streamers and balloons decorated the big machine shop on our family farm for the gathering. We found bandanna-print paper napkins to use along with red and blue plastic dinnerware.

Our buffet included Country Baked Beans, Grandma's Potato Salad, Haystack Supper, fresh fruit and tomatoes, plus a selection of yummy homemade desserts. Picnic Pecan Pie was among the favorites.

The recipe for Country Baked Beans came from our local John Deere dealership. I requested it after tasting the flavorful blend they served at a customer appreciation dinner. Added ingredients give extra zip to canned beans.

Grandmother has always made her delicious potato salad by adding "a little of this and a little of that". I wrote down the recipe for Grandma's Potato Salad while observing her prepare it.

Everyone loved Haystack Supper! This hearty layered main dish is great for a group. Similar to taco salad, it includes a medley of ingredients popular with all ages.

In our family of pie lovers, everyone tries several kinds for dessert. I've never come away from any gathering with leftovers of Picnic Pecan Pie.

The day was a great success. Relatives enjoyed being together again and went home filled with country-fresh memories and delicious, down-home food.

I'd be delighted if my recipes and ideas spark your plans for a summer gathering!

Country Baked Beans

After sampling these savory beans at our local John Deere dealer's open house, I asked for the recipe. To my surprise, they started with canned beans.

4 cans (16 ounces *each*) baked beans, drained
1 bottle (12 ounces) chili sauce
1 large onion, chopped
1 pound sliced bacon, cooked and crumbled
1 cup packed brown sugar

In two ungreased 2-qt. baking dishes, combine all of the ingredients. Stir until blended. Bake, uncovered, at 350° for 45-60 minutes or until heated through. **Yield:** 10-12 servings.

Grandma's Potato Salad

My grandma makes the best potato salad—but she doesn't use a recipe! So I carefully watched while she made it and jotted a recipe that comes close.

8 medium red potatoes, cubed
4 to 5 hard-cooked eggs, chopped
1-1/2 cups mayonnaise
2/3 cup sour cream
3 tablespoons sugar
3 tablespoons cider *or* red wine vinegar
2 teaspoons prepared mustard
1-1/2 teaspoons dried minced onion
1 teaspoon celery seed
Salt and pepper to taste

Place the potatoes in a saucepan and cover with water. Cover and bring to a boil; cook until tender, about 15-20 minutes. Drain and cool. Place in a bowl; add eggs. Combine the remaining ingredients; pour over potato mixture and toss to coat. Cover and refrigerate for 6 hours or overnight. **Yield:** 8-10 servings.

Haystack Supper

Served as the entree at our family reunion buffet, this flavorful layered taco-style dish is a crowd-pleaser. Folks are pleasantly surprised to find a rice layer, and everyone enjoys the creamy cheese sauce.

1-3/4 cups crushed saltines (about 40 crackers)
2 cups cooked rice
3 pounds ground beef
1 large onion, chopped
1-1/2 cups tomato juice
3/4 cup water
3 tablespoons taco seasoning mix
Seasoned salt, salt and pepper to taste
4 cups shredded lettuce
3 medium tomatoes, diced
1/2 cup butter *or* margarine
1/2 cup all-purpose flour
4 cups milk
1 pound process American cheese, cubed
3 cups (12 ounces) shredded sharp cheddar cheese
1 jar (10 ounces) stuffed olives, drained and sliced
1 package (14-1/2 ounces) tortilla chips

Divide crackers between two ungreased 13-in. x 9-in. x 2-in. baking dishes. Top with rice. In a skillet, cook beef and onion until meat is no longer pink; drain. Add tomato juice, water and seasonings; simmer for 15-20 minutes. Spoon over rice. Sprinkle with lettuce and tomatoes. In a saucepan, melt butter. Stir in flour until smooth. Gradually add milk. Bring to a boil; cook and stir for 2 minutes. Reduce heat; stir in American cheese until melted. Pour over the tomatoes. Top with cheddar cheese and olives. Serve with chips. Refrigerate any leftovers. **Yield:** 10-12 servings.

Picnic Pecan Pie

Topped with ice cream or whipped cream, this timeless treat is delectable.

3 eggs
1 cup dark corn syrup
1/2 cup sugar
2 tablespoons butter *or* margarine, melted
1 teaspoon vanilla extract
1/8 teaspoon salt
1 cup chopped pecans
1 unbaked pastry shell (9 inches)

In a bowl, beat the eggs lightly. Stir in corn syrup, sugar, butter, vanilla and salt. Add pecans and mix well. Pour into pie shell. Cover edges loosely with foil. Bake at 350° for 20 minutes. Remove foil; bake 20 minutes longer or until a knife inserted near the center comes out clean. Refrigerate any leftovers. **Yield:** 6-8 servings.

'Fishing' Luncheon Nets Compliments

By Martha Conaway, Pataskala, Ohio

LET'S GO FISHING! was the whimsical theme I used when hosting my card group at our lake cottage.

My guests were greeted by a sailboat flag and a fish mobile hanging outside. Inside, a "Welcome" lighthouse wall hanging and a fish throw rug continued the theme.

For the table, I made a candle centerpiece with shells and sand in a glass bowl. More shells, plus duck and fish salt and pepper shakers, added to the lakeside atmosphere. Small shells printed with each guest's name served as place cards.

On the menu were Pierside Salmon Patties, Angler's Gelatin Delight and Smooth Sailing Sugar Cookies.

In addition, I baked banana and corn muffins in a cast-iron seashell muffin pan. For a beverage, I offered "fisherman's brew" of iced tea or coffee.

Pierside Salmon Patties were a hit with their crispy golden coating and pleasant salmon flavor. My friends said the dill sauce was the perfect complement.

I had copper molds in the shape of a fish and a crab to use for the Angler's Gelatin Delight. But if you don't, you can use cake pans to form an eye-catching fish salad (like the one pictured above).

Using my old favorite sugar cookie recipe, I cut out and decorated colorful sailboats and fish for the Smooth Sailing Sugar Cookies.

The nice thing about this menu was that most of the food preparation could be done the day before, leaving me free to enjoy the summer gathering.

You're welcome to cast my ideas and recipes into a party of your own. Good luck!

Pierside Salmon Patties

A lemony dill sauce enhances the flavor of the salmon in this enjoyable entree.

2 eggs
1 cup milk
2 tablespoons lemon juice
3 cups coarsely crushed saltines (about 66 crackers)
2 teaspoons finely chopped onion
1/4 teaspoon salt
1/4 teaspoon pepper
2 cans (14-3/4 ounces *each*) salmon, drained, bones and skin removed
DILL SAUCE:
2 tablespoons butter *or* margarine
2 tablespoons all-purpose flour
1 teaspoon snipped fresh dill *or* 1/2 teaspoon dill weed
1/4 teaspoon salt
Dash *each* pepper and nutmeg
1-1/2 cups milk

In a bowl, beat eggs; add the next six ingredients and mix well. Add salmon; shape into 12 patties, 3 in. each. Place in a greased 15-in. x 10-in. x 1-in. baking pan. Bake at 350° for 30-35 minutes or until lightly browned. Meanwhile, melt butter in a saucepan. Stir in the flour, dill, salt, pepper and nutmeg until smooth. Add milk; bring to a boil. Cook and stir for 2 minutes or until thickened and bubbly. Serve with the patties. **Yield:** 6 servings.

Angler's Gelatin Delight

Get in the swim with this refreshing cucumber-lime molded salad, a hit at my theme party!

✓ Uses less fat, sugar or salt. Includes Nutritional Analysis and Diabetic Exchanges.

1 medium cucumber, peeled
1 package (3 ounces) lime gelatin
1 cup boiling water
1 cup chopped celery
1 small onion, chopped
1 cup small-curd cottage cheese
3/4 cup mayonnaise
1 tablespoon lemon juice
1 raisin
1 sweet red pepper strip
Lemon and lime slices and celery leaves, optional

Cut one slice from center of cucumber for fish's eye; refrigerate. Peel and chop remaining cucumber. In a bowl, dissolve gelatin in water. Add celery, onion and chopped cucumber. Stir in cottage cheese, mayonnaise and lemon juice; mix well. Pour into one 8-in. round pan and one 8-in. square pan (or a fish and lobster mold) coated with nonstick cooking spray. Refrigerate overnight or until set. Unmold round pan onto a 14-in. round serving platter. Unmold square pan onto a cutting board; cut in half diagonally to form two triangles. Position one triangle on the platter so tip touches circle, forming the tail. Cut remaining triangle in half. Place one half on top of the circle and the other on the bottom for fins; gently curve fins toward the tail. For the eye, place reserved cucumber slice on the side of the circle opposite the tail; place raisin in the center. Add red pepper strip for mouth. If desired, garnish with lemon and lime slices and celery leaves. Refrigerate until serving. **Yield:** 6 servings. **Nutritional Analysis:** One 3/4-cup serving (prepared with sugar-free gelatin, fat-free cottage cheese and light mayonnaise) equals 111 calories, 316 mg sodium, 3 mg cholesterol, 6 gm carbohydrate, 5 gm protein, 8 gm fat. **Diabetic Exchanges:** 1-1/2 fat, 1 vegetable.

Smooth Sailing Sugar Cookies

I cut out sailboats and frisky fish, frosting them brightly for my nautical gathering.

1 cup butter (no substitutes), softened
3/4 cup sugar
1 egg
2 tablespoons milk
1-1/2 teaspoons vanilla extract
3 cups all-purpose flour
1 teaspoon baking powder
1/2 teaspoon salt
FROSTING:
1 cup confectioners' sugar
1/2 teaspoon vanilla *or* almond extract
1/4 teaspoon salt
1 to 2 tablespoons milk
Food coloring, optional

In a mixing bowl, cream butter and sugar. Add egg, milk and vanilla. Combine flour, baking powder and salt; gradually add to the creamed mixture. Chill for 1 hour or until easy to handle. On a lightly floured surface, roll out dough to 1/8-in. thickness. Cut with cookie cutters of your choice. Place 2 in. apart on greased baking sheets. Bake at 375° for 5-8 minutes or until lightly browned. Remove to wire racks to cool. In a mixing bowl, combine sugar, extract, salt and enough milk to achieve spreading consistency. Add food coloring if desired. Frost cookies; decorate as desired. **Yield:** about 4 dozen.

Family Dinner's a Bushel of Fun

By Nadine Brimeyer, Denver, Iowa

IN HONOR of our new grandson's first visit to Grandma's house, I created a "Corny" Classic Celebration. I want him to know that his roots are in the "Corn State" of Iowa!

Son Chad and his wife, Tamie, brought little Brennan—the guest of honor—from Madison, Iowa. Daughter Shonda with her husband, Jay Bravinder, also joined us.

To decorate the dining table, I used a harvest print cloth with bright yellow place mats. On each mat, I placed a large autumn leaf under a glass plate and scattered more colored leaves on the table.

For a centerpiece, I used a toy John Deere corn sheller, since Grandpa Ronald works at the company in Waterloo. Other accents were a ceramic pumpkin and a toy John Deere wagon loaded with seed corn packets, cobs of Indian corn and apples.

Tiny baskets filled with candy corn plus cans of whole kernel corn at each place were fitting favors.

The menu was corny, of course! Corny Vegetable Salad is tasty, crisp and pretty with sunny kernels.

Corn State Broccoli Bake gives a double dose of the highlighted ingredient, calling for both whole kernel and cream-style corn. The broccoli adds contrast.

Buttery-rich and slightly sweet, Sunflower Corn Muffins have a custard-like consistency similar to spoon bread. They made just the right accompaniment for Stuffed Corn-ish Hens.

Although our grandson was still too little to appreciate all of this, we adults had a memorable meal.

Corny Vegetable Salad

Bright yellow kernels perk up this cool, crisp vegetable medley. Since this dish needs to be chilled, you can make it the day ahead.

 Uses less fat, sugar or salt. Includes Nutritional Analysis and Diabetic Exchanges.

1 package (10 ounces) frozen corn
2 pounds fresh broccoli, broken into florets (8 cups)
1 medium head cauliflower, broken into florets (6 cups)
6 green onions, sliced
1 envelope ranch salad dressing mix
1 cup (8 ounces) sour cream

Cook corn according to package directions; drain and cool. In a large bowl, combine the broccoli, cauliflower, onions and corn. In a small bowl, combine dressing mix and sour cream; mix well. Pour over vegetables and toss to coat. Cover and refrigerate for at least 2 hours. **Yield:** 12-14 servings. **Nutritional Analysis:** One 1-cup serving (prepared with fat-free sour cream) equals 90 calories, 250 mg sodium, 2 mg cholesterol, 18 gm carbohydrate, 6 gm protein, trace fat. **Diabetic Exchanges:** 1 starch, 1 vegetable.

Corn State Broccoli Bake

A double dose of corn teams up with broccoli in this colorful side dish. The green and yellow went well with my table decorations.

1 package (8 ounces) Chicken in a Biskit crackers, crushed
1/2 cup butter *or* margarine, melted
1 package (10 ounces) frozen chopped broccoli, thawed
1 can (15-1/4 ounces) whole kernel corn, drained
1 can (14-3/4 ounces) cream-style corn

Combine cracker crumbs and butter; reserve 1/2 cup for topping. In a bowl, combine broccoli, both cans of corn and remaining crumbs. Transfer to a greased 2-qt. baking dish. Sprinkle with reserved crumbs. Bake, uncovered, at 375° for 25-30 minutes or until lightly browned. **Yield:** 6-8 servings.

Sunflower Corn Muffins

New grandmothers sometimes get a little goofy—in my case it was "corny". These golden cheesy mini muffins with a rich corn taste were a fun part of the meal.

1 cup (8 ounces) sour cream
1 can (8 ounces) whole kernel corn, drained
1 can (8 ounces) cream-style corn
1/2 cup shredded cheddar cheese
1/4 cup sliced green onions
1/4 cup butter *or* margarine, melted
1 egg, beaten
1 package (8-1/2 ounces) corn bread/muffin mix
3 tablespoons sunflower kernels

In a bowl, combine the first seven ingredients; stir in corn bread mix just until moistened. Spoon into greased miniature muffin cups. Sprinkle with sunflower kernels. Bake at 375° for 30-35 minutes or until muffins test done. Cool for 2 minutes before removing from pans to a wire rack. Serve warm. **Yield:** 3-1/2 dozen mini muffins.

Stuffed Corn-ish Hens

Okay, so I cheated just a little on the entree, using a play on words to link it to my corn theme. This recipe's delicious blend of rice, almonds and mushrooms is a nice change from bread stuffing. Fit for a celebration, these savory stuffed hens tasted so good with the other menu items.

1 cup uncooked long grain rice
1 can (4 ounces) mushroom stems and pieces, drained
1/2 cup slivered almonds
3 tablespoons chopped onion
3 tablespoons butter *or* margarine
2 cups water
2 chicken bouillon cubes
2 tablespoons minced fresh parsley
1 tablespoon lemon juice
1 teaspoon salt
1 bay leaf
6 Cornish game hens (22 to 24 ounces *each*)
6 bacon strips, halved

In a saucepan, saute rice, mushrooms, almonds and onion in butter for 5 minutes or until rice is lightly browned. Stir in water, bouillon, parsley, lemon juice, salt and bay leaf; bring to a boil. Reduce heat; cover and simmer for 25 minutes or until liquid is absorbed. Discard bay leaf. Spoon about 3/4 cup rice mixture into each hen. Place breast side up in a large roasting pan; tie drumsticks together. Place two bacon pieces over each hen. Cover and bake at 375° for 45 minutes. Uncover; bake 45 minutes longer or until a meat thermometer reads 185° for hens and 165° for rice stuffing. **Yield:** 6 servings.

General Recipe Index

This handy index lists every recipe by food category and/or major ingredient, so you can easily locate recipes.

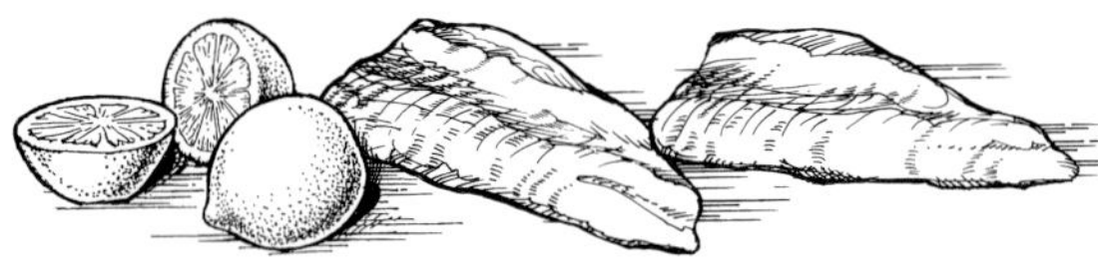

Issue-by-Issue Index

Do you have a favorite dish from a specific Taste of Home issue but can't recall the recipe's actual name? You'll easily find it in this categorized listing of recipes by issue.

Nutritional Analysis Recipes Index

This index lists recipes that use less fat, sugar or salt and include Nutritional Analysis and Diabetic Exchanges. These good-for-you recipes are marked with a ✓ throughout the book.

The Cook's Quick Reference

From the Taste of Home Test Kitchens

Substitutions & Equivalents

Cooking Terms

Guide to Cooking with Popular Herbs

Substitutions & Equivalents

Equivalent Measures

3 teaspoons	=	1 tablespoon	**16 tablespoons**	=	1 cup
4 tablespoons	=	1/4 cup	**2 cups**	=	1 pint
5-1/3 tablespoons	=	1/3 cup	**4 cups**	=	1 quart
8 tablespoons	=	1/2 cup	**4 quarts**	=	1 gallon

Food Equivalents

Grains

Macaroni	1 cup (3-1/2 ounces) uncooked	=	2-1/2 cups cooked
Noodles, Medium	3 cups (4 ounces) uncooked	=	4 cups cooked
Popcorn	1/3 to 1/2 cup unpopped	=	8 cups popped
Rice, Long Grain	1 cup uncooked	=	3 cups cooked
Rice, Quick-Cooking	1 cup uncooked	=	2 cups cooked
Spaghetti	8 ounces uncooked	=	4 cups cooked

Crumbs

Bread	1 slice	=	3/4 cup soft crumbs, 1/4 cup fine dry crumbs
Graham Crackers	7 squares	=	1/2 cup finely crushed
Buttery Round Crackers	12 crackers	=	1/2 cup finely crushed
Saltine Crackers	14 crackers	=	1/2 cup finely crushed

Fruits

Bananas	1 medium	=	1/3 cup mashed
Lemons	1 medium	=	3 tablespoons juice, 2 teaspoons grated peel
Limes	1 medium	=	2 tablespoons juice, 1-1/2 teaspoons grated peel
Oranges	1 medium	=	1/4 to 1/3 cup juice, 4 teaspoons grated peel

Vegetables

Cabbage	1 head	=	5 cups shredded	**Green Pepper**	1 large	=	1 cup chopped
Carrots	1 pound	=	3 cups shredded	**Mushrooms**	1/2 pound	=	3 cups sliced
Celery	1 rib	=	1/2 cup chopped	**Onions**	1 medium	=	1/2 cup chopped
Corn	1 ear fresh	=	2/3 cup kernels	**Potatoes**	3 medium	=	2 cups cubed

Nuts

Almonds	1 pound	=	3 cups chopped	**Pecan Halves**	1 pound	=	4-1/2 cups chopped
Ground Nuts	3-3/4 ounces	=	1 cup	**Walnuts**	1 pound	=	3-3/4 cups chopped

Easy Substitutions

When you need...		*Use...*
Baking Powder	1 teaspoon	1/2 teaspoon cream of tartar + 1/4 teaspoon baking soda
Buttermilk	1 cup	1 tablespoon lemon juice *or* vinegar + enough milk to measure 1 cup (let stand 5 minutes before using)
Cornstarch	1 tablespoon	2 tablespoons all-purpose flour
Honey	1 cup	1-1/4 cups sugar + 1/4 cup water
Half-and-Half Cream	1 cup	1 tablespoon melted butter + enough whole milk to measure 1 cup
Onion	1 small, chopped (1/3 cup)	1 teaspoon onion powder *or* 1 tablespoon dried minced onion
Tomato Juice	1 cup	1/2 cup tomato sauce + 1/2 cup water
Tomato Sauce	2 cups	3/4 cup tomato paste + 1 cup water
Unsweetened Chocolate	1 square (1 ounce)	3 tablespoons baking cocoa + 1 tablespoon shortening *or* oil
Whole Milk	1 cup	1/2 cup evaporated milk + 1/2 cup water

Cooking Terms

HERE'S a quick reference for some of the cooking terms used in *Taste of Home* recipes:

Baste—To moisten food with melted butter, pan drippings, marinades or other liquid to add more flavor and juiciness.

Beat—A rapid movement to combine ingredients using a fork, spoon, wire whisk or electric mixer.

Blend—To combine ingredients until *just* mixed.

Boil—To heat liquids until bubbles form that cannot be "stirred down". In the case of water, the temperature will reach 212°.

Bone—To remove all meat from the bone before cooking.

Cream—To beat ingredients together to a smooth consistency, usually in the case of butter and sugar for baking.

Dash—A small amount of seasoning, less than 1/8 teaspoon. If using a shaker, a dash would comprise a quick flip of the container.

Dredge—To coat foods with flour or other dry ingredients. Most often done with pot roasts and stew meat before browning.

Fold—To incorporate several ingredients by careful and gentle turning with a spatula. Used generally with beaten egg whites or whipped cream when mixing into the rest of the ingredients to keep the batter light.

Julienne—To cut foods into long thin strips much like matchsticks. Used most often for salads and stir-fry dishes.

Mince—To cut into very fine pieces. Used often for garlic or fresh herbs.

Parboil—To cook partially, usually used in the case of chicken, sausages and vegetables.

Partially set—Describes the consistency of gelatin after it has been chilled for a small amount of time. Mixture should resemble the consistency of egg whites.

Puree—To process foods to a smooth mixture. Can be prepared in an electric blender, food processor, food mill or sieve.

Saute—To fry quickly in a small amount of fat, stirring almost constantly. Most often done with onions, mushrooms and other chopped vegetables.

Score—To cut slits partway through the outer surface of foods. Often used with ham or flank steak.

Stir-Fry—To cook meats and/or vegetables with a constant stirring motion in a small amount of oil in a wok or skillet over high heat.

Guide to Cooking with Popular Herbs

HERB	APPETIZERS SALADS	BREADS/EGGS SAUCES/CHEESE	VEGETABLES PASTA	MEAT POULTRY	FISH SHELLFISH
BASIL	Green, Potato & Tomato Salads, Salad Dressings, Stewed Fruit	Breads, Fondue & Egg Dishes, Dips, Marinades, Sauces	Mushrooms, Tomatoes, Squash, Pasta, Bland Vegetables	Broiled, Roast Meat & Poultry Pies, Stews, Stuffing	Baked, Broiled & Poached Fish, Shellfish
BAY LEAF	Seafood Cocktail, Seafood Salad, Tomato Aspic, Stewed Fruit	Egg Dishes, Gravies, Marinades, Sauces	Dried Bean Dishes, Beets, Carrots, Onions, Potatoes, Rice, Squash	Corned Beef, Tongue Meat & Poultry Stews	Poached Fish, Shellfish, Fish Stews
CHIVES	Mixed Vegetable, Green, Potato & Tomato Salads, Salad Dressings	Egg & Cheese Dishes, Cream Cheese, Cottage Cheese, Gravies, Sauces	Hot Vegetables, Potatoes	Broiled Poultry, Poultry & Meat Pies, Stews, Casseroles	Baked Fish, Fish Casseroles, Fish Stews, Shellfish
DILL	Seafood Cocktail, Green, Potato & Tomato Salads, Salad Dressings	Breads, Egg & Cheese Dishes, Cream Cheese, Fish & Meat Sauces	Beans, Beets, Cabbage, Carrots, Cauliflower, Peas, Squash, Tomatoes	Beef, Veal Roasts, Lamb, Steaks, Chops, Stews, Roast & Creamed Poultry	Baked, Broiled, Poached & Stuffed Fish, Shellfish
GARLIC	All Salads, Salad Dressings	Fondue, Poultry Sauces, Fish & Meat Marinades	Beans, Eggplant, Potatoes, Rice, Tomatoes	Roast Meats, Meat & Poultry Pies, Hamburgers, Casseroles, Stews	Broiled Fish, Shellfish, Fish Stews, Casseroles
MARJORAM	Seafood Cocktail, Green, Poultry & Seafood Salads	Breads, Cheese Spreads, Egg & Cheese Dishes, Gravies, Sauces	Carrots, Eggplant, Peas, Onions, Potatoes, Dried Bean Dishes, Spinach	Roast Meats & Poultry, Meat & Poultry Pies, Stews & Casseroles	Baked, Broiled & Stuffed Fish, Shellfish
MUSTARD	Fresh Green Salads, Prepared Meat, Macaroni & Potato Salads, Salad Dressings	Biscuits, Egg & Cheese Dishes, Sauces	Baked Beans, Cabbage, Eggplant, Squash, Dried Beans, Mushrooms, Pasta	Chops, Steaks, Ham, Pork, Poultry, Cold Meats	Shellfish
OREGANO	Green, Poultry & Seafood Salads	Breads, Egg & Cheese Dishes, Meat, Poultry & Vegetable Sauces	Artichokes, Cabbage, Eggplant, Squash, Dried Beans, Mushrooms, Pasta	Broiled, Roast Meats, Meat & Poultry Pies, Stews, Casseroles	Baked, Broiled & Poached Fish, Shellfish
PARSLEY	Green, Potato, Seafood & Vegetable Salads	Biscuits, Breads, Egg & Cheese Dishes, Gravies, Sauces	Asparagus, Beets, Eggplant, Squash, Dried Beans, Mushrooms, Pasta	Meat Loaf, Meat & Poultry Pies, Stews & Casseroles, Stuffing	Fish Stews, Stuffed Fish
ROSEMARY	Fruit Cocktail, Fruit & Green Salads	Biscuits, Egg Dishes, Herb Butter, Cream Cheese, Marinades, Sauces	Beans, Broccoli, Peas, Cauliflower, Mushrooms, Baked Potatoes, Parsnips	Roast Meat, Poultry & Meat Pies, Stews & Casseroles, Stuffing	Stuffed Fish, Shellfish
SAGE		Breads, Fondue, Egg & Cheese Dishes, Spreads, Gravies, Sauces	Beans, Beets, Onions, Peas, Spinach, Squash, Tomatoes	Roast Meat, Poultry, Meat Loaf, Stews, Stuffing	Baked, Poached & Stuffed Fish
TARRAGON	Seafood Cocktail, Avocado Salads, Salad Dressings	Cheese Spreads, Marinades, Sauces, Egg Dishes	Asparagus, Beans, Beets, Carrots, Mushrooms, Peas, Squash, Spinach	Steaks, Poultry, Roast Meats, Casseroles & Stews	Baked, Broiled & Poached Fish, Shellfish
THYME	Seafood Cocktail, Green, Poultry, Seafood & Vegetable Salads	Biscuits, Breads, Egg & Cheese Dishes, Sauces, Spreads	Beets, Carrots, Mushrooms, Onions, Peas, Eggplant, Spinach, Potatoes	Roast Meat, Poultry & Meat Loaf, Meat & Poultry Pies, Stews & Casseroles	Baked, Broiled & Stuffed Fish, Shellfish, Fish Stews